Modern Greece:
A Short History

MODERN GREECE
A Short History

C. M. WOODHOUSE

faber and faber

LONDON · BOSTON

First published in 1968
as *The Story of Modern Greece*
by Faber and Faber Limited
3 Queen Square London WC1N 3AU
Revised and first published as
Modern Greece a Short History in 1977
Third edition, revised, published in 1984
Fourth edition, revised, published in 1986
Fifth edition, revised, published in 1991

Printed in England by Clays Ltd St Ives Plc

A CIP record for this book is available from the British Library

ISBN 0–571–16122–7

Contents

Maps

Introduction

W hat is the subject of the history of Greece: a people, a race, a country, a language, a religion, a culture, an idea? It has been called all of these. Something of each of them must go into the answer, but none of them is adequate by itself, and their inadequacy varies.

As a complete answer, some of them can be ruled out at once. A country, for instance: the boundaries of what might be called Greece have long fluctuated over a very wide area, and have not ceased to change, though by smaller variations, even in the present century. Or a religion: for the Orthodox Church, which has been the religion of most Greeks for sixteen centuries, is also the religion of millions of non-Greeks, particularly among the Slavs. Or a race: ever since the work of Jakob Fallmerayer in the nineteenth century, it has been unreasonable to think of the inhabitants of Greece (however defined) as racially homogeneous and lineally descended from the ancient Hellenes. It would be equally unreasonable, however, to assert dogmatically that no Greek living today could possibly have had a direct ancestor living in Greece 2,500 years ago.

To illustrate the intractability of the problem of definition, it is interesting to reflect on the many significances of the word Rûm (that is, Rome) and its derivatives. The word Greece and its derivatives are unknown in the languages of the Middle East, including that which we call Greek. The name Rûm, on the other hand, has been applied to the Greeks, the Orthodox community (whether Greek or not), the territory in Asia Minor once occupied by the Greeks (even after it became a Turkish sultanate), and other parts of the Balkans such as Rumania and

Rumelia (now part of Bulgaria). Romaic was even distinguished from Hellenic as a language; and this makes the linguistic criterion also inadequate by itself to define the Greek identity.

Nor can refuge be found, though it has been sought, in thinking of the history of Greece as the history of the embodiment of an idea. It is true that what has separated Greek history from the Latin West, the Slavonic North and the Muslim East has been basically ideological. But what coherent ideology runs through Greek history for the last sixteen hundred years? The answer is none, but rather a conflict of ideas: Hellenism *versus* Byzantinism, to put it in its most abstract form. Sometimes the internal conflict of ideas has been more powerful and destructive than the external conflict. Certainly there has never been a time when the Greek soul has been impervious to external penetration by the ideologies of its Latin, Slavonic or Muslim neighbours.

Yet there is a sense in which an idea is at the root of the whole matter. It is a simple, almost naive idea, which can best be put like this: the only practicable definition of a Greek is that he is somebody who thinks he is a Greek; and it is the Greek people as so defined, neither more nor less, that is the subject of this history.

Refinements can be added to the definition, of course. A Greek must have some grounds for thinking himself a Greek. His grounds will include language, consciousness of history, almost inevitably religion, but not necessarily place of birth. None of the refinements is decisive, however. The consciousness of history may be based on what that sardonic philhellene, George Finlay, called 'Homer, Plato & Co.' or it may be on the glories of Byzantium, or on an amalgam of both. The geographical criterion is the weakest of all, for it would be hard to identify a span of fifty years in the last sixteen centuries in which the boundaries of the Greek world remained unaltered; and the expatriate communities (for instance in Cyprus or Alexandria or Istanbul) are as much part of the story as the Greeks of Athens, Epirus or the Peloponnese.

The simple definition is therefore best. This is the history of the Greek people—those who called themselves Greeks and thought of themselves as Greeks—during the sixteen centuries which separate the foundation of the Greek Empire from the present day. It might well be sub-titled 'from Constantine to

Constantine', for the rulers at the beginning and end of the story happened to bear the same name; and so did the last Emperor of Constantinople in 1453. For the Greeks there is deep significance in the continuity implied by that name, and the coincidence is no accident. But what the significance of it will be in the next stage of Greek history, it is not the historian's task to divine.

CHAPTER I

The Foundation of Constantine
(324–641)

The history of the Mediterranean world forms a natural whole. Separate histories can be written of each of the lands and peoples that surround it, but so far as they are separate they will be incomplete. Greek history begins in the Levant as well as the Balkans; it spreads westwards to the Pillars of Hercules and grows into the history of republican Rome. Roman history floods over into North Africa, where it rejoins the history of the Levant at Carthage, and moves eastwards across the Balkans into Anatolia. As it turns into the history of imperial Rome, it merges again with the history of Greece. This is not to deny that there are deep incompatibilities and antagonisms between the tides of Greek and Roman history. They do not merely converge but clash and split furiously; but they are part of one and the same story. The ebb and flow and confluences of these tides are often imperceptible, but sometimes there is a distinct moment of change that can be identified without hesitation. Such a moment came with the accession to power of Constantine the Great early in the 4th century A.D.

Constantine left three indelible marks on the history of the Mediterranean world, two of which can be precisely dated. He inaugurated the toleration of the Christian religion by inspiring the Edict of Milan (313). He founded the new capital of the Roman Empire at Byzantium, to which he gave his own name, the City of Constantine—Constantinople, the foundations of which were laid in 324. And he took the first steps, by his personal example and by his legislation, towards that fusion of three separate cultures—the pagan hellenistic, the Roman, and the orthodox Christian—which created what we know as the Byzantine Empire. He was neither a religious man by nature, nor a Greek nor even a Roman by patriotic instinct. He was a soldier of ferocious and ruthless ability, and a cunning politician of immense ambition. But whatever his motives, he is rightly looked upon by the Greeks as the founder of the greatest era in their post-classical history and their Church. Constantinople is to this day known to them simply as 'the City', though it has been a foreign capital for half a millennium.

What led Constantine to his fateful decisions? Both in founding the new capital and in adopting the new religion, his motives were practical and political. The Roman Empire was undergoing a process of diffusion which brought it near to disintegration. Rome had long ceased to be the effective capital of the Empire. The capital was in the Emperor's military camp, wherever it might be. Constant threats to the security of the Empire from the north and east meant that there had to be many alternative centres of command—at Milan, at Trèves (Trier) in Germany, at York, at Salonae (Split) in Dalmatia, at Nicomedia (Izmit) in Bithynia, but seldom at Rome itself. The Emperors, too, had long ceased to be Romans or even Italians by birth, and they had no sentimental attachment to the eternal city. Since Caracalla had conferred Roman citizenship on every free inhabitant of the Empire (212), the name of 'Roman' had ceased to have any national connotation. The Greeks call themselves Romans (*Romioi*) to this day; and *Rûm* (Rome) became in due course the name of Anatolia, where the majority of Greeks lived.

Of Constantine's immediate predecessors, few had any personal connexion with Rome. Maximinus (235–8) was the son of a Goth and an Alan, born in Thrace; Philip the Arab (244–9) was a Syrian; Diocletian (284–305) was the son of a Dalmatian slave; several were born, like Constantine himself, in the region known as Illyria, which came to include the whole territory bounded by the Adriatic and the Black Sea. When Diocletian divided the administration of the Empire between four Emperors—two senior, with the title of Augustus, and two junior, with the title of Caesar—all four colleagues were natives of the Balkan lands. Rome was no more than a name to them. The Senate still sat there, and commanded respect. But senators could hold no military commands, and the few posts to which they could elect each other were empty honours without real functions. They even sought to intervene in the election of new Emperors when the *imperium* was vacant, but never with any success that was not soon undone by civil war. The centre of gravity of the Empire had shifted away from the ancient capital.

It had shifted away, but it had yet to settle elsewhere. The shift was part of the Empire's endless quest for security. Neither as a centre of power within the Empire nor as a command-post for the protection of the frontiers was Rome a natural site. Power passed increasingly into the hands of the army, which no longer consisted chiefly even of Italians, let alone Romans. Celts, Sarmatians, German tribesmen, Dalmatians, Thracians and other non-Italians manned the armies. Control of the Empire depended on control of its armed forces. When the Emperor Decius was killed in battle with the Goths (251) and again when Valerian was captured by the Persians (260), claimants to the Empire emerged from all quarters, backed by their local armies. On each occasion, too, the Senate tried in vain to assert its right of election. It was usually troops who had been proved in battle on the frontiers that carried the successful claimant to power, and his camp was always far from Rome.

The power of the frontier armies lay in the vital need for security from enemies without. The history of Rome is the history of a perennial quest for external security. To the west and south all was well since the conquests of the republican era. Behind the North African littoral lay barely inhabited desert, beyond Spain and Gaul lay the sea. The British Isles were never completely conquered: hence the importance of the head-quarters of York, where Constantine's father had held command. But much more dangerous was the undemarcated frontier in Central Europe, beyond which the Goths were growing in power and militancy. Even more dangerous was the fluctuating frontier to the east, because there the enemy consisted not simply of barbarian tribes but of another highly developed and sophisticated power, the Sassanid Persians. From the Rhine and the Danube to the Taurus mountains, there was no sector where the imperial arms could rest unalert, even in the intervals between open conflicts. War was a perennial state.

Such distant frontiers could not be defended from an imperial

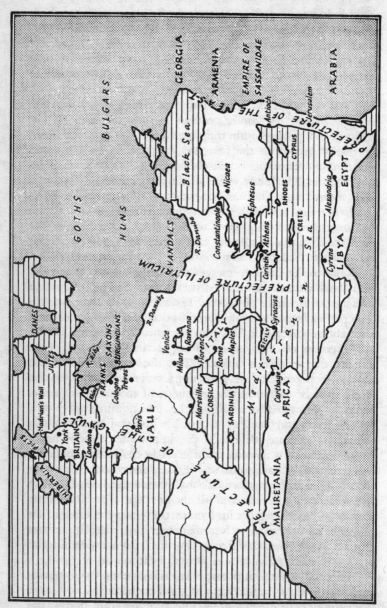

THE ROMAN EMPIRE IN THE 4TH CENTURY A.D.

headquarters at Rome, nor from any single capital. That Rome was inadequately situated had been recognized long before Constantine. If Mark Antony had not lost the Empire to Augustus Caesar, he would probably have transferred his capital to Alexandria, and that for more serious reasons than merely the company of Cleopatra. Later Emperors were guided by the dictates of current compaigning. By the end of the third century, there was a good case for Salonae or Nicomedia as alternative capitals. Certain things were clear that had to be taken into consideration. One was that any movement of the centre of power from Rome would have to be eastwards, since that was the direction in which the line of communications with Rome was longest and most uncertain. Another was that there would have to be at least two capitals: the Roman Empire was too large to be administered from a single centre. The division of the Empire was a fact long before it was recognized.

Diocletian had divided the Empire between four colleagues. He had further tried to establish a limited monarchy which would be held only for a fixed period of twenty years by each Emperor. One of his junior colleagues, Constantius I, was the father of Constantine, who himself became Caesar in 306 and Augustus in 308; but he had no intention of preserving Diocletian's system. Constantine destroyed each of his rival co-rulers in a bloody civil war; he re-established the hereditary principle; and he re-united the Empire under his own dominion. But no sooner had he done so than he found it necessary to divide it again for administrative convenience. For administrative purposes he established four great provinces divided approximately as the commands of the four Emperors had been divided under Diocletian: Gallia (which included also Spain and Britain), Italia (which included North Africa), Illyricum (which included all the Greek mainland and most of the Balkan lands), and Oriens (which included all the crescent of territory from Thrace to Egypt). Under his successors the two western and the two eastern provinces were sometimes united and sometimes grouped under separate Emperors, until the western Empire was overrun by the Goths in the 5th century.

Over each of the four provinces a civil governor was appointed, who held no military command. The armed forces were placed under the command of two senior generals, one for the cavalry (*magister equitum*) and one for the infantry (*magister peditum*). All these office-holders, civil and military, were directly responsible to the Emperor and had no jurisdiction over each other. The separation of powers was clearly intended to make another usurpation impossible. That was also why Constantine dissolved the Praetorian Guard. He had learned the hard lesson of the civil wars by which he had himself reached power. He had also learned from the same experience where the centre of gravity of the Empire now lay. It was in the so-called 'Illyrian triangle', bounded by the Black Sea and the Aegean and Adriatic. This area happened to include territorial Greece, though the Greeks of Hellas were now a minority in the Greek-speaking world. Illyricum was predominant rather because it was the nursery of tough soldiers and forceful leaders. It was an accident that the primacy of the Illyrian triangle meant that Constantinople was sited among the Greeks.

Constantine required a capital and a populace wholly dependent on himself, thus making a clean break with the past. He had climbed to power by bloodshed and treachery, in which he slaughtered both enemies and friends, and even his own family. Weary of the succession of civil wars in which he had himself been the final victor, he determined to set the civil above the military power. That could not be done in a capital which was also an armed camp, such as Nicomedia. There were other motives besides security for choosing a new site. A simple one was for the personal glory of Constantine and the immortality of his name. Another, more complex, was to provide a focus for the re-integration of the diverse peoples of the Empire, which was to be achieved, though not in Constantine's lifetime, through the Christian religion. To this religion Constantine himself was undergoing a gradual but politic conversion, impelled by reasons of state rather than by the miracles with which later piety garnished the story.

Constantine's instinct in choosing the site of his new capital was sound for another reason, which probably he could not have formulated himself. The ancient and medieval history of the Mediterranean world is the history of a flow of dynamic ideas—philosophical and religious, political and economic, technical and scientific. The flow was longitudinal, sometimes from east to west, sometimes from west to east. The earliest Emperor known to have explicitly recognized this tide in the affairs of men was Alexius I in the early twelfth century, who wrote that 'once science was transmitted from the East to the West: now on the contrary, it is the Latin, coming from West to East, who descends upon the Greeks'. Sometimes, as in the days of which Alexius wrote, the ideological tide was associated with physical power, sometimes not. Nor was its flow uniform at any given time. There might be a confluence of different but powerful tides at the same moment; and territorial Greece was where such a confluence was most likely to occur.

The western tide carried to the East the principles of Roman law and administration, and the power of civil and military technology. The eastern tide carried to the West the influences of Greek philosphy and oriental religion. The two tides met along an axis running through the Greek-speaking lands, with its southern pole at Alexandria and its northern pole among the Greek colonies of the Black Sea, such as Cherson or Khersón-nisos, in the Crimea. Constantinople lay near the centre of this axis. But the city was also ideally situated in a more practical sense at the confluence of two tides which, in the nature of things, flowed with equal and opposite force. The principal trade-routes between Asia and Europe passed through Byzantine territory. It was well furnished with ports, all of them in Greek hands. Constantinople, with its superlative harbour, became the natural centre of a system comprising a circle of ports which were in turn the natural outlets of vast commercial hinterlands. The site of the city was also eminently defensible. Indeed, there were times when it alone held out after all its territory had fallen into enemy hands.

Constantinople thus occupied a key point on the map not only strategically but ideologically and economically. Here, or approximately here, was the natural meeting-point of the tides of East and West, Christianity and paganism, Roman and Hellenistic and even oriental tradition. This is another reason why a new site had to be found. Athens, for instance—still a cultural centre of great wealth and influence, with its own university until the 6th century—was as closely associated with the past as the old Rome; Nicomedia was a military camp; Alexandria was too exclusively Greek. The city on the Bosporus had none of these defects. Its population, being entirely new, could be genuinely eclectic. Apart from senators and officials recruited from Rome, it was populated from all over the Empire. 'Constantinople is dedicated, while almost all other cities are denuded,' St. Jerome wrote half a century later. Equally there is no doubt that Constantine intended his new capital to be completely assimilated to the Roman tradition.

His intention was defeated within a few generations. Latin might be the language of the courts and the administration, but Greek was already the language of the Church. It was also the *lingua franca* of the Near East: hence its name, the *koiné* or common tongue. It was unavoidable in the cosmopolitan atmosphere of the new capital that it should become a Greek city. This was the certain consequence of Constantine's own choice of the Christian religion, which attracted him because of its highly organized character. How long the transition from a Latin to a Greek character took at Constantinople is not easily settled. Most scholars would agree that, although the legal conceptions of Rome continued to form the basis of the Byzantine constitution, Latin elements in the language and culture were fast disappearing by the 7th century. The eastern tide prevailed over the western, and Constantine unconsciously willed it so. Christianity was both the motive and the undoing of his plan.

In the 4th century Christianity was still only the religion of a minority, but it was a powerful and well-placed minority. Even in the reign of Diocletian, who somewhat reluctantly persecuted the Christians in the early years of the 4th century, they held influential posts at court and in the army. Proportionately they were more numerous in the eastern provinces, and Greek was the language of the church. Rome, despite the eminence of its bishopric, was still essentially a pagan city, where the old religion had its most lasting roots and the Vestal Virgins still performed their duties. It has been estimated that the proportion of Christians was about one in fifteen in the west, but nearer to one in ten in the east. Perhaps the decisive factor for Constantine was not, as he claimed, his vision of the monogram of Christ's name with the words 'In this sign conquer' on the night before his victory over one of his rivals for the empire (312). It was rather the knowledge that the enemy forces contained a large proportion of Christian troops. He saw the value not only of their predominance in the army, but of their ecclesiastical organization as the framework of a civil administration. Moreover, the last of his rivals, Licinius, made the mistake of persecuting the Christians, and thus gave Constantine another motive for conciliating them.

By such accidents, which Christians accepted as the will of God, was the great decision made. To say this is not to belittle the doctrinal power of Christianity, but to emphasize that it was, at the turn of the 3rd to the 4th century, only one among many competing religions. Rome had always been hospitable to foreign cults, ever since the sacred stone of the Magna Mater was brought to Rome from Phrygia during the second Carthaginian War (204 B.C.). Isis from Egypt, Mithras from Asia Minor, and other foreign deities were admitted at the same time as Christianity. The profounder philosophies of Manichaeism and Neoplatonism attracted thoughtful pagans, and never entirely lost their charm. Christianity, to become acceptable, had to compromise with other popular creeds. Its angels were assimilated to the pagan *daimones*, and its elements of superstition, including necromancy and magic, were given more emphasis than devout Christians would have wished. Its deeper mysteries were a closed book to the first Christian Emperor.

Constantine's religious convictions are still something of a puzzle, as they probably were to himself. He retained pagan inclinations, especially towards Mithraism, which had come near to defeating Christianity as the established religion of the Empire. But in fact there was no established religion in Constantine's day. Not until the reign of Theodosius I, more than a generation later, did Christianity achieve that status (380). The effect of Constantine's edict of toleration (313) was simply that there was no official religion at all. He himself was baptised only on his death-bed—a not unusual practice. At his funeral the ceremonial was pagan rather than Christian. Ambiguity, also, enveloped his intentions towards his new capital. He called it the 'New Rome', and wished it to be unsullied by pagan cults. But temples as well as churches were allowed to be built there. Though it might be a replica of Rome even to the point of being built on seven hills, it was only under Constantine's successors that the city was invested with the trappings of a capital—a senate and magistracies. He claimed to have received the command of God to build Constantinople, so it must be primarily a

Christian city. But Christianity was to prevail only gradually, and not by enforcement.

In the meantime religion had become a cause of bitter conflict, which was at least as much political as spiritual in character. Christianity was already torn by schism and heresy before Constantine adopted it. Churches took on local characteristics wherever they were founded. The Armenians, who were officially converted a little earlier than Constantine, formed a distinct sect from the first. So did the Georgians and Abyssinians, both converted in Constantine's life-time. Gnosticism, Montanism in Phrygia, Donatism in Africa, were deep-rooted survivals from the age before Constantine. He was himself obliged to intervene in the great controversy caused by the followers of Arius, who maintained that Christ was only of 'like substance' with God (*homoioúsios*) and not 'consubstantial' (*homooúsios*). Arianism was condemned by the bishop of Alexandria, whose orthodoxy was confirmed at the Council of Nicaea (325) under the personal chairmanship of Constantine; but it was only after a bloody conflict, which continued into the following generation. Constantine himself weakened later, when he belatedly appreciated how deeply entrenched Arianism was in the eastern provinces. It had to be condemned afresh at the second of the Church's seven Councils, held at Constantinople in 381; and even so it survived.

The ecclesiastical wrangle had also a political significance. It was in part a dispute between rival bishoprics, notably Antioch and Alexandria, and in part the first harbinger of the struggle between the eastern and western churches. Only a small minority of western bishops attended the Council of Nicaea, though the few that came were gratified to find that Constantine took their side. They resented the intrusion of Constantinople into a leading role in ecclesiastical affairs. It was an upstart see, not to be compared in status with Rome, Alexandria, or Antioch, and not yet even associated with the name of any great saint, though St. Andrew was later to be claimed as the founder of the Church at Byzantium. A long and intricate battle was to be fought before Constantinople came to be recognized as a patriarchate equal, and eventually superior, to the other eastern patriarchates; and Rome never fully accepted it. The irresoluble character of this contest for primacy first became apparent at the Council of Sardica (343), on the frontier between east and west, which also left the issue between homoiousians and homoousians in suspense.

One reason for the deadlock was that the sons of Constantine, between whom he divided the Empire on his death, were themselves divided by force of circumstances on the doctrinal issue. Constantius II, who ruled in the east, was an Arian, though a vacillating one; his brother Constans, ruling in the west, supported the Alexandrian orthodoxy embodied in the Nicene creed. Their personal relations were amicable, and each acted as spokesman for the view held by influential opinion in his own provinces. But it is hardly surprising that men of a spiritually thoughtful nature were shocked by the worldly wrangling of the new religion. Such a man was the nephew of Constantine the Great, known to history as Julian the Apostate, who succeeded to the Empire after the death of his two cousins, Constans and Constantius, and ruled for three years (361–3). Although (or perhaps because) he had been brought up to the Christian priesthood, Julian reacted violently against it and tried to restore the old pagan religion. But his life was cut short in battle, and legend has it that he died acknowledging the victory of Christ.

After the pagan reaction had proved abortive, the internal disputes of the reinstated Church continued, though with temporarily abated force. The next Emperors were devout Christians. Valens (364–78) was an Arian, but he had other preoccupations than theological controversy. A fresh and more formidable invasion of the Goths brought about his defeat and death at the battle of Adrianople (378). Their western cousins, the Visigoths, poured into peninsular Greece before moving westwards towards Italy and Spain. A still greater danger to the Empire was the advent of Alaric, who made a feint at Constantinople itself (395) before moving on into Macedonia and Thessaly. The Danube frontier crumbled, never to be completely restored. Unable to resist the invaders, the Emperor Theodosius I (379–95) compromised with them and enlisted barbarian generals to command the imperial forces. Alaric himself was appointed military commander of Illyricum. Whether for this expedient, or because he made Christianity the official religion of the Empire, Theodosius earned the title of 'the Great'. He was also the last to rule the Empire as an undivided whole.

The formal division of the Empire on Theodosius' death (395) between his sons, Arcadius in the east and Honorius in the west, was an important event in the history of the Greeks. Although they were not numerically predominant, they were diffused throughout the eastern Empire; trade with Asia was in their hands; theirs was the prevalent language, and especially that of the Church. In the undivided Empire, although not oppressed and allowed to retain their municipal institutions, they could not hope to compete for political influence with the Italians, nor could their language prevail against Latin, the language of the law-courts and administration. Although the Empire was administered in four great provincial subdivisions, none of the four closely corresponded to Greek territorial limits. But the division into two separate sovereignties contributed to the polarization of the Mediterranean world between a Latin and a Greek sphere of influence. One of the two poles was naturally Constantinople, which was becoming an increasingly Greek-speaking city.

The first Emperor at Constantinople who thought of himself as a Greek rather than a Roman came to the throne in 408. He was Theodosius II, the son of Arcadius, known to the Greeks as *Kalligráphos*, the 'penman'. The nickname indicates his attachment to the cultivated arts, which held an increasingly honourable place at Constantinople. Unlike the West, the East enjoyed a golden age of peace and prosperity in the first half-century after the Empire was officially divided. A cultured aristocracy was emerging. The law was codified. Education enjoyed the highest prestige, and the university of Constantinople was founded in 425. The late 4th and the 5th centuries were also the period of a great expansion of monasticism, which played a powerful part in the intellectual life of the Empire, as well as in its politics and religion. Monasticism had originated in Egypt, and moved in a slow circle through Palestine, Syria, and Anatolia, to arrive in Greece under Theodosius the Great. A century later there were at least a hundred monasteries in or near the capital. While Constantinople was growing in spiritual strength and the arts of peace, the western empire was bearing the brunt of the barbarian invasions. Gradually the tribal leaders usurped control of the empire which they had first entered as vassals and allies.

The western empire was effectively ruled for thirteen years after the division (395-408) by the Vandal general, Stilicho. Still worse was to follow. Rome itself was taken by the Visigoths under Alaric in 410. For two more generations, a nominal Emperor was allowed to reign in the West, until the last puppet, appropriately named Romulus Augustulus, was deposed by Odoacer (who still acted nominally as viceroy of the eastern Emperor) in 476. Meanwhile the eastern empire had been more successful at controlling its unwelcome guests from the north. The power of the barbarian commanders of the Germanized imperial armies was broken by a massacre of the Goths at Constantinople (400). A more menacing enemy, the Huns under Attila, swept across the Danube a generation later, and threatened Constantinople itself (447). They were followed by the Vandals and the Ostrogoths, who reached the gates of the city more than once. But Constantinople was in no danger from the techniques of 5th-century warfare. In the reign of Leo I (457-74) the power of the barbarian troops and commanders was again broken by the importation of savage Isaurian mercenaries from Asia Minor. It was an expedient fraught with consequences for the future of the Empire, but it worked.

In the century following the accession of Theodosius I (379) and the adoption of Christianity as the official religion (380), Constantinople was troubled more by religious controversy than by foreign invasions. The Arian heresy was ended by the first Council of Constantinople (381), but the passion of all classes for religious debate, deriving as it did from a longing for the certainty of immortality, was not abated. A contemporary writer, Gregory of Nyssa, describes the theological ferment of the times:

'The whole city is full of it, the squares, the market places, the cross-roads, the alleyways; old-clothes men, money-changers, food-sellers: they are all busy arguing. If you ask someone to give you change, he philosophises about the Begotten and the Unbegotten; if you enquire about the price of a loaf, you are told by way of reply that the Father is greater and the Son inferior; if you ask 'Is my bath ready?' the attendant answers that the Son was made out of nothing.'

It must never be forgotten that the theological controversies of Byzantium were matters of intense and agonizing reality to everyone, for all regarded their souls as being at stake, as well as the physical security of the Empire, which doctrinal error would put at mortal risk.

The fierce interest of public opinion was not the only reason why religious controversy was a political matter. The Church began at an early date to take on national characteristics, partly because its leaders allowed and even encouraged the use of the vernacular for ecclesiastical purposes. Hence the separation of local churches—in Egypt, Syria, Armenia, Georgia, Persia, and Abyssinia as well as the west. Because there was a close connexion, from the time of Constantine the Great, between ecclesiastical and civil administration, local diversity helped to lead to political nationalism. Even within the Greek-speaking Church administration, there were rivalries between the great bishoprics of Jerusalem, Antioch, Alexandria and Constantinople, the last of which was long looked on as an upstart by the eastern as well as the western churches. At Constantinople itself religious disputes led sometimes to persecution and sometimes to bloody riots, which on occasion took on the character of class warfare.

For all these reasons the Emperor could not remain indifferent to the theological quarrels of which Gregory of Nyssa wrote. He was also obliged to take a stand by his own position in relation to the Church, which Constantine bequeathed to his successors. Although Constantine was personally indifferent to theology and inclined sometimes to heresy and sometimes to paganism, he felt compelled to play a dominant role in controlling ecclesiastical politics in the interests of peace and good order. He described himself as 'a common bishop', but the Church more extravagantly described him as 'the thirteenth Apostle' or even as 'God's living image on earth'. His successors inherited a position not very different from that of head of the established Church, in a far more effective sense than that of the sovereign in the Church of England. The allegation of theocracy or 'Caesaropapism' (meaning an identification of Emperor and Pope) was a much later exaggeration. But the Emperor had a crucial, if ill-defined, position in the Orthodox hierarchy.

It has been said that the relation of the Emperor and the Church was the only constitutional problem at Constantinople.

Their powers were closely intertwined. The Emperor could, for instance, convene a Council and even try (not always successfully) to dictate a dogma, as Constantine had done at Nicaea. He could receive communion in the manner of a priest; he could preach sermons; on certain feasts he could serve at the altar. The vestments now worn by Orthodox bishops are identical with those once worn by the Emperor. He was the symbol of the fact that, in Greek eyes, the world had reached its final order. Both the Pope and the Patriarch were nominally his subjects, and did not deny it. The Emperor could always interfere in elections to the patriarchate, and later Emperors actually appointed their Patriarchs. In the 6th century Pope Gregory still acknowledged his subordination to the Emperor: 'whatever he should do, we follow, if it is in accord with canon law,' he wrote to one of his deacons. The qualification was important, for it was also possible for either Pope or Patriarch to excommunicate the Emperor, as not infrequently happened. Equally, the Church exercised its influence in civil affairs as much as the Emperor did in ecclesiastical affairs. The good order of Byzantine life depended on an indissoluble harmony between Church and state.

The equality and harmony of the imperial and ecclesiastical power, first formulated by Pope Gelasius in the West (494), was again clearly expressed by a later Emperor, John I Tzimiskes:

'I recognize two authorities, priesthood and empire. The Creator of the world entrusted to the first the care of souls and to the second the control of men's bodies. Let neither authority be attacked, that the world may enjoy prosperity.'

Tzimiskes reigned in the 10th century, but such was the conservatism of Byzantium that his words can be taken as simply a re-formulation of a doctrine established by Constantine the Great. Neither the Emperor nor the Church could willingly allow inroads into their power, least of all from each other. Any such attempt on ecclesiastical authority by the Emperor (for instance, the reforms launched in the 8th century by the Iconoclast Leo III, the Isaurian) could be relied upon to unite the Pope of Rome and the Patriarch of Constantinople in a way that no other force could do. The Emperor was the source of all authority, but he could only undermine the harmony of Church and state at his peril.

In later generations, the disturbance of this harmony came chiefly from the monasteries, which became immensely wealthy and a law unto themselves. But in the early centuries of Byzantium the source of disturbance was the emergence and re-emergence of heresies. The sincerity of religious belief, and the vital concern of every Christian for his immortal soul, made matters of correct doctrine truly matters of life and death. No man could take them lightly, least of all the Emperor. Any Emperor who doubted this fact would be reminded of it by a dogmatic theologian, as Nestorius reminded Theodosius II (408–50):

'Give me the earth purified of heretics, your Majesty, and I will give you heaven in return. Subdue the heretics with me and I will subdue the Persians with you.'

The essence of Orthodox belief was that with the confluence at Constantinople of Roman and Christian theories of terrestrial and celestial empire, the world had achieved its final order, of which the Emperor was the symbol. Not only were Orthodox Christians superior to the rest of mankind; not only was all future improvement or innovation impossible; but also error was unthinkable. It was an unfortunate fact that Christianity was already divided when Constantine adopted it, so that it fell to him to arbitrate between equally dogmatic and irreconcilable factions. The same task fell to his successors.

Half a century after the Council of Constantinople (381) and more than a century after the Council of Nicaea (325), the issues had changed but the ferment was still there. In 431 a Council was convened at Ephesus, the third of the seven Councils recognized by the Orthodox Church as 'oecumenical' or world-wide in authority. The crisis which had to be resolved at Ephesus was precipitated by Nestorius, the Patriarch of Constantinople, who insisted on the humanity of Christ and refused to call the Virgin Mary the 'Mother of God' (*Theotókos*). He was defeated by St. Cyril of Alexandria—a victory not without political significance in view of the rivalry of the two patriarchal sees—and Nestorianism was condemned. But that did not end the matter: the schism had a political sequel of great importance. Nestorianism attracted many of the eastern churches, and took root particularly in Persia, whence Nestorian missionaries spread as far afield as China. The victory of the Alexandrians also led them to carry their arrogance too far. At the second Council of Ephesus (449) the followers of Cyril insisted that Christ had but a single nature. This doctrine, Monophysitism, became a heresy in its turn.

The Emperor Marcian (450–57), asserting his right as the civil head of the established Church, convened another Council at Chalcedon (451), the fourth Oecumenical Council, in order to condemn the Monophysite heresy. It was the end of the domination of Alexandria, though not of the controversy. The official proclamation that Christ possessed two natures, not simply one, antagonized the Christians of Syria and Egypt, and consequently the Abyssinians too, who were converted by the Copts from Egypt. A large part of the eastern world was thus alienated from Constantinople no less decisively than Constantinople from Rome, with incalculable consequences when the onslaught of Islam began two centuries later. A vain effort was made by the Emperor Zeno (474–91) to reconcile the difference by means of his *Enotikón*, or Edict of Union (484), which sought to reverse the decisions of Chalcedon without denying their validity. But this desperate effort only resulted in the first formal schism with Rome, where the Pope denounced the Edict. The schism lasted till the accession of Justin I (518).

The barbarian tribes from the north had meantime taken complete control of the western empire, which they found an easier prey than Constantinople. The Visigoths had overrun the Iberian Peninsula, the Ostrogoths Italy, the Vandals much of North Africa. The Roman army was disbanded and barbarian kings replaced the Emperor—chief among them Clovis of the Franks and Theodoric in Italy—by the end of the 5th century. The eastern empire had not been immune, but Constantinople was never in real danger of sharing the fate of Rome. The raids of the Slavs into Greece first began in the early 6th century, and they reached Corinth in 540. The Huns and the Bulgars also ravaged the territory of the eastern empire. At the same time it was engaged in perennial warfare with the more civilized power of Persia. But just when there appeared to be a prospect that the Empire might actually disintegrate, in the 6th century an exceptional ruler came to power, Justinian the Great (527–65). He reformed the administration, recovered much of the lost lands of the West, and immortalized his name by codifying the Roman law and by building one of the great churches of the world, Sancta Sophia, the Church of the Holy Wisdom (537).

Every few generations the Empire was similarly saved from collapse by the emergence of a ruthless and able Emperor: Constantine, Justinian, Heraclius, Basil the Bulgar-slayer, and a handful of others. It is a tribute to the system of succession and constitutional power, which was never precisely formulated and worked only intermittently. Theoretically the Senate elected a new Emperor, and its election was ratified by popular acclamation. This pretence of constitutional procedure was punctiliously carried out long after it had ceased to have any real significance. In fact the succession was neither elective nor simply hereditary. It was a system of co-option modified by usurpation. Emperors usually, but not always, co-opted their sons or nephews or relatives by marriage. Constantine virtually restored a hereditary system, but it lasted only a few generations. There were other attempts to found hereditary dynasties in later centuries, which in some cases lasted longer. But although a strong Emperor could usually make sure of his nominee's succession by carrying out the ritual for his heir in his own life-time, none could take it for granted.

Justinian in this way succeeded his uncle, Justin I (518–27), and was similarly succeeded by his own nephew, Justin II (565–78), after a reign of nearly forty years. During those years the Empire was saved from disintegration and re-constructed, but the revival proved transitory. The most lasting effect of Justinian's reforms was to strengthen the power of the Emperor himself. His power became increasingly absolute. The civil and military administrations were kept strictly separate; and no one below the Emperor could exercise both powers. He was the source of all legislation: constitutional theorists called him 'the living law', just as theologians called him 'the image of God'. The government was based upon the Emperor's personal household. Many of its most senior officials bore titles reflecting this association, such as the *protovestiarius* (keeper of the wardrobe) or the *parakoimómenos* (literally, one who slept next to the imperial bed-chamber) or Grand Chamberlain. It was in keeping with this system of family despotism that Justinian gave extraordinary authority to his wife, the Cypriot courtesan

Theodora, who became the first of many politically powerful Empresses in the East.

His contemporaries and subjects would have regarded Justinian's posthumous fame as dearly earned. From their point of view, his administration was expensive, oppressive, and effective chiefly as a tax-gathering machine. He squandered the surplus built up by more frugal predecessors, notably the able administrator, Anastasius I (474–91). The public works for which he was celebrated extended to all parts of the Empire, and included a reconstruction of the military fortifications on the northern frontier; but they were costly and largely failed of their purpose. The centralization of the government was carried further at the expense of those parts of the Empire, like the Greek provinces, which still nominally enjoyed their ancient privileges of local government. Constantinople itself absorbed enormous revenues to pay for a highly organized bureaucracy and the heavy cost of defence, which included the hire of mercenaries and the payment of subsidies to potential enemies. Most expensive of all was the war in the west to recover the provinces lost by Rome, including Italy and North Africa. The fruits of this war, temporarily successful though it was, were also short-lived.

It was not a popular war with the rest of Justinian's subjects. The lost provinces in the West were Latin-speaking, whereas the eastern provinces which formed the Empire at his succession were already predominantly Greek. As the psychological gulf between Latins and Greeks had already begun to open, the Greeks looked without enthusiasm upon the consequences of the re-conquest of the Latin West, which would alter the cultural balance of the Empire to their disadvantage again. This is not to say that nationalism was a potent factor in the Empire. Greek was the common language of the imperial territories from the Adriatic Sea to the Taurus mountains, but the people who used it did not think of themselves as Greeks by nationality in the modern sense. What united them apart from the language was another factor related to language—their common membership of the Orthodox Church. Differences in interpretation of religious doctrine were therefore also at work in widening the gulf between East and West.

The eastern empire was unselfconsciously cosmopolitan.

There was no hostility to alien races at Constantinople, though the Jews as usual kept themselves a race apart. It would be impossible to assign a distinct nationality to the majority of the half-million inhabitants of the capital itself: they simply called themselves 'Romans', and did so in Greek. They accepted cultural influences as readily as traders from the east, with a justified conviction that Greek culture and Greek commercial enterprise were strong enough to match and assimilate any rivals. The great church of Sancta Sophia was largely built by Asian architects in a style owing little to classical models. Oriental influences had helped to pave the way for Christianity. Literature in the Greek language ceased to be associated with either territorial Greece or Greek nationality: it was the literature rather of a cosmopolitan governing class and of the Orthodox Church. The word 'Hellene' no longer meant Greek but 'pagan'. Yet Hellenism was steadily taking over the Empire.

Although he married a Greek, Justinian was at heart a Roman. He would have liked to stem the rising tide of Hellenism at Constantinople. He closed the schools of philosophy at Athens (529) and the law school at Beirut (551). When he set about the vast codification of the laws of Rome, it was natural that they should be published in Latin; and this was the case with the Codex, the Digest, and the Institutions. But Justinian's original contributions to the corpus of imperial legislation, known as the Novels, were mostly issued in Greek. To those who would be governed by them, Latin was increasingly a foreign language. The original collections were also translated into Greek, and Greek commentaries were written on them. To the Greeks, Roman law was an alien imposition. They clung to their ancient municipal institutions so long as the growing centralization of the Empire allowed them to do so. But it was rather through the Church, whose language was their monopoly, that their predominance over the Latin elements of the Empire was built up.

Justinian offended the Greek hierarchy by reaffirming the primacy of the Pope in his Novel 131 (545). He further alienated the masses of the capital by his brutal insistence on the strictest orthodoxy (which meant alliance with Rome) in opposition to the Monophysite heresy, even though his Empress Theodora was a devoted Monophysite. The supporters of the Council of Chalcedon (451) and their Monophysite opponents continued to contend for the adherence of the population of Constantinople. Social and even sporting issues became entangled with religious. The two factions had become identified with the rival colours of the Circus, the Blues and the Greens. The Blues were dominated by the orthodox upper classes, the Greens by the Monophysite lower classes. In 532 riots broke out between them and the government in the capital, and lasted for five days. From the watchword '*Nika*—vanquish!' they became known as the riots of Nika. The riots were suppressed only with great difficulty, and severe punishment was imposed on the Monophysite leaders of the Greens. In 553 Justinian called a second Council at Constantinople (the fifth of the seven Oecumenical Councils) to complete the restoration of orthodoxy.

The second Council of Constantinople was notable for the attendance in person of the Pope. This was made possible by the success of Justinian's most ambitious project—the re-conquest of the western Empire from the barbarians. It had been achieved at heavy cost. Thanks to the ability of two great generals, Belisarius and Narses, Justinian had recovered North Africa from the Vandals (534) and Italy from the Ostrogoths (537). He even had the satisfaction of ratifying the establishment of the French monarchy (536) under the descendants of the Frankish king Clovis, who were destined to re-found the western Empire. But Justinian's bloody victories were won at an exorbitant price. The other frontiers of the eastern Empire were neglected. The Huns overran the northern shores of the Black Sea, where Cherson was almost isolated as an imperial outpost. Armenia revolted in 539, and appealed to the Persians for help. The Persians under Chosroes invaded Syria and devastated Antioch in the same year (540) in which the Slavs raided Greece as far south as the Isthmus of Corinth. The Avars joined in the flood of invaders from beyond the Danube.

Eastern Emperors were to become famous for their crafty diplomacy, which often involved payments of a kind known in English history as Danegeld. Such subsidies, which their recipients would call tribute, were not considered humiliating by even the most arrogant of Emperors. Justinian made peace with the Avars (558) and also with the Persians (562) at the expense of such subsidies. But he left his successors with insoluble problems. The weight of taxation necessitated by his wars and subsidies was intolerable. It fell especially heavily on the agricultural population, at a time when the land was becoming exhausted. The conquests were themselves ephemeral. Justinian's nephew and successor, Justin II, tried new tactics. He made an alliance with a martial tribe from Central Asia, the Turks, in order to harass the Huns and keep open the trade-route to China without passing through Persia (568). 'It was thus that the Turkish nation became friends with the Romaioi,' wrote the historian Menander, little guessing the bitterly ironic sequel to his words in a later generation. Justin II then refused to pay the subsidies to either the Avars or the Persians, and both wars were renewed (572).

Justin's boldness failed to pay. The Turks denounced their alliance when they found out that the Greeks were also negotiating with the Avars (576). The Avars joined forces with the Slavs (usually known to Greek historians as the Sclavonians), who poured into northern Greece about 580 in numbers estimated at a hundred thousand. In 597 they attacked Salonika (Thessaloniki), the second city of the Greek mainland. They overran the whole peninsula of Greece while the bulk of the imperial armies were in Asia Minor, confronting the threat from Persia. Peace was made between the Empire and Persia for a time in 591, but in 604 the war broke out again and lasted for a quarter of a century. It was during this war that Jerusalem was lost by the Empire for the first time (614), but by no means the last. Meanwhile the re-conquests of Justinian in the West were being lost again to the invading Lombards. The new generation of barbarians were not content, like the Goths before them, to be assimilated into the Empire: they wanted to take it over. Justinian's successes were shown to be built on sand. From his death in 565 there followed almost half a century of chaos and anarchy.

There was little reason for the Emperor's subjects to feel loyalty towards him. They were heavily taxed, and there was much illicit extortion on top of the taxation. The tax system was based on agricultural land, the peasants being virtually tied to the soil. A large and centralized bureaucracy, supported by crushing taxation, gave the ordinary subjects of the Empire little in return. Outside the major cities, which enjoyed baths, bread and circuses, the common man had few pleasures. He was liable to conscription into the armed forces, which became a hereditary service. Justice was slow and the legal system clumsy. A Greek who defected to Attila in the 5th century was reported to have declared that he did so because of the burden of taxation and the inequality of rich and poor under the law: 'an injured party cannot get a hearing unless he pays money to the judge and his officials.' Justinian's contemporary, John of Lydia, wrote that 'a foreign invasion seemed less formidable to the taxpayer than the arrival of the officials of the Treasury'. There was a deep gulf of antipathy between the capital and the provinces, which was accentuated by religious differences and even by language. To add to the troubles of the Empire, in the middle of the 6th century it was swept by bubonic plague.

Only the natural strength of Constantinople saved the Empire once more from disintegration. Apart from the main cities, territorial Greece was almost entirely lost to the barbarians, as was Italy again, and this time for generations. The barbarians are not easy to distinguish: many names appear in the records—Slavs, Antae, Bulgars, Huns, Turks, Avars, Magyars, Patzinaks or Petchenegs—and some of the names are used interchangeably. Others, though once distinct, became assimilated in the course of time: for example, the Bulgars, a non-Slavonic people, adopted a Slav culture and language, as well as eventually the Christian religion; and the same was later to be true of the Russians, a Scandinavian people who were soon to appear on the scene of south-east Europe. But through the confusion of aggressive tribes at the end of the 6th century, it is the Slavs who stand out most clearly. They are the 'Sclavonians' of the Greek records; and for at least two centuries they, with their satellites, the Avars, were virtually masters of mainland Greece.

Both the historical and the archaeological records of this long obliterated conquest are unmistakable. The arrival of the Avars in the Peloponnese is approximately dated to the year 590 by the testimony of a 9th-century Patriarch, Nikolaos the Grammarian, writing about 808:

'These Avars had held possession of the Peloponnesus for two hundred and eighteen years, and had so completely separated it from the Byzantine Empire that no Byzantine official dared to put his foot in the country.'

The arrival of the Slavs is no less precisely established by the historian Isidore of Seville in the year 615. The completeness of their conquest is confirmed, at least at Athens and Corinth, by the evidence of excavation. The after-effects are equally clear from contemporary records. An 8th-century pilgrim from the west landed in Lakonia in what his biographer calls 'the land of the Slavs'; and the 10th-century Emperor, Constantine Porphyrogennitos, speaks of the Peloponnese as having been 'Slavised' in the mid-8th century.

In the long run, the foreign invaders were to be civilized, converted to Christianity, and eventually even transformed into Greek-speaking Byzantines. But at the end of the 6th century there was no effective will to resist either the northern or the eastern aggressors. A part of the reason no doubt lay in the alienation from Constantinople of the vast mass of the Emperor's subjects, both in Europe and Asia. This alienation was due not only to the fact that Justinian was an oppressive and rapacious administrator, but also to a lack of sympathy with his brutally imposed solution to the great religious controversy. The Monophysite heresy was widely accepted by ordinary people, especially in the eastern territories. Justinian's determination that it should be condemned contributed to a sense of defeatism everywhere, and even to a desire to secede from the Empire on the part of Egyptians and Syrians. It was for this reason that the Patriarch of Jerusalem cared little about being overrun by the Persians in 614. A generation later even the Muslims were widely welcomed.

The successive heresies which the Church condemned were consequently more effective than Orthodoxy in propagating Christianity among the pagans. Like Nestorianism among the Persians, the Monophysite heresy in particular had a great appeal to the Arabs, and undoubtedly influenced their prophet Muhammad. Religious divisions thus helped to disrupt the Empire, and the process was to be repeated again in the 8th century with the Iconoclast controversy. On the other hand, the missionary effort of the Orthodox Church itself was still in its infancy. Some attempts were made to convert the northern invaders who had actually settled within the Empire, not without success. Some attempts were also made further afield. There is evidence of missionary contact with the Magyars, who

38

were settled to the north of the Black Sea, in the late 6th century. But the great days of Orthodox missionary activity lay in the future. Meanwhile the souls of the Emperor's eastern subjects were irrecoverably alienated, and awaited only the inspiration of Islam.

The ruinous heritage of Justinian was finally exposed a generation after his death. His three immediate successors, Justin II (565–78), Tiberius (578–82) and Maurice (582–602), made valiant efforts to restore the defences of the Empire on the northern and eastern frontiers, which had been sacrificed to the wars in Italy and North Africa. Maurice probably initiated the re-organisation of the Empire for defence, which his successors in the 7th century completed. In particular, he established the Exarchates or subordinate capitals of Ravenna and Carthage. But in 602 a military rebellion overthrew him, and he was murdered with all his family. There followed eight years of disastrous civil war, which were exploited by both the Persians and the Slavs. The Persians overran the outlying provinces and penetrated deep into Anatolia. The Slavs again attacked Salonika (609). Constantinople itself was not free from danger. The Empire was virtually bankrupt. It would have been a brave man who would have forecast the possibility of revival. But such a man was found, in the person of Heraclius (610–41), whose reign marked a turning-point in Byzantine history. It began in chaos, and achieved a triumphant climax; but it also coincided with the emergence of the greatest of all militant religions, Islam.

Although less celebrated in history, Heraclius has a better claim than Justinian to be regarded as the restorer of the Empire. Like Justinian, he felt as a Roman. By descent he was an Armenian, which is to say that he felt little sympathy with Greeks. But he came to power from the western or Latin-speaking part of the Empire—specifically from North Africa, which was its most Roman province. His father held the Exarchate of Carthage. At one time Heraclius contemplated moving the capital from Constantinople to Carthage, but he abandoned the plan under pressure from the Patriarch. His motive was no doubt a conviction in his early days that it was impossible to restore the eastern Empire or even to hold the capital itself; and with Rome in the hands of the Lombards, Africa was the last stronghold that could be defended. He suffered at first, in fact, from a lack of resolution which makes his later achievements all the more remarkable. There was good reason for a man to despair on inheriting the Empire in the first quarter of the 7th century. But Heraclius had not so much inherited as usurped it. If he were not to suffer the same fate himself, he had to show himself capable of counter-attack.

The tide of war ran uniformly against him for more than a decade. The Persians overran Syria and Egypt, carrying off the True Cross from Jerusalem in 614. The Avars, now the mightiest power in Central Europe, swept over the Empire in a series of tidal waves. They even reached the suburbs of Constantinople in 619 and again (with their Slav and Bulgar allies) in 626. The Slavs raided Crete in 623, showing that the imperial fleet had even lost control of the Aegean. Hostile tradition has it that Heraclius was inactive during these years. But it is inconceivable that an idler or a coward should have wanted to seize the throne at such a time, or that he would have held it without showing himself capable of counter-attack. Heraclius was in fact preparing his forces for a crushing revenge. His hour struck when he renewed the war with Persia in 622, and successfully overran Armenia. In 626 he beat off simultaneous attacks by the Persians and the northern invaders. Constantinople itself was at stake, and narrowly but decisively survived.

A year later Heraclius had not only secured Anatolia but was ready to march into the heart of Persia. He defeated the Persian army near Mosul, and was rewarded in 629 with a revolution in the Persian capital which overthrew the Great King. The Persian threat to the Empire was destroyed for good. Peace was made on humiliating terms, including the restoration of Syria and Egypt to the Empire. Heraclius was able to bring back the True Cross to Jerusalem and to celebrate a brilliant triumph at Constantinople. As a permanent recognition of his defeat of the Persian King, he was the first Emperor to take the Greek title of *Basileus* (King), which the Greeks had once held in horror. In 630 the Empire reached a new pinnacle of power and magnificence. Yet an even more portentous event took place in the same year—the first armed clash between Roman forces and the Arab followers of Muhammad. History records that soon after his victory over Persia, Heraclius received an embassy from Muhammad, but he did not yet recognize the new force that had arisen.

Muhammad died in 632, and Heraclius outlived him by nearly ten years. During that time the first waves of the Arab inundation lapped against the outskirts of the Empire, and Heraclius had a foretaste of what was to come. The Arabs captured Damascus in 635 and Jerusalem in 637. They defeated Heraclius himself at the battle of the River Yarmuk (636). By the time of his death (641) they held all Palestine and Syria. It is notable that Heraclius devoted much time in his last ten years to religious questions, as if aware that Islam could be looked on as a particularly attractive new heresy. He sent missionaries among the Slavs, and he asked that they be supplied from Rome as a token of harmony between the eastern and western churches. In collaboration with Pope Honorius, he tried again to resolve the vexed question of the nature of Christ by means of the doctrine that there was in Him only a single energy (Monoenergism) and a single will (Monothelitism). But the attempt at such a compromise, though it appealed to the Armenians, offended both Jerusalem and Alexandria. Once more the grand design of Christian union collapsed.

The collapse was dramatically marked by a close succession of dates: the fall of Jerusalem (637) and Alexandria (640) to the Arabs, the death of Pope Honorius (638) and Heraclius (641). While the Caliph Omar, Muhammad's father-in-law and second successor, was sweeping away Heraclius' conquests, the Greeks and the Latins continued bickering about the nature, the will and the energy of Christ. Honorius' successors recoiled in horror from his Monothelite doctrine. Monophysites rallied in thousands to the standards of Islam. Heraclius' successor, Constans II (641–68), found the whole controversy so embarrassing that in 648 he issued an edict forbidding discussion of the disputed doctrines. Pope Theodore disapproved of the edict so violently that he excommunicated the Patriarch—a gesture which was to be repeated and reciprocated many times. In the middle of the 7th century the Empire was once again threatened by internal disruption as much as by external aggression. Yet once again it was to rally.

The Empire had great reserves of underlying strength, which could survive superficial disturbances almost unscathed. Although it never achieved the stability of secure frontiers, the capital itself was still impregnable to the weapons of the day.

Its geographical situation assured it enormous wealth from trade, so that it could afford to hire mercenaries or to buy off aggressors almost at will as its frontiers contracted. In economic sophistication as in military technology it was by far the most advanced state of the day, having left western Europe behind and not yet been overtaken from the East. It had an efficient civil service, which successfully operated the two most important functions of collecting taxes and exercising central power. Above all it was reinforced by the conviction of enjoying the favour of heaven and having God's representative in its midst. Individual Emperors and Patriarchs were expendable, but the system of which they were the outward and visible sign was recognized as immutable. Byzantium, as it must now be called, was there to stay.

CHAPTER II

The Byzantine Ascendancy
(641-1071)

The underlying strength of the Empire showed itself in the half-century after the death of Heraclius, and not least in the twenty years around the turn of the following century (695–717), when half a dozen Emperors were dethroned or murdered in rapid succession without seriously undermining it. The wars with the northern invaders continued, subject to fluctuating fortunes. Constans II regained some ground from the Slavs in the middle of the century, though they continued to occupy most of mainland Greece. For two years (675–7) they almost continously invested Salonika, but without success. Their allies the Bulgars settled south of the Danube at about the same time. Constans reverted to the notion of shifting the capital back to the West again for greater security. To return to Rome itself was impracticable, so he settled at Syracuse. But he was murdered for his pains, and the capital returned to Constantinople. His successors concentrated on converting the Slavs and Bulgars instead of retreating from them.

The Arabs were not susceptible to conversion. But their tidal wave of aggression, which looks so spectacular in the retrospect of a dozen centuries, was by no means without setbacks and hindrances. They experienced their first great defeat in a naval attack on Constantinople (678) after a four-year blockade, when modern technology in the form of 'Greek fire' was decisive for the defence. It was not their only setback. On several occasions in the 7th century, it is recorded, local Muslim commanders paid tribute to the Emperor to avert counter-attack. As on the occasions when the Empire paid what its enemies called 'tribute' to them, the term would not have been admitted by the payers. It was simply a recognition of a temporarily adverse balance of power, just as the transfer of gold by modern states is the recognition of an adverse balance of trade. But it is evidence that the Arab advance was not uniform or uninterrupted. There were even occasions when the balance of power was so exactly equal that the two sides accepted a condominium over a given territory, as they did in the case of Cyprus (688).

Nor were relations between the Arabs (or Saracens,[1] as the Greeks called them) and Constantinople uniformly hostile. They had been in contact since the early days of the Roman Empire. Arab horsemen had served in the Roman armies. Christian Arabs made pilgrimage to the Holy Places under Roman control. More than one Arab actually sat on the throne of the Empire. Even in the centuries of warfare, peaceful traffic continued between Saracens and Greeks in trade, in the arts and scholarship. The Saracens who overran Spain and established the Umayyad dynasty there were never at war with the Empire: trade continued between them even during the battles for the control of Italy. Mosques were built in Constantinople, just as Christian churches remained open in Muslim territory. Rarely were either attacked or desecrated. On the contrary, Christendom and Islam were both more intolerant of their own heretics within than either was of the other.

A Greek in the Middle Ages would have found himself more at his ease in Cairo or Baghdad than he would have in Paris or Rome. Many did so; and Christian pilgrims still visited the Holy Places. Christian artists and civil servants were employed by the Caliphs. In Egypt, Greeks rose to high office under the Muslim Fatimids. In Damascus, St. John (a Christian Arab, known as the Damascene) lived and wrote under Muslim rule more unrestrictedly than he could have done at Constantinople in the 8th century, for his views were then regarded as heretical at the Christian capital. Rome and Constantinople were already temperamentally alienated long before their final rupture. They were divided in ways that Greeks and Saracens were not: by mutual contempt, by language, by the intrusion of barbarians down the east flank of the Adriatic, by competition to convert

[1] Probably derived from the Arabic *Sharc* = east.

those barbarians to Christianity, by rivalry between the two patriarchal sees, by centuries of history. Between Greeks and Saracens there was no such incurable bitterness as between Orthodox and Catholics. This was to become paradoxically apparent in the era of the Crusades.

The paramount issue between the Empire and the Muslims was the possession of Asia Minor, which was the chief recruiting ground of the imperial forces. Armenia, the source of both man-power and gold, submitted to the Arabs in 653—a disastrous loss to the Empire which took long to recover. Half a century later, the massacre of the Armenian princes by the Arabs led to the flight of the survivors (705), who settled in Cilicia, which became known as Little Armenia. The Muslims' attempt to penetrate the Caucasus was frustrated by the Khazars, who were the allies of the Emperor though they preferred the Jewish to the Christian religion. Their alliance enabled Constantinople to keep open its trade-routes with eastern Asia after the loss of Egypt and Syria. By the beginning of the 8th century most of Asia Minor and North Africa had fallen to the Arabs. They took Carthage in 698 and Sardinia in 711 during the period of anarchy in which the dynasty of Heraclius finally collapsed. But in 717 they were again repulsed from Constantinople.

That year marked a turning-point in history. Some historians have dated from it the emergence of a distinctively Byzantine rather than an East Roman Empire. It was not the victory over the Arabs that led to this designation but the accession of a new and powerful Emperor, Leo III (717–41), known from the home of his ancestors as the Isaurian. The Isaurians were a people of Asia Minor, neighbouring Cilicia, who already enjoyed a legendary fame as soldiers and pirates. The fact that Leo came from Anatolia[1] was historically important in two respects. First, he naturally wished to expel the Saracens from his home-land; and in this task he laid the foundations on which his successors were able to build decisive victories later in the century. Secondly, he wished to reform the Church in a way which would make it possible to attract the lost peoples of Asia back to the Christian fold. In this endeavour he roused a controversy which lasted a century and a half, and ended in failure.

[1] Although he certainly came from Asia Minor, it is in fact doubtful whether he was an Isaurian.

45

The political undertone of all the religious controversies of Byzantium was now undisguised. There was the problem of reconciling the eastern Christians of Asia and Egypt to orthodoxy, in competition with Islam. There was also the problem of reconciling Constantinople and Rome, which was not merely a matter of interpreting a common doctrine in two increasingly separate languages but also of settling the primacy in status between the Patriarch and the Pope. Overlaid on the unsettled rivalry between Pope and Patriarch was that between both and the Emperor, though this was not a perennial feud but simply a personal affair which arose from time to time between particular incumbents. No way was ever found of solving all these problems simultaneously. The result was a threefold fragmentation of mediaeval Christendom. The separation of the eastern Churches began in the 5th century and was completed in the 8th. The schism between Rome and Constantinople was already latent in the 7th century, though not complete till the 11th.

So far as theology was concerned, the repudiation of the Monophysite and Monothelite heresies completed the spiritual secession of the Asians and Egyptians, and thus facilitated their surrender to Islam, at the same time as it effected a superficial reconciliation with Rome in the 7th century. The crucial date was the year 681, when the third Council of Constantinople (the sixth of the seven recognised Oecumenical Councils) re-affirmed the condemnation of Monophysitism that had been formulated at Chalcedon in 451, and also condemned the more recent heresy of Monothelitism as well. The effect was to alienate the East and conciliate the West. But what the hierarchy at Constantinople further wanted was to affirm its own supremacy over Rome. To this end a further Council was convened at Constantinople by the Emperor Justinian II in 692, which was known as the Council of the Dome (*in Trullo*), from the shape of the building in which it was held. Here the Greeks tried to impose their own ritual on Rome; but the Latin bishops neither attended the Council nor recognized its validity.

For the time being ecclesiastical controversy had reached a dead end. The east was virtually lost: three of the five historic patriarchates (Antioch, Jerusalem, Alexandria) were in Muslim hands. The rivalry between the remaining two, Constantinople and Rome, was all the keener for that reason, but there was no decisive way of settling it. The city of Rome was reduced to a shadow of its ancient glory. It was nominally subject to the Emperor's deputy, the Exarch at Ravenna, though much of its territory was in the hands of the Lombards. But the Popes continued to assert the primacy of their see as well as their loyalty to the Emperor. It was not always easy to reconcile these two positions, as the Council *in Trullo* had painfully shown. The difficulty was to be far more seriously exposed when Leo the Isaurian, with his eye on the lost sheep of Asia and Egypt, launched a new controversy which the Roman Church found harder to stomach than even the Monophysite heresy. In the tenth year of his reign (726) Leo the Isaurian became also the Iconoclast.

Those who called themselves Iconoclasts believed that the presence of representations of the deity in places of worship was idolatrous. All the *icons* of Christ, the Virgin Mary and the Saints must therefore be destroyed. Their opponents, who clung to the veneration of *icons*, were known as Iconodules. It was a deep controversy between two conceptions of Christ's human nature and of the relation between the material and the spiritual elements in religion. Orthodox belief, both before and after the Iconoclast controversy, was that Iconoclasm rested on a misconception which amounted to a betrayal of the doctrine of incarnation. The Iconoclasts wanted a religion purged of all material contamination; but Orthodoxy had traditionally been a religion of the physical as much as the spiritual side of humanity. The greatest of the 8th-century opponents of Iconoclasm, St. John of Damascus, wrote that 'the Word made flesh had deified the flesh'. That was and is Orthodox doctrine, which the puritanical Iconoclasts sought to repudiate as though it were a defilement of their spirituality.

It is not certain whether, in adopting Iconoclast prejudices, the Emperor Leo III was influenced by Asian conceptions derived from his own homelands. Certainly the Iconoclastic doctrine was one that would have been acceptable to Jews and Muslims, and to the Christians of Egypt and Syria who were wavering in their loyalties. Leo was presumably not indifferent to those considerations when he issued the decrees concerning the destruction of icons, starting in 726. If so, the outcome was not what he expected. Instead of winning back subjects in the East, he merely further antagonized the West. Pope Gregory II opposed Leo's decrees and witheld the revenues under his control. His successor, Gregory III, who was confirmed in the papacy by the Emperor for the last time in Byzantine history (731), excommunicated his sovereign. The rebellions in the West led to the political independence of Rome, and eventually also of Venice. Even the Patriarch of Constantinople opposed Leo's decrees, and was deposed in retaliation.

In the East, the Iconoclastic decrees had no decisive effect. The tide of Muslim advance had already been turned, nearly a decade before Iconoclasm became official, by Leo's great victory over the Arabs before Constantinople in 717, the first year of his reign. The Arabs were still able to occupy much of the Empire's Asian territories for another century and a half; and there were to be further massive invasions of Asia Minor within Leo's own life-time; but the survival of the Empire itself was now assured. Leo's victory in 717 was not less decisive in European history than the later victory of Charles Martel at Poitiers (732), won over the Arab armies advancing into France from Spain. Both battles marked the limit of Arab advance, though neither broke Muslim power. It is significant that within a generation of Leo's victory, the Umayyad rulers of the Arab world suffered a revolt at the hands of the Abbasids (747), which was tantamount to a revival of Persian power; and in 750 the Muslim capital was shifted eastwards from Damascus to Baghdad. These dramatic changes were symptomatic of a Byzantine revival, but not of a decay of Islam.

The salvation of the Empire lay in Leo's military reforms. Reorganization began in the century before Leo, and continued under his successors, but his was the inspiration which gave it the greatest impetus. The contraction of the frontiers, both in the East and the West, made the armed forces increasingly dependent on mercenaries; and this dependence in turn placed a still heavier burden on the tax-payer. Far-reaching consequences, both good and bad, followed from the increasing concentration of policy upon defence. Provinces were re-organized as military districts (*thémata*) in which the governors exercised both military and civil functions—a combination which the earlier Emperors had tried to avoid. Small proprietors were squeezed out of their properties by the fiscal rapacity of the Emperor, who became virtually his own minister of finance.

The distinction between slaves and the impoverished freemen began to wither away. At the other end of the scale, large estates became larger and their proprietors increasingly independent. In between there grew up a quasi-feudal class of farmers who received grants of land on hereditary tenure with the obligation of military service.

Growing numbers of these new classes were foreigners to the Empire in origin. The depopulation of formerly Greek lands and islands by the Arab wars and recurrent plagues had encouraged the influx of foreign mercenaries who settled for good —Avars in Dalmatia, Bulgars in modern Bulgaria and further south, Slavs in Greece itself, and also in Asia Minor. Gradually these were assimilated to the Greek language, religion and culture, though not without continuing hostilities from time to time. The Bulgars, for instance, fought under Leo III as mercenaries against the Arabs, but a generation later they were at war with his son Constantine V (755). Such hostilities had rather the character of a civil war than a foreign war. There was no sense of nationality within the Empire: what the Bulgars and the Slavs were trying to do, when not fighting for pay under the Emperor's command, was to take over the Empire from within. It was not so paradoxical as it might seem when a Bulgar Khan, defeated in 777 by the Emperor, fled to Constantinople and accepted baptism and a Greek bride.

Leo the Isaurian had died in 741, leaving his work unfinished in both the military and the ecclesiastical sphere. Perhaps his most important legacy was an abridgement of the voluminous body of post-Justinian law, published in Greek under the title of the *Ecloga*. The language of the people thus displaced the traditional Latin for legal purposes. The change emphasized the widening gulf between the East and the West, which Iconoclasm had aggravated. Nor did the controversy abate. Leo's death was followed by a rebellion under an Iconodule pretender, supported by the Pope. But Leo's son successfully overcame the rebels and ascended the throne as Constantine V, to continue his father's work. In 754 he convened a Council at Constantinople to re-affirm the denunciation of images. It was repudiated by the Pope, by three of the eastern Patriarchs, and above all by the monasteries, which were the mainspring of opposition to Iconoclasm. Actual persecution of the adherents of *icons* followed (765). By now reconciliation seemed impossible between the rival doctrines.

In Italy a new combination arose to contend with the unorthodox Emperors in the East. Pépin, the son of Charles Martel, invaded Italy with his army of Franks in 754, the year of the Iconoclast Council at Constantinople. His antagonists were the Lombards, who had taken even Ravenna (751), and his ally was the Pope, to whom he granted the duchy of Rome. The last thing that he and his successors intended was to restore the eastern Empire in Italy. His son Charlemagne defeated the Lombards decisively in 774, and continued the alliance with the papacy, in which he was the dominant partner. It was Charlemagne who destroyed the chance of reconciliation between Rome and Constantinople, abetted by the first woman who ever ruled as Emperor (not Empress) in her own right— the Athenian Irene, widow of Leo IV. She lived up to her pacific name by an attempt to secure the toleration of *icons*, though in most other respects her influence was disastrous. In 787, at her behest, the second Council of Nicaea was convened (the seventh and last Oecumenical Council). It authorized the restoration of images, and earned the approval even of the Pope. But Charlemagne personally dissented.

The Iconoclast controversy was now near to achieving the fatal result of separating the Greek and Roman Churches irreconcilably. The separation was the outcome of secular events as much as religious controversy. Faced by the aggression of the Lombards, the Pope could no longer turn to Constantinople for succour, partly because the Emperor was unorthodox and partly because Byzantine arms were too feeble. He had turned instead to the rising power of the Franks, who had no patience with the minutiae of the iconoclastic squabble, and whose ambition was to usurp the Empire. It was they who make the Pope a temporal ruler in return for his moral support. At some date around the turn of the 8th to the 9th century, an ingenious forgery was put into circulation known as the Donation of Constantine, by which the founder of Constantinople was alleged to have transferred the secular power over the western Empire to the papacy. Charlemagne, overriding this docile Pope, now began to assert the same combination of secular and ecclesiastical power as that claimed by the Byzantine Emperor.

Charlemagne published a refutation of the doctrine adopted at Nicaea (787), in which he criticized impartially both the superstitious bigotry of the Icondules and the misguided zeal of the Iconoclasts. In short, his quarrel was with the Greeks as such, and it was embittered by a personal antagonism to Irene. Irene, being an Athenian by birth, was a Greek by sentiment as well as religion. At one time a marriage was projected between Charlemagne's daughter and her son, which would have united the two halves of the Empire under a remarkable partnership. When this plan broke down, Charlemagne pursued his own ambitions along another course. With the support of the Pope, he convened a Council of western bishops at Frankfurt (794) at which it was decreed that images should continue to be placed in churches but not worshipped.

The Council of Frankfurt also sowed the seeds of another bitter dispute by deciding that the word *filioque* ought to be included in the Creed, and that the Greeks were wrong to recite it in its original form without this word. The point at issue was whether, in the words of the Creed, the Holy Spirit proceeded from the Father only or from both the Father *and the Son* (*filioque*). The *filioque* had been adopted in Spain over two centuries earlier, but Rome had not yet approved it; nor did the Popes formally decide to do so for another two centuries, though they held it to be doctrinally sound. At the end of the 8th century the *filioque* was therefore not yet a bone of contention between Rome and Constantinople. What drove them apart was rather the personal ambition of Charlemagne.

Having defeated the Lombards, Charlemagne turned on the Byzantine armies in Italy. In a series of campaigns between 788 and 798, he virtually ended the Emperor's rule in the West. He recovered Ravenna and handed it over to the Pope. Only a few coastal cities remained in Byzantine hands, together with Sicily, until it fell to the Arabs from North Africa. The climax of Charlemagne's career came on Christmas Day, 800, when the Pope crowned him Emperor in Rome. Two years later he presumed to make an offer of marriage to the Emperor Irene, who would probably have accepted if she had not been overthrown by a usurper, Nicephorus I, her own Minister of Finance. In 803 the Treaty of Aix-la-Chapelle settled the boundaries between the two Empires, and in 812 Byzantium recognized Charlemagne's title of *Basileus* or Emperor.

The eastern Empire now had no alternative but to acquiesce in the secession of the west. At the beginning of the 9th century, the new Emperor Nicephorus I (802–11) was beset with dangers and anxieties on all sides. Rome and Venice were already lost, as an indirect result of the Iconoclast quarrel. After a respite in the middle of the 8th century, the tide of Saracen advance swept on again under the Abbasid dynasty. Its most celebrated Caliph, Haroun al-Rashid, invaded Asia Minor repeatedly between 782 and his death in 809. In the following generation Saracen raids spread still further to the west. They occupied Crete in 826 and began the long-drawn-out conquest of Sicily next year. About the year 840 they landed in southern Italy, and penetrated nearly to Rome by 846. The islands of Greece were largely depopulated by Saracen naval raids. On the mainland there was even one occasion when Slavs and Saracens concerted operations, in an attack on Patras (about 807). The Bulgars also harried the Empire at the same time under their outstanding national leader, Krum, who defeated and killed the Emperor Nicephorus in 811.

Reduced on all sides, the Empire was forced to recognize its western rival, and then to negotiate a peace for thirty years with the Bulgars (815–45). A new policy was gradually evolved for taming the Empire's Balkan neighbours—to convert them rather than to defeat them. The 9th century was the pioneering era of Byzantine missionary activity. The Slavs settled in Greece were the first to be assimilated in this way, and the Bulgars a generation later. But the work of conversion was carried on against a background of continuing dissension within the Orthodox Church. Iconoclasm was far from defunct. The Emperor Nicephorus I, though not himself violently partisan, was anti-ecclesiastical. When the throne was usurped in 813 by Leo V (an Armenian general), the restoration of Asian influence led to a revival of Iconoclasm. After Leo's death in 820, there was an Iconodule rebellion, whose leader, very significantly, was a Slav called Thomas. Though finally defeated, he had much support among Greeks, Slavs and Arabs. Leo's own successors, who were also Asians, continued and intensified the persecution of those who tolerated images, until at last the controversy gradually lost its virulence and was finally laid at rest in 843. Since that date the presence of images in places of worship has always remained part of Greek Orthodoxy.

The credit for reconciling the two factions in 843—for it was rather a reconciliation than a total defeat of Iconoclasm—goes partly to the Patriarch of the day, but chiefly once more to a woman. The Empress Theodora was the widow of Theophilus, the second Emperor of a dynasty known as the Amorian, from its centre of origin at Amorium in Phrygia. Theophilus (829–42) was himself the last of the Iconoclasts, but he tolerated his wife's adherence to the Iconodule creed. She in her turn, after his death, made it a condition of the restoration of icons that Theophilus' name should be exempted from the general anathema pronounced against the Iconoclasts. In fact, the heat and bitterness had at last died out of the controversy. The reconciliation opened the way for a revival of Byzantine power, which made itself strongly felt in the second half of the 9th century.

Under the Amorian dynasty, Egypt was invaded by a Byzantine army in 852; both Crete and Cyprus were recovered, though only temporarily; and in 863 a crushing defeat was inflicted on the Saracens at the battle of Poson, which marked a turning-point in their history. Theodora's brilliant brother, Bardas, was one of the chief architects of victory, and for ten years (856–66) he was Emperor in all but name. On the other hand, success was not unmixed: even the city of Amorium, the cradle of the dynasty, was taken and sacked by the Saracens in 838. But although the Empire never recovered all the territory that it had lost, there was no longer a united Arab world ranged against it, only a number of independent Muslim states. Unfortunately the Christian world chose this particular moment of returning strength to split itself again on a religious issue: not this time only within the Orthodox Church, but once again between Rome and Constantinople.

Religious controversy had developed a new character. Theology and politics were still intertwined, but the balance between them had shifted. Formerly theology had dominated politics; now politics dominated theology. A new type of cleric was emerging, whom strict ecclesiastics regarded as a secular politician. It would be fairer to call this new type, in modern parlance, a 'broad' churchman. Such men could believe, in matters of controversy, that one side or the other was unmistakably in the right, yet for neither side was it worth going (or sending others) to the stake. Their favourite doctrine was called *Economy*, which may be translated as management, dispensation, or compromise. It was this doctrine that had laid the Iconoclast controversy to rest. In the following centuries it was to be the established device for dealing with a succession of bitter controversies of different kinds. But always it was opposed by the austere, uncompromising extremists, to whom the slightest deviation from orthodoxy was mortal sin. A fresh example came within a generation of the end of Iconoclasm.

What is known to history as the Photian schism was a long-drawn-out wrangle lasting some thirty years (857–87) with marked political and international overtones. It began with a relatively trivial event. Bardas, the brother of Theodora and uncle of the Emperor Michael III (842–67), was suspected of incest. The Patriarch Ignatius imposed a penance on him. In retaliation, Ignatius was exiled by the Emperor and resigned his office. He was replaced by Photius, a layman (as Patriarchs not infrequently were) and a man universally admired for his scholarship and diplomatic skill. The Pope, encouraged by the supporters of Ignatius, expressed doubt about the validity of Photius' election. He sent legates to Constantinople to investigate the case (861). Photius treated them with great respect, and they returned to Rome satisfied. But the Pope rejected their conclusions, re-tried the case himself in Rome (863), and declared Ignatius the legitimate Patriarch. Constantinople ignored the Pope's declaration. The dispute was already bad enough, but it was soon to be made worse by two new factors: a rivalry in missionary activities abroad, and a change of dynasty at Constantinople.

The dispute coincided with a time of intense activity in the missionary field. The Slavs settled in Greece had already been converted to Christianity: it was time to press further afield, and the missions were closely connected with diplomacy. Cyril and Methodius, two brothers from Salonika, were sent on their first mission in 860, to the Khazars north of the Black Sea. It had no permanent results, partly because the Khazars were already under pressure from the Varangians (later to be known as Russians), and partly because they eventually preferred

Judaism to Christianity. The next expedition of Cyril and Methodius, which was to Moravia, seemed at first more promising. Here, however, they met competition from German missionaries, sent out under the authority of the Pope. They withdrew to Bulgaria (863). It was difficult to avoid a conflict because of the doctrinal differences which already separated the Churches: over marriage of the clergy, rules of fasting, and above all the *filioque* in the Creed. The Bulgar Khan Boris at first accepted baptism from the Greeks (864); then he turned to Rome, no doubt because Rome was further off and therefore more likely to leave his Church independent (866). The Patriarch Photius was alarmed both by the extension of Roman influence and by the question of the *filioque*, which now became more than academic.

Photius published an encyclical letter to his fellow Patriarchs in the East, denouncing both Rome and the *filioque* (867). He summoned a Council at Constantinople, which supported him in excommunicating the Pope. But in the same year a dramatic reversal of fortunes took place. The Emperor Michael III was deposed and murdered by his general and former groom, Basil, the founder of the Macedonian dynasty, who was in fact Armenian by descent. Basil I sought a reconciliation with Rome by deposing Photius and restoring Ignatius to the Patriarchate. In 869 a further Council was convened at Constantinople, which reversed all the decisions of the Council of 867. Yet the gratification of the Pope was shortlived. Boris of Bulgaria changed his mind again in 870: he expelled the German missionaries whom Rome supported, denounced the *filioque*, and returned to Byzantine jurisdiction. Meanwhile, Photius and Ignatius had reconciled their differences at Constantinople. When Ignatius died in 877, Photius again succeeded him as Patriarch. Peace was proclaimed at another Council of Constantinople (879), and a new Pope refrained from trying to interfere.

The religious issues remained unsettled between East and West. It was only a matter of time before they caused fresh controversy, though in a different form. Nor was the internal peace of the Eastern Church undisturbed. New heresies—or old ones in a new guise—were active in the 9th century. In Armenia there were the Paulicians, who believed (like the Manichaeans before them) in a duality of equal powers for good and evil, ruling respectively over the world of the spirit and the world of the flesh. Their rebellion in 871 was severely repressed by Basil I, himself of Armenian descent. The doctrines of the Paulicians spread to Bulgaria, where they were preached by a village priest called Bogomil. His followers, who called themselves Bogomils, were in part reacting against the Byzantinisation of Bulgaria, after the conversion of Boris. But the durability of the dualist doctrine itself is shown by its re-appearance in different guises in many parts of southern Europe for centuries. The Cathari and the Albigenses in southern France were among the later examples.

Two centuries were to pass, however, before another religious dispute seriously shook the stability of the Empire. These were the great days of Byzantium, and the Macedonian dynasty founded by Basil I was its most powerful and durable epoch. Though the Macedonian dynasty succeeded the Amorian by violence, the process of imperial consolidation was continuous from the one to the other. The friendship of the Emperors was solicited, or at least their influence was accepted, throughout the Mediterranean world. In the 870's Basil's armies were campaigning in Italy against the Saracens, in alliance with the western Emperor Louis II. A long peace with the Bulgars was only briefly interrupted in 846, and again for five years in 888–93. The Serbs—a Slavonic tribe—followed the Bulgarian example in accepting Orthodox Christianity by the end of the 9th century: their assimilation was now virtually complete. Other newcomers from the north made their appearance: the Magyars (commonly called Turks by Byzantine historians), the Petchenegs, the Vlakhs, the Croats—all of whom were eventually baptised, though the Magyars and Croats preferred the Roman to the Greek Church.

Most important of all the newcomers were the Russians, originally known to Byzantium as Varangians. Their importance in the history of Greece, whether political, military, or religious, cannot be overstated. Each decisively affected the history of the other in innumerable ways, from the 9th to the 20th centuries. The Russians' first appearance in Byzantine history was probably in 839, when small groups of Russian mercenaries came to the aid of Constantinople against the Saracens. Between 850 and 860 they had established themselves in the modern Ukraine, where they captured Kiev from the Khazars. When next they came to Constantinople, it was as a more formidable force, which turned against their allies and almost captured the capital itself (860). From then onwards, the Empire had to deal with them on something nearer to equal terms. A treaty was signed with them by Basil I (874), who was allowed to send an Archbishop to Kiev. Relations continued to oscillate uneasily. Further treaties were signed at intervals in the 10th century, often under threat of Russian attack, which sometimes turned from a threat to actuality. But Russian mercenaries were regularly recruited into the armies of Byzantium from about 900, and formed what was known as the Varangian Guard, one of the most dependable forces in the service of the Empire.

The historical importance of the Russians could not yet be foreseen, any more than could that of the Turks, on whom the Abbasid rulers of the Saracens increasingly depended as mercenaries. If the Emperors of the 9th century had had to name their most dangerous rivals in Europe, they would have named the Bulgars, not the Russians, still less the Turks. Despite their acceptance of Christianity, the Bulgar Khans did not cease to attack the Empire: rather, because of their conversion they regarded themselves as having a claim to be its heirs. Bulgaria reached its zenith under Symeon, who first took the title of Caesar or Tsar around the turn of the 9th to the 10th century. In 914, when the Empire was ruled by the Empress-Regent Zoe on behalf of the infant Constantine VII Porphyrogennitos, Symeon's armies invested Constantinople itself. His object was to take over the Empire either by force or by marriage during Constantine's minority. Repeated attacks were repulsed during the next decade, but the territory of the Bulgars expanded further and further into Greece. Adrianople fell to them in 923.

So many were the enemies of Constantinople in the 10th century that it seemed as if the only question was which would take the capital first. But the ingenuity of Byzantine diplomacy and the strength of the city's walls frustrated them all. Basil I and his son, Leo VI (886–912), strengthened the reduced Empire by an immense but little-publicised work of re-organization, including the administration, defence, the Church and the law. An able general, Romanus Lecapenus—yet another Armenian by descent—cheated the Tsar Symeon of his prize by marrying his daughter to the boy-emperor Constantine VII. Symeon's last assault on Constantinople failed in 924, and he died three years later. Thereafter peace was signed, and the Bulgarian Empire declined; but it secured the recognition of an autocephalous Church in 945. The Magyars, whom Byzantium had enlisted as allies against the Bulgars at the end of the 9th century, turned on Constantinople in their turn a generation later, but besieged it in vain (934). The Russians similarly failed in 941. They made peace a few years later, and by the middle of the century they had been allowed to establish a Russian quarter in Constantinople for trading purposes. Thus did Byzantium tame and frustrate her enemies.

The credit for saving the Empire goes chiefly to Romanus Lecapenus, who exercised power on behalf of the Emperor Constantine VII Porphyrogennitos for twenty-five years. Although his struggle with the northern invaders was largely defensive, he carried Byzantine arms successfully to the offensive against the Saracens. Victories were won against them in Italy (915) and Asia Minor (929), where Romanus compelled the Saracens to pay tribute and recovered both cities and sacred relics from the infidels. Not less important were the measures of domestic reform initiated by Romanus and continued by Constantine VII himself when he assumed sole power in 945. The backbone of Byzantine society had once been the small peasant farmer, holding his land directly from that state, usually in return for military service. But in times of insecurity, when land was the only safe investment, it had gradually passed into fewer hands, particularly those of the monasteries and the great officers of state. There thus grew up a land-owning aristocracy powerful enough to defy the Emperor himself. Romanus began the task of reversing this trend.

Romanus, however, was overthrown by a revolution in 945, which brought his son-in-law Constantine VII Porphyrogennitos (913–59) to effective power. Hitherto Constantine had been more interested in scholarship and the arts: it is to his pen that we owe much of our knowledge of mediaeval Constantinople. Even when he assumed power, it is doubtful whether his interests greatly changed. But it was during his reign that legislation to protect the small land-holder was strengthened and the rights of the peasant-soldier were restored. The good sense of

Constantine and his father-in-law were rewarded in the second half of the 10th century. From 955 there began a period of almost unbroken advance against the Saracens under the command of a series of able and aggressive Emperors— Nicephorus Phokas (963–9), John Tzimiskes (969–76), and Basil II (976–1025)—of whom the first two were both usurping generals. Nicephorus recovered Crete in 961 and Cyprus in 965, thus re-asserting Byzantine sea-power. His successors pushed back the Muslims from Asia Minor and Syria. The crowning triumph of the recovery of Antioch came in 969. Basil II added the restoration of Armenia to the Empire (1021).

The triumphs of Byzantium in the East were not uniformly matched elsewhere. In the West, the Saracens were still established in southern Italy, where the Emperor had to pay tribute for his few remaining possessions. Venice had become an independent Republic. Nicephorus Phokas was unsuccessful in his attempts to recover Sicily (967). In the South, a strong Muslim dynasty, the Fatimids, who had established themselves as an independent power in Egypt, forestalled Tzimiskes' ambition to recover Jerusalem by themselves taking control of Palestine (969). Early in the 11th century Basil II was obliged to recognize the Fatimid domination of southern Syria by treaty (1001). This setback was rendered doubly bitter by the accession of a mad Fatimid Caliph, Hakim, who departed from the tradition of Muslim tolerance by persecuting the Christians in his dominions and even destroying the Church of the Holy Sepulchre at Jerusalem (1010). Such experiences showed that it was impossible for even the strongest and ablest Emperor to dominate his enemies in every direction at once. But while the Fatimid power was reviving in the south, Basil II was earning himself glory in the opposite direction.

The power of the Bulgars had only temporarily been checked upon the death of Symeon (927). A new age of Bulgarian imperialism began under the Tsar Samuel, who usurped the throne in the same year in which Basil II succeeded John Tzimiskes (976). Tzimiskes had invited the Russians to help him keep the Bulgars under control, but they did the job too thoroughly for his liking, and in 972 he was forced to drive them back to the Danube. The Bulgars were not content to submit to Byzantium again. Samuel took advantage of the rebellions by which Basil II's early reign was plagued to build up a new Bulgarian Empire as extensive as Symeon's had been. Basil's first efforts to contain the Bulgarian expansion were unsuccessful: it was only later in his long reign that he earned the formidable title of *Voulgaróktonos*, the Bulgar-slayer. His first campaign against them in 981 ended in a defeat from which he narrowly escaped with his life. For several years afterwards he was too preoccupied with internal problems to renew the attack.

The numerous rebellions by which Basil was plagued were the bitter fruit of the growth of a landed aristocracy under earlier emperors. Like Romanus Lecapenus and Constantine Porphyrogennitos, their successors had tried vigorously to check the growth of great estates and to restore the imperial army on its old basis. Nicephorus Phokas, for instance, had forbidden the establishment of new monasteries, which were among the greatest independent land-owners. John Tzimiskes and Basil himself both legislated to curb the great estates. But the evil was actually growing as the imperial frontiers extended again. The war on the frontiers had given rise to a legendary class of warriors, the *akrítai* (frontiersmen), of whom the most celebrated was Dighenis Akritas, the hero of an 11th-century epic poem. Characteristically, his name (*dighenís* = born of two races) reveals the curious fact of inter-marriage across the frontiers of geography and religion, and illustrates the independence of such men from national commitments. When they settled on their lands as the frontier moved beyond them, they considered themselves as good as the Emperor, if not better.

A series of rebellions by such great land-owners shook the throne of Basil II for more than a decade. In the end he enlisted the help of Russian mercenaries to defeat them in 989, for the Russians still seemed a lesser evil than the Bulgars. Moreover, the Russians were on the brink of accepting Christianity. During the reign of Constantine VII Porphyrogennitos the Dowager Grand Duchess Olga had visited Constantinople and become the first convert in the ruling family (957). Her son refused to follow her example, saying that his men 'would laugh him to scorn'. But a generation later his own son Vladimir took a different view. He accepted baptism in 989, and married a sister of the Emperor Basil II. He even went so far as to restore to Byzantium the Greek city of Cherson on the Black Sea, which he had seized in 988 as one of the perquisites of his campaign in support of Basil against his domestic rebellions. Now at last after twelve years of precarious survival, Basil II had freedom of action to turn against his foreign enemies.

Basil's great tide of military success began with his campaign in Armenia (991), though it took another generation before the Armenians renounced their vassalage to the Saracens and submitted again to the Empire (1021). He fought several other campaigns in the East, notably in Syria (995). But in that direction the power of the enemy had already been broken by his predecessors. It was mainly against the Bulgars that he had to turn the full strength of his re-organized armies after the Russians had been brought to heel. Since the defeat of his first Bulgarian campaign in 981, Basil did not venture against them again until nearly ten years had passed. Between 990 and 995 his armies were almost continuously in action against the Bulgars. In 996 the Tsar Samuel felt strong enough to counterattack, not in the direction of Constantinople but through mainland Greece towards the Peloponnese. Basil's army came upon the Bulgars returning northwards after plundering Attica and Boeotia. On the banks of the River Sperkheios they inflicted a crushing defeat on Samuel and his son, who barely escaped with their lives.

The battle of the River Sperkheios (996) was a turning-point in the history of both Bulgaria and Greece. Basil carried the war again into Bulgarian territory between 998 and 1003, and in the latter year he won another decisive victory on the banks of the River Vardar. The hardy Bulgarian kingdom still survived for another fifteen years, though reeling under a succession of blows. In 1014 Basil won his greatest triumph and committed the atrocity which made his name a legend. The battle was fought in a narrow valley of the River Strymon. Basil's overwhelming victory brought him some 15,000 prisoners, all of whom he blinded, leaving only one man in every hundred with one eye so that he could lead his companions home. The spirit of the Bulgars was crushed, and four years later they accepted subjugation anew to the rule of Constantinople (1018). Bulgaria was not to appear again as a name on the map for two centuries. Basil returned to celebrate a triumph in Constantinople (1019) and to complete the re-conquest of Armenia (1021).

The Byzantine Ascendancy (641-1071)

At his death in 1025, Basil II left the Empire at its apogee. The whole Balkan peninsula came once again under the domination of the Byzantium for the first time in more than three centuries. The northern neighbours of the Empire—from west to east: the Serbs, the Magyars, the Petchenegs, the Russians—were all at peace with Constantinople, if not in alliance. As far as Azerbaijan to the east and Palestine to the south, the Emperor was absolute master. Neither the Fatimids in Egypt nor the successors of the Abbasids in Persia constituted any menace to the Empire. In the West, the remains of the Empire in Italy at least held its ground. Imperial forces crushed a revolt of the Lombards in 1011; and although Venice no longer recognized the sovereignty of Constantinople, they had been in treaty relations since 992. Basil succeeded even in imposing his will on the Patriarch, and avoiding a fresh quarrel with the Pope. After an unfortunate incident in 1009, when the Patriarch of Constantinople omitted the Pope's name from the Diptychs in which he traditionally recorded the names of the Patriarchs whom he recognized as orthodox, a formula of compromise on the *filioque* was devised in 1024.

Basil II was happy in the timing of his death. Under the Macedonian dynasty, Byzantium was the richest, most powerful, most civilized state on earth. Never had the arts and scholarship flourished so securely, not least thanks to the enlightened policy and taste of Constantine VII Porphyrogennitos. A fresh codification of the law was carried out by Basil I and his son, Leo VI. Education was universally respected and almost universally available. The university of Constantinople had been re-founded by Bardas in the middle of the 10th century. Literature never achieved much originality of expression in the Byzantine Empire, but the 11th century was the age of compilations such as the Greek Anthology and Constantine's own works. It was also an age of great architectural design: St. Mark's at Venice, Sancta Sophia at Salonika; the mosaics of the monastery church at Daphni near Athens; and many of the monasteries on Mount Athos and on the pinnacles in Thessaly (known as the *Metéora*, from their appearance of 'hanging in the air'.) It was the pre-eminent age, too, of illuminated manuscripts and luxurious silk embroideries. Constantinople was looked upon from both the East and the West as a unique city of marvels, which set the standard of civilization to Europe and Asia. But there were already sown, still undetected, the seeds of future troubles. The security of Constantinople was again to be threatened both from without and within.

The successful wars of the Macedonian dynasty had been paid for at a high price. The coinage was debased by Nicephorus Phokas to pay his mercenaries, and the bad example was contagious. All reforms were resisted by the landed aristocracy, who succeeded in rendering largely ineffective the legislation intended to break up their great estates for the benefit of the peasantry. A fierce rivalry developed between the military caste, based on the aristocracy, and the civil service composed of scholarly officials. The latter were successful in cutting back expenditure, but only at the cost of weakening the imperial defences. With Basil's powerful influence removed, quarrels broke out again between church and state. What was worse, the Patriarch was allowed to renew the ancient quarrel with Rome. The compromise of 1024 on the *filioque* proved abortive. When a bigoted and dogmatic Patriarch, Michael Cerularius, ascended the throne in 1043, it was only a matter of time before the ecclesiastical feud between East and West again came to a head.

The enemies and dissident subjects of the Empire were not slow to exploit its inner stresses. The Petchenegs invaded Byzantine territory within two or three years of Basil's death. In 1030 the Saracens defeated the Emperor Romanus III near Antioch, but lost Edessa to the Empire two years later. The Bulgars and Serbs rebelled about the year 1040, and at about the same date a revolt at Athens was put down by the Varangian Guard under Harald Hardrada, the gigantic Norseman who fell a quarter of a century later at the battle of Stamford Bridge (1066). In 1043 men of the Varangian Guard itself revolted at Constantinople with the support of their Russian kinsmen, and three years elapsed before peace was restored. The Petchenegs invaded Byzantine territory again in 1048. In the same year new enemies appeared in the East. These were the Seljuq Turks, who had already begun the conquest of Armenia. Two fearsome names now stand out for the first time in Byzantine history: the Normans in the West and the Turks in the East.

Devastating blows were struck at the Byzantine Empire from

east and west by the Seljuqs and the Normans, though neither was destined to give it the *coup de grâce*. The Normans first appeared on Greek soil as pilgrims on their way to the Holy Places in the 10th century; then as mercenaries in the Empire's service in the 11th century; finally as crusaders—which is to say as would-be conquerors, for the Crusades were essentially a campaign of aggressive imperialism, at least so far as the Normans were concerned. The Seljuqs, on the other hand, had no ambition to destroy the Byzantine Empire: they were rather predatory raiders. They first appeared as mercenaries in the armies of the Abbasids, but by the 11th century they had established an independent power in Anatolia, based on Iconium and known as the Sultanate of Rûm. By the middle of the 11th century, the Seljuqs took over Armenia (1045) and the Abbasid Empire based on Baghdad (1055).

Both Norman and Seljuq raids on opposite ends of the Byzantine Empire were increasingly frequent and damaging. The Normans had aided the rising of the Lombards against the Empire in 1011. It was they, and not the Byzantines, who were recovering Sicily from the Arabs of North Africa. In 1081 they invaded Greece by way of Corfu, and seized Dyrrhachium (Durazzo). Over the same period the Seljuqs repeatedly invaded Byzantine territory. They seized Syria and Palestine from the Fatimids of Egypt, including Jerusalem (1070). The Empire was harassed at the same time by invasions of the Magyars and Petchenegs from the north. Apart from Venice—a former vassal, but now an independent ally—the Emperor had hardly a friend in the world. Yet the rulers of Christendom chose these perilous years to tear themselves apart with yet another ecclesiastical quarrel between Rome and Constantinople. The schism of 1054 was perhaps the severest in Christian history. If not final, it was certainly disastrous and decisive.

The fault lay principally with one man: the Patriarch, Michael Cerularius, who was determined to re-assert the independence of Constantinople from the Papacy. By implication, this had been compromised two centuries earlier when the Emperor sought the Pope's intervention in the dispute between the adherents of Photius and Ignatius. Ecclesiastical memories were long, and great importance was attached to the minutiae of protocol. At Rome a series of strong, reforming Popes had restored the prestige and ambitions of their office, but at Constantinople these changes had passed with little notice. In 1050 a papal synod at Siponto passed decrees disallowing Greek usages in Italy. Michael Cerularius retaliated by ordering the Latins at Constantinople to practise only the Greek Orthodox rite. He also warned his Emperor against attempting any compromise or reconciliation: 'I made him an Emperor and I can unmake him,' he declared. When the Latin Churches refused to conform, he ordered them to be closed. His uncompromising firmness was in part dictated by the fact that Rome had recently been seized by the Normans, so that the Pope was again under barbarian control.

Nevertheless a year or two later the Patriarch showed himself willing to bargain. He wrote to the Pope offering to restore his name to the diptychs—in other words, to recognize him as a patriarch. In return, the Pope sent three legates to Constantinople to negotiate (1054). Unfortunately, the leading legate was Cardinal Humbert, a man as bigoted and intemperate as Michael Cerularius. The exchange of views on the minutiae of unleavened bread and the procession of the Holy Spirit quickly degenerated into a renewed exchange of discourtesies. Cardinal Humbert brought about the final breach by laying a papal Bull of excommunication on the altar of the Church of the Holy Wisdom (Sancta Sophia) and leaving Constantinople without another word. The Bull had no sanction from the Pope, but it was not withdrawn. The Patriarch held a synod to repudiate the Bull and to re-affirm the Greek position on the disputed issues, but he pursued the quarrel no further. Other patriarchal sees took no part in it.

Although the year 1054 is now looked upon as the date of the final rupture between the eastern and western Churches, it was not so seen at the time. Christendom was largely unconscious of it. The Latin Churches in Constantinople were re-opened a few years later without opposition. Michael Cerularius was deposed in 1059, and died soon afterwards. All might have been well if the aggressive persistence of the Normans had not provoked a further crisis of confidence in the succeeding generation. Their advance through the Mediterranean gradually turned from a welcome counter-attack against the Saracens into a threat against the survival of the Byzantine Empire under the mask of the Crusades. After gaining control of the Pope's dominions in 1053, they took Otranto from the Emperor's garrison in 1055 and reduced the Byzantine foothold in Italy to the single garrison of Bari by 1060. The next year they began the invasion of Sicily, which took them thirty years to complete. Their leaders were Robert Guiscard and his brother Roger, who was proclaimed Count of Sicily in 1071. Their next ambition lay in the East.

The Byzantine Empire seemed once again to be ripe for seizure. The long line of the Macedonian dynasty, which had begun with Basil I in 867, ended with the death of an Empress Regent in 1057. A period of anarchy followed, from which eventually emerged a new dynasty, the Comneni in 1081. During the calamitous interval of a quarter of a century, the Empire was subjected to a succession of foreign attacks. Besides the Normans in the west, there were invasions from the north by the Magyars, who had by now formed the Kingdom of Hungary and accepted baptism from Rome, and the Petchenegs, who stood once more before the walls of Constantinople in 1064. An even graver threat were the Seljuq Turks, whose Sultan had virtually taken over the Abbasid empire in 1055. Their greatest leader, Alp Arslan, succeeded as Sultan in 1063. Within a few years, he completed the conquest of Armenia (1064) and took Jerusalem from the Fatimids of Egypt (1070). Only the extraordinary resilience of the Empire could enable it to survive yet again.

In 1071 the Emperor Romanus IV, a soldier who had usurped the throne by the familiar process of marrying a widowed Empress, marched across Asia Minor to chastise the Seljuqs. As he set out from Constantinople, the bitter news arrived from Italy that Bari, the last Byzantine stronghold in the west, had fallen to the Normans. His expedition to the east was not without hope of success: it was not his first, and he had defeated the Turks before. But he commanded a motley army, at least half of whom were mercenaries. The largest contingent were themselves Turks, and they were ready to desert in the moment of crisis. That moment came at Manzikert in August 1071, where Alp Arslan fell on the Byzantine army. This first decisive battle between Greeks and Turks ended in overwhelming victory for the latter. The Emperor Romanus was wounded and captured, later to be contemptuously ransomed. The Normans and the Seljuqs between them, aided by internal divisions, had reduced the Empire to its lowest ebb within half a century of its zenith. Early in the 12th century Anna Comnena, the daughter of Alexius I, wrote that 'the neighbouring Bosporus was the frontier of the Roman Empire in the east, and Adrianople in the west'.

Such a rapid crumbling of the Empire can only have been the symptom of a deep-seated demoralization. Many factors contributed to it. The religious schism played only a small part: few Greeks outside the hierarchy of church and court can have been seriously concerned in it, though all abominated Rome. Economic deterioration was probably the most serious factor, in which something like a multiplier effect was at work. Norman and Seljuq conquests simultaneously contracted the Empire and disrupted its trade. The Emperor was at one and the same time deprived of his recruiting grounds, made more dependent on mercenaries, and less able to pay them. Debasement of the coinage led to lack of confidence in financial rewards. It was the discontent of the mercenaries that precipitated the disaster of Manzikert. To secure native recruits for the army within the Byzantine Empire, a new system was introduced which approximated to the feudal system of western Europe. Large landed properties known as 'provisions' (*prónoiai*) were granted to senior officers with an obligation in return to supply soldiers. The independent peasant-soldier belonged to the past.

The Empire was now deeply and tragically divided, on many different lines of fission. Between the army and the citizens of Constantinople there was a complete alienation of sympathy, reflecting the antagonism of the military aristocracy and the civil bureaucracy. Between Church and state there was an unresolved rivalry for predominance, which came to the surface in frequent disputes between Emperor and Patriarch—for instance, over the Emperor's right of re-marriage in order to procure an heir. Among the results of such dogmatic feuds was the fact that Constantine VII Porphyrogennitos was born a bastard and Leo VI was excommunicated for contracting a fourth marriage. The Church itself was divided not only by the breach with Rome, but also by the antagonism between the moderates, with their favourite doctrine of Economy, and the extremists or zealots who abominated all compromise. The city of Constantinople itself was a nest of hostile factions, among which racial or national bitterness was fortunately absent, but the Latin colonies of Venetians and Genoese were hated for their religion and their arrogance, and the Varangians were feared for their violence.

With the development of huge quasi-feudal estates, whose owners felt themselves increasingly independent of the bureaucracy at Constantinople, the traditional rivalry between the military aristocracy and the civil service took a decisive turn under weak Emperors in favour of the former. The advent of the new dynasty of the Comneni—beginning with Isaac I in 1057 (but only for two years), later followed by his nephew Alexius I in 1081—marked the victory of the landed magnates. Such a victory, with the promise of at least a relative stability, was preferable to the state of anarchy which preceded it, though it did no more than stem the tide of history which was to sweep over Byzantium little more than a century later. It was not easy to foresee in the last quarter of the 11th century whether destruction would finally come from the east or the west. But there were at least some in the Christian world of the west who believed that it would be a crime to allow the Empire to be destroyed by infidels. Such a one was Pope Gregory VII, who was elected in 1073. He soon afterwards began to contemplate what came to be called a Crusade—a new idea destined in the end to spell the doom of the civilization which it was once sincerely intended to save.

CHAPTER III

The Decline and Fall of Byzantium
(1071-1453)

The Byzantine Empire was probably doomed from the day of Romanus' defeat at Manzikert in 1071. But it was a long time perishing, and more than once the spark of life was re-kindled. Another period of civil war followed the defeat and capture of Romanus, before Alexius I (1081-1118) consolidated his hold on the Empire. In the meantime a truce was made with the Seljuqs, who turned eastwards towards Transoxiana. Alp Arslan died a year after his great victory (1072), and his successors continued the conquest of Asia Minor. They were themselves troubled by a rebellion in Armenia (1077), which took four years to crush. Syria and Palestine were also overrun by the Turks: Antioch and Aleppo fell to them in 1085. But the Seljuqs were not by nature an imperialist power, and their conquests soon began to split up among semi-independent leaders. Among those leaders were the tribe of Othman, settled in north-west Anatolia, and destined to be the greatest of all.

The Seljuqs themselves declined to a minor threat almost from the moment of their greatest triumph. But no one could have foreseen so rapid a decline at the time. To Pope Gregory it seemed that the infidels in the East were about to overthrow the capital of the Christian Empire. Hence his call for a Crusade. If he had been more far-sighted, he would have recognized that the true threat lay on his own doorstep, with his Norman allies. While the Pope was meditating on the possibilities of assembling an alliance to save the Empire from the Muslims, Robert Guiscard led an expedition across the

Adriatic to attack Durazzo (1081). Alexius I, who succeeded to the throne in that very year, was unable to save the great fortress which stood at the western terminal of the main highway into Greece. It fell in 1082, and the Normans marched towards Constantinople, under Robert's son Bohemond. A year later another Norman expedition seized Corfu and Cephallonia.

The Emperor was already plagued by internal rebellions, as he was to be throughout his long reign of thirty-seven years. He made a fresh treaty with the Seljuqs and an alliance with Venice to safeguard himself against the Normans. The price of Venetian help was a high one: Alexius granted their traders concessions within the Empire which were eventually to make Venice the greatest commercial power in the Mediterranean. He also made his peace with the new Pope, Urban II, who succeeded Gregory VII before the project of a Crusade had matured into reality. Through no fault of his own, Alexius had inherited a state of papal excommunication which was an indirect consequence of the breach of 1054. The excommunication was formally lifted by Pope Urban in 1089. In return, Alexius saw that the name of the Pope was restored to the patriarchal diptychs. All these manoeuvres were designed to ensure that the Emperor was not left friendless to face the Normans.

Apart from a Venetian fleet, which was sunk by the Normans off Corfu in 1084, very little help came to Alexius. His throne was saved from the Normans not by his allies but by the death of Robert Guiscard in 1085. Meanwhile the eastern Empire had been almost entirely overrun. The Seljuqs had established their capital at Nicaea. In Asia Minor there remained under imperial control only the environs of Trebizond, which was later to take on an independent sovereignty of its own. It was a situation in which only the devious diplomacy characteristic of Byzantium could save the Empire. To this task Alexius devoted prodigies of intrigue, which contributed skilfully to the division of the Turkish tribes, setting off one leader against another, and preventing the consolidation of a Seljuq Empire. But these were no more than delaying manoeuvres. The question was whether Christendom could make a better display of unity than Islam, for thus alone in the long run could Constantinople be saved.

To explore that crucial question, the Emperor sent an embassy to the Pope in 1090. Both sides showed cautious good will. Papal

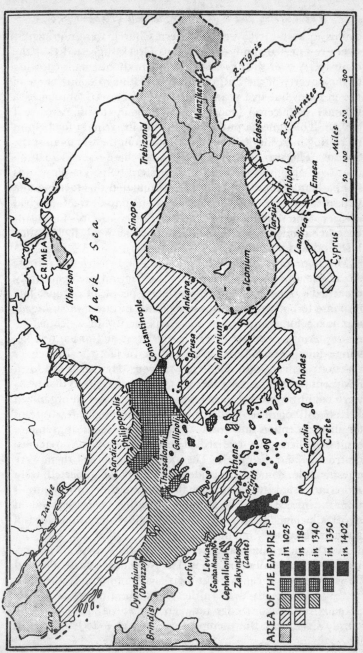

THE BYZANTINE EMPIRE 1025–1402

AREA OF THE EMPIRE

in 1025
in 1180
in 1340
in 1350
in 1402

Miles
0   50   100   200   300

R. Danube

Zara

Brindisi

Dyrrachium (Durazzo)

Corfu

Levkas (Santa Maura)
Cephallonia
Zakynthos (Zante)

Corinth

Athens

Thessalonik

Gallipoli

Phillippopolis

Sardica

Constantinople

Kherson

CRIMEA

Black Sea

Sinope

Trebizond

Manzikert

R. Tigris

R. Euphrates

Edessa

Antioch

Emesa

Laodicea

Tarsus

Cyprus

Rhodes

Candia

Crete

Iconium

Ankara

Amorium

Brusa

R. Danube

claims to authority over the eastern Church were not aggressively re-asserted; and an ingenious Greek suggested that the controversy over the *filioque* was no more than semantic, owing to the poverty of the Latin language. Nothing definite came of the mission, but five years later Pope Urban II summoned a Council at Piacenza (1095) to which again the Emperor sent envoys. This time he put forward a specific request for help in recruiting mercenaries from the West to join the war against the Seljuqs. The war was going well, and there seemed to be a chance of ending it for good with western help. The Pope was sympathetic. He had not yet fully formulated the doctrine of a Crusade, but service in the East would help to distract the rival leaders of the West from fighting each other. Towards the end of 1095 he summoned a further Council at Clermont. By this time his mind was made up.

The Pope proclaimed the First Crusade in November 1095. At about the same time Peter the Hermit independently preached a Crusade among the ordinary people of Europe. The response to both appeals was immediate and overwhelming. It was taken for granted that the Emperor would welcome the motley army which set out from the West at Constantinople, where they were ordered to assemble. In fact the Emperor's reaction was cautious, not to say nervous. He had asked for a few thousand mercenaries; he was taken aback to find that what were coming were vast armies of predatory and ill-organized Franks. Although he made careful and thorough preparations for their reception and conduct through his territory, some of his worst fears were realized. The Crusaders were rapacious, destructive and disorderly. The motives of many of them were questionable. Some of the leaders, the Emperor suspected, were more interested in taking over the Empire than in rescuing it from the infidels. He was careful to insist that the leaders should swear allegiance to himself, acknowledging him as overlord of any territories they might conquer.

Most of the leading Crusaders accepted the oath of allegiance, but by no means all respected it. The Normans in particular had no scruples about carving out their own dominions in the East, as they had already done in the West. The Emperor was perpetually on a razor's edge between war and alliance with the unruly Crusaders. But there was no alternative to letting them go forward into Asia Minor and Syria, with a nominal blessing and reluctant help. Operations against the Seljuqs were undertaken almost independently by the Byzantine and crusading armies. When both encamped before Nicaea, the Seljuq capital, the Turks hastened to surrender to the Emperor alone (1097). He prevented the Crusaders from looting the city, and horrified them by his magnanimous treatment of the enemy. In the following year, the Emperor gave the Crusaders no help at all in their capture of Antioch, which they ruthlessly pillaged, regardless of the religion or nationality of the inhabitants. A similar massacre marred their capture of Jerusalem in 1099.

With the recovery of Jerusalem by a Christian power, the object of the Crusade was nominally achieved. But that was far from being the end of the matter; nor had it ever been intended to be. A further wave of belated Crusaders swept eastwards like jackals after a defeated prey: the Lombards in 1100, and three separate Crusading armies of Franks and Germans in 1101, all of which met with severe defeats at the hands of the Turks. Relations between the Emperor and the western leaders were now critical and frigid. They were to grow even worse as the Crusaders set about carving out their own sovereign principalities in Syria. Alexius' particular enemy was the Norman Bohemond, son of Robert Guiscard, who had already distinguished himself in the wars with Byzantium twenty years earlier. Disregarding his nominal allegiance to the Emperor, Bohemond proclaimed himself Prince of Antioch. After many vicissitudes, including two years of captivity by the Turks, he succeeded in establishing his claim to Antioch, and even in gaining the recognition of it by the Emperor.

These were galling experiences for Alexius I and his successors. Instead of recovering territory for the Empire, the Crusaders had created a number of independent kingdoms of their own: in particular, the Kingdom of Jerusalem, the Principality of Antioch, and the County of Edessa. Although parts of Asia Minor had been restored to Byzantine rule, this was due rather to the Empire's own exertions than to the Crusaders. The Seljuqs, aware of the quarrels among the Christian powers, counter-attacked in the years 1112–15, and were held by the Emperor only with difficulty. Other foreign invaders again beset the Empire. The Petchenegs attacked in 1122, the Hungarians in 1128; and the Venetians began to infiltrate the Greek mainland through the Ionian Islands, capturing the port of Modon (Methóni) in the Peloponnese in 1125. Of all the troubles brought upon the Empire by the Crusades, perhaps the most serious was that it imported the ecclesiastical disputes of east and west into the Levant.

So long as the rival dogmas were separated by the Adriatic, it was possible to mitigate their antipathy. But in the Levant they were living cheek by jowl, with tragic effect. Centuries of bickering were devoted to the control of the Holy Places or the appointment of the Patriarch of Antioch by followers of the Greek and Latin rites. The Emperor Alexius devoted sincere efforts to reconciling his subjects and the Franks. In 1108 he negotiated a *modus vivendi* in the Treaty of Devol, but it proved to be no more than an agreement on paper. A few years later he attempted to negotiate a settlement at a higher level through the Pope himself, but he was too preoccupied with the Turkish wars to carry it through to a successful conclusion. It is possible that at the beginning of the First Crusade a secret agreement had been made on reunion between the Pope and the Emperor; but if so, the death of Urban and the misbehaviour of the Crusaders nullified it. A generation after Alexius' death in 1118, the Empire was in as sore straits as ever.

Alexius' son, John Comnenus (1118–43), came into an unhappy inheritance. Under attack from all sides, he tried in vain to secure the support of the Pope against the Normans of Sicily (where Roger, the nephew of Robert Guiscard, was proclaimed King in 1130) and to recover possession of Antioch. In 1143, after reigning for twenty-five years, he died with nothing achieved. Two years later the Turks re-captured Edessa, and a year later (1146) Roger of Sicily invaded Greece by way of Corfu and Itea. It was a brutally destructive campaign, in the course of which the Normans took Thebes and Corinth, and sacked both with greedy thoroughness. But a new Emperor, John's youngest son Manuel (1143–80), had succeeded with better promise for the future. He was tough, charming, diplomatic, and gifted with an unusual sympathy both for the Latins and for Islam. Although inevitably on the defensive in his earliery ears, he had learned from his grandfather's experience how to handle the complexities of a Crusade. It was just as well, for a Second Crusade was to be launched in 1147.

The West was roused to a Second Crusade by the shock of the fall of Edessa to the Turks (1145). The Crusade was first preached by St. Bernard of Clairvaux; then it was promoted by the Pope, and organized by the Kings of France and Germany, Roger of Sicily also wanted to take part, but was looked on with disapproval by his western colleagues, not to mention the Emperor Manuel, with whom he was still at war. The Crusaders gathered in 1147 and entered Byzantine territory overland in the late summer. Emissaries from the Emperor tried unsuccessfully to divert them along a route into Asia Minor by-passing Constantinople. He also annoyed the two western Kings, who did not understand Byzantine diplomacy, by making a treaty with the Seljuqs (1147). Conrad of Germany and Louis VII of France distrusted each other as much as they both distrusted Manuel. Not surprisingly, the Crusade ended in a disastrous defeat at the battle of Attalia (1148). The only benefit gained from the fiasco was an alliance by marriage between the Emperor and Conrad, which was primarily directed against Roger of Sicily.

It was characteristic of the supple Emperor Manuel to seek security by negotiations in preference to force. Such were his treaty with the Turks in 1147 (renewed in 1159); the marriage alliance with the King of Germany (1149); his commercial treaties with the rising city-states of Genoa (1155) and Pisa (1169); his own marriage to a Frankish princess of Antioch (1161); and his attempt, when conquest failed, to incorporate Hungary in the Empire by another dynastic marriage (1169). Sometimes he could not avoid war, however. There were long campaigns against his northern neighbours between 1149 and 1168, and a last attempt to recover Italy in 1154. But this united the Normans and Venetians against him; so in 1158 he made peace with the Normans and withdrew the Byzantine armies from the west for good. Diplomacy became again his chosen instrument. The schism in the western Church which led to the election of two rival Popes (1159) persuaded Manuel that he could exploit the weaknesses of Rome to reunite Christendom; and he sought the same goal of reunion even in Armenia. His cosmopolitan outlook was also reflected in the establishment of the first Russian monastery on Mount Athos (1169).

But in the last resort ingenuity could not be a permanent substitute for power. No negotiation could recover Antioch from the Franks, and no Byzantine Emperor could acquiesce in its alienation. Manuel set out through Asia Minor at the head of a great army in the same year in which he withdrew from Italy (1158). Next year the show of force was sufficient to bring about the surrender of Antioch. The achievement was sufficient for him without further conquest. He married Maria, the daughter of the Princess-regnant of Antioch, who later became the first Frankish Empress to sit on the throne of Constantinople (1180); he re-instated a Greek Patriarch, renewed his non-aggression treaty with the Turks, and abandoned his campaign. A few years later he entered into an alliance with the Franks to share the conquest of Egypt (1168), but they were forestalled by Saladin, the great Kurdish leader, who became master of Egypt in 1170 and deposed the last Fatimid ruler. Manuel's star of success now began to wane.

Within the Empire, the central power was being progressively weakened by the growing independence of the landed aristocracy. Manuel had aggravated the process by making large grants of land with rights of collecting taxation. The trading concessions which he had granted to the Italian commercial cities were also disadvantageous to the Empire. The Genoans and Venetians and other Italians had established self-contained colonies with special privileges inside the city walls, where they were becoming bitterly unpopular with the Greeks. A quarrel between the Venetians and the Lombards at Constantinople (1171) led to reprisals by the Emperor against the Venetians, which were ill-judged and resulted in an unnecessary war. To make matters worse, when peace was made in 1174, restoring their privileges to the Venetians, subsequent Emperors evaded the terms of peace. The consequent bitterness between Venice and Byzantium played a part in the events leading to the catastrophe of the Fourth Crusade a generation later.

Manuel's diplomatic touch was failing at the same time as his military power dwindled. After the failure of his alliance with the Franks aimed at Egypt, and the futile war with Venice, he undertook a last expedition against the Turks in 1176. The Turks won a crushing victory at Myriocephalum, which Manuel himself compared to Manzikert a century earlier. It was not the end of the campaign, for Manuel won a partial revenge on the banks of the River Maeander a year later. But it was the end of his will to victory. He died in 1180 after a reign of thirty-seven years, conscious that his life's work was a failure. Not only had he been compelled to abandon his claims in Italy and in the Frankish states of Outremer: the Empire could no longer enforce any claim to control the Balkans. Serbia was completely independent by the end of the 12th century; the attempt to annex Hungary had proved abortive; and a second Bulgarian Empire was beginning to emerge.

Manuel's death was the beginning of a grave time of troubles. His son being only eleven years old, the throne was occupied by his widow, but for less than two years. In 1182 Manuel's cousin Andronicus usurped the throne, murdered the widowed Empress and her son, and condoned a massacre of the Latins resident at Constantinople. His reign was short and calamitous. Rightly expecting attack from the West in revenge for the massacre of the Latins, he made a treaty with Saladin, which proved of no effect. He tried to reduce the power of the landed magnates by breaking up their estates, also without success. The Normans invaded Greece and looted Salonika in 1185. In the same year a prince of the royal house, Isaac Comnenus, declared himself an independent Emperor in Cyprus. Before the end of the year, Andronicus in his turn had been overthrown and murdered. His descendants were later to rule in Trebizond; but the throne of Constantinople returned to the line of Alexius in the person of Isaac II Angelus (1185–95).

The Normans, the Bulgars, the Seljuqs had all taken advantage of the confusion in the Empire to erode its frontiers. But the greatest blows were struck by the rising power of the Kurdish leader, Saladin. Already master of Egypt since 1170, he achieved the crowning triumph of capturing Jerusalem from the Franks in 1187. The effect in the West was electric. Pope Gregory VIII proclaimed a Third Crusade. Frederick Barbarossa, the Western Emperor, personally took the Cross. So did many other western princes, including Richard I of England. Even the Norman King of Sicily made peace with the Emperor. But once more the Emperor had a legitimate suspicion that the real object of the Crusade was to take over his Empire. To avert an attack on

Constantinople, he negotiated a treaty with the Crusaders (1190). It was a timely precaution, for no doubt Barbarossa had precisely such an attack in mind. But he died in the East in the same year, and the Empire was spared again.

The ultimate achievements of the Third Crusade were slight. Richard I of England captured Cyprus from the usurping Emperor Isaac Comnenus, but ceded it to the family of Lusignan and went on to campaign in Palestine (1191). He took Acre and other coastal towns from Saladin, but failed to press home the attack on Jerusalem. In 1192 he made a truce for five years with Saladin (who died in 1193) and returned to Europe, never to revisit the East. From the Byzantine Emperor's point of view, the principal outcome of the Crusade was to confirm the loss of Cyprus, though now it was lost to the Franks instead of a rival Greek. It was not the only loss to the Empire at this time. In 1194 an Italian adventurer, Matteo Orsini, who was not even nominally a Crusader, seized the islands of Cephallonia, Zante and Ithaca, over which he later acknowledged the sovereignty of Venice. Once more Byzantium had learned to 'trust not for freedom to the Franks'. In 1197 the Empire purchased a peace treaty with the Turks on humiliating terms.

Meanwhile the deposition of Isaac II in 1195 had left a disputed succession which brought calamitous results in the guise of a Fourth Crusade. Pope Innocent III sincerely wished to bring about a reunion of the Greek and Latin Churches, but the western leaders wanted only to gratify their jealousy and desire for revenge against Constantinople. Their excuse lay in the person of Isaac II and his young son Alexius. Both had taken refuge in the West, and Alexius' sister was married to the German Prince Philip. Confusingly, the usurping Emperor at Constantinople bore the same name: he was Isaac's brother, Alexius III. The western leaders originally determined to depose Alexius III in his turn, and to establish as their puppet on the throne of Constantinople his nephew and namesake as Alexius IV. The Pope's half-hearted approval was gained by the willingness of the young Alexius to accept the reunion of the Churches on Rome's terms, for which he was implacably hated by the other Greeks. In the event, the Fourth Crusade turned out differently from anybody's anticipations.

By the end of the 12th century Byzantium's deadliest enemies in the west were no longer the Normans but her former subjects, the Venetians. They had not forgotten the war of 1171–74, the evasion of the peace terms, the humiliation of their fellow-citizens at Constantinople, and above all the massacre of the Latins in 1182. The disputed succession in 1195 coupled with the proclamation of a new Crusade gave them the opportunity for revenge. Moreover, they held a dominant position in relation to any future Crusade, because Venice alone could provide sufficient ships to transport the Crusaders. The French and German leaders, chief among whom were Baldwin of Flanders, Geoffrey of Villehardouin, and Boniface of Montferrat, had decided to avoid the immensely long overland route to Palestine, and to attack first the heart of Muslim power, which was now in Egypt. The Venetians drove a hard bargain when their help was sought in 1199. When the Crusaders found it hard to fulfil their obligations, the Venetians unscrupulously diverted the crusading force first to seize the island of Zara on the Adriatic coast (1202) and then against Constantinople itself.

The ostensible object of the diversion to Constantinople was to restore either Isaac II or his son Alexius to the throne. It was difficult for the Pope to denounce this purpose, since the young Alexius had agreed to reunion, but he was deeply uneasy. The fact was that he could no longer control the driving force of the Crusade. Nor was Constantinople in any condition to resist. The usurping Emperor Alexius III fled from the city, which then opened its gates to his nephew, the Crusaders' candidate, who was crowned as Alexius IV (1203). But Alexius IV was unable to carry out his undertakings to the Crusaders, and he had for-forfeited all support from his subjects by his sympathies with Rome. Two sons-in-law of Alexius III contested the succession. One, Theodore Laskaris, withdrew from the capital and pre-pared himself for resistance in Asia Minor. The other succeeded in overthrowing Alexius IV and obtaining his own coronation as Alexius V. This palace revolution brought down the wrath of the Crusaders on Constantinople and precipitated the final calamity (1204).

The Crusaders had no difficulty in capturing the demoralized city in April 1204, one of the most tragic dates in the history of Europe. They looted and massacred with their usual thorough-ness; they desecrated the altar of Sancta Sophia; the horror of

their conduct left the Muslims aghast and was never to be forgotten by the Greeks. After much unseemly wrangling between
the leading Crusaders, they elected Baldwin of Flanders to be
the first Latin Emperor, with a Venetian as the first Latin
Patriarch. All thought of continuing the Crusade into Egypt or
Palestine was abandoned. The Pope's legate was induced to
absolve them from their Crusade, for which he was rebuked by
the Pope; but the Pope raised no objection to the seizure of
Constantinople, nor would he have been in a position to frustrate it. The conquerors proceeded to carve up the Empire on
a plan which they had probably long meditated and discussed.
But events did not proceed according to plan. The Latin Empire was never more than a ramshackle collection of semi-independent succession-states, some of which lasted less than a
generation. The Crusaders did not inherit the Byzantine Empire
but broke it up.

The reaction to the Crusaders' treachery came from many
directions. Only a year after the seizure of Constantinople, the
revived Bulgarian power invaded Byzantine territory, and
defeated and captured the Latin Emperor Baldwin (1205). This
setback helped Theodore Laskaris (1204–22) to consolidate his
position in Anatolia, where he established a rival Empire with
its capital at Nicaea. Another descendant of the legitimate
dynasty founded an independent dominion in the west of Greece,
known as the Despotat of Epirus. Yet another established a
separate Greek empire on the Black Sea, based at Trebizond.
There was resistance to the Latins, too, in many other parts of
Greece, though most of it proved fruitless. An adventurer called
Leo Sgouros, based on the Peloponnese, tried to take over Attica
and Thessaly, but he was forced back by the Latin Emperor.
The Seljuqs meanwhile took every advantage of the disarray of
Christendom. They enlarged their control of Anatolia to the sea
on both sides, by capturing Attalia in 1207 and Sinope in 1214.
Only the emergence of the Mongol power in their rear frustrated
still more damaging advances.

The area of Byzantine territory available for the Crusaders to
carve up was thus disappointingly diminished, Encroachment
by Serbs and Bulgars to the north and Seljuqs in Asia, added to
the survival of three distinct succession-states under more or less
legitimate Greek rulers, limited the Latin Empire in effect to the

Peloponnese, Attica and Thessaly, parts of Macedonia and Thrace, the north-west corner of Anatolia, and the principal islands. From these territories were created half a dozen semi-autonomous dominions. First in importance was the Empire of Romania, based on Constantinople, under the successors of Baldwin of Flanders. Neighbouring it to the west was the Kingdom of Salonika, created for Boniface of Montferrat as a vassal of the Emperor. Attica and Boeotia became the Duchy of Athens under the Burgundian family of de la Roche, and most of the Peloponnese formed the principality of Achaea under the family of Villehardouin. Venice retained Modon as well as Corfu, and gained possession of Crete, Euboea and other islands. The rest of the islands, though nominally Venetian, were parcelled out among private Italian adventurers. The most important groupings among them were the County Palatine of Cephallonia (including Zante and Ithaca) and the Duchy of the Archipelago (including Naxos, Andros and Tinos).

Few of the Latin possessions were long-lived. The kingdom of Salonika was the first to vanish. In 1223, it was overrun by the Greek Despotat of Epirus; but this first re-conquest was also short-lived. The future of Byzantium, at first in doubt, was destined in the end to lie with Theodore Laskaris and his successors at Nicaea. With intervals of co-existence to safeguard its rear from the Seljuqs, the Empire of Nicaea was continuously at war with the Latin Empire of Romania from 1214 onwards. In 1236 John Vatatzis, the successor of Theodore Laskaris, almost took Constantinople itself; in 1246 he recovered Salonika from the Greek Despot of Epirus. These wars produced strange alliances. The Greek Empire of Nicaea allied itself with the Bulgars against the Latin Empire of Constantinople. The Latins allied themselves with the Greek Empire of Trebizond against the Greeks of Nicaea. In 1241 the Emperor of Nicaea kidnapped his Greek rival, the Despot of Epirus. He even sought, though unsuccessfully, to negotiate a reunion of the churches with the Pope, at the expense of his Latin rival.

The Papacy was in despair at the turn events had taken. One of the few welcome results of the seizure of Constantinople was the recognition of Constantinople as the second see after Rome, made at the Lateran Council in 1215; and this survived the Greek recovery of their capital. But the whole concept of crusading was irremediably discredited. New Crusades were indeed launched. There was the strange venture of the Children's Crusade, launched by the boy Stephen in 1212. There was the Fifth Crusade in 1217, which captured Damietta in Egypt, but ended in failure (1221). There was the Crusade of the Emperor Frederick II, which actually recovered Jerusalem (1229), but only for a decade. (A singular feature of Frederick's success, which was achieved by negotiation and not by force, was that he was excommunicated at the time.) There was another abortive Crusade in 1239, and the gallant Crusade of the saintly King Louis IX of France, who was taken prisoner and ransomed in Egypt (1250). All were unsuccessful in the end. Nor were they of the least interest or moment to the Greeks, to whom all Franks were now an abomination far more detestable than the Turks.

The counter-attack of the Greek Empire of Nicaea was built up slowly but efficiently in the half-century following the fall of Constantinople. The Bulgars were alternately wooed and fought. The Despotat of Epirus was driven back upon the shores of the Adriatic. A foothold was gained in the south-east Peloponnese, including the new capital which the Villehardouins were building for themselves at Mistra (1250). A new dynasty was founded at Nicaea by Michael VIII Palaeologus (1259–82) who usurped the throne by the customary steps of treachery and murder (1259), but proved himself a dynamic and successful leader. He even achieved a treaty with the Genoese, who were at war with Venice and not disposed to come to the rescue of the Latin Empire (1261). Only in his own Anatolian territory was he unsuccessful and unpopular, because of the means by which he usurped power and his oppression of his Greek subjects. The rival Greek Empire of Trebizond never submitted to him. The Seljuq Empire of Rûm also remained a threat in his rear—a diminishing threat, but one which Palaeologus' own policies kept alive.

The Seljuq threat would have been more damaging had it not been for the emergence at the same time of the Mongols from Central Asia. They overran Georgia by 1236 and entered Russia in the following year, thus cutting off the Greek and Russian branches of Orthodox Christendom for many centuries. In 1240 they took Kiev and advanced into Central Europe; in 1242 they invaded the Seljuq sultanate; in 1258 they took Baghdad, and in 1260 Damascus. The Turkish power was far from broken, but it was so neutralized as to cease to be a factor that the Greeks of Nicaea needed to take into their calculations. When a revival took place in the following generation, the Seljuqs had been replaced by the descendants of Othman—the Osmanlis or Ottomans—as the leading Turkish tribe. Meanwhile Michael Palaeologus had achieved the greater part of his ambitions. He decisively defeated both the Latins and the Epirote Greeks at the battle of Pelagonia (1259), where he took prisoner William of Villehardouin and all his barons from Achaea. Two years later, with naval help from the Genoese, he re-captured Constantinople.

The end of the Empire of Romania in 1261 did not eliminate the Latins from the Levant as completely as they deserved. The Duchy of Athens and half the Peloponnese remained in Latin hands; so did Crete, Cyprus, Euboea, the Ionian Islands, and many lesser islands. Other beneficiaries of the confusion which followed the collapse of the Latin Empire were the Vlakhs, who established an independent principality in Thessaly, and the Serbs under Stephen Dushan, who carved out a vast but short-lived Empire in western Greece as far south as the Gulf of Corinth. In the following century a fresh wave of western adventurers was to descend upon the luckless body of Greece: the Catalan Company of piratical mercenaries, the Florentines in the Duchy of Athens, the Navarrese in the Principality of Achaea, the Genoese in numerous islands, and the Knights of St. John in Rhodes. The Genoese in particular were principal beneficiaries of the new order. In 1267 they occupied Galata on the Golden Horn at Constantinople and soon established a powerful position in the Black Sea trade. The restored Greek Empire was little more than a pawn in the imperialist struggle between Genoa and Venice.

There was, however, a more immediately obvious danger in the first generation after the recovery of Constantinople. In 1263 Charles of Anjou, the brother of King Louis IX of France, became King of Sicily and soon showed that he did not intend to acquiesce in the total loss of the Latin Empire. The last Latin Emperor had taken refuge at the court of Charles's predecessor. In 1267 Charles entered into a treaty with him at

Viterbo, by which he took over all the fallen Emperor's claims. He married his daughter to the Latin Emperor's son, and also established a claim to the principality of Achaea by marrying his son to the Villehardouin heiress. Next he formed alliances with the Bulgars, the Serbs and the Vlakhs; and his troops occupied Corfu (1267), Durazzo (1271) and the coast of Epirus. So obviously did he mean aggressive business that Michael Palaeologus decided to renew overtures to the Pope for a re-union of the Churches in order to secure allies against the impending Sicilian attack. Terms of submission to the Papacy were agreed in 1274 at the Council of Lyons. In return the Pope undertook to give the Emperor a free hand east of the Adriatic.

The immediate result was to release Michael to counter-attack the conquests of Charles of Anjou. But his submission to the Pope cost him the loyalty of his Greek subjects. There was a schism in the eastern Church, a bitter quarrel between the Emperor and the Patriarch, and a sharp disillusionment for the Pope. By 1276 Charles was ready to renew his campaign of conquest, no longer restrained by the Pope. Five years later he achieved an alliance with the Pope and Venice (1281) which must have proved fatal to the precariously restored Byzantine Empire. In desperation Michael Palaeologus responded with all the traditional ingenuity of Byzantine diplomacy. By means of an infinitely crafty and complex conspiracy which can never be completely unravelled, the aggressive power of Charles of Anjou was undermined by the Sicilian Vespers at the very moment in March 1282 when it was about to deliver Constantinople its death-blow. Every Frenchman within reach was massacred by the Sicilians in an outburst of nationalist fury which Byzantine gold had undoubtedly helped to finance.

It was the end of Charles's pretensions to restore the Latin Empire at Constantinople. It was also the last of Michael Palaeologus' triumphs, for he died in the same year (1282). He left a precarious succession in the hands of weaker men than himself. The same year saw the accession to power of an ambitious prince in Serbia, who was to be followed by the even more dynamic Stephen Dushan in 1331. Still more alarming was the rise of the Ottoman Turks, who first appear in history in the second half of the 13th century. Othman, the founder of their dynasty, reigned from 1289 to 1326. In that time they captured

Tripoli in Syria (1289), Acre and Jerusalem (1291), many towns on the coast of Asia Minor from 1308 onwards, and Brusa, which became their capital in 1326. In the following reign, under Orkhan, they added Nicaea (1329), and Nicomedia (1337). Having overrun Asia Minor, they took to the sea and began to harass the islands. The Byzantine Empire, fatally weakened by its fellow-Christians from the West, now faced its final, mortal enemy in the East.

Yet more Crusades were preached, with little effect; in 1290, as soon as the Ottoman menace appeared, and again in 1343, when the Crusaders briefly recaptured Smyrna from the Turks. But during the hundred years before the Ottomans first invaded the European mainland (1354), the Christian powers were almost constantly engaged in internal feuds or wars against each other. The chaos of Christendom gave the Turks their opportunity. The restored Byzantine Empire hired Turkish mercenaries to help push back the Serbs and Bulgars. Venice and Genoa were at war from 1296 to 1302, with Constantinople engaged on the Genoese side. In 1302 the Emperor hired the Catalan Company as mercenaries; but they soon turned against their employer and remained as a scourge in Greece for a generation, taking over the Duchy of Athens in 1311. From 1315 to 1328, and again in 1341, there was civil war within the Empire, both sides unscrupulously hiring Turkish mercenaries against each other. The Serbs, having crushed the Bulgars at the battle of Velbuzd in 1330, took advantage of Byzantium's time of troubles to carve out their empire under Stephen Dushan between 1333 and 1355. Albanians as well as Serbs flooded into Greek territory to settle.

Despite their orgy of self-destruction, the Greeks were not wholly unsuccessful in regaining lost ground. They recovered Chios from the Genoese (1329); Thessaly from the Vlakhs and the Latins (1333) and the Despotat of Epirus (1337); and they established a Greek Despotat at Mistra (1348). But all except the last were short-lived. The Genoese took Chios back in 1346, and ruled it for more than two centuries through a commercial company. Thessaly and Epirus fell to the Serbian Empire of Stephen Dushan, who proclaimed himself Emperor of the Serbs and Greeks in 1346. But his empire in its turn crumbled away on his death (1355). Meanwhile a vigorous new Emperor, John VI

Cantacuzene, had come to the throne of Constantinople in 1347 and once more opened up the hope of revival. He was a usurper, who had displaced but not eliminated the child Emperor John V Palaeologus (1341–91), and the two reigns overlap. But it was only during the years of Cantacuzene (1347–55) that the dying Empire had its last chance of survival.

In the year Cantacuzene was overthrown (1355), a Venetian envoy wrote home from Constantinople to report that:

'This Empire is in a bad state, even, to be truthful, in a desperate one, as much because of the Turks who molest it sorely on all sides, as because of the Prince and his government with which there is general discontent; the people would prefer the rule of the Latins, mentioning as their first choice our seigniory and commune, if they could obtain it. For in truth they cannot remain as they are for anything in the world.'

The growing power of the Latin states was a fact, but there was no love for them. Cantacuzene preferred the Turks. He married his daughter to the Sultan Orkhan—the first of several such mixed marriages between the dynasties—and he hired Turkish mercenaries to fight the Bulgars. His successor, John V Palaeologus, tried the alternative policy of reunion with Rome, but his subjects bitterly resisted it. Eventually he acknowledged himself a vassal of the Sultan (1381). His son Manuel became a hostage at the Sultan's court, until he escaped to claim the succession as Emperor in 1391.

The Turkish power was becoming irresistible. During the reign of Cantacuzene they entered Europe for the first time—at his invitation, about 1354. Within a decade they had established their capital at Adrianople and captured Philippopolis (the modern Plovdiv). From their base in north-west Anatolia they were now expanding in two directions. On their eastern front, they took Ankara (the modern capital of Turkey) in 1361. On the western front, they crushed the Bulgars on the River Maritsa (1371) and the Serbs at Kossovo (1389). They overran all Macedonia, except Salonika, and the rest of mainland Greece, except the Peloponnese. By 1391 the Sultan Bayazet was ready to besiege Constantinople itself. These successes were not achieved without setbacks. One was a concerted rebellion of the Greek and Turkish heirs against their respective fathers (1373), which the Sultan and his loyal vassal, the Emperor, combined to crush. There were also several more attempts to organize crusades against the Muhammadan invasions.

In the main, however, both the will and the capacity to come to the rescue of the Greeks were lacking in western Europe. For this there were numerous reasons, both physical and political. Chief among the physical reasons was the Black Death, which spread westwards from the Black Sea in the middle of the 14th century, with devastating effects in Italy, France and England. Such energies as the western princes and leaders had left were devoted to internecine feuds. Venice and Genoa were interested only in destroying each other's commercial interests in the near East. The papacy, which had provided the driving force of the Crusades, was rent by the Great Schism: for forty years from 1378 there were two rival popes in Rome and Avignon. France and England were engaged in the Hundred Years War (1138–1453), which ended only in the year that Constantinople fell. The Balkan neighbours of the Greeks were equally enfeebled by civil wars. Only during occasional intermissions in these struggles were the peoples of Europe able to gather their pitiful forces to confront the dynamic thrust of Turkish power as it rose to the peak of its ascendancy.

Even if the Franks had been capable of organising an effective Crusade in the 14th century, their good faith was suspect at Constantinople. Memories of the Fourth Crusade were long and its results were not yet extinguished. Large areas of Greece remained under Latin occupation. The Principality of Achaea survived, though under different families and reduced in size, until 1432. The Duchy of Athens was held for two and a half centuries (1205–1456) by a succession of Latin rulers: French, Catalan, Sicilian, Navarrese and Florentine. The County Palatine of Cephallonia, with its neighbouring islands, was held by Italian families from 1194 to 1483, and the Despotat of Epirus was usurped by the same rulers for a short period in 1318. The Duchy of the Archipelago was held by a succession of Italian dynasties under Venetian sovereignty for three and a half centuries (1207–1566). Genoa acquired several Aegean islands, covering the approaches to the Black Sea, notably Chios and Lesbos (Mytilíni), after helping to restore the Greek Empire in 1261. Corfu was held by a succession of Latin families after the Greek Despot of Epirus lost it in 1259, finally passing under Venetian sovereignty in 1386 for four centuries to come.

Venice was the arch-imperialist power in the Greek lands at this time. Apart from the territories already mentioned, the Republic held numerous colonies in Greece for varying periods. Some were forts on the mainland: Modon and Coron (1206–1500), Argos (1388–1463), Nauplia (1388–1540), Monemvasia (1464–1540), Lepanto or Navpaktos (1407–99). Others were strategic islands: Negroponte or Euboea (1209–1470), Aigina (1451–1537), Tinos (1390–1715), Mykonos (1390–1537), as well as Crete (1204–1669) and later Cyprus (1489–1571). There were also shorter occupations by the Venetians of Athens (1394–1402), Patras (1408–13 and 1417–19) and the promontory of the Peloponnese known as the Maina or Mani (1467–79). The Greeks could not be expected to regard these Latin imperialists as Crusaders in any but a cynical sense. Those who were morally capable of a genuine Crusade, on the other hand, were physically and materially incapable of the effort.

The revived Crusades were thus mostly feeble efforts, though King Peter of Cyprus did succeed in capturing Alexandria in 1365. The most hopeful effort was that organized in response to an appeal from the Hungarians in 1390, after the disastrous defeat of the Serbs at Kossovo. It produced by 1395 the largest crusading army ever to march to the east, and Sultan Bayazet took it so seriously as to break off his siege of Constantinople. In 1396 he met the Crusaders at Nikopolis and decisively defeated them. But although he resumed the siege of Constantinople, its defences still frustrated him, strengthened by the arrival of the French Marshal Boucicault and 1,200 men. In desperation, the Emperor Manuel II (1391–1425) visited western Europe to seek fresh aid in 1402, but obtained no more than a courteous welcome and vague promises in Venice, Paris and London. A respite came from an unexpected quarter. The Mongols under Timur the Lame (Tamerlaine) fell upon the Turks from the East. They defeated Bayazet at the battle of Ankara (1402) and took him prisoner. The Empire, though reduced to Constantinople, Salonika and the Peloponnese, considered itself saved.

Historians have detected a strange mood in Byzantium during the last century of its existence: a mood which reached its splendid and melancholy climax in 1453. It was not defeatism, though it included an awareness of the desperate situation recorded by the Venetian envoy in the middle of the 14th century. It could not indeed be defeatism, since the metaphysical foundation of Byzantium was the belief that the Empire was the final perfection of human achievement, the immutable embodiment of God's will on earth. The Orthodox Church, too—the spiritual aspect of that same achievement—was insusceptible to change or improvement. As St. John of Damascus had written in the 8th century: 'We do not change the everlasting boundaries which our fathers have set, but we keep the Tradition, just as we received it.' The changelessness, the permanence, the supremacy of Byzantium, in both its outward and its spiritual manifestions, were regarded as beyond challenge. Either Byzantium would survive for ever, or it would be the end of the world. No one could foresee which, and no need was felt to do so.

The mood of the 14th and early 15th centuries expressed this deep dichotomy between doubt and certainty. On the one hand it was a backward-looking period, in which men reflected on the glories and agonies of the past. There was a revival of classical scholarship, led by Gemistus Pletho, the last great theorist of Byzantine philosophy, who lived not at Constantinople but at Mistra in the Peloponnese. He spent some time at Florence, where he contributed to the revival of Platonic studies. He also drew up a plan for the political and economic regeneration of the Peloponnese, where Byzantine power was growing again almost independently of Constantinople. Like other outlying provinces of the restored Empire, the Peloponnese was taking on a life of its own, only nominally under the Emperor's control, though often ruled by one of his sons in the capacity of Despot. Its capital at Mistra was one of the great glories of the last centuries of Byzantium.

Another sort of reversion to the past found its focus at Salonika, the other major province of the Empire which was increasingly cut off from Constantinople. Here recurred in the 14th century that common phenomenon of earlier centuries, the outbreak of a fiercely contested theological controversy with marked social and political overtones. Hesychasm (or 'quietism'), as it was called, was initiated by the Archbishop of Salonika, Grigorios Palamas, who claimed to be able to achieve a direct communion with God and to enjoy the vision of 'the uncreated light which shone on Tabor' by a combination of mystical contemplation and physical exercises at prayer. He was supported by the powerful monasteries of Mount Athos as well as by the usurping Emperor, John VI Cantacuzene. But the Hesychast doctrine was bitterly attacked by a rival party of theologians, brought up in the traditions of Latin rationalism, and led by a Greek monk from Calabria called Barlaam, who enjoyed the support of Rome and advocated a reunion of the Churches.

The controversy thus had political significance from the first. Moreover, its lines of division roughly corresponded to a social cleavage, since in general the aristocracy supported the Hesychasts and the lower classes opposed them. The social conflict was brought to a head in the middle of the 14th century by a party known as the Zealots (a confusing term, since it was also applied to the reforming monks who supported the Hesychasts). The Zealots succeeded for a few years (1342–49) in expelling the aristocrats from Salonika and setting up an independent republic. A contemporary writer described Salonika as 'the teacher of other cities in popular rebellions against the aristocracy'. John Cantacuzene was eventually successful in regaining control of Salonika, and also in maintaining the position of Grigorios Palamas as Archbishop. In the end, therefore, Hesychasm became a part of orthodox theology. But the upheavals of the 14th century still further weakened the crumbling Empire.

At the same time, however, Byzantium was showing signs of a renaissance which seemed to pre-suppose a glorious future. Both at Constantinople and at Mistra in the Peloponnese, the last century of the Empire produced new and original works of art which show no sign of decline. New and splendid churches were built at this period; Byzantine iconography, though not uninfluenced by Italian painters, took on a new lease of life; and the mosaics which decorated the church of the monastery of Khora at the capital in the 14th century are among the finest in the history of Byzantine art. These are not the works of a people conscious of living in an age of decline and approaching extinction. On the contrary, a new and almost nationalist pride was being born. Yet the odds against survival were to prove insuperable. The west was more sympathetic to Byzantium than it had ever been, partly because the communication of ideas, cultural influences and scholarship was steadily enlarged. But active help was only to be obtained at the price of submission to Rome. Meanwhile the Turks recovered from their defeat by Tamerlaine with staggering rapidity.

The capture of Sultan Bayazet by the Mongols (1402) left the Ottoman conquests at the mercy of civil war between his sons, from which the Emperor Manuel profited temporarily. But the ephemeral empire of Tamerlaine disintegrated after his death in 1405, and the control of the Ottoman dynasty was reunited under Mehmet I (1413–21). These were years of relative peace between Greeks and Turks, which Manuel put to good use. He ceased to pay tribute to the Sultan; he visited the Peloponnese and reinforced its defences; he sent his son John, the future Emperor John VIII, to Buda to negotiate for help from the Hungarians; he even recovered Salonika from Mehmet after it had been taken from the Greeks by a pretender to the sultanate. But a more determined policy was pursued under Mehmet's son, Murad I, who succeeded in 1421. He invaded the Peloponnese and renewed the siege of Constantinople (1422), bringing cannon into use against the city for the first time. The Hungarians under Hunyadi and the Albanians under Skanderbeg were still to prove a thorn in his flesh, and he failed to capture Belgrade, but Salonika and Ioannina both fell to him.

The Greeks were not yet a spent force. Even while they were losing the last of their northern territories, they almost completed the re-conquest of the Peloponnese from the Latins, with the capture of Patras in 1430. The Venetians, however, still held their key-points—Modon and Coron, Argos and Nauplia, and Lepanto (Navpaktos) across the Gulf of Corinth. Venice and Genoa fought out their own imperialist struggle over the dying body of the Empire; and this was why the Greeks were understandably reluctant to pay the price demanded for western help. But the Emperor John VIII (1425–48) was finally convinced that he had no alternative but to capitulate to Rome. In 1438 he set out for Italy, accompanied by his Patriarch. At the Council of Florence (1439), terms were agreed for the reunion of the churches. The basis of agreement was ingenious. The Greeks accepted the papal doctrines and claims, including the *filioque.*

But they were left free in matters of ritual—for instance, to use leavened instead of unleavened bread in the Communion—and these were matters to which the Orthodox Church has always attached great importance.

Both good and bad results flowed from the reunion at Florence, but there is no doubt that the bad predominated. The Pope obliged by preaching a new Crusade (1440), which was led by Hunyadi. The Crusaders twice defeated the Turks in 1443–4, but were finally crushed at the battle of Varna (1444). Hunyadi lived to fight another day, but was again defeated at the second battle of Kossovo (1448). Even if this last organized attempt to relieve Byzantium from the west had been successful, it could still hardly have counter-balanced the harm done to the Empire by the domestic consequences of the Council of Florence. Both Church and people were bitterly divided. The Emperor's brother led a rebellion against him; and John himself never dared to promulgate the Union at Constantinople. Of the bishops who accompanied him to Florence, most accepted the union but almost all later recanted; while learned laymen such as Gemistus Plethon and George Scholarius (the latter a future Patriarch) had reservations. The Russian Church absolutely rejected the Union, although their Greek Metropolitan, Isidore, was a signatory. He escaped back to Italy in 1441, and the Russians elected their own Patriarch from 1448 onwards.

John VIII died in 1448, leaving a tragic inheritance to his younger brother, Constantine XI (1448–53)—the last Greek ruler of that name for nearly five hundred years. Constantine was crowned at Mistra in 1449 by the local Metropolitan—in itself a unique beginning to a brave but hopeless reign. If he ever had any doubts that his capital was mortally threatened, they must have been soon removed on the accession of Sultan Mehmet II in 1451. Murad had not been implacably hostile to the Christians: he had even married a Serbian wife. Mehmet was very differently disposed towards the Greeks. Although he began his reign with conciliatory gestures, confirming all his father's treaties and receiving homage from all his Christian vassals in amiable fashion, this was no more than outward show. He distrusted his father's Vizier, whom he suspected of taking bribes from the Greeks; and he resented the asylum given at Constantinople to a pretender to his own throne. His first preparatory moves against Constantinople began in 1451. In the following year he made a diversionary raid into the Peloponnese.

Constantine XI naturally renewed urgent appeals to the west. He sent an embassy to Rome in 1452, carrying a letter from the bishops who were opposed to the Union. They invited the Pope to send delegates to a new Council at Constantinople, where inevitably the Roman representatives would hold a less dominant position. The Pope ignored the letter and pressed the Emperor to take the only course that would ensure speedy help, namely to promulgate the decree of union. This Constantine dared not do, so strong was the opposition. It was now led by the future Patriarch Gennadius, the last Patriarch of independent Constantinople having fled to Rome in 1451. Constantine remained loyal to the Union, but he stood almost alone. His Megadux (commander-in-chief), Lucas Notaras, uttered the memorable phrase that he would 'rather see the Muslim turban in the midst of the city than the Latin mitre'. He spoke for most of the Greeks, who had never been allowed to forget the atrocities committed by the Latins in 1204.

A last attempt at reconciliation was made by the despatch of Isidore, the former Metropolitan of Kiev, as a papal envoy to Constantinople towards the end of 1452. He brought token aid in money and a small contingent of troops, to embolden the Emperor to proclaim the Union. Being a Greek himself, he was warmly received and knew how to handle his fellow-countrymen. He seems even to have suggested that mere lip-service to the Council of Florence would suffice. Committees of the nobles and the people were formed to accept the Union, and did so; but it was a half-hearted affair, and the absentees were more weighty than the adherents. There were anti-Latin riots in the streets. Gennadius and his supporters formally dissociated themselves from the proclamation, which was finally made at the end of 1452. Nor did the Emperor gain effective help by his surrender of Greek principle. The only western ruler to send an organized force was the King of Aragon and Naples, and his fleet was soon withdrawn for other purposes. Genoa, Venice, and other cities whose traders had established themselves at Constantinople, remained neutral until too late.

There is a curious similarity between the attitudes of western Europe to the destruction of Greek independence in 1453 and to its restoration nearly four centuries later. The rulers were indifferent to the last; but their subjects felt no such constraint. A group of Venetian sailors at Constantinople put their ships at the Emperor's disposal 'for the honour of God and the honour of all Christendom'. A Genoese contingent of volunteers came to join them, ashamed of the neutrality of their fellow-countrymen in the suburb of Pera across the Golden Horn. They were led by a gallant young soldier called Giustiniani, who played a crucial and unfortunately fatal role in the siege of the city; and they included an engineer called Johannes Grant, who is said to have been German but may perhaps really have been a Scot—the first, in that case, of the splendid line of Scots philhellenes. There were Castilians and Catalans and Germans and other Italians in the defending forces. There were also Hungarians and Serbs, though their rulers respected their status as vassals of the Sultan; and there were even renegade Turks, under a pretender to the sultanate.

Mehmet invested Constantinople at the beginning of April 1453. The siege lasted two months, and once at least it was almost raised in despair. But in the end the Turkish superiority was irresistible. In numbers they had considerably more than ten times the defending force. They also had immensely powerful artillery of a kind which had never been brought against the city by any previous attacker; and they had command of the sea. On 28th May the Greeks knew that their last hour had come. A last, moving, brilliant service was held in the Church of the Holy Wisdom, attended by all the clergy of both the Greek and Latin rites, who buried their centuries of futile antagonism at the eleventh hour. The final assault began on the next day, a Tuesday, which has ever since been a day of ill omen to the Greeks. Giustiniani was wounded early in the fighting: his withdrawal broke the nerve of the Italian contingents. The Greeks fought on alone until the walls, the suburbs, and the centre of the city were overrun in turn. Constantine XI is assumed to have died at his post, though no one saw him fall and devout Greeks still await his return.

Muhammadan law prescribed that a city which had refused to surrender should be sacked. So it was with Constantinople. But the city was large and contained numerous small townships within it, which could and in some cases did surrender individually. Some parts, including a surprising number of churches, thus survived intact. Sancta Sophia became a mosque no less glorious than it had been as a church, until it was secularized in the twentieth century. Gennadius became Patriarch under his new master, the Sultan Mehmet II; and Mehmet himself installed the new head of the Orthodox Church with full Byzantine ritual and enhanced powers. By this calculated gesture the Sultan emphasized both his conception of his own role as the heir of the Byzantine Empire, and his intention to rule the Greeks through their Patriarch. Towards the other surviving leaders of the Greeks, the Sultan showed first clemency and then harsh brutality: such was his arbitrary and unpredictable character. 'What a city we have given over to plunder and destruction!" he mused as he rode out of Constantinople some three weeks after its capture.

Western Europe was awakened too late to the tragedy it had condoned. The obstacle to the task of concerting a rescue operation, even after the Emperor had satisfied the Pope by promulgating the decree of Union, lay in the mutual suspicions and jealousies of Rome, Venice and Genoa. A Genoese fleet was finally manned in the spring of 1453 at the Pope's expense, and arrived in time to fight one successful action in the Bosporus, but no more. Even then the Genoese in the city remained neutral, and handicapped the defence by quarrelling with the Venetians. A Venetian fleet, also commissioned by the Pope, arrived only after the fall of the city. In September the Pope went further and issued a Bull calling for another Crusade; but there was virtually no response. The rulers of Europe soon acquiesced in the tragedy and accepted the change of sovereignty at Constantinople: they had no alternative. So did the minor potentates surviving in eastern Europe, including the cadet branches of the imperial family ruling in Epirus and Trebizond. The Genoese at Pera and in the Aegean islands were quick to submit, and their commercial domination of the Black Sea was soon extinguished.

There was still parts of the former Empire to be conquered by force. The Peloponnese resisted two campaigns personally led by Mehmet, and succumbed only in 1460, still with the exception of the Venetian strongholds. Athens was taken in 1456 and Trebizond in 1461. The conquest of the Aegean islands was begun at about the same time, and proved a long-drawn-out process:

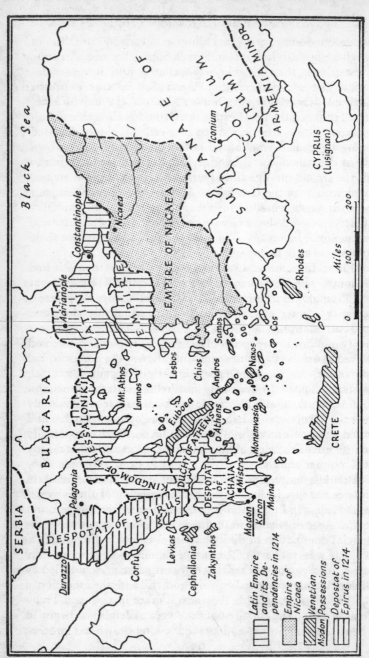

THE EMPIRE UNDER THE LATINS
in the 13th century

Legend:

Latin Empire and its Dependencies in 1214

Empire of Nicaea

Venetian Possessions
Modon

Despotat of Epirus in 1214

Miles
0   100   200

some of the most important survived into the 16th century and a few even later. Crete was not conquered till more than two centuries after Constantinople; Tinos fell only in 1715. In the north, Serbia and Bosnia were overrun during the decade after 1453, but Albania only after the death of Skanderbeg (1467), whom Mehmet never completely defeated. Vallachia and Moldavia, the core of modern Rumania, accepted the status of vassals to the Sultan soon after 1480, but were allowed to retain their own governmental institutions, with vital consequences to the Ottoman Empire three centuries later. Not the least momentous of the events by which power was re-distributed in the near East was the capture of Azov by the Turks (1475), who were then in a position to close the Black Sea entirely to Christian traders.

The year 1453 was thus neither the beginning nor the end of the great shift in power from Christian to Muslim hands in the Byzantine lands of the eastern Mediterranean. Nor was it a cardinal date, as it has sometimes been represented, in the Renaissance of western Europe; for intellectual interchanges had been going on between Italy and Byzantium for more than a generation before the Greek professors escaped from Constantinople to carry their precious manuscripts to the West. Nevertheless 1453 is rightly chosen to mark the end of an era. For the city on the Bosporus was the one fixed point in the Empire, its physical heart and spiritual soul. While it survived, no one could call the Empire defunct; after it fell, no one could deny that it had long been so, perhaps ever since 1204. And none of the other calamities suffered by Christendom, whether self-inflicted (as most of them were) or due to foreign hands, could be compared in finality or dramatic intensity to the fall of Constantinople. It was the 'triumph of barbarism and religion' in a more exact sense than Gibbon intended by his memorable phrase.

Western Europe has been slow to recognize its debt to Byzantium. The emergent nations of the western Empire surpassed the Greeks in material power and commercial enterprise from the 13th century onwards, but they did so behind the shield of Constantinople's walls. Byzantium bore the brunt of the Muhammadan invasions, from the Arabs to the Ottoman Turks, and served as a breakwater which enabled the West to turn the tide. There were other incalculable debts: the preservation of classical literature and Roman law; the systematic study of history, the foundation of universities and the promotion of science; the rise of monasticism and missionary activity; the evolution of a religious art and architecture which left their mark not only on Italy but in the Norman West. In return, the West sent to Byzantium its Crusaders and traders, between whom it is hard to distinguish for unscrupulous rapacity. It is little wonder that many Greeks accepted the Turkish conquest not only as a punishment for the heretical Union of 1439, but as a merciful release from Latin domination.

CHAPTER IV

The Dark Age of Greece
(1453–1800)

The framework of organization which was to be imposed on the former Byzantine Empire was already prepared. Indeed, on most of the Greek-speaking lands it was already imposed before 1453. It was a simple system which showed clear traces of its origins in the past history of the Ottoman Turks, first as a nomadic tribe and then as a military organization inspired by a religious mission. Among many relics of the restless past, two were of particular significance for the subject peoples. One, which was essentially symbolic—though it symbolized an attitude of great psychological importance—was the Turks' custom of referring to their Christian subjects as 'cattle' (*rayah*). It was not a term that implied brutal oppression or even indifference, for such is not the attitude of a nomad to his animals. But it did imply a sense of natural and permanent superiority which was particularly humiliating to proud peoples such as the Greeks, the Armenians and the Slavs. They construed the word as equivalent to 'slaves' (a word which itself derives from the Slavs), though the implications were far from exact.

The second respect in which the Turks' view of their historic role was significant to their subjects lay in the belief that they were in a state of permanent religious war with the non-Muslim world. The world was divided, on this view, into two parts: the House of Islam (*Dar-ul-Islam*) and the House of War (*Dar-ul-Harb*). It was the continuing duty of the latter to conquer and absorb the former. Consequently there were no permanent frontiers: the territory of the House of Islam must unendingly expand. A further consequence was that the administration of the Ottoman Empire was organized on a permanent war-footing. There was no real distinction between military and civil administration. All provincial governors were military commanders, responsible to the Sultan as commander-in-chief. The structure of the empire was highly centralized, and therefore became increasingly difficult to operate as its territory grew larger. Since there was no alternative to continuous expansion, it contained within it the seeds of its own decay. Only Sultans of the highest ability could control the system effectively at all. In this respect the Turks were amazingly well served up to the latter half of the 16th century.

Although the Sultan was an absolute ruler, he was to some extent bound by tradition and convention, mainly of religious origin. There was, for instance, the sacred law (*sheri*) based on the Koran, which served as a constitution. But it was archaic, inelastic and unworkable unless it were supplemented by new decrees (*kanun*—a word adopted from the Greek *kanón* or canon), which the Sultan could promulgate in his capacity as Caliph or successor of the Prophet[1]. He was also circumscribed by the existence of the Muslim establishment—lawyers, teachers, theologians—known collectively as the *ulema* with the Sheikh-ul-Islam at the head of the pyramid. Over against the Muslim Institution there was the Ruling Institution under the Sultan's absolute command. This comprised the military commanders and administrators who were, in contrast to the Muslim Institution, nominally slaves. But slavery was not a degrading condition. The Sultan's slaves could achieve immense power and might even marry into the Sultan's family. The majority of the Grand Viziers in the first two centuries after the fall of Constantinople belonged in this category.

The two Institutions of the Ottoman government met at the apex in the *divan* (cabinet). But subject to their advice, which he might or might not take at his own discretion and his own risk, the Sultan's power was absolute. He exercised it through the Ruling Institution, which alone had any direct impact on the lives of the subject peoples. Its operation was organized through a clearly articulated hierarchy of essentially military character. At the time of the conquest, the Empire was divided into a European province under the *Beylerbey* (lord of lords) of Ru-

[1] The title was formally adopted by the Sultans only in 1517.

melia, with his headquarters at Sofia, and an Asiatic province under the *Beylerbey* of Anatolia. As the Empire expanded, the number of provinces grew until eventually there were more than thirty, the title of the *beylerbey* being changed to *veli*. Next below the *beylerbey* came the *sanjakbey*, administering a *sanjak* of which there were a variable number in each major province. Greece was originally divided into six *sanjaks*, to which five more (three of them in Crete) were eventually added as the islands were conquered. The life of the subject peoples under this system varied greatly from area to area and with the personal whims of the governors.

The principal functions of the administration in the conquered provinces were two: to maintain a military establishment and to collect taxes. The military establishment was basically feudal. The Sultan's cavalry (*spahi*), who were all Muslims —indeed, a non-Muslim was forbidden by law to ride a horse— were allotted land in fiefs, either large (*ziamet*) or small (*timar*) according to rank. The *spahi's* duty was to bring a prescribed number of troops onto active service when required. In the meantime he and his men lived at ease on the proceeds of his estate, tilled by non-Muslim peasants. The system was not a harsh one so far as the Greek peasant was concerned, for the *spahi* had his fief only for life whereas the peasant's tenure was hereditary and inalienable. Nor was the peasant ever called upon for military service: in fact he was forbidden to carry arms. It is likely that the Greek peasant of the 15th–17th centuries was better off than his counterpart in western Europe. He was, it is true, heavily taxed; and one of the taxes, usually known as the 'tribute of children' was of a peculiarly oppressive kind. Yet there is no evidence that it was deeply resented.

The 'tribute of children' had been instituted about the middle of the 14th century as a means of recruiting a regular infantry force. It required that one male child in five of every Christian family between the ages of ten and twenty should be taken away to be enrolled in the corps of Janissaries (*yenicheri*, or 'new force') from which they might later graduate into the Sultan's civil service. The Janissaries were an *élite* force which had played an important role in the Ottoman conquests, including that of Constantinople itself. Later they were to become a menace to the security of the empire—corrupt, inefficient and without discipline. But in the early days it was a matter of pride to become a Janissary. It was in fact the one certain prospect of a good career open to the children of a peasant family, and was generally welcomed as such. Nor did parents generally resent giving their daughters to become *odalisques* in Ottoman harems. A proud minority might resist and lament, but there was little pride left among the Greeks of the 15th century.

Other forms of taxation were not numerous, though they were supplemented by arbitrary exactions and forced labour. The main tax on non-Muslims was the *kharaj* or capitation-tax, which literally entitled the tax-payer simply to retain his head on his shoulders. The existence of this tax is itself a refutation of the myth that the Turks attempted forcible conversions to Islam, for if they had done so they would have been depriving themselves of revenue. Two other regular taxes also bore heavily on the Greeks. One was the land-tax, which varied between a tenth and a third of the annual crop. The other was a tax on imports and exports. The significant point about the latter was that the rate of tax was doubled for non-Muslims. In fact few Muslims engaged in trade, which was regarded as an undignified occupation not to be compared with the profession of arms. Trade thus gradually passed into the hands of Greeks, Jews and Armenians, who flourished in spite of the tax, with important consequences in the later stages of the Ottoman Empire.

In return for taxation, the subject peoples enjoyed no services whatever from the Ottoman administration. What they did enjoy, however, which was more important in the long run, was relative freedom to manage their own lives as they thought fit. Since Islam made no distinction between religious and secular law, it was impossible to apply the legal system of the Ottoman Empire in its entirety to the subject peoples. It was tacitly assumed that the same identification of the secular and religious law applied to Greeks, Jews and other non-Muslims, as to some extent was indeed the case. Each such religious community was regarded by the Turks as an autonomous *millet* (nation) under its religious leaders, supervised at the top (in the case of all Orthodox Christians, and not merely the Greeks) by the Patriarch of Constantinople. The *millet* system implied no connotation of national identity, though in the later age of nationalism it was to become invested with that idea. Still less did it imply national boundaries. It was simply a convenient administrative device which worked in fact remarkably well.

The Turkish attitude towards secular and religious administration accounts for the extraordinary privileges conferred by Mehmet the Conqueror on the Patriarch Gennadius, and never withdrawn from his successors. In return for guarantees of obedience and regular payment of taxes, the Patriarch was given rights and privileges which went beyond the requirements of the Koran. Moslem tradition required that the Christians, like the Jews and the Zoroastrians of Persia, being 'People of the Book' (that is to say, possessing divinely revealed scriptures) should be treated with special tolerance. There was also a political motive for tolerance, in the case of the Greeks: by favouring the Orthodox religion, the Turks could expect to widen the gulf between the rival Churches and thus weaken the combined resistance of Christendom. Consequently the position of the Church became extremely powerful. It became also an instrument of alien rule, which made it unpopular when nationalist feeling began to revive. But at the same time it was the main vessel for preserving the culture, education and traditions of hellenism. Ecclesiastical leaders were never able to reconcile the ambiguities of their situation.

The powers of the Patriarch, and through him of the hierarchy, were laid down in a warrant conferred on Gennadius by Mehmet II. It declared him to be exempt from taxation and irremovable from the patriarchate, though as a matter of fact he later resigned and was reinstated twice. It empowered him to control not only all the Orthodox clergy throughout the empire, but to levy dues on laity and clergy alike. It guaranteed full religious freedom. It also invested him with civil powers, especially to establish tribunals which could decide matters of marriage, divorce and inheritance. In course of time these tribunals took over virtually all civil cases between Christian litigants, who preferred the verdicts of their bishops to those of Turkish judges. Some of the Church's civil powers were shared with elected authorities in the villages, for the residual municipal institutions of the Byzantine Empire were not abolished. There was in fact a fair degree of autonomy in the *millet* system. Provided the taxes were paid, the Turks did not care what their subjects did with themselves. Local administration, trade and education were entirely their own affair. The centuries of foreign oppression are therefore exaggerated, though not wholly mythical.

That the *millets* were in many respects autonomous did not meant that the peasant was free from oppression. From the impossibility of effective central control of so large an empire it followed that circumstances varied very greatly from area to area. There were some areas where the Turkish administration seldom ventured at all, and failed to impose itself when it did The most famous were the districts of Souli in Epirus, Maina in the Peloponnese, and Agrapha (which literally means 'un-registered') in the Pindus mountains. Such areas might be con-sidered in a sense to be free, but their freedom might be subject to the domination of a powerful local family, as the Maina became under the clan of Mavromikhalis. Even in areas where the writ of the Ottoman administration still ran, local adven-turers might take advantage of Turkish tolerance to acquire fortunes and power, as happened in the Peloponnese, where the local institutions became so strong that they were entitled to send their own ambassadors (*vekils*) to Constantinople to report on their Turkish masters.

Again the Greek peasant did not necessarily benefit from the system. A Greek *kodjabashi* or primate could be as oppressive as a Turkish *pasha;* so could an Orthodox bishop. Probably those who were best off were the inhabitants of areas excluded from the feudal system, either because they belonged to Moslem religious foundations (*vakouf*), of which there were many, or because they were private appanages of the Sultan's family. A most notable example of the latter kind was the island of Chios, which was for centuries the most prosperous and civilized com-munity in the Aegean. Athens and Rhodes enjoyed similar status. It was certainly preferable for a Greek peasant to be under the direct control of the Sultan's house than under a Roman Catholic domination (as in Tinos, Crete, or the Ionian Islands) or at the mercy of some of his own fellow-Greeks. This was the case at any rate in the early years of the Ottoman occu-pation, before the seeds of corruption which were already latent in the system had begun to sprout. Clear evidence that Ottoman rule was not in itself intolerable is to be found in the large influx into Greece (especially Salonika) of the Jews.

The Dark Age of Greece (1453–1800)

But the subject peoples were never allowed to forget that they were, in the eyes of their conquerors, simply 'cattle'. They had to dress differently from the Turks; they could not bear arms or ride a horse; they paid higher taxes; they might not build their houses higher than their Muslim neighbours; they could not repair their churches or ring their bells without official permission. At least two Sultans seriously contemplated exterminating the Greeks altogether. They were subject to mass-deportations in the early days of Turkish rule, though not later. Hence came the movement of Greeks out of the towns, the renewed influx of Albanians into Greece (which had already begun in the 14th century), and the re-population of Constantinople itself from Serbia, Albania and Greece. These movements were in part enforced and in part spontaneous but caused by the conditions of life under Ottoman rule. For if not systematically oppressive, its total indifference to the welfare of its subjects was itself productive of discontent and even despair. Ottoman administration was never a settled system, only a by-product of war; and war was virtually continuous from the 14th century, when the occupation of Greece began, to the 19th, when it ended.

The Greeks as a people were seldom directly involved in this unending procession of wars. For three centuries they were a people without history, whose fortunes fluctuated with the ebb and flow of Ottoman warfare. During the early period, when the Ottoman armies were advancing on all fronts, the state of Greece was relatively secure. The people were demoralized but not oppressed. There followed a period when the tide of conquest was contained and the latent seeds of decay began to do their inevitable work. In this period the Greeks suffered from mis-government, depopulation and economic depression, without yet enjoying any compensatory improvements. Then came the period of headlong decline of the Ottoman Empire, which the Greeks exploited to the full. They both accelerated the decline and profited from it. On the Turkish side, vindictive oppression alternated with sudden relaxation. It is impossible to assign precise dates to these tidal movements; nor was their effect on the condition of the Greeks instantaneous. But the ebb and flow of Ottoman warfare was the decisive factor in determining the context of their lives. From 1453 to 1821, it was never wholly static.

The Dark Age of Greece (1453–1800)

Although the capture of Constantinople had been much the greatest episode in the advance of the flood of Ottoman conquest, it was no more than an episode. The flood which had swept across the straits into Europe in the 14th century continued to advance for another two hundred years after 1453. It is not possible to say precisely when it reached its high-water mark, because it was still advancing in some directions even after it had begun to recede in others. This was natural to the Ottoman genius as well as to the Muhammadan religion. The concept of fixed geographical frontiers permanently separating sovereign states was alien to both. The Turks were in origin fighting nomads: their capital was their camp, and their territory was what they currently occupied by force of arms. Their religion imposed an eternal duty to extend the House of Islam. To draw a precise line on the map demarcating the Ottoman Empire from other states was thus to them a pointless exercise.

Subject to this reservation, however, it is clearly to be seen that the momentum of their advance changed and slowed down. There was a moment of maximum extent, even if it is hard to identify it. It came with the conjunction—itself difficult to date precisely—of two factors which operated with varying efficacy to weaken the dynamism of the Ottoman Empire. One was the growth of resistance in Europe, as the powers of western and central Europe belatedly recognized the menace and developed their forces to confront it. The other was the decline of ability in the Ottoman leadership, which was due partly to social changes and partly to anomalies in the hereditary system within the dynasty of Othman. The two counter-productive factors made themselves felt at different times and with varying intensity. The decline in the capacities of the ruling family is generally dated from the death of Suleiman I (known to the Turks as the Lawgiver and to the west as the Magnificent) in 1566. The resistance of the Christian powers had already begun to become effective well before that date.

So long as the Turks had only the indigenous armies of the Balkans against them, they suffered no more than temporary checks, inflicted by local heroes like John Hunyadi and Skanderbeg. But the tide of conquest soon swept their local enemies aside. All Serbia (except Belgrade) was conquered by 1459; almost all the Peloponnese by 1461; Bosnia by 1463; Albania by

1468; Herzegovina by 1483. Vallachia and Moldavia were gradually brought under control between 1456 and 1512, though they were allowed to elect their own princes, subject to the Sultan's suzerainty, for another two hundred years. The Aegean islands (except Rhodes, Crete, Cyprus and some smaller ones) were overrun during the second half of the 15th century. In the same years the Ottoman conquests spread to outlying posts both in the further East and in the further West; Trebizond on the Black Sea fell in 1461, Azov in the Crimea in 1475, Otranto on the heel of Italy in 1480. The setbacks were few and seemed to be temporary. Belgrade resisted siege in 1456; so did Rhodes in 1480. Ragusa (now Dubrovnik) remained autonomous, though tributary, and Montenegro clung to its independence. But in general it was only where the powers of western Europe had established a foothold first that Ottoman conquest was resisted with success.

Austria retained Slovenia, Hungary retained Croatia, Venice held a number of islands encircling the Greek mainland as well as some fortified ports in the Peloponnese. These possessions in European hands marked the limits of Ottoman expansion, even if only temporarily. The frontiers between them and the Turks were a kind of no-man's-land, across which the tide of war lapped to and fro without making any very great advances or retreats, or any that were seen as permanent. Of all the limitations imposed on their advance, the Venetian possessions were the greatest irritant to the Turks, since they were enclaves within what was otherwise wholly Ottoman territory. In the centuries that followed, other European powers were to take the leading role in warfare against the Turks in succession to Venice: first Austria and then Russia. But it was natural that in the centuries of Ottoman conquest the Venetians were the first and closest enemy. For the same reasons they were the closest to the Greeks, since they were the only European power with Greek subjects under their rule.

Apart from the last ineffective attempts to organize a Crusade in the west, the first war between Venice and Turkey broke out in 1463. It lasted sixteen years, and left the pattern of power little altered. The Venetians briefly seized Athens in 1466, and the Turks equally briefly seized some of the Ionian Islands in 1479. But apart from Euboea, which the Turks captured permanently, and some of the Ionian Islands, which they retained for varying periods, the war ended with few territorial changes. The Venetians' standing in the Levant was severely shaken, however, and they had to agree to pay tribute to the Turks for the return of some of their possessions and the right to resume their commerce in the near East. A second war between Venice and Turkey (1500–3) led to further small losses among the islands, and a further deterioration in the Venetians' prestige. Navpaktos (Lepanto), Coron and Modon fell to the Turks, but they were unable to capture Cyprus, which had been bequeathed to Venice by its last independent ruler in 1489.

Circumstances conspired to make Venice the principal defender of what remained to Greek Christendom against the Turks, but little love was lost between the Catholic Venetians and the Orthodox Greeks. The conviction that the turban of the Prophet was preferable to the Cardinal's hat was reinforced by the experience of Venetian rule, especially where it could be contrasted with Turkish rule in the immediate vicinity. In Cyprus, Crete, the Ionian Islands and the fortified ports on the coasts of the Peloponnese and Epirus, Venetian rule was found more oppressive than that of the Turks. Taxes were heavier, self-government was entirely denied, Greek trading was strictly controlled, and the Catholic priests were encouraged to proselytize among the Orthodox population. These were intolerable indignities which had no counterpart among the Greeks in Ottoman territory. From Gennadius onwards, the Patriarchs encouraged their obedient flocks to regard the Ottoman government as their protectors against Catholic subversion. Nor was there any alternative protector yet to be found among the European powers.

Not yet—but far away to the north there was the one Orthodox people in the world which was not under Ottoman domination. The Russians were not yet in a position to emerge as the champions of Orthodox Christendom, for they were themselves under the domination of the Mongols since the 14th century. But the links between Russia and Greece had never been entirely broken by the subjugation of either. Russian monks were established on Mount Athos since the 12th century; Russian mercenaries had served the Byzantine Emperors since the 10th century; Russian gold had been sent to maintain Sancta Sophia in 1350; and it was only as late as 1448 that the Russians first elected their own Metropolitan, having hitherto always accepted a Greek. After the Ottoman conquest, the link was maintained, and was indeed as important to the Russians as to the Greeks. In 1472 Ivan III, Grand Prince of Moscow, married Sophia Palaeologus, niece of the last Emperor of Byzantium. This dynastic connexion provided the basis for the claim, reinforced by the Orthodox faith, that Moscow was the legitimate successor to the Empire.

The claim was given its most celebrated formulation in 1510 by the monk Theophilus of Pskov in a letter to the Tsar Basil III:

'I wish to add a few words on the present Orthodox Empire of our ruler. He is on earth the sole Emperor of the Christians, the leader of the Apostolic Church which stands no longer in Rome or in Constantinople, but in the blessed city of Moscow. She alone shines in the whole world brighter than the sun. . . . All Christian Empires are fallen and in their stead stands alone the Empire of our ruler in accordance with the Prophetical books. Two Romes have fallen, but the third stands and a fourth there will not be.'

These ambitious claims were symbolized by the assumption of the title of the Tsar or Caesar. They were never entirely forgotten in the following centuries, though the time when they could be effectively asserted was still far off. It was not until the middle of the 17th century that direct conflict between Turks and Russians began.

Meanwhile, the champions of Christendom against the Turks were still the heretical Venetians, later joined by the equally heretical but more distant Austrians. In the 16th century, Venice could hold her own but no more. The Turco-Venetian war at the beginning of the century, ending in deadlock, turned the ambitions of the Ottoman leaders temporarily in other directions. Sultan Selim I (1512–20) conquered Syria and Egypt, and fought a victorious war against the Persians. But he failed to gain control of the Indian Ocean, where the Portuguese were establishing themselves in the wake of Vasco da Gama's discovery of the route to India *via* South Africa. Selim's successor, Suleiman the Magnificent, opened his triumphant reign of forty-six years (1520–66) by capturing Belgrade (1521) and Rhodes (1522), both of which had defied his predecessors. Enormous conquests followed: most of Hungary, the Crimea, much of Mesopotamia and Armenia, the Yemen and Aden, much of North Africa. The Black Sea, the Red Sea and the eastern Mediterranean (except Cyprus and Crete) could now be counted as Turkish lakes.

The European powers at last learned to treat the Ottoman Empire as an equal. Francis I of France sought a Turkish alliance against the Holy Roman Emperor in 1525—the first such sign of recognition. Only a few years later, the first treaty between the Turks and the Austrians was signed in 1533. But although the Turks were thus accepted as diplomatic equals, they were no more than equals. The balance of forces was now very even. The armies of Suleiman defeated the Hungarians at Mohacs in 1526—one of the decisive battles of European history —but the score was levelled when they were repulsed from Vienna in 1529. Another war between Venice and Turkey (1537–40) ended in the loss of still more Venetian islands; but Suleiman's great reign ended in 1566 with the task of conquest still incomplete. Malta defied his attack in 1565; Venice still held Cyprus, Crete, most of the Ionian Islands and a few in the Aegean. The death of Suleiman is generally held to mark the Ottoman Empire's apogee. Thereafter corruption set in at home, and few victories remained to be won abroad.

The symptoms of decline were naturally not immediate. Suleiman's successor, Selim II (amiably known as 'the Sot'), was not without ability, though far inferior to his father. He reigned for only eight years (1566–74), but during that time he gained territory from both Persia and Venice, and achieved the triumph which had eluded his predecessors with the conquest of Cyprus in 1571. That year itself marks a turning-point in the balance of power between Europe and the Ottoman Empire. It was not only the year in which Cyprus fell to the Turks, but also the year of the battle of Lepanto.[1] The two events were connected, for the Christian fleet gathered by the Pope and commanded by Don John of Austria, which defeated the Turkish navy at Lepanto (Navpaktos) in the Gulf of Corinth, had been

[1] Both events have literary connexions of a curious kind. The first provides the setting of Shakespeare's *Othello*; the second, which is the subject of Chesterton's *Lepanto*, was the battle in which Cervantes lost his arm.

raised for the purpose of saving Cyprus; but it arrived too late. The battle of Lepanto was not itself decisive, since the Turks soon recovered from their defeat, and the Venetian and Spanish commanders quarrelled incessantly about their objectives. Peace was made in 1573 on terms favourable to the Turks. The only interest of Lepanto to the history of Greece is that many of the galley-slaves in both fleets were Greeks, who anonymously lost their lives.

The war of 1570–74 between Turkey and Venice was the last in which the balance between the Christian and Muhammadan powers still lay with the latter. It was not the end of the Turks' conquests—Crete was still to fall to them a century later; nor did they lose any territory to their enemies during the century after the death of Suleiman. Given the unmistakable signs of deterioration in the Ottoman Empire during the 17th century, the outcome seems paradoxical. The explanation is that Venice was still the principal enemy, and Venice too was in decline; whereas Austria, which was to inherit the leadership of the resistance of Christian Europe, was not yet ready for the role. Consequently the succession of contemptible Sultans who followed Selim II between 1574 and 1623 did less damage to the Empire than might have been expected. But their fatal subservience to the Janissaries, who were allowed to marry and to recruit their own children from the second half of the 16th century, created insuperable problems for their successors.

Twice in the course of the 17th century the emergence of an able man helped the Empire momentarily to rally. One was the Sultan Murad IV (1623–40), who had to undo the effects of a succession of voluptuaries and lunatics. Another was the Albanian, Muhammad Kiuprili, who became Grand Vizier in 1656 and passed the succession to his son. To these two men belongs the credit for the ultimate success of the long-drawn-out campaign to wrest Crete from the Venetians (1645–70). It was not quite the last territorial gain by the Turks: they won part of the Ukraine from the Poles in 1672, and the island of Tinos in 1715. But it was the last time they had Venice alone to deal with. Other more formidable foes were arising on other fronts, sometimes in isolation and sometimes in alliance with each other or with Venice. Under pressure from Austria and Russia in the north, as well as from Persia in the east, the ill-defined frontier of the Ottoman Empire began gradually to retract from the second half of the 17th century.

The dates speak for themselves. In 1664 an Austrian army decisively defeated the Turks at St. Gotthard. The battle marked the end of the Turks' military supremacy. An inconclusive war between Turkey and Russia ended in 1681. In 1683 the Turks failed in their last attempt to capture Vienna. During the war of the League of Augsburg (1683–99), which united Austria, Poland, Venice and Russia against the Turks, Prince Eugène of Savoy defeated them again on the River Theiss in Croatia in 1697. In the same war the last great Venetian commander, Francesco Morosini, overran the Peloponnese and made very extensive conquests from the Turks on the Greek mainland, including Athens, where his artillery destroyed the Parthenon (1687). The war ended with the Peace of Carlowitz (1699), by which for the first time the Ottoman Empire ceded substantial territory without compensation. One of the principal beneficiaries was Venice, which acquired the Peloponnese and most of Dalmatia. In this way a considerable number of Greeks came back under Christian rule, but there is no doubt that most of them greatly disliked it. When a further succession of wars beginning in 1710 resulted in the re-conquest of the Peloponnese by the Turks in 1714, there is evidence that the Greeks welcomed their return.

There is evidence to the same effect in connexion with the conquest by the Turks from the Venetians of both Cyprus (1571) and Crete (1669). An Austrian embassy chaplain wrote in 1575:

'. . . the Venetians kept their subjects in Cyprus (like the Genoese theirs in Chios) worse than slaves. . . . After the Turks came, the poor people are freed of their burden, and are equally free, but their masters, who had tortured them, were caught and sold in Turkey.'

The story was clearly the same in Crete, which was in fact the one part of Greece in which apostasy to Islam took place on a considerable scale after the Turkish conquest. In both islands, however, as in the Ionian Islands and the Peloponnese, there were exceptions. The upper classes were more ready to side with the Venetian aristocracy which ruled them. At this level social and cultural relations between two Christian societies, even though they regarded each other as heretics, were possible in a way which was not possible with the Turks. It is significant that the one masterpiece of Greek literature during these centuries, the epic poem *Erotókritos*, was written in Crete in the 17th century by a poet with an Italian name, Vincenzo Kornaros (Cornaro).

Even if, on balance, the Greeks preferred the Turks to the Venetians as masters, it was only a choice of evils. The increasing inefficiency and oppressiveness of the Ottoman government, particularly in the hands of the Janissaries, led to frequent revolts and internal disturbances, from which the Christian population were invariably the chief sufferers. The Albanians revolted against the tribute of children by which the Janissaries were recruited in 1575, though many Christian families accepted it as offering a unique prospect of a career for their children. (It was abolished a century later, because the reduction of the Christian population was depriving the state of too much tax-revenue.) There was a revolt in Akarnania and Aitolia in 1585, another in Epirus in 1611, and a rising of the Albanians in the Peloponnese in 1647. The declining revenue of the state led to an intensification of oppression. Areas which had never paid the *kharaj*, like the Maina, were at last forcibly brought under control; and the collection of the tax was entrusted to the army —a sure sign that it was proving difficult to collect.

Greece and the other Balkan lands were in fact becoming progressively depopulated, and therefore incapable of producing increased taxation. Of many accounts which illustrate the condition of the Balkans in the 17th century, one of the most striking is that of Sir Thomas Roe, British Ambassador at Constantinople in 1622:

'. . . all the territory of the grand signor is dispeopled for want of justice, or rather by violent oppressions, so much as in his best parts of Greece and Natolia, a man may ryde 3, and 4, sometimes 6 daies, and not find a village able to feed him and his horse. . . .'

Oppression there no doubt was, but it seems likely that it was sporadic and temporary, and related mainly to the collection of taxes. An almost equal evil, and perhaps a more serious charge against the Ottoman administration in the days of its decline, was neglect. In return for taxation, governments have a duty to provide security and justice; but the Turks provided neither.

The only functions of the Turkish officials in Greece were to collect taxes and to raise troops.

The Turkish system was in fact wholly unsuited to a settled way of life. Its merits were those of a machine for waging permanent war and maintaining a continuous expansion. Only such a condition could provide the supply of slaves needed to man administration and the forces, and the booty and tax-revenue necessary to support them. Once the process of expansion began to slow down, the machine began to deteriorate. From the middle of the 17th century, the Ottoman Empire ceased to expand. It had already become too large to be administered by so centralized a government as the Sultanate necessarily was, especially when the process of selection which produced the successive Sultans was so arbitrary and uncertain. Both at the centre and the periphery the system began to break down as the momentum of conquest became exhausted. At the centre, the Muslim institution began to challenge the basis of the ruling institution, which consisted almost entirely of ex-Christian slaves directly dependent on the Sultan. At the periphery, the feudal system began to disintegrate as its foundations in successful warfare and conquest crumbled away.

The latter change was the more immediately serious for the *Rayahs* or Christian subjects of the Empire. The original system of fiefs (*timars* and *ziamets*) was congenial to the peasants, since their tenure of land under their overlords was inalienable and hereditary. Moreover, all the feudatories held their fiefs direct from the Sultan: there was no sub-infeudation, as in western Europe. The feudatories could thus be held strictly to their responsibilities. Nor could they sell or bequeath their fiefs, which were attached to the offices they held as military commanders, administrators, officers of the Sultan's domains or religious foundations. So long as there was a continuing supply of new land becoming available by conquest, the system worked comfortably. But again the waning momentum of successful war brought about a change. Once the Janissaries were allowed to marry and became a hereditary service, they needed land to support them. The Sultan also needed more land in his private domain as his revenue declined. Both needs were satisfied at the expense of the feudal soldiers, whose fiefs were sequestrated to meet them when they died.

The evil of the new system, which substituted *chifliks* or private estates for the feudal *timars* and *ziamets*, was that the peasants living on the land found themselves deprived of their former rights. The new landlords had acquired their *chifliks* as an investment, not as the basis of a responsible way of life. The Janissaries in particular, having virtually abandoned their role as the Sultan's infantry, had become a hereditary corps of traders and profiteers. Prices were rising, partly because no new land was becoming available and partly in response to the economic impact of western Europe. The new landlords did not hesitate to do with their *chifliks* what the former feudatories could not do with their *timars*: to evict their tenants, or alternatively to reduce them to the status of serfs bound to the soil by irredeemable debts. The consequence again was widespread depopulation of the countryside. A vicious circle was thus set in motion: the failure of the central government caused depopulation, which deprived the government of further revenue and obliged it to act still more oppressively. Inefficiency bred oppression and oppression inefficiency. Only a successful renewal of war and conquest could have revitalized the system.

Inevitably relations between the Ottoman administration and its subjects further deteriorated. At least two Sultans seriously considered systematically exterminating the Greek population. Men took to the hills rather than submit, and the title of *kléphtis* (brigand) became one of honour. The Turks armed other Christians, known as *armatoli* (*gendarmes*), to suppress the *kléphtes*, but in course of time there came to be little difference between them. Piracy became rife in the waters round Greece, particularly towards the end of the 17th century. Revolts continued to break out—there was a grave one in the Maina in 1659—though still spontaneously, from local motives, rather than by foreign inspiration, as was to happen in the 18th century. The Turks began to realize that something other than oppression was needed to contain them, especially as their own power was weakening under foreign pressure and frequent disturbances in the army and the corps of Janissaries. The Greeks were still in a sense their favourite Christians, as they showed by supporting them against the Catholics in all disputes over the Holy Places. Now they decided to make use of them.

In earlier centuries, the posts in the Ottoman service open to

Christians by birth had been filled more or less indiscriminately by Greeks, Serbs, Bulgars or Albanians. Under the Albanian Grand Vizier, Muhammad Kiuprili, an important innovation took place which put the Greeks in a different class from the rest. In 1669 Panagiotaki of Chios, a Greek who had not renounced his religion, was appointed Dragoman of the Porte—literally 'interpreter', but in effect a secretary of state. Soon afterwards a similar post was created under the naval commander-in-chief (the *Capudan-pasha*) known as the Dragoman of the Fleet. Other posts also fell almost permanently into the hands of the Greeks: the governorship of the Peloponnese, for instance, and the posts of *hospodar* (prince) of Moldavia and Vallachia from 1711. A group of Greek families, living near the Patriarchate in the Phanar (light-house) quarter of Constantinople, gradually acquired almost a monopoly of these posts. Among the Phanariotes, as they were called, were names later to be famous in the war of independence, like Ypsilantis and Mavrokordatos; but for the present they were collaborators with the Turks.

Even before the Phanariotes came to dominate the administration, they already held an important position both in the Church and in foreign commerce. Both brought them into specially close contact with the world and ideas of Europe. In the case of trade, the nature of the connexion is obvious. Greek communities of merchants were establishing themselves in major ports and cities throughout Europe—Moscow, Geneva, Trieste, Ancona, Marseilles, London and elsewhere—without hindrance from the Turks, who regarded commerce with contempt but derived satisfaction from the imports and taxes which accrued. These connexions were to have important consequences in the future. But less conspicuous were the connexions gradually established by the Orthodox Church. Naturally they were first and foremost between the Greeks and the Russians, but the Patriarchate, conservative and self-centred though it was, never entirely neglected the other Christian communities. With the Roman Catholics, so long as the Venetian possessions survived, it was in one sense unnecessary and in another sense too painful to pursue any liaison. But with other churches it was not so.

The first recorded contact between Orthodox and Protestants began in 1573, when a delegation of Lutheran scholars from

Tübingen visited Constantinople. Their interchanges were courteous and inquiring, in marked contrast to the Orthodox hostility to the creation of the Uniate Church in 1596 at the Council of Brest-Litovsk. Within a generation the influence of Protestantism on Orthodoxy began to show its effect, for instance in the *Confession* of the Greek priest Cyril Lukaris, published at Geneva in 1629, which showed a marked Calvinist influence, though it is true that a succession of Orthodox councils condemned it as heretical. With the Church of England contact was established almost at the same time, when Cyril Lukaris corresponded with the Archbishop of Canterbury, and a future Patriarch of Alexandria, Metrophanes Kritopoulos, studied at Oxford from 1617 to 1624. But the experiment of opening an Orthodox Church in London for the first time proved a failure, owing to Anglican prejudice: it lasted only from 1677 to 1682.

The Orthodox hierarchy was thus never entirely shut off from the outside world. Monks from Mount Athos stimulated the religious revival in Russia during the 18th century; and at about the same time the Church was in correspondence with the Non-Jurors in England (a group of Anglicans who regarded William III as a usurper), though the attempt to establish communion between them broke down. Even the most tenuous connexions of this kind were important in view of the powerful position occupied by the Church within the Ottoman Empire. The Sultan looked on the Patriarch as the head of the entire Orthodox *millet*, whether Greek-speaking or not. It was therefore essential to the administration that a suitable man should occupy the Patriarchate; and there were frequent changes, accompanied by intrigue, murder and bribery as a result. It was also natural that the Patriarchate, like other positions of trust, should come to be dominated by the influential Greeks of the Phanar. By the beginning of the 17th century, when the Phanariotes were promoted to the top of the administrative hierarchy, they already held innumerable threads of power in their hands.

The promotion of the Phanariotes had diverse consequences. On the one hand, it widened the separation between the Greek aristocracy of Constantinople, including the upper hierarchy of the Church, from both the rest of the Greeks and the other Christian subjects of the Sultan. There was nothing in common except the name between the peasant Greeks with their village-priests and the sophisticated, wealthy, powerful Greeks of the Phanar. Equally the Rumanians and Slavs identified their Greek princes and bishops with their oppressors. At Greek instigation, for example, the Serbs lost their independent patriarchate in 1766, and the Bulgars lost theirs a year later. On the other hand, power was now gravitating into the hands of Greeks who were both better educated and more worldly-wise than their Turkish masters. Through their diplomatic contacts with European governments and their personal connexions with Greek merchants established in Russia, Germany, France, Italy and England, the Phanariotes were moving into a position of great strength. Eventually, it seemed, they might even have taken over the Ottoman Empire as a going concern. In this way the innovations at the beginning of the 18th century contained within them the seeds of still further decline for the Turks.

They were a long way from being finished, however. In the first half of the 18th century, a series of wars with Venice, Austria and Russia resulted in the recovery of the Peloponnese (1714) offset only by the loss of Azov (1736). There followed three decades of peace, during which another shift in the balance in forces took place on the European side. Venice was no longer a great power, and Austria was already tending to take second place to Russia. Since the reforms of Peter the Great (1682–1725), Russia had begun to emerge as the predominant Christian power in eastern Europe; and being an Orthodox instead of a Catholic power, Russia had a special affinity with the Greeks as well as a deep hostility to the Turks. Peter himself tried to exploit this affinity by appealing to the Balkan Christians to revolt during his own wars with the Turks, but without success. The first systematic attempt to subvert the Ottoman Empire by means of the Orthodox religion was made a generation later by Catherine the Great (1762–96), who was German by birth and Russian only by marriage.

After three decades of peace, Catherine's first war with Turkey broke out in 1768. The war sprang from a compact between Catherine and Frederick the Great of Prussia for the partition of Poland, which was put into effect in 1772. Under French incitement, the Turks joined in to harass the Russians' southern flank. Catherine took the opportunity to exploit the pro-Russian sympathies of the Sultan's Orthodox subjects, particularly in Greece. She sent a fleet to the Mediterranean by way of the Atlantic, and two brothers, Gregory and Alexei Orlov (who had previously obliged her by murdering her husband, Peter III), to stimulate a rising in the Peloponnese. The fleet arrived off the west coast of Greece early in 1770 under the nominal command of Alexei Orlov, though his effective officers were British. His brother meanwhile had been in contact with potential leaders of the Greeks, and hopes were high on both sides. Catherine's friend Voltaire was so optimistic that he predicted Constantinople would soon become the capital of the Russian Empire—a tactless boast which certainly did not correspond with the aspirations of the Greeks.

Disappointment was speedy and mutual. The Greeks had asked for very substantial Russian forces, including up to 10,000 troops. They were dismayed to welcome four ships, a few hundred soldiers, and forty boxes of arms and ammunition. Alexei Orlov for his part was soon writing back to his mistress that 'the natives here are sycophantic, deceitful, impudent, fickle and cowardly, completely given over to money and to plunder'. However, the arrival of reinforcements induced the Greeks to mount a half-hearted rebellion. The fort and harbour of Navarino were captured in April 1770—the only success of the campaign—and the Greek and Russian forces pressed on into the interior of the Peloponnese. At Tripolitsa they were met and defeated by a largely Albanian force mustered by the Turkish governor. The rebellion instantly collapsed. Reprisals were extremely severe. The Albanians were allowed to run riot in the Peloponnese, which they pillaged and terrorized for ten years, until the Turks themselves were obliged to intervene and forcibly deport them back to Albania. The Russians abandoned the Greeks to their fate.

The disaster to the Peloponnese in 1770 was by no means the end of the war. The Russians continued their campaigns against the Turks both in the Mediterranean and on the Danube. In July 1770 Alexei Orlov redeemed his failure by a decisive naval victory at Cheshmé on the coast of Asia Minor, thanks largely to his British officers. He than occupied a number of Aegean islands, which the Russians held until the end of the war in

1774. Catherine's successes in the Aegean and further north finally compelled the Turks to make peace on unfavourable but not entirely humiliating terms. The treaty signed at Kütchük Kainardji in July 1774 deprived Turkey of important territories, particularly on the north of the Black Sea, but its territorial provisions were not so important as some others. One gave the Russians the right to appoint consuls anywhere at will in the Ottoman Empire. Another gave them the right to 'make representations' on behalf of the Christian subjects of the Empire. Vague though the latter phrase was, it opened up endless opportunities of Russian intrigue.

Catherine's appetite was not satisfied but whetted by the Treaty of Kütchük Kainardji. She began to formulate plans for the partition of the Ottoman Empire on the same lines as Poland. Her fellow-empress, Maria Theresa of Austria, opposed her plans, but when the latter was succeeded by the Emperor Joseph II, Catherine renewed correspondence on the subject in even more precise terms. By September 1782 she had formulated a detailed project which included the establishment of an autonomous buffer state between Russia and Austria, formed out of Bessarabia with the principalities of Moldavia and Vallachia; a restored Greek Empire with its capital at Constantinople, under her grandson Constantine, who was to be brought up as a Greek; and a sop to the French, who opposed the whole project, in the form of an offer of Egypt and Syria. The correspondence dragged on fruitlessly through 1783–84, but the plan was finally abandoned only in 1792. There was no chance of inducing the Greeks to rise again on behalf of Catherine. Meanwhile she pursued her imperial plans in other directions.

In 1783 she seized the Crimea, which had been virtually isolated by Russia's territorial gains at Kütchük Kainardji. The Turks had now finally lost control of the Black Sea, which for two centuries had been a Turkish lake. In the same year Catherine forced on the Turks a commercial convention, supplementing the Treaty of 1774, which gave the Greeks the privilege of trading under the Russian flag. Under this protection, the Greek merchant navy developed extensively. The Turkish navy had no such mercantile support, a difference which was to have a profound importance in the struggle that was to come a generation later. Not content with the effect of these pressures, Catherine went to war with Turkey again in 1787. She was at first supported and then deserted by Austria; and the Turks were supported in arms by Sweden. The war also brought Russia and Britain into a state of tension, though not of armed conflict, for the first time. It ended in a compromise, with territorial exchanges on both sides, by the Treaty of Jassy in 1792. Catherine's major success lay not in the Balkans but in the second partition of Poland. Her Greek dream was over.

Indecisive though its outcome was, the war of 1787–92 was of great importance for the Balkans. It led to the abandonment of Catherine's plan for the partition of the Ottoman Empire. It aroused the British government for the first time to an awareness of the potential conflict of British and Russian interests in the Near East. It coincided with the French Revolution, an event which profoundly stirred the Balkan peoples. In the words of Theodore Kolokotronis, one of the leading *kléphtes*, who also served as an officer in the British army, 'according to my judgment, the French Revolution and the doings of Napoleon opened the eyes of the world.' The impact was reinforced by the publication in 1788 of the Abbé Barthélemy's *Le Voyage du Jeune Anacharsis*, which was widely read by educated Greeks. They were also familiar with the works of Voltaire and Rousseau. Paris, where the leading Greek intellectual, Adamantios Koraïs, settled in 1788, was now beginning to rival St. Petersburg as the centre of Greek aspirations. Nor were these ideas merely vague abstractions: they were reciprocated by the French. The first study on paper by the French Foreign Office of the possibility of annexing the Peloponnese was probably dated as early as 1786.

Both Russian and French interest in the southern Balkans remained keen and competitive in the last decade of the 18th century. Russian agents were again active in the Peloponnese, based upon the consulate at Patras; and a Greek deputation visited Catherine's court in 1790 with an offer to recognize Constantine (then aged ten) as their Emperor. But Catherine was ready to abandon her plans for Constantine, who never himself developed any interest in being Emperor of the Greeks or even Tsar of Russia. The French established a consul at Ioannina, where Ali Pasha of Tepeleni became *veli* (governor) of Epirus in 1788 and gradually created a virtually independent state.

The Dark Age of Greece (1453–1800)

After Napoleon had conquered northern Italy, he expressed a strong interest in the Ionian Islands (which were still a Venetian possession) and sent a staff officer to visit Ali Pasha at Ioannina in 1796. Next year, by the Treaty of Campo Formio, he acquired sovereignty over the Ionian Islands. He told the Directory that 'Corfu, Zante and Cephallonia are of more interest to us than all Italy'. One of his advisers at this time was the Greek revolutionary poet, Rhigas Pheraios, who was later to be executed by the Turks.

There was now a triangular rivalry for control of the southern Balkans between the French, the Russians and the rising power of Ali Pasha. Ali Pasha, an Albanian by birth, was an able and ruthless tyrant who made Ioannina the most influential and in a curious way also the most civilized capital of south-east Europe. He had no scruples in playing off the rival contenders against each other, and never kept his word for longer than it suited him to do so. He intrigued with the French, the British, the Russians and the Greeks. He ignored the Sultan, executed his emissaries, and treated all his rivals with impartial treachery. His particular ambitions were first to crush the independent Greek community of Souli, against which he waged a series of wars in the closing years of the 18th century, and then to acquire control of the Ionian Islands and their mainland dependencies, including Parga, Butrinto and Preveza. Napoleon's ambitions, coming from the opposite direction, were in direct conflict with those of Ali Pasha. He was already planning to control not only the Adriatic but also the Levant. Inevitably therefore he was also bound to collide with Russia.

Napoleon's invasion of Egypt in 1798, after seizing Malta on the way, involved him in war not only with Britain but also with an unnatural coalition of Turkey and Russia. Ali Pasha took advantage of the war to seize some points on the Epirus coast with the help of French troops from Corfu, and others (notably Preveza) in the teeth of French opposition. His further plans were frustrated for the time being by the seizure of the Ionian Islands from the French by a Russo-Turkish fleet (1799). The islands were jointly occupied for a short time by this strange condominium, which turned into a Russian protectorate in 1801. In name the Ionian Islands became an autonomous state known as the 'Septinsular Republic' under a treaty signed at

Constantinople in March 1800. It had its own flag, the right to establish diplomatic relations (which it did with France), and an aristocratic constitution; but it remained subject to Turkish suzerainty, paying a triennial tribute. Russian forces remained in occupation for the islands' protection, without which they might well have been seized by Ali Pasha. Even this show of autonomy was extinguished in 1807, when the Russians ceded their rights to the French by the Treaty of Tilsit, and Napoleon interpreted the rights he had thus acquired as a title to complete sovereignty.

One episode at this date deserves special mention because of its later consequences. Early in 1807 Ali Pasha, being already master of Preveza, decided to seize the island of Levkas (Santa Mavra), which is separated from Akarnania only by a narrow and shallow strait. The Septinsular Republic entrusted its defence to a young aristocrat, Count John Capo d'Istria,[1] who was already Secretary of State at the age of thirty. He conducted the defence with vigour and success. During the campaign, he became acquainted with a number of the *kléphtes*, who had taken refuge in the island from the mainland. They included Theodore Kolokotronis and Marko Botsaris, both of whom were later to earn fame in the war of independence. These rugged adventurers and the cultured aristocrat found a common bond in their devotion to Greek independence, which they are said to have taken an oath together to promote with all their powers. The Treaty of Tilsit ended their immediate campaign, and Capo d'Istria's destiny took another course. He emigrated to Russia, where he followed a distinguished career in the diplomatic service, rising to become the Tsar's joint Secretary of State at the Congress of Vienna. But he never forgot his ambitions for Greece, nor did the *kléphtes* to whom he had bound himself by oath.

In other ways, too, the short-lived Septinsular Republic was a phenomenon of more than symbolic importance. The islanders were the first Greeks for three and a half centuries to enjoy even the pretence of governing themselves. They did so, it is true, under a very restrictive constitution and merely as the playthings of the great powers. But the great powers had set in motion forces whose outcome lay beyond their control. They

[1] He later adopted the Greek spelling, Kapodistrias.

had in fact inaugurated the so-called Eastern Question, which was to bedevil their relations for more than a century. So far as the Greeks were concerned, the question was whether Greece should become an annexe of Russia or even conceivably of Austria; a colony of Britain or France; a private empire of Ali Pasha of Ioannina; or whether it should even remain, by virtue of the mutual cancellation of contending forces, a province of a salvaged Ottoman Empire. The last thing anybody contemplated was an independent nation-state. It was disputed in the early 19th century whether there even was such a people as the Greeks. But one thing became certain with the emergence of the great powers' rivalry: nothing could ever be quite the same again. Greece had re-entered history.

CHAPTER V

The Struggle for Independence (1800–1832)

By the end of the 18th century, the signs of a Greek renaissance were unmistakable, and the possibility of a successful revolution leading to national independence could not be discounted. A great change was forecast in the condition of the Greeks, but no one could guess with confidence quite what the nature of the change would be. Western travellers, particularly the English aristocrats whose Grand Tour had been diverted from France and Italy by the Napoleonic Wars, visited Greece in increasing numbers around the turn of the century. There was probably much wishful thinking in their minds, filled as they were with the dreams of classical education; but they had no doubts that the Greeks must and therefore would recover their national pride. Expatriate Greeks in Paris and Geneva and Moscow shared the same conviction. But what form would the revival take? There were as many different possible answers to that question as there were symptoms of the revival itself.

A Greek renaissance need not necessarily take the form of national independence. Certainly it was the doctrine of the French Revolution that such ought to be the outcome; and that Revolution had reached the fringes of Greece in 1797, when Napoleon's forces occupied the Ionian Islands and pushed their clandestine tentacles into Peloponnese and the court of Ali Pasha at Ioannina. But this was not the only possible outcome, nor was it the most widely expected. To achieve national independence meant violent revolution and the use of force. Many Greeks of the Enlightenment regarded this prospect with abhorrence. They included influential men like the expatriate scholar, Adamantios Koraïs, born in Smyrna and settled in Paris, whose life was devoted to the revival and purification of the classical language; the young Count John Capodistria from Corfu; and the young scholar Spyridon Trikoupis, who served as Lord Guilford's secretary and was later to be Secretary of State, Minister in London, and the first modern historian of his native country. To these men education was the key to all development for their fellow-countrymen. But it was difficult to see how it would work as a liberating force in practice.

The cultural revival for which they were working was indubitably coming about. The symptoms were marked in education, literature, journalism and the Church. Greek schools there had always been: now their quality was improving, particularly in a few cultural centres like Ioannina. Between the middle of the 18th century and 1821 some 2,500 books were published in Greek, but all of them abroad; and it was abroad—at Vienna, in 1784—that the first Greek newspaper appeared. For higher education, too, the Greeks had to go abroad, which their growing wealth from trade enabled a minority to do. They brought back from the West the ideas of liberal philosophers such as Rousseau and Bentham, whose works made a powerful impact in translation. The poems of Byron also struck an immediate chord within a few years of his first visit to Greece (1809). Nor did the Greeks have only foreign impulses to stir them. Their own first national poet, Rhigas Pheraios, had published his superb songs in the last quarter of the 18th century; and Koraïs read his 'Memoir on the Present State of Civilization in Greece' to a learned audience in Paris in 1803. There were intellectual stirrings even in the Church, a traditionally conservative and even reactionary institution, which had maintained for generations that orthodox doctrine was a final and complete perfection, to which nothing could be added and from which nothing must be taken away.

The attitude of the Church towards the Greek renaissance was consistently ambiguous. It already had all that it could reasonably desire under Turkish rule, including doctrinal authority over Slavs and Rumanians as well as Greeks. It was accustomed to being a part of the civil establishment, enjoying protection under the Sultan against rivalry within the Ottoman

Empire and heretics abroad. Why should it seek or tolerate change? In 1789 – the date could hardly be more significant—a work known as the *Paternal Teaching* was published at Constantinople, discouraging revolutionary ideas and praising the Sultan as the protector of Christianity. Its author was probably the future Patriarch Grigorios V, who was nevertheless to be one of the first victims of Turkish vengeance in 1821. Such was the tight-rope on which the Orthodox clergy walked. On the other hand, they were also the main vehicle of Greek education and therefore peculiarly exposed to liberal ideas from abroad. That such ideas were penetrating their minds was soon to be shown by the revolutionary activity of many of the lower clergy. There was also some fresh attention given to the minutiae of orthodox doctrine, as shown in the publication in 1800 of the *Pedalion* ('Rudder') by a monk on Mount Athos.

But where did such intellectual activity lead? The learned Greeks abroad might insist that education was the right road for the new generation of Greeks; but to what goal would education carry them? The intellectuals had no precise answer. It was not clear whether they thought in terms of national independence at all. Those who did so had no expectation that it would come in their life-time, nor any idea how it would be brought about. Another class of educated Greeks, who had a different approach to the matter, were the Phanariotes of Constantinople. Their approach was more subtle and practical, but equally non-violent. During the 18th century their position in the Ottoman government service had been growing progressively stronger, since they had the contacts with the Christian powers, the diplomatic skill and linguistic abilities which the Turks despised. Some of the chief posts at court were already their monopoly. It might be only a matter of time before they took over the Ottoman Empire in its entirety.

Besides the Phanariotes, there were other prominent Greeks who were in two minds about the direction which the national renaissance ought to take. Among them naturally were the leaders of the Church, to whom Greek independence on a purely national basis would mean the loss of their authority—as indeed it eventually did. While some ecclesiastics hesitated on these grounds, as did many Phanariotes, others took a more intransigeantly nationalistic line. One of them was Bishop Ignatios of Arta, who was obliged to take refuge in Italy. There he collaborated with a leading Phanariote who had taken the same course, Prince Alexander Mavrokordatos. The latter also became a close friend of Byron's during his Italian sojourn. Thus were some of the threads of revolution interwoven outside the boundaries of Greece. But inside the country there was still a strong, inarticulate feeling that a national revolution was not the most desirable outcome.

Doubt was felt chiefly by those who feared that a national revolution would turn into a social revolution: in other words, those who enjoyed position and privilege under the Turks, which would be at risk if the Greeks became independent. Naturally the priests and the land-owners or village headmen (*kodjabashis* in Turkish, *proestótes* in Greek) had most to lose. To many Greeks, these were the real enemy. Adamantios Koraïs wrote in 1788:

'. . . instead of a Miltiades and Themistocles, whom Europe still admires, we are governed by scoundrels and stupid men as well as by an ignorant clergy who are even worse than our foreign tyrants the Turks'.

The same attitude was reported thirty-five years later by a British traveller, Sir William Gell, who wrote in 1823 of:

'a saying common among the Greeks, that the country labours under three curses, the priests, the *cogia bashis* and the Turks; always placing the plagues in this order'.

There were later to be found heroes among the priests and the land-owners, but many of them were reluctant adherents to the struggle.

The primates of the Peloponnese and the islands were among those who felt the deepest doubts. The independence they wanted was more local and personal in character. Men like Petrobey Mavromikhalis of the Maina or wealthy merchants like George Koundouriotis of Ydra wanted to feel that they were masters in their own house rather than to become cogs in a national machine. Many of the *kodjabashis* were fairly known as 'Christian Turks': they simply wanted to usurp their masters' place. The notion of a Greek state as a new sovereign power in the Concert of Europe was to most Greeks too remote to be real. Among those who seriously envisaged it from the first were the few professionally educated men in Greece like John Kolettis, who was Ali Pasha's official doctor at Ioannina. Of the land-owning primates, the first to declare for the cause was Andreas Zaïmis, ancestor of a family greatly distinguished in public life. A few inspired patriots of humbler origin had the same vision—notably Makrigiannis, the author of a remarkable volume of *Memoirs* written after independence. But at the beginning of the 19th century even the most visionary had little idea how independence would come about.

It could in practice come about only by force. This was the fact to which the theorists of national revival blinded themselves. Two widely scattered groups of people had no illusions about it: the *kléphtes*, to whom violence was a way of life, and the founders of the *Philikí Etairía*, or 'Friendly Society'. The *kléphtes* were already active all over the country, including the islands, many of them following a hereditary profession: Kolokotronis in the Peloponnese, Botsaris in Epirus, Odysseus Androutsos in Rumeli, and the legendary men of Sphakia in southern Crete. Their counterparts were active at sea as privateers, notably Andreas Miaoulis and Constantine Kanaris from Psara; but they were also merchantment for whom piracy was an almost indistinguishable side-line. There was a particular affinity between these picturesque adventurers and the British in the Mediterranean. Miaoulis is said to have been once captured by Nelson, and to have captivated him in return. Kolokotronis served in the Greek regiment raised by Sir Richard Church in the Ionian Islands. The British seizure of these islands from Napoleon in 1814 was one of the events which gave the Greeks their most powerful stimulus to revolution.

When the task of organizing and co-ordinating the many forces at work came to be undertaken, it is not surprising that the initiative came from the merchant community. Merchants had the advantage of equally wide-spread contacts both inside and outside Greece. The economic development of the country, though still unsophisticated, was surprisingly well advanced by the beginning of the 19th century. Manufacturing industry was limited to a few simple goods—dyed cotton from Ambelakia in Thessaly, soap from Crete, weapons from Ioannina and Naoussa—but some of them (particularly the first) reached a wide market. Trade in primary products, particularly from agriculture—wine, currants, olive oil, resin—was more highly deve-

loped. The carrying trade by sea was virtually a Greek monopoly, generally under the Russian flag. Others, based on the
Ionian Islands, enjoyed the protection of the British flag.
Colonies of Greek merchants, many of them very wealthy, were
established in all the major countries of Europe, particularly in
Russia. Nothing was easier than for communication following
the natural trade-routes to lead to conspiracy, financed and
supplied from abroad.

The decisive step was taken by a group of three merchants in
Russia, who formed the *Philiki Etairia* at Odessa in 1814. Their
names, scarcely known outside Greece and almost forgotten
even there, were Nicholas Skouphas, Emmanuel Xanthos, and
Athanasios Tsakalov. The *Philiki Etairia* was not the first such
organization. Rhigas Pheraios had founded an *Etairia* twenty
years before, but it lapsed after he had been trapped by the
Austrian police in Vienna and handed over to his death at the
hands of the Turks (1798). Vienna was also the scene of the
foundation of a new *Etairia*, of a more harmless and respectable
kind: this was the Philomuse Society, founded during the Congress of Vienna in 1814, and supported by many eminent philhellenes, including the future King Ludwig I of Bavaria and the
Tsar Alexander I of Russia. Its president was Count John
Capodistria, then the Tsar's joint Secretary of State; and although its purposes were quite innocent, it provided a convenient screen for the activities of the *Philiki Etairia*, with which it
was often confused. Capodistria was widely believed (perhaps
correctly, though it was vigorously denied at the time) to be a
secret member also of the more revolutionary *Etairia*. Certainly his two brothers in Corfu, Agostino and Viaro, were
active members.

Plans for revolt were not confined to the Greeks. There were
two competing impulses at work in the Balkan territories of the
Ottoman Empire: one purely nationalist, aiming at the liberation of Greeks, Serbs, Albanians or Rumanians as such; the
other aiming at a Balkan federation of autonomous states, not
necessarily severed from Turkish suzerainty. Rhigas Pheraios
(who was by birth a Vlakh) was a supporter of the latter aim. He
wanted a multi-national Balkan State in which Greek would be
the language of administration and the Church—a replica in
miniature of the Byzantine Empire. That such dreams were

shared by many potential leaders of the several peoples should not be forgotten, even though nationalism eventually prevailed and made the word 'Balkan' a by-word for petty chauvinism. The first rising came in Serbia (1804), where the leaders—first Karageorge and then his rival and murderer, Milosh Obrenovich—sought not to throw off Turkish sovereignty but to end the tyranny of the Janissaries, whom the Sultans found equally intolerable and uncontrollable. Karageorge was actually initiated into the *Philiki Etairia* before his death in 1817. Ali Pasha also made overtures to the *Etairia*, though probably with little sincerity.

The existence of the *Philiki Etairia* and its conspiratorial activities in Greece soon became an open secret. The organizers were bold to the point of rashness. They exuded plots and promises for which they had little authority. They intrigued with potential rebels throughout the Ottoman territories in Europe, including the Serbs, Bulgars, Rumanians, and Ali Pasha in Ioannina. In particular they persuaded their thousands of followers in Greece that the Tsar was their secret patron, whose armies would see that they did not fail. Capodistria gave them little encouragement, but it took little to persuade the Greeks that the head of the greatest Orthodox power in the world would come to their rescue. Russian consuls in various cities, particularly Patras, made no secret of their sympathies. The Russian monks on Mount Athos were equally assumed to be a symbol of indissoluble religious bonds. The leaders of the *Philiki Etairia* convinced themselves that they had only to choose the right moment to ensure success. That moment seemed to be near at hand in the years 1819–20, when much revolutionary movement was afoot throughout Europe. There were rumblings or outbreaks of revolt in Germany, Spain, Piedmont and Naples: even in France and Russia; and above all in Epirus, where Ali Pasha was openly challenging the Sultan's authority and drawing off large Turkish forces from the Peloponnese to curb his independence.

The Greeks were over-optimistic, however, in believing that they could count on the support of European powers. After the defeat of Napoleon in 1815, the major powers were anxious to avoid further turmoil. The Tsar had invented the strange project of a Holy Alliance (reluctantly drafted on his instructions by

Capodistria himself) as a league of sovereigns for the suppression of liberalism and revolution. Few governments took it seriously, and the British government refused even to be associated with it; but its spirit dominated European policy for a decade. So far as the eastern Mediterranean was concerned, British policy was no more sympathetic to Greek nationalism than that of Metternich, who contemptuously pointed out that it was impossible even to define what was meant by the word 'Greek'. Two anxieties dominated British policy: to keep the Russians out of the Mediterranean, and to safeguard the Ionian Islands, over which Britain had assumed a protectorate after evicting the French in 1814. The Greeks, including Capodistria, had at first welcomed the British presence in Corfu, but they were soon to regret it. Under its autocratic High Commissioner, Sir Thomas Maitland, the protectorate's neutrality in the coming struggle was far from benevolent towards the Greeks.

The Greeks had been encouraged in their expectations of the West, and of Britain in particular, by the contacts formed with official and unofficial travellers in south-eastern Europe. During the Napoleonic Wars, the French consul Pouqueville and the English topographer Colonel Leake became well known in Greece; so did many Russian consuls established under the treaty of Kütchük Kainardji. English aristocrats began to include Greece in their Grand Tour, especially after Napoleon's conquests closed the way to Germany and Italy. Apart from Byron in 1809, there were also the Earl of Aberdeen ('Athenian Aberdeen', later Foreign Secretary and Prime Minister), Frederick North (later Earl of Guilford, a convert to the Orthodox Church and the founder of a university at Corfu), and many classical scholars and collectors of antiquities, who were astonished to find that Greece was actually inhabited by Greeks. Even the depredations of the Earl of Elgin on the Acropolis had the result of awakening cultured opinion in London to the importance of Athens as a fountain-head of European civilization. Philhellenism became fashionable in Britain, but mainly in Whig or radical rather than Tory circles; and the same was true, *mutatis mutandis*, in continental Europe.

The value attached to these attentions was enhanced by the contacts of the Greek merchant communities overseas: in London and Manchester, Paris and Geneva, Moscow and Odessa, and many cities in Germany and Italy. There was also a natural freemasonry among sailors which stood the Greeks in good stead. Both the British and the French navies had squadrons in the eastern Mediterranean, many of whose officers were openly sympathetic to the Greeks: notably the British Captain Hamilton and the French Admiral de Rigny. The same was true of at least a number of army officers stationed in the Ionian Islands: in particular Sir Richard Church, who had raised and commanded a Greek regiment in the assault on the islands under French occupation, and Colonel Charles Napier, who was at one time invited to become Commander-in-Chief of the Greek army (a post later held by Church) before departing to win greater glory in India. Nevertheless the hopes founded by the Greeks on these sympathetic connexions were to prove delusive, at least initially. The official policy of all the governments concerned was resolutely neutral, with an inclination towards the Turks as the wielders of a legitimate authority.

A severe shock to Greek faith in the West came in 1819, when the British government allowed Ali Pasha, the ruthless and treacherous governor of Epirus, to take possession of the port of Parga. Parga had been one of Venice's possessions on the coast of Epirus until the destruction of the Venetian Republic in 1797. It was an appendage of the Ionian Islands, but the resolution of its inhabitants enabled it to escape the fate of the seven islands after the fall of Venice. The islands were occcupied in succession by the French (1797–99), by a Russo-Turkish condominium (1799–1807)—a fantastic arrangement which ended as an exclusively Russian protectorate—by the French again (1807–14), and finally by the British for another half century. The people of Parga welcomed the British forces which arrived in 1814 in the course of the conquest of the Ionian Islands from the French. They feared no change, even though a Russo-Turkish convention in 1800 had nominally transferred their town to the Ottoman Empire. So things remained until the British High Commissioner in Corfu, Sir Thomas Maitland, persuaded his government to carry out the convention of 1800 by ceding Parga to Ali Pasha, as the Sultan's nearest representative.

Britain has never appreciated the bitterness which this decision caused among the Greeks. Capodistria, on a visit to his aged father in Corfu at the time, was a witness of the tragedy, for almost the entire population of Parga emigrated to Corfu rather than remain under Ali Pasha's tyranny. Capodistria complained to the British government about the conduct of Maitland, who may fairly be judged the worst colonial governor ever appointed (even though in name he was not a colonial governor at all, but High Commissioner of a protecting power). But all was in vain. A lasting suspicion of British intentions grew in Capodistria's mind. It was reciprocated, and only partially dispelled by later events. There is evidence that at this time Capodistria secretly met again with several leaders of the *kléphtes* (including Kolokotronis and Botsaris) who had sought refuge in Corfu from the mainland. It appears that he encouraged their plans for action, but carefully dissociated his master, the Tsar, from any commitment. The Greeks, however, no longer had any doubt that they had a powerful ally in the background.

In 1820 the leaders of the *Etairia* made a fresh attempt to secure Capodistria as their leader. When he refused, they turned (possibly on his advice) to Alexander Ypsilantis, a Phanariote Greek whose family had held the office of *hospodar* in Vallachia and Moldavia. Ypsilantis was an officer in the Russian army and A.D.C. to the Tsar, but he readily resigned his commission and accepted the leadership of the *Etairia*. In March 1821 he courageously but foolishly led a motley force across the River Pruth into Rumanian territory, where he found little sympathy for the Greek cause. The Tsar disowned him; Capodistria convinced his master and the European powers that he was not implicated; and Ypsilantis' force was soon routed and dispersed. He himself escaped to Vienna, where he died in exile, protesting that Capodistria had betrayed him. But the fiasco in Rumania was not the end. In the same month as Ypsilantis' rising, the Metropolitan of Patras, Germanos, proclaimed the rising in the Peloponnese on 25th March, which is now traditionally celebrated as Greece's national day.

The revolution was co-ordinated so far as it lay in the power of the *Philiki Etairia* to make it so. The intention is plain from the fact that it took place simultaneously over so wide an area: in Epirus, the Peloponnese, Macedonia, Thessaly, Rumeli; in the mountain ranges of Olympus, Pindus and the Maina; in the islands, where these were occupied by the Turks, such as Crete and Samos and even Cyprus; and at sea, based on the islands which were practically autonomous, such as Psara, Ydra, Spetsai, Kasos and Chios. Almost the only neutrals were those islands which had remained longest under Latin occupation, such as Tinos and Naxos where the population was predominantly Roman Catholic. These relied on French protection and took no part in the struggle.

The co-ordination with Alexander Ypsilantis' incursion into Rumania was made plain by the despatch of his brother, Dimitrios, as military commander in the Peloponnese. Other leading Greeks were sent to Greece by the *Philiki Etairia* to take control of the struggle, or made their own way there independently. They included the Phanariotes, Prince Alexander Mavrokordatos and Theodore Negris. Others emerged from among the native population, either because they were traditional leaders or because they had proved themselves in action: primates like Andreas Zaïmis and Petrobey Mavromikhalis in the Peloponnese and George Koundouriotis of Ydra; chieftains of the *kléphtes* like Theodore Kolokotronis, Marko Botsaris and Odysseus Androutsos. There was in fact a surplus of leaders, but little leadership. The backbone of the struggle, without which it could not have succeeded, was from first to last the Greek people.

The Greeks started their revolution with a number of advantages. There was the advantage of surprise, which enabled them to overwhelm most of the Turkish garrisons in the Peloponnese while the Commander-in-Chief, Khurshid Pasha, was absent in Epirus on a campaign to crush Ali Pasha. The advantage of surprise was a symptom of the decay and lethargy into which the Ottoman administration had sunk. Another symptom of it was the almost complete control of the sea which the Greek privateers established, making skilful use of the fire-ship against the cumbrous Turkish battle-ships. Control of the sea enabled the Greeks to hold and supply a number of key-ports around their coast-line—and most of the major towns in Greece were ports—while the Turks could only bring reinforcements and supplies overland, through mountainous country ideally suited to guerilla attack. These advantages account for the Greeks' early successes, but they could not offset the greater resources and manpower of the Turks in the long run.

In the long run, however, the Greeks had another asset which was not at first apparent. There was a strong sentiment of philhellenism at work in Europe, based partly on the recognition that the Greeks were Christians but much more substantially on the belief that they were the lineal descendants of the heroes of Thermopylae and Marathon. Learned scholars soon came to repudiate this belief, and most of the European travellers tended to pour scorn on it. Even more damaging was the attitude of the governments of the great powers, who were assembled in conference at Laibach (Ljubljana) when the revolution broke out, and quickly denounced it with contempt. But public opinion felt differently. In Paris and Geneva, in many cities of Italy and Germany, and in London and Edinburgh under the influence of Byron, philhellenic committees were formed to collect funds for the Greeks. Young men from Britain, France, Germany, Switzerland, Italy and America volunteered to fight in Greece, many of them risking the wrath of their governments or resigning their commissions to do so. Rich expatriates, particularly in Russia, also sent liberal contributions, undeterred by their rulers' prejudices. Even more important than their money was the moral support of the philhellenes, which was to ensure in the end that it was impossible to allow the Greeks to be crushed.

It was as well that this resource remained to be tapped in the long run, for the Greeks quickly squandered their initial advantages and the Turks retaliated with great savagery as soon as they had recovered from their first shock. On both sides atrocities were appalling. At least one Scots philhellene, Thomas Gordon, abandoned the cause after seeing what the Greeks had done to their enemies in the capture of Tripolitsa (1821). The Turks in revenge hanged the Patriarch Grigorios of Constantinople and massacred the population of Chios, among many other brutalities. They succeeded in crushing the revolution almost everywhere north of the Gulf of Corinth, but even their most bloodthirsty triumphs redounded to their eventual disadvantage. How could the Turks appreciate the reaction in western Europe to their destruction of the first contingent of philhellenes at the battle of Peta in Epirus (1822), or to the massacre of Chios, immortalised by Delacroix? The names of Byron and Shelley, Goethe, Schiller and Victor Hugo meant nothing to the Sultan, but these were his real enemies. He was left to depend on Metternich and Castlereagh—an unequal match, as history was to show.

But the Greeks were their own worst enemies. Before their long-term advantages could begin to take effect, they had almost dissipated their short-term assets. In the first elation of success, rather than consolidating their victories, they devoted their energies to two activities, one premature and the other disastrous—constitution-making and civil war. The one led naturally on to the other, given the difference of background, aims and temperament that were at work. Local assemblies were convened for the purpose of imposing political control in accordance with rival ambitions: a Senate of Messenia (April 1821), a 'central government' of the Peloponnese (June 1821), an Assembly of western Rumeli at Mesolonghi and an Areopagus of eastern Rumeli at Amphissa. Each of these represented different claims to authority—by the primates, the land-owners, the Church, the Phanariotes (Mavrokordatos at Mesolonghi and Negris at Amphissa). Also competing for the leadership were the *kléphtes* (outstanding among them Odysseus Androutsos and Kolokotronis); the wealthy islanders such as George Koundouriotis; and Prince Dimitrios Ypsilantis, younger brother of the late leader of the *Philiki Etairia*, who claimed the succession as of right.

To reconcile the aspirations and methods of all these potential leaders was an impossible task. The primates and the leaders of the Church were used to holding authority under the Turks: all they wanted was the same authority without the Turks over them. The island merchants wanted to increase their profitable trade overseas without paying Turkish taxes. The Phanariotes were by temperament partly Europeans, with affiliations in Russia or the West, and partly Ottoman officials, accustomed to arbitrary rule. The *kléphtes* were a law unto themselves. They fought when they pleased and obeyed no man. If they chose not to fight, they readily made accommodations (*kapákia*) with the enemy. Some of them—Gogos in Epirus, Karaiskakis at Mesolonghi, Odysseus Androutsos in Boeotia—sometimes carried their accommodations to the point of treachery. But this was in part because none of them yet felt themselves to be Greeks in a national sense. There was a Greek language and a Greek Church: there was not yet a Greek nation.

A first attempt to reconcile the rival interests was made by convening a National Assembly near Epidaurus at the end of

1821, which proclaimed a Constitution on New Year's Day, 1822. It was largely drafted by Mavrokordatos, who became the first President; but it was a presidency only in name and a constitution only on paper, though full of noble aspirations. Mavrokordatos returned to Mesolonghi, which he rightly recognized as a key-point interrupting Turkish communications with the Peloponnese. The government of which he was titular head vainly addressed appeals to the Great Powers. Meanwhile the fortunes of war were evenly balanced. The Turks finally destroyed the power of Ali Pasha in Epirus (February 1822), but failed in successive expeditions against the Peloponnese. The Greeks wrought havoc in the Turkish fleet with fire-ships under Miaoulis and Kanaris, but lost control of most of the islands other than those that formed their naval bases. They captured Athens (July 1822), which was no more than a provincial town without military importance, whatever its symbolic significance; but they could not prevent the Turks moving freely across the isthmus of Corinth.

The Greek leaders' attempts to realize their assets in the west were equally unsuccessful. Apart from appeals for intervention —the earliest of which had been addressed to the governments of Britain and the USA in April 1821—they had the optimistic notion of offering the crown of Greece to suitable candidates among the minor royalties of Europe. Unfortunately the rival leaders had different ideas on the suitability of candidates, and between them they found even more candidates than there were factions to support them. Three different names were canvassed in the first eighteen months of the war, and three more were added to the list by 1825. Of these half-dozen, the most interesting were Leopold of Saxe-Coburg, the son-in-law of King George IV, and the Duke of Nemours, son of the Duke of Orléans (who later became King Louis-Philippe). Leopold, while pretending to have no interest in the Greek crown, in fact angled for it with some avidity. Later (in 1830) he first accepted it and then withdrew, subsequently becoming King of the Belgians.

The approaches by different Greek leaders to different royal candidates naturally carried political implications, as also did their contacts with Capodistria. Leopold was the favourite of the pro-British faction, as the Duke of Nemours was of the pro-

French. The British government was aware of the Greeks' communications with the French royalists, through intercepted correspondence. So was the rival Greek faction, headed by Mavrokordatos. As a compromise, the pro-French faction offered to consider Leopold for the still non-existent throne, if he could be induced to marry an Orléanist princess (his English wife, Princess Charlotte, being already dead). There was little need for the British government to pay serious attention to these unofficial intrigues, which had no prospect of fruition. At most, Leopold's name was established as an acceptable candidate for official consideration in later years. But in the meantime the Greek revolution was to be all but extinguished.

The great tragedy of these years began to unfold when Nauplia fell to the Greeks in the late summer of 1822. It was a major prize: the chief port of the eastern Peloponnese, strongly fortified, and the natural capital of the infant state. But the Turkish garrison surrendered it to Kolokotronis, who had no respect for the titular government and refused to admit them when they wished to hold a second National Assembly there in December 1822. The Assembly met instead at the nearby village of Astros, where two important decisions were taken: to send representatives to London to seek a loan, and to curtail the powers of Kolokotronis by imposing new organs of government on him. Kolokotronis showed his contempt for the latter decision by kidnapping four members of the government and carrying them off to Nauplia. The remnants moved first to Argos, and then to a remote promontory of the Peloponnese where they could enjoy the protection of the neighbouring islands, Ydra and Spetsai. In gratitude for this protection, they elected as their new President the wealthy ship-owner from Ydra, George Koundouriotis. But Kolokotronis was now the real master of the Peloponnese.

It is a striking fact that the leading defenders of Greek liberty at this time were largely non-Greek. Koundouriotis was descended from the Albanian invaders of Greece in the 14th century, and spoke Greek only with difficulty. His principal colleague was John Kolettis, a Vlakh who had been Ali Pasha's court doctor at Ioannina. One of the few leaders who maintained resistance far to the north of the Gulf of Corinth was the Souliote, Marko Botsaris, whose followers were largely Albanian. By a strange chance, it happened that two of the Turkish commanders-in-chief during the war, Khurshid Pasha and Muhammad Reshid Pasha (known to the Greeks as Kiutahi), were by birth Orthodox Christians, who had been converted to Islam for the sake of a career in the Sultan's service. The Sultan had some grounds for insisting, as he did to the Powers whenever they remonstrated with him, that he was faced by a series of rebellions for the sake of personal ambition, not by a genuinely national rising.

In the third year of the war (1823), the prospects of the Greeks momentarily brightened. The Sultan was handicapped by a disastrous fire at Constantinople, which destroyed the naval arsenal, and by his own justified suspicions of the loyalty of the Janissaries. The annual campaign to invade the Peloponnese by parallel marches down the eastern and western routes through Greece was pursued in a half-hearted and ineffective fashion. Kolokotronis broke off his feud with the titular government in the Peloponnese and marched across the Isthmus of Corinth to meet and defeat the Turks on the eastern front. On the western front they were similarly defeated by the brilliant leadership of Marko Botsaris, who was tragically killed in the hour of victory at the battle of Karpenisi. Only a few days earlier, he had written a letter to the Englishman on whom the Greeks' hopes now increasingly turned—Lord Byron, who had arrived in Cephallonia in the summer of 1823 as the emissary and financial agent of the Greek Committee in London.

Philhellenism in western Europe, as the Greeks correctly saw, was beginning to be an important factor in the struggle. At the level of combat in the field, there was little to choose, and little need to do so, between the disinterested enthusiasts of France, Britain, Italy, Switzerland and Germany. (Russian volunteers were few, though there were some Poles.) At first the British and French were the least conspicuous. Then came a few regular officers dissatisfied with the peace following the Napoleonic Wars: notably Captain Frank Hastings of the Royal Navy, who was to introduce the most modern techniques of naval warfare to the Mediterranean, and Colonel Fabvier, who introduced French standards of training and discipline to the Greek forces while his fellow-countrymen did the same thing for the naval forces of their enemies. It was the arrival of Byron on the scene, however, that transformed the philhellenic movement into the great romantic crusade of the early 19th century. Though he died at Mesolonghi within four months of his arrival (April 1824), his brief intervention made it certain that Europe could not forget or abandon the Greeks.

The governments of the Great Powers would gladly have done so. At Vienna, Metternich spared no effort to strengthen the Turks' resistance and to undermine the position of Capodistria at St. Petersburg. In the middle of 1822 Capodistria, who had pressed a forward policy on the Tsar since 1812, felt compelled to resign his post as Secretary of State. He retired to Geneva, where he became a discreet focus of Greek intrigues and encouraged his Swiss friend, the banker Eynard, to send copious funds to his fellow-countrymen. In London, although the anti-Greek foreign secretary, Castlereagh, was succeeded on his death in August 1822 by George Canning, there were few early signs of British policy moving towards the Greek cause. (One of the few was that in December 1824 Canning at least acknowledged, even if non-committally and after four months' delay, a letter from the Greek government appealing for recognition.) Paris, where there were many Greek sympathizers, was preoccupied with the problems of the restoration of its monarchy and the instability of Spain. The Greeks were sufficiently well-informed to be aware of all these uncertainties. Though welcoming philhellene volunteers and financial loans from all quarters, they were divided in their estimates of the reliability of the Great Powers. Mavrokordatos favoured the British, Kolokotronis the Russians, Kolettis the French. These were the nuclei of the three main political parties in the early years of independence.

Their frequent appeals to the powers only taught them the bitter truth of Byron's warning to 'trust not for freedom to the Franks'. The conference at Laibach had denounced their rising in 1821; the conference at Verona refused to receive their delegates in September 1822. The Greek delegates in 1822 also carried an appeal to the Pope, and they were shortly followed by a further delegation, including Bishop Germanos, which was authorized to discuss a reunion of the churches; but, under Metternich's influence, the Pope declined to receive them. A new initiative was tried in January 1824, when the Tsar proposed that three autonomous principalities should be established in Greece under Turkish suzerainty; but the British government suspected the plan of being a ruse to establish Russian control, and rebuffed it. The Tsar then abandoned all discussion of the Greek problem with Britain, and attempted to concert a policy with France, Austria and Prussia through a conference at St. Petersburg in the early months of 1825. These negotiations also failed to produce any result. The Tsar was thus unable to find any partners with whom he could cooperate (admittedly on his own terms) in settling the Greek question. For a year he gave up trying. To the Greeks, this series of failures was deeply disappointing, even though there had been some progress, from talk of requiring their 'pacification' (meaning submission) in 1821 to autonomy and mediation in 1825.

Unfortunately the one thing they could not achieve was national unity against the Turks. The arrival in 1824 of the first British loan under Byron's charge momentarily helped to promote reconciliation, because the only Greek named among the three commissioners authorised to spend it was Koundouriotis, whose status as head of the titular government was thus reinforced. Kolokotronis reluctantly surrendered Nauplia to him in the early summer of 1824, in return for an amnesty and a share of the money. But it was only a short respite. The Turks did little in the campaigning season of 1824, leaving the Greeks to destroy each other. Before the end of the year they had duly begun to do so. The primates, joined by Kolokotronis, rebelled against Koundouriotis' government, but were vigorously suppressed by Kolettis. Kolokotronis was captured and held prisoner on Ydra. Other leading figures, notably Mavrokordatos and Petrobey Mavromikhalis, retired in disgust from the unseemly scene. Meanwhile the Turks prepared a devastating counter-blow which was to prove almost fatal to the revolution.

Being short of resources and having little confidence in his own forces, the Sultan called on his vassal, Mehmet Ali of Egypt, to help crush the insurgents. In return, Mehmet Ali was offered the *pashalik* of Crete and the Peloponnese. He sent his able son, Ibrahim Pasha, with the most powerful naval force that had ever been launched in the Mediterranean by any non-European power. Ibrahim sailed from Alexandria in July 1824, devastated the island of Kasos while a Turkish fleet did the same to Psara, and landed on Crete at Suda Bay in the early winter.

In January 1825 he sailed on to the Peloponnese and established his headquarters at the fortified harbour of Modon (Methoni). From there he dominated the Peloponnese for the next
three years with fire and the sword, spreading terror and destruction everywhere. In May 1825 he captured the fort of Navarino,
overlooking the splendid bay and the island of Sphaktiria,
where the Athenians had trapped the Spartans in 425 B.C., and
the abortive Russian expedition had landed in 1770. A year
later he helped the Turks capture Mesolonghi (April 1826), and
it seemed that all was over with the Greeks.

By this time, however, the activities of the philhellenes, and
particularly the death of Byron, had shamed the Christian rulers
of Europe into recognizing that the war in Greece was a disgrace
to civilization. In the latter half of 1825 'Acts of Submission'
were separately addressed by different Greek factions to all
three great powers. Although they were ignored, the powers
began at last to move. April 1826 was in fact a turning-point in
Europe as well as Greece. While Mesolonghi, immortalized by
the fate of Byron, was suffering its last indescribable agonies at
the hands of Kiutahi and Ibraham Pasha, and another National
Assembly at Epidaurus was ending in melancholy confusion, the
Duke of Wellington was in St. Petersburg congratulating the
new Tsar, Nicholas I, on his accession and his survival of the
Decembrist plot. Wellington was authorized to sign a Protocol
with the Russians, which offered the Powers' mediation between
the Turks and the Greeks, but without any sanction to enforce
it. Though secret at the time, it soon became known to the
Greeks, who saw it as an important step forward and a partial
reward for their long struggle to gain recognition by the Powers.
Different factions had offered their submission to Britain, France
and Russia in turn. They now redoubled their efforts to solicit
funds and moral support from each of the powers, but the pro-
British party was decidedly in the ascendant. In 1825 and 1826
they repeatedly threw themselves on the mercy of the British
government, which still maintained an embarrassed silence.

The year 1826 brought them no further comfort. In October
the Russians signed the Convention of Akkerman with the
Turks, settling on paper all outstanding issues between the two
governments. The terms were humiliating for the Sultan, but
they gave the Ottoman Empire a brief respite. Earlier in the

summer the Janissaries had revolted at Constantinople: they were slaughtered and suppressed for ever, which was also a relief to the hard-pressed Sultan. While he tried desperately to put his house in order and his vassal Ibrahim devastated the Peloponnese, the Greeks added to their own miseries by another outbreak of political quarrelling. The fall of Mesolonghi led to the fall of Koundouriotis' government and cut short the first session of a third National Assembly. Violent recriminations throughout 1826 culminated in the emergence of two rival Assemblies under rival Presidents, one on the island of Aigina and one at Kastri, on the coast of the Peloponnese opposite Ydra. Only the imminent arrival of two distinguished British officers persuaded them temporarily to forget their differences and reunite.

Before Koundouriotis fell, he had communicated officially with Sir Richard Church and Lord Cochrane, inviting them to command the Greek army and navy respectively. Both were officers of the greatest ability and men of remarkable, not to say eccentric character. Their chief honours were won outside the British service: Church under the King of Naples, in whose forces he learned to command Mediterranean troops, with good effect in his later operations among the Ionian and mainland Greeks; Cochrane in South America, where he fought in the wars of liberation, after being cashiered from the Royal Navy on a trumped-up charge of fraud. Like many other British participants in the wars of independence, neither was English by birth: Church was born in Ireland, Cochrane was a Scot. Such men perhaps found in foreign causes a sublimation for their own suppressed nationalism; they also found excitement, high responsibility denied to them at home, and in some cases a prospect of lucrative rewards. In other respects they differed. Church was a competent soldier who admired the Greeks and made not a penny out of them; Cochrane was a naval genius second only to Nelson, but he regarded the Greeks with contempt and took a large slice out of their borrowed funds.

Neither man would accept his appointment so long as the Greeks squabbled with each other. Their insistence on unity as a pre-requisite compelled the rival Assemblies to come together in a re-convened session of the third National Assembly at Trozene in March 1827. Here the temporarily re-united leaders took three momentous decisions. They formally invited Church and Cochrane to be their commanders-in-chief; they elected Capodistria president[1] for seven years; and they drafted a new constitution. The constitution was highly liberal and ill suited to the character of the provisional president, who ignored it when he accepted his own election. But the consequential conflicts and problems still lay in the future. The immediate sequel to the arrival of the new commanders-in-chief was a major disaster for which neither of them was wholly exempt from blame, and in the course of which the best of the surviving Greek chiefs, Karaiskakis, was killed. After a series of ill-controlled skirmishes, in June 1827, the Acropolis of Athens fell to the Turks under Kiutahi, its surrender being negotiated by the French Admiral de Rigny. Greek resistance was now at its last gasp, and it seemed as if the Powers were too late to intervene.

Salvation came in the end from the direction the Greeks had always foreseen. Not for the last time in their history, they knew instinctively what the Powers would eventually have to do better than the Powers knew themselves. If the Turks had been able to crush the rebellion quickly, the Powers would have done nothing. But the long-drawn-out agony of six years' anarchy and bloodshed was intolerable. At first the Powers merely resented the disruption of trade: that was why the British government recognized the Greeks as belligerents in 1823, in order to impose international standards of conduct on their privateers. In the following years mutual distrust between the Powers frustrated more than half a dozen tentative propositions of intervention. The Russians were the most active in taking the initiative against Turkey, but the French and British governments feared the consequences of a Russo-Turkish war. The Austrians, ruled by Metternich, were even more uncooperative: they positively wished the Ottoman Empire to crush the rebels. It was, after all, a political fabric similar to their own, and the example of its disintegration might be catching.

A variety of motives gradually converted the French and British governments to intervention. King Charles X, who came to the French throne in 1824, prided himself on his liberal opinions. The French and British naval forces in the Mediter-

[1] The Greek word *kyvernitis* literally means 'Governor'.

ranean were sympathetic to the Greeks and anxious to prevent a further degeneration into chaos and piracy. The death of Byron stirred the whole of Europe. The succession of Canning to Castlereagh as Foreign Secretary (August 1822) and later his brief tenure as Prime Minister (April 1827) heralded the end of reactionary Toryism in England; and his cousin, Stratford Canning, a known philhellene, replaced a Turcophil ambassador at Constantinople. Above all, the conduct of Ibrahim Pasha in the Peloponnese became a scandal to Christian consciences. He was reputed to have the intention of totally depopulating the region, carrying the Greeks into slavery and replacing them with Egyptians. This rumour, which was in fact unfounded, stirred the British government to send instructions to the commander-in-chief of the Mediterranean squadron to frustrate the operation by force if necessary. The instructions never needed to be carried out, but they played a part in the downfall of the next commander-in-chief, Sir Edward Codrington.

To restrain Ibrahim from atrocities was only part of the problem. What was needed was a general pacification of southeast Europe, which it was clear that the Sultan himself no longer had power to impose. To this was annexed the problem of achieving a local pacification with the minimum damage to the Ottoman Empire, whose survival was still considered desirable, in varying degrees, by all the powers. From the point of view of those concerned with the Greeks, the problem thus resolved itself into the questions, how large a Greece would have to be detached and how autonomous should it be? At the time of the signature of the Protocol of St. Petersburg (April 1826), there was no question of independence for Greece. But the Protocol bound only Britain and Russia, and it contained no provision for enforcement. The Greeks recognized it as an essential step in the right direction, but only a step; and the Convention of Akkerman in the same autumn was a long step backwards. They rightly saw that only collective action by all the sympathetic powers would save them, and they therefore appealed for mediation not only to Britain and Russia on the basis of the Protocol, but also to France.

The powers likewise realized that action would have to be collective in order to be effective, and that the vague provisions of the Protocol would have to be equipped with teeth. Negotiations to this effect began on Canning's initiative early in 1827. They were delayed by the desire of the French government to include the Prussian and Austrian governments, both of which eventually declined, and by the Tsar's insistence on strong sanctions to compensate him for sacrificing the benefits of the Convention of Akkerman. At last a treaty was signed by the three powers in London on 6th July 1827, only a few weeks before Canning's death. The essential advance made on the Protocol of St. Petersburg was a provision for the enforcement of an armistice by a combined fleet, qualified by the almost irreconcilable phrase: 'without however taking any part in the hostilities'. The Russians, who alone of the three powers had as yet no fleet in the Mediterranean, hastened to send one there under the expatriate Dutch Admiral Heiden; and the Tsar plainly indicated in a farewell address that he would not be sorry if it came to a fight.

The three Admirals in the Mediterranean came together for the first time only in early October 1827. They were Sir Edward Codrington, who was the senior, though he had taken over his command only six months earlier: de Rigny, who had five years' experience in command; and Heiden, who had formerly served in the British navy. Codrington and de Rigny distrusted each other, but both found Heiden an easy colleague. They had difficulty in interpreting their instructions, which was not dissipated by the glosses put upon them by their governments' respective ambassadors at Constantinople. They also had difficulty in establishing reasonable communication with Ibrahim, whose fleet was still in Navarino bay while his army, based on Methoni, was devastating the Peloponnese. Ibrahim refused to accept the proffered armistice without explicit orders from the Sultan, especially as he contended that the Greeks were ignoring it. This was true, for although the Greek government at Nauplia had readily accepted the armistice, Church was reforming the shattered army to attack the Turks in western Greece, Cochrane was cruising aggressively round the Peloponnese, and Captain Hastings with his powerful frigate, the *Karteria* (*Perseverance*), was harassing the Turks in the Gulf of Corinth.

It is undeniable that the three Admirals, horrified by Ibra-

147

him's atrocities on land, stretched their neutrality in favour of
the Greeks at sea. Twice Codrington prevented the Turco-
Egyptian fleet from sailing out of Navarino bay, intent to supply
the garrison of Patras or to chastise Hastings in the Gulf. Finally
the Admirals decided that they had no alternative but to sail
into the bay and insist at gun-point that Ibrahim should accept
the armistice and return to Alexandria; for it would be impossible to blockade the harbour throughout the coming winter.
The fateful confrontation took place on 20th October. An
Egyptian ship foolishly shot down the occupants of an open boat
sent to parley, and a general action immediately followed, in
which Ibrahim's fleet was virtually annihilated. Reactions to
the battle were mixed, though no one doubted its decisive
character. The Tsar and the French were delighted; Metternich
called it an 'épouvantable catastrophe'; and Wellington (who
became Prime Minister soon afterwards) called it an 'untoward
event' in the Speech from the Throne at the opening of Parliament in January 1828. The Duke of Clarence (soon to be King
William IV) insisted on awarding Codrington the Grand Cross
of the Order of the Bath, but failed to defend him in 1828 when
he was removed from his command, ostensibly for having failed
to carry out the order to prevent the deportation of Greek slaves
from the Peloponnese to Egypt.

The Greeks had a clearer view of the outcome: they knew that
they were free. Capodistria, who had been touring the European
capitals since his election, in order to ensure the moral and
financial support of the powers, arrived at Nauplia early in
1828 to take up his duties as President. He applied his skill and
international experience disinterestedly to improving the prospects of his people, by gaining the maximum possible boundaries, by extracting money from the powers, and by imposing
discipline on the Greeks. But he was to suffer bitter disappointments. The powers soon lost interest in Greece, once Ibrahim
had been dislodged from the Peloponnese by a combination of
pressure from Codrington on Mehmet Ali and the intervention
of a French military expedition (October 1828). They overruled
the recommendations of a conference of their own Ambassadors,
held on the island of Poros in 1828, because it proposed too
generous an extension of Greece's boundaries. Their main pre-
occupation was with the Russo-Turkish war, which broke out as

a delayed consequence of Navarino, from April 1828 to September 1829.

It was an unhappy period for the infant state. Free they might be, but only within limits, and it was still impossible to say how narrow those limits were. First, there were geographical limits. The Greeks were certain only of the Peloponnese and a few adjacent islands. Crete, though recommended by the Ambassadors at Poros, was almost certain to be lost. Attica was highly doubtful, though powerful philhellenes (including Palmerston) argued on grounds of history and sentiment that Athens could not be excluded. North of the Gulf of Corinth was debatable ground: if they made gains there at all, it was likely to be without the province of Akarnania, lying between the River Aspropotamos, the Gulf of Arta and the Ionian Sea, because Wellington feared for the security of the Ionian Islands. Capodistria rightly saw that the matter was likely to be settled in the end on the principle *uti possidetis*. He therefore encouraged Church to occupy Akarnania, Dimitrios Ypsilantis to advance north through Attica and Boeotia, and the French expeditionary force to extend its area of operations north of the Isthmus of Corinth. He also sent Mavrokordatos to try to bring Crete under control, and the French philhellene Colonel Fabvier to seize Chios.

The policy was well conceived, though not all of it succeeded. Church did well in the north-west, though he quarrelled with the Rumeliote chieftains and with Capodistria's tiresome brother, Agostino, who was sent as Lieutenant Plenipotentiary to receive the surrender of Navpaktos and Mesolonghi. The saddest setback was the death in action at Anatoliko of Captain Hastings (May 1828), who had far surpassed the ineffectual services of Cochrane and might well have become the founder of the Greek Navy. Cochrane and Church both found Capodistria hard to work with, and resigned their commands; but in Church's case not until he had successfully asserted a strong claim to Greek possession of territory up to the Gulf of Arta by the summer of 1829. The French in the Peloponnese were forbidden to cross the isthmus of Corinth, but Dimitrios Ypsilantis held his ground in Attica and Boeotia, and won the final battle of the war between Thebes and Levadeia in September 1829. The attempts to gain Crete, Chios and other islands all failed.

Capodistria reinforced his dynamic measures with diplomatic argument. He pointed out that a state confined to the Peloponnese, as Wellington intended, would be too weak to be viable. It would be unable to resist Turkish pressures, to control piracy, to protect its frontiers, or to maintain internal order. The last point was sharpened by the presence in the Peloponnese of numerous refugees from north of the Gulf, including many armed and undisciplined Rumeliote troops who would not rest so long as their home-land was under Turkish rule. Capodistria's persistence was only gradually and partially rewarded. The Conference of London in March 1829 proposed, as a basis for negotiation, to give Greece a northern boundary from Arta to Volos, but excluded Crete and Samos. It also required the withdrawal of Greek troops from Akarnania, even though the province was to be part of Greece. A year later, in February 1830, the Conference issued a further protocol excluding Akarnania from Greece. Only two years later, in the final settlement which created the new Kingdom of Greece, were Akarnania and the Arta-Volos line restored by the Convention of 7th May 1832.

The protracted delay of the final settlement was due to two complicating factors. The first was the Russo-Turkish war of 1828–29. This ended with the peace of Adrianople (September 1829), by the terms of which the Sultan accepted the treaty of London of July 1827, together with any settlement of the Greek question that the powers might impose under that treaty. The second difficulty was that of agreeing on the status of Greece. Size and sovereignty were bargained against each other: if a vassal status was accepted, then a larger Greece might be permitted; but a fully independent Greece must be kept small. The Greeks themselves would have none of this bargaining. Their constitution of 1827 proclaimed them independent, and they expected Capodistria to assert that independence in its entirety. He, on the other hand, regarded himself as equally bound by the treaty of London, which said nothing about independence. His enemies accused him of being in league with his late master, the Tsar, to subject Greece to Russian suzerainty in place of Turkish.

Justice has been done only posthumously to Capodistria's reputation. He thought and acted as a Greek, not a Russian agent. He genuinely sought independence for Greece within the maximum obtainable frontiers, but he did not wish to relinquish personal power. If Greece was to be independent, there was the choice of a sovereign to be settled. The London Protocol of March 1829 proposed that there should be a hereditary prince, subject to the suzerainty of the Sultan, and chosen by the three protecting powers. Capodistria reacted angrily to the protocol. Apart from his customary demands for wider frontiers and financial support, he argued that the Greeks must have a say in the choice of their prince, and he must adhere to the Orthodox Church. Hostile critics believed that Capodistria wished to be the sovereign himself. Certainly, when Leopold of Saxe-Coburg was selected by the powers, Capodistria presented him with a most discouraging account of the prospects, as a result of which Leopold resigned in May 1830, four months after he had accepted, without ever setting foot in Greece.

Capodistria's manoeuvres were disconcerting to the powers and damaged his own reputation. But they benefited Greece in the long run. It took the powers two years after Leopold's withdrawal to settle the destiny of Greece, but when they finally did so it was on the basis of an enlarged kingdom and complete independence from Turkey. Unfortunately Capodistria did not live to see his achievement. Like other national leaders, he was unable to match his skill in international dealings with the necessary measure of control over his fellow-countrymen. The Greeks were peculiarly ungovernable, and beset with internal rivalries. From the day of his first arrival, Capodistria made up his mind that it was impracticable to allow the Constitution of Trozene to operate. He postponed the National Assembly which was about to meet, persuaded the provisional government and legislature to dissolve themselves, and set up a body of his own choice, 27 strong, which he called the *Panhellinion*, with a 'General Secretariat' of 11 secretaries to act as his personal cabinet. But all effective power remained in his own hands. These were decisions for which three and a half years later he paid with his life.

With almost no one to share his responsibilities, Capodistria was soon held to blame for everything that went wrong; and internally very little went right. He distrusted almost all those who had exercised power before his arrival in Greece: the primates, the ship-owners of the islands and land-owners of the Peloponnese, the chieftains of the *kléphtes*, the Phanariotes, the philhellenes, the constitutionalists and intellectuals. Only Kolokotronis, whom he had known since his younger days in the Ionian Islands, and the gallant Admiral Kanaris commanded something of his confidence. It was to the Ionian Islands and the Greeks scattered across Europe that he particularly looked for help. From Corfu he brought his brothers, Viaro and Agostino, among many others. With the Greeks of Russia, Italy and Central Europe he carried on a vast correspondence, seeking loans, assistance in kind, and help in placing young Greeks in European schools. Education preoccupied him more than any other subject. But these were plans for the long term. Meanwhile the jealous and suspicious leaders whom he had displaced intrigued against him and subverted his schemes for establishing a civilized state.

He was plagued by the quarrels of the rival factions literally from the day of his arrival in Greece, when he found two Rumeliote chieftains bombarding each other from opposite ends of Nauplia. His presence was enough to induce them to desist, but it was an ominous beginning which remained typical of his luckless presidency. While he grappled with the problems of organizing a civil administration, collecting revenue, housing refugees, promoting trade and agriculture, establishing discipline in the army and navy, creating an educational and ecclesiastical system, founding law-courts, reforming local government, evicting the remaining Turkish garrisons and negotiating compensation for their property, the leaders of the revolution pursued their anarchic feuds. It is not surprising that Capodistria once incautiously remarked that 'il faut éteindre les brandons de la révolution', but the phrase was long remembered against him. Only the peasants and the refugees and perhaps the children looked on Capodistria as their saviour from anarchy and pillage. To be called *Barba Yanni* ('uncle Johnny') by them was one of his few consolations.

The principal contenders for power were the three factions which associated themselves with their particular choices among the protecting powers: the pro-British under Mavrokordatos, the pro-French under Kolettis, and the pro-Russian under Kolokotronis. The last naturally expected special favours from Capodistria, whom they looked on as an emissary of the Tsar;

the first two were then drawn together in opposition and in a common demand for a constitution. But there were many other cross-currents. There were the military leaders, divided between the Rumeliotes (who were also homeless refugees, displaced from north of the Gulf of Corinth) and the Peloponnesians, who expected enormous rewards for their services and a permanent condition of armed irresponsibility. There were the semi-feudal magnates like Petrobey Mavromikhalis and the island capitalists like Koundouriotis, who demanded huge compensation for their losses during the war. There were the Philhellenes and Phanariotes with their powerful western connexions; and there were the Residents of the three protecting powers, who interpreted the role of protection as one of almost unlimited interference.

The first two years of Capodistria's presidency were nevertheless reasonably successful. The eviction of Ibrahim from his last strongholds in the Peloponnese was achieved without bloodshed in 1828, and the campaigns of Church and Ypsilantis in the north in 1829 were a satisfaction to Greek pride. An outbreak of plague was brought under control by a strict quarantine, which Capodistria's opponents mischievously criticized. The French army in the Peloponnese, debarred from helping to enlarge Greece's frontiers, won golden opinions by helping to build roads and carry out other public works. Even when they were recalled, cadres were allowed to remain behind to train a modern army for the Greeks, to Capodistria's great satisfaction. His tours of the Peloponnese and the islands were hugely successful. In July 1829 he was able to convene a fourth National Assembly at Argos with the certainty that his personal rule would be overwhelmingly endorsed. So it was, though not without complaints that the election of representatives had been unduly influenced by Capodistria's agents. At this date his prestige was at its height, but the fatal decline was about to begin. Even his most trusted colleagues, such as Spyridon Trikoupis, the Secretary of State, found it increasingly impossible to cooperate in his arbitrary system of government.

Capodistria's training was that of an official, not a politician. He argued that Greece could only be governed by a strong central power, not through the patchwork of arbitrary despotism and local autonomy which he had inherited. He had the official's weakness of believing that if he acted honestly, efficiently and reasonably, all would be bound to recognize that he was right. In fact the result was to antagonize almost everybody, particularly the pro-British faction, since the mutual suspicions generated by the British occupation of his native island were never to be dissipated. Of the protecting powers, he probably found the French the most congenial, but they were the least able to help him, especially after the revolution of July 1830 overthrew Charles X. He was naturally close to the Russian party, especially when the Tsar astutely appointed a fellow-Greek in the Russian service as Resident. In any emergency, he could rely on Russian support more readily than British or French; and inevitably he did so. But the pro-Russian faction among the Greeks, led by the uneducated ex-brigand Kolokotronis, was no match for the more sophisticated leaders of the British and French factions.

Two causes, finally, conspired to bring about Capodistria's downfall in 1831. One was the pressure of the constitutionalists for liberal reforms, including freedom of the press. The other was an accumulation of personal grievances on the part of those whose claims to power and financial reward could not be satisfied, particularly the family of Mavromikhalis in the Maina and the leading islanders of Ydra. Ydra became the centre of the opposition when Mavrokordatos and the editor of an independent journal, which Capodistria had suppressed, took refuge there. Petrobey Mavromikhalis was arrested on Capodistria's orders, escaped on the ship of the British philhellene Thomas Gordon, and was caught again and imprisoned at Nauplia (March 1831). Simultaneous revolts broke out in the Mavromikhalis' family domain in the Peloponnese and in Ydra, as well as north of the isthmus. Capodistria's retaliatory measures were not ineffective, but a disastrous incident followed the attempt of Admiral Miaoulis to seize the Greek fleet at Poros on behalf of the rebels on Ydra. At Capodistria's request, the Russian Admiral Ricord intervened (alone of the three protecting powers), and Miaoulis, rather than surrender, blew his flagship and other vessels skyhigh.

With the help of loyal sailors under Kanaris and regular troops under Colonel Kalergi, both veterans of the war of independence, Capodistria was able to re-assert his control at Poros. But Ydra remained unsubdued and his personal prestige was destroyed. One or other of his many enemies was certain to make an attempt on his life, but he refused to take special precautions. It is doubtful whether there was a far-reaching plot against him: that he had given mortal offence to the family of Mavromikhalis was sufficient excuse for assassination, by the social canons of the Maina. Petrobey's brother and son, though technically under arrest, were allowed to move freely about Nauplia. On Sunday 9th October 1831 they took advantage of their freedom to assassinate Capodistria on his way to church. There followed another period of total anarchy while the powers tried to formulate a new policy. At first they recognized Capodistria's brother Agostino as his successor: he was duly elected as such by a new National Assembly in December. But civil war soon broke out between the pro-Russian troops of the Peloponnese under Kolokotronis (who supported Agostino) and the Rumeliotes under Kolettis. Two rival governments were formed, and the protecting powers were divided between them.

The Russians naturally sympathized with Agostino, but Kolettis had the support of French troops in seizing control of Argos, Tripolitsa and Nauplia (April 1832). Agostino fled to Corfu, taking his brother's corpse with him for burial there. Kolettis soon gained a further advantage. The powers' search for a sovereign prince had at last hit upon Otto, the seventeen-year-old son of King Ludwig I of Bavaria; and Ludwig's private emissary to Greece, the philhellene Professor Thiersch, had reported favourably on Kolettis. When the choice of Prince Otto was announced in July 1832, it seemed that Kolokotronis' days of power were numbered. He did not yield easily. While Kolettis held a National Assembly at Pronoia, which welcomed the choice of Otto, Kolokotronis held a rival gathering which offered the presidency to the Russian Admiral Ricord. Ricord prudently declined, but Kolokotronis nevertheless broke up the Assembly at Pronoia by force, and even attacked the French at Argos early in 1833. By that time, however, Otto was already on his way to Greece in a British frigate. He landed at Nauplia at the end of January 1833 accompanied by three Bavarian regents and 3,500 Bavarian troops. Once more, as upon Capodistria's arrival five years before, the forces of anarchy temporarily collapsed.

The protecting powers had at last decided not only on the sovereignty but also on the boundaries of Greece. The new kingdom was not to be subject in any way to the Ottoman

Empire, but it could hardly be called independent while it was subject to a Bavarian Regency and to the arbitrary interference which was disguised under the name of 'protection'. The boundaries were larger than those which had been offered to Leopold of Saxe-Coburg in 1830, but less than those proposed by the three Ambassadors on Poros in 1828. The northern frontier was enlarged to run from the Gulf of Arta to the Gulf of Volos, as Capodistria had demanded, though the Turks retained the northern shores of both Gulfs. In other words, Epirus and Thessaly were excluded, although largely Greek in population. So were Crete, which remained under Mehmet Ali until 1840, and Samos, which was made autonomous under a Christian governor. Chios recovered a similar status; but no other islands, except those immediately adjacent to Greece, formed part of the new kingdom. The one certainty about the settlement was that the Greeks would not regard their frontiers as permanent. Irredentism was born in Greece as the Convention was signed in London[1] on 11th May 1832.

---

[1] It was antedated to 7th May, the British government having fallen in the meantime.

CHAPTER VI

The Emergence of the Greek Kingdom
(1833–1908)

King Otho[1] (as young Otto became on his accession) reigned for almost thirty years, and his successor, King George I, for almost fifty. Their long span is worth recalling in the light of Balkan monarchy's reputation for instability. Yet both reigns ended tragically in spite of their long duration, Otho's by deposition and George I's by assassination. Not until the death of King Paul in 1964 could it be said that a Greek king had both enjoyed an uninterrupted reign and died from natural causes. These vicissitudes show at least that, whatever might be thought of particular monarchs, there was an instinctive attachment in Greece to the principle of monarchy. Republican institutions had only a limited attraction, and never for long. The Greek constitution became known as 'a democracy under a king' (*vasilevoméni dimokratía*) and it is a significant paradox that in modern Greek the word *dimokratía* is used indifferently to mean either 'democracy' or 'republic'. But the former sense has generally prevailed.

It was not for many years after the accession of King Otho, however, that Greece could really be called a democracy. The Greeks had been led to expect that a constitution would soon be promulgated under the new king. This was implicit in the terms of the announcement by the three powers of his nomination; and it was confirmed in writing by the Bavarian Foreign Minister in July 1832. But the three Regents proceeded to rule absolutely, as Capodistria had done, though with less wisdom. Of the three— Count Armansperg, Georg Maurer, and General Heideck—

[1] The Greek form of the name is Othon.

only the third had any previous experience in Greece. He had fought as a philhellene in the war of independence, and had served Capodistria well as commander of the garrison at Nauplia. It was natural that he should confine himself largely to the re-organization of the army. Knowing the Greek irregulars from bitter experience, he had no hesitation in disbanding them at once and creating a regular army on the basis of strong Bavarian cadres. In the political domain, Armansperg—the president and dominant figure of the Regency—acted no less autocratically but without the wisdom of experience.

Of a constitution there was not a word, though Greek Ministers were retained in office. Capodistria's centralized system of power was retained, giving the Greeks little say even in the choice of their local magistrates. Even some features of the Turkish system of taxation were retained. When they had neither the precedents of Capodistria nor the Turkish system to follow, the Regents were at a loss. But there were two exceptions where they had ideas of their own. In education they followed the German system, whereas Capodistria had followed the Swiss; similarly in military organization, where Capodistria had preferred the French. Nor were their troops so useful as the French had been in laying the physical foundations of administration— roads, fortifications and other public works. The Bavarians, unlike their predecessors from western Europe, were a drain on the country's resources, which depended in their turn largely on loans from the protecting powers. Taxation imposed on the Greeks was nevertheless exceedingly onerous, and so badly administered that it was not until the end of the fourth year of the Regency that any public accounts were published. It is no wonder that the Regency was exceedingly unpopular. The Regents made themselves even more so by muzzling the press, by slighting the philhellenes and heroes of the revolution, and by pursuing undignified quarrels with each other and intrigues with the three Residents.

Clumsy and insensitive as the Regents were, it would be wrong to suggest that their rule was devoid of merit or that they were to blame for all the woes of Greece. The fate of Capodistria was evidence enough that the Greeks were hard to govern, though it was no proof that they would have been un-governable under a constitution. The Regents saw that if they were to govern at all, they must do so firmly. The speedy dissolution of the irregular bands was a necessary measure, and Armansperg was unwise to go partially back on it a few years later under the influence of Church. An improved system of justice was introduced by Maurer, a professional lawyer, who laid an enduring foundation for the Greek legal code. The Regents also took a necessary step in the direction of establishing a national church, independent of the Patriarch of Constantinople, on the ground that the church could not be subordinated to a subject of a foreign, hostile and non-Christian power (August 1833). Although the process of obtaining the consent of the patriarchate to the establishment of an 'autocephalous Church' in Greece, with its own Holy Synod, was not completed till 1850, it probably could not even have been started by an Orthodox ruler. Otho in fact never renounced his Roman Catholic faith, and could therefore never be crowned under the Orthodox rite.

But he was spared the odium of his Regents' unpopularity. He was received with enormous warmth in 1833, and being still a minor (until June 1835) he could not be held responsible for Armansperg's misdeeds. A number of events in the early years of his reign fortuitously helped to promote public goodwill towards him. In March 1833 the Turks were forced to evacuate the Acropolis of Athens, which was soon to be designated as the capital. This was a happy omen coming so soon after Otho's accession. His name was also associated a few years later with the foundation of a University at Athens, opened in 1837 in the vicinity of the over-splendid palace built for the king. The juxtaposition of the two buildings led to a pungent comment from the rough tongue of Kolokotronis. Looking from one to the the other, the old *klépht* remarked: 'This house will eat that house!'—by which he meant that graduates of the university would overthrow the royal dynasty. His prediction was not far off the mark. But the young king's early years were still bright with promise.

So far Otho had held little or no responsibility. In this he was lucky, for the state of his country under the Regency was miserable and disordered. Kolokotronis made another attempt to seize power with Russian help in the summer of 1833. He was arrested with his accomplices, tried and sentenced to death, but reprieved by the king. Sporadic rebellions and brigandage continued. As Capodistria had predicted, there was no security on the frontiers with Turkey. The Sultan, shattered by a rebellion of his Egyptian vassal and rescued from the armies of Ibrahim Pasha only by the intervention of the powers, was in no position to guard his borders. Greek irregulars crossed into Turkish Epirus to sack Arta (May 1833), and others crossed the frontier at will in the opposite direction to harass Otho's kingdom. There was a serious rebellion in the Maina in 1834, where Bavarian troops were defeated and sent home stripped of their equipment. Another in Akarnania in 1836 was put down only by the skill and energy of the Scots philhellene, Thomas Gordon, who had returned to become a General in the Greek army. Brigandage grew yearly more formidable.

The Regents meanwhile continued their undignified intrigues. In 1834 Armansperg procured the recall of Maurer, and reduced Heideck to a cipher. He was virtually the unchallenged ruler of Greece for the next three years, although Greek ministers continued to be appointed and to hold titular office. Armansperg removed Kolettis from the scene by sending him to Paris as Minister; Mavrokordatos he retained as a willing tool. Although King Otho reached his majority in June 1835, and thereafter presided at his own cabinet, Armansperg retained power with the enhanced title of Arch-chancellor. But the arrogance and incompetence of his administration at last brought about his own downfall. In 1836 the king paid a visit to Germany, principally to seek a wife. While he was at Munich, it was agreed that his father should replace Armansperg. Otho returned to Athens in February 1837 bringing not only a bride, Amalia of Oldenburg (who was a Protestant), but also a new prime minister, the Bavarian Chevalier Rudhart. Armansperg was abruptly recalled, and the post of Arch-chancellor was abolished.

Rudhart did not last long. He attempted to rule Greece with the same arbitrary absolutism as his predecessor. This was no longer tolerable either to the Greek constitutionalists or, more important, to the British government, which was now the most influential of the protecting powers. On the insistence of the British Minister, Rudhart resigned within a year, and was succeeded by the first Greek to hold the chief office since independence, Constantine Zographos (December 1837). But the Greeks were still little nearer to a constitution. The king continued to preside in the cabinet, and rejected the repeated pressures of Palmerston and his representatives to hold the constituent assembly which had long been promised. Bavarian officials still dominated the ministries over which Greeks nominally presided. In the armed forces, Bavarian officers held the key-posts and a Bavarian minister was in charge of the war department. Otho himself was a well-meaning but weak-minded young man, of whom it was said that he was dominated by his wife, in political as well as social affairs. As they had no children, the succession remained in permanent and unhappy doubt.

The internal condition of the country was now pitiful. No progress had been made with Capodistria's systematic plans for developing a modern state. On the contrary, things were now worse than under Turkish rule, as was recognized by a new generation of European travellers who had the opportunity to compare the life of the Greeks under Turkish and Bavarian government. In *Eothen*, based on journeys in the 1830's, A. W. Kinglake reported that there was more migration of Greeks from Greece to Turkey than *vice versa*. In the early years of independence the population actually fell, and almost no new industry was established in the 1830's. Several of the philhellenes who had fought for Greece's independence, notably George Finlay and David Urquhart, lived to form a more favourable opinion of their old enemies, the Turks. The predominance of brigandage in the mid-19th century was satirically immortalized by Edmond About in *Le Roi des Montagnes*. Even as far away as Spain, George Borrow's Greek servant was proud to call himself a Turkish subject. His contempt for the Spaniards as Roman Catholics was an echo of the feelings of Otho's subjects towards their Bavarian masters.

The Greeks had still not forgiven Catholic Europe for the crimes of the past. A conspiracy to replace Otho with an Orthodox prince was formed around the remnants of Capodistria's following and the pro-Russian faction, led by Andreas Metaxas after the death of Kolokotronis. But its object was in the nature of things unattainable, for only Russia could have supplied an Orthodox prince, and the three protecting powers had agreed to exclude from the Greek throne any connexion of their royal families. The anti-Catholic movement then joined forces with the constitutionalists, with the common object of getting rid of the Bavarian ministers and officials rather than the king himself. They could claim the support and even the inspiration of the British government, which constantly reminded Otho of the undertaking made in his name to grant a constituion. A new High Commissioner in the Ionian Islands set an encouraging example of liberal reforms in the spring of 1843, and later in the summer the House of Commons openly debated the desirability of representative institutions in Greece. These hints were lost on the Bavarians, but not on the constitutionalists.

On 3rd September 1843 a bloodless revolution in Athens compelled the king to yield to what was represented as the popular will. The people had been conditioned to shout 'Long live the Constitution!' (*zíto tó sýndagma*) for years before many of them knew what it meant, just as they were later to shout *zíto* for other abstract causes. But the revolution of 1843 was a victory for the leaders of the war of independence rather than for constitutional democracy. The ringleaders were all men who had made their names in the rising of 1821: on the military side, Makrigiannis, General Kalergi (who had loyally served Capodistria) and Captain Botsaris (the son of the hero of Souli); on the political side, Andreas Metaxas, Mavrokordatos and Kolettis. After a brief show of resistance, Otho agreed to dismiss his Bavarian advisers and to call a National Assembly. The Assembly met in November 1843, with the participation of Greeks from Thessaly, Epirus and Macedonia. It framed a constitution to which the king swore his oath in March 1844. In theory, parliamentary government was now established, under a bicameral system of lower house (*voulí*) and senate (*gerousía*).

In practice the Greeks had only exchanged arbitrary rule by Bavarians for arbitrary rule by others scarcely closer to themselves. The first six prime ministers under the new constitution were all war-time leaders, several of them only nominally Greek. They included the Phanariote Mavrokordatos, the Vlakh Kolettis, and the Albanian Koundouriotis. With the exception of the last prime minister of Otho's reign, Admiral Kanaris, all of them paid little regard to the constitution which had cost them so much toil and intrigue. Mavrokordatos in particular culpably betrayed his trust as Greece's first constitutional prime minister (March 1844), and was compelled to resign within six months. Kolettis, who succeeded him in August 1844, remained in office until his death three years later. Neither took naturally to democratic principles, though both had a superficial acquaintance with western Europe. Mavrokordatos' background was the Phanariote society of Constantinople and the Rumanian principalities; Kolettis' was the court of Ali Pasha at Ioannina. The paradoxical result of their supposedly constitutional administration was to increase the popularity of the king.

Otho's reputation had suffered surprisingly little from the upheaval of 1843. In part this was due to his naive character, which created the false impression that he was incapable of intrigue. By wearing the national dress, conducting his miniature court with childlike simplicity, and mixing easily with his people all over the country, the king won all hearts, except those of the foreign diplomatists. The British Minister in particular was continually insisting on the payment of interest on his country's loan, demanding liberal reforms (such as were rarely in evidence in the British protectorate of the Ionian Islands), complaining about petty insults, and insinuating that Otho was mentally deficient. But these irritations, combined with the king's stubbornness in standing up to the British government, only served to increase his popularity. So did his ill-judged quarrel with the Turkish government in 1847, which led to a temporary rupture of diplomatic relations over the Turks' refusal to grant a visa to a notorious brigand, Karatassos, who had frequently raided their territory before receiving an appointment at King Otho's court. The king was beginning to realize that there was profit to be made out of Greek irredentism. In this he was encouraged chiefly by Kolettis.

Greece included considerably fewer than half of those who regarded themselves as Greeks by virtue of their language, their religion, and (less plausibly) their race. It was easy to stir up agitation in favour of enlarging Greece's frontiers by a progressive extension of *énosis* (union). Cretans were always ready to rise in revolt, and did so in 1841 after the Sultan had resumed control of the island from Mehmet Ali. The northern territories had been encouraged to demand *énosis* by the activities of Karatassos and his like, and by invitation to the National Assembly of 1843. In March 1845 the Turkish government complained officially that the Greek press was inciting Ottoman subjects to revolt; and this was perfectly true. The year of European revolution, 1848–49, was marked by nationalist risings in the Ionian Islands, particularly Cephallonia, where a period of liberal administration had the usual effect of whetting the appetite for more. The sympathy of the British government for the European revolutionaries in 1848 did not extend to the Ionian Islands. On the contrary, they were seeking to enlarge their protectorate by claiming two additional islets off the coast of the Peloponnese.

Antagonism between the British and Greek governments came to a crisis in 1850, from which once again Otho emerged with increased popularity. It was a sorry affair from which the Greeks emerged on balance with credit only because Palmerston behaved in a manner unworthy of the Foreign Secretary of a great power. The British government had a number of claims against the Greek government. They included the possession of the two Peloponnesian islets which were alleged to form part of the Ionian islands, and compensation for a piece of land belonging to the historian George Finlay, which had been seized to become part of the king's country property. But the most notorious issue was the case of Don Pacifico, whose house in Athens had been plundered during anti-Jewish demonstrations at Easter a few years earlier. The undeniable outrage had been a substitute for the usual practice at Easter of burning Judas Iscariot in effigy—abandoned on this one occasion in deference to the arrival in Athens of a member of the Rothschild family, from which a substantial loan was hoped. Don Pacifio, having been born at Gibraltar, was a British subject. Palmerston therefore supported his exorbitant claims, and sent the Mediterranean squadron to blockade Piraeus (January 1850) in enforcement of the whole series of demands.

Otho and his government at first treated the claims with frivolous evasiveness, and then with despairing obstinacy. They were encouraged to resist by the intervention of the newly established republican government of France under Louis Napoleon, which offered its mediation in a manner suggesting that it would not regret a humiliation for Palmerston. Reports of the strength of feeling in Athens induced Palmerston to agree to the

French offer. But the French emissary to Athens made himself so offensive to the British Minister that the latter ignored his good offices, renewed the pressure on Otho, and compelled him to agree to pay a substantially higher sum by way of compensation than the Frenchman had negotiated. When Palmerston informed the French Ambassador in London that there could be no revision of the terms imposed, the Ambassador was withdrawn in protest by his government. Palmerston was censured in the House of Lords in June 1850, but won a vote of confidence in the Commons ten days later after the longest and most brilliant speech of his career, which culminated in the famous claim on behalf of Don Pacifico to be entitled to say, like St. Paul, '*Civis Romamus sum.*'

Although Otho had been finally compelled to give way to threats and force, his people credited him with a moral victory. The financial claims of Don Pacifico were eventually whittled down to a derisory sum; the other claims were dropped; and Palmerston was forced to resign a year later after another ill-judged *contretemps* with the French. National emotion was now thoroughly aroused among the Greeks, and the king and queen were identified with it. Otho believed that he had hit upon the key to lasting popularity by setting himself at the head of the patriotic movement. But the trouble with such waves of popularity is that they have to be kept flowing constantly forward if they are not to ebb. It is true that there were almost unlimited claims to *terra irredenta* that could be advanced, and were so. The only logical conclusion to such a movement, however, was the reconstruction of the Byzantine Empire with its capital at Constantinople. Such in fact was the Great Idea (*Megáli Idéa*), with which Otho and Amalia identified themselves in the 1850's.

There were other by-products of the crisis. One was an improvement in relations with the Tsar, who was naturally more sympathetic than the British government to Greek irredentism. He was also in favour of reconciliation between the various sections of the Orthodox Church, which had been seriously divided ever since the war of independence. Because the Patriarchate was situated in the Turkish capital, where the Sultan tried to use the Patriarch as an instrument of policy, the Greek rebellion in 1821 had led to a breach between the clergy in Greece and the hierarchy at Constantinople, which still remained. Consequently there had been no valid ordinations of Greek bishops for nearly thirty years, and the problem of filling vacant sees was acute. The Tsar had worked hard for reunion, but the Russian party in Athens was suspected of disloyalty to the throne, occupied as it was by a Roman Catholic king with a Protestant queen. The affair of Don Pacifico helped to launch a new wave of nationalism in which Orthodox solidarity became emotionally involved and Russia temporarily replaced Britain as the natural protector of Greek interests.

The ecclesiastical schism between Athens and Constantinople was virtually ended in 1850, with the help of the Russians' good offices. The Patriarch issued a Synodal Tome which recognized the Church in Greece as 'autocephalous' under a Synod presided over by the Archbishop of Athens, subject to various conditions on the Greek side. The conditions, which displeased the Greek government and also the British and French governments, because they would have restricted the growing power of the state over the church, were never fully put into effect. A somewhat unsatisfactory statute based on the required conditions was finally passed into law in 1852, and rather surprisingly accepted as adequate by the Patriarch. The reconciliation solved a part of Greece's religious problem, though it could not touch another part, which arose from the fact that there was no prospect of an Orthodox heir to the throne. However, King Otho had improved in cunning as a result of his battle with Palmerston over Don Pacifico, and he saw in the *Megáli Idéa* the opportunity to distract attention from the domestic problem, with the help of his new champion, the Tsar.

The time was opportune, for the dissolution of the Ottoman Empire seemed chronically imminent. Only the intervention of the great powers had saved the Sultan from defeat and overthrow in his civil wars with his Egyptian vassal, Mehmet Ali, in 1831–33 and 1839–41. Ten years later Tsar Nicholas I was openly talking about the partition of the Empire. A brief war between Montenegro and Turkey in 1852 almost precipitated a major war with Austria. Even though that was averted, the consequence was to convince the Tsar that Turkey would yield to any pressure, and to intensify Turkish resentment of foreign interference. A year later the Tsar's ambassador at Constantinople tested his calculation by demanding the right to protect all Orthodox subjects in the Empire. The Sultan was encouraged to resist by the French government, which claimed only a much more limited right on behalf of Roman Catholics, and by the British government, which preferred a weak and docile government at Constantinople to the prospect of a Russian occupation. The dispute moved by inexorable stages to the outbreak of the Crimean War in March 1854, ranging France, Britain and Austria with Turkey against Russia.

The Greeks were delighted. The moment seemed to have arrived to realize the Great Idea. Turkey and Russia were at war from the summer of 1853, and irregular bands were formed in the following winter to raid across the Greco-Turkish frontier. The Greek government denied complicity, but the king and queen were less inhibited. By the spring of 1854, despite stern remonstrances from the French and British Ministers, the government allowed the army to reinforce and support the irregulars. By April it was clear that the attempt to conquer Thessaly and Epirus was a complete failure, gaining almost no support from the Greek population. The Turks routed the Greeks in two battles, which quickly ended an affair too brief and futile to be called a war. Nevertheless the French and British governments retaliated by occupying Piraeus and compelling Otho to renounce his alliance with Russia. The occupation lasted from May 1854 to February 1857, being prolonged ostensibly as a guarantee against the continued threat of brigandage. It was reasonably suspected that the royal court was itself implicated with some of the brigand-leaders.

Allied interference did not end with the withdrawal of the occupation. After the Crimean War ended in 1856, Russian resumed her partnership with Britain and France as a protecting power. The three powers sent a commission to examine the financial administration of Greece. It sat from 1857 to 1859, but produced little effect. In 1858 a sincere effort was made by the British government to end the grievances of the Ionian Islands, from which large numbers of volunteers had crossed to the mainland to join the recent attack on Epirus. Gladstone was sent as High Commissioner Extraordinary, but he learned only that the sole satisfaction of the islanders' grievances would be *énosis* (union with Greece). This course he refused to recommend, assuring the House of Commons in 1861 that it would be 'nothing less than a crime against the peace of Europe'. The Greeks thus learned from their humiliation that their future success must depend upon association at the moment of crisis with a victorious great power. The lesson was painfully emphasized by the fact that the main beneficiaries of the Crimean War had been Rumania, Serbia and Piedmont, all of which had made substantial advances towards fully independent status.

The first chance to apply the lesson came in 1859 with the outbreak of war between Austria and the Italians. But the crisis unfortunately divided King Otho from his people for the first time in foreign policy. The Greeks naturally identified themselves with the cause of Garibaldi, with whom the Ionian islanders had been clandestinely in touch. The king supported his fellow-German, the Austrian Emperor, on the reasonable assumption that the big battalions must win. But the intervention of France under Louis Napoleon (now Napoleon III) upset the balance of calculations, and incidentally showed the Greeks how fickle and unreliable were the friendships of great powers. The outcome of the French victory at Solferino (July 1859) was a setback for the Greeks as well as the Italians. Otho vainly tried to restore his popularity and to distract his people's attention by proposing a new attack upon Turkey; but he failed to stir any sympathy. The Greeks were temporarily tired of foreign adventures. A new generation educated at the University, as Kolokotronis had foreseen, was entering public life. On a sober calculation, it was clear that the only great power in a position to afford Greece real protection was Great Britain, with her naval control of the Mediterranean. The days of the Bavarian dynasty were numbered.

It might have been otherwise if Otho and Amalia had had an heir. But they had no son, and none of Otho's brothers was prepared to accept the constitutional condition that the successor to the throne must be a member of the Orthodox Church. Although the question of the succession was much debated in Athens, the king chose to ignore its significance. He also refused to recognize the significance of the entry of a new generation of politicians into parliament. The crisis of the Crimean War had ended the era in which politics were dominated by the British, French and Russian parties in Athens. They were replaced by fluid groups attached to individual leaders of a new generation:

Dimitrios Voulgaris, Thrasyvoulos Zaïmis (son of the war-time leader), Epaminondas Deligiorgis, Alexander Koumoundouros —all men of greater sophistication than the previous generation. But the king continued to believe that administration consisted simply in the wily manipulation of elderly politicians less sophisticated than himself. Early in 1862 he brought ruin on himself by trying the trick once too often on the much-admired figure of Admiral Kanaris. When Kanaris, called upon to form a government, presented him with a memorandum of proposed reforms, the king accepted the memorandum but contrived to ensure that no men of substance would serve under Kanaris. It was his last superficial victory. In February revolts occurred simultaneously in a number of military garrisons, but were successfully suppressed. Eight months later a more general revolution overthrew the king for good.

Otho and Amalia were on tour at the time of the rising, having been assured by obsequious ministers that the rumours of revolution were without foundation. Their antagonists were able officers of the middle ranks, not superannuated leaders of the war of independence, as in 1843. They tried to return to Athens, but were debarred from landing at Piraeus. As the protecting powers refused to intervene, the king had no choice but to leave Greece, which he did, as he had arrived, on a British warship. He never gave up his claim to the throne, though he lived only five years more, constantly asserting his affection for Greece. It was a genuine feeling, and history has judged him less unfavourably than his contemporaries. But he brought about his own downfall by gravely underrating the forces at work in his adopted country: in particular, the emergence of a new generation of leaders, the revival of British ascendancy in Greek affairs, and the discontent caused by a monarchy which professed an alien religion and held no prospect of an heir. The interim government thrown up by the revolution, which was dominated by Voulgaris, Koumoundouros and Deligiorgis, took care to ensure that these forces were not neglected in the determination of the succession.

The protecting powers immediately recognized the right of the Greeks to expel their king and to select another, but reaffirmed their ban upon any member of their own royal families. The Greeks nevertheless voted by an overwhelming majority in favour of Queen Victoria's second son, Prince Alfred. After re-asserting the impossibility of this choice, the British government undertook to select an alternative king. The task was not easy, but the choice finally fell on Prince William George, the second son of the King of Denmark, who was, like his predecessor, a boy of 18 at the time of his accession. Although he did not completely satisfy all the conditions, he was to prove a successful choice. He was proclaimed King George I of the Hellenes by unanimous election on 30th March 1863. There were two significant differences from his predecessor's case: he was elected by the Greeks, not imposed upon them; and he was to be king of the Hellenes, not simply of Greece. Both points were intended to mark the constitutional and democratic character of the new monarchy. But to the Greeks a more significant feature of the title was that it comprehended all the Hellenes, whether living in Greece or not.

The significance of the latter point was underlined in two ways. First, the kingdom of the Hellenes acquired an immediate extension of its frontiers by the decision of the British government to cede the Ionian Islands, barely a year after Gladstone had declared that it would be a crime against the peace of Europe to do so. The strategic value of the islands, particularly Corfu, which had enticed both Napoleon and Nelson, had long become unimportant since they last played a part in the operations leading up to the battle of Navarino. Now they could safely be handed over to the Greeks, provided that the fortifications of Corfu was dismantled. It was taken for granted that this would not be the last increment to the kingdom of Greece. The same assumption underlay the second significant change in King George I's early years, which was to provide under the new constitution of 1864 for the election to parliament of representatives from the expatriate colonies of Greeks wherever they might be. Unfortunately the provision was abused to elect place-men of the government in power rather than eminent residents abroad; though there was one notable exception— Kharilaos Trikoupis, the son of Spyridon, who was elected by the London Greeks in 1863.

There was a danger that history might repeat itself in other ways besides the choice of an eighteen-year-old prince. As before, a period of acute anarchy and bloodshed marked the interval before the new king arrived, as rival factions sought to gain control. Like his predecessor, the king was accompanied to Greece by a foreign adviser, the Danish Count Sponneck, who was no more tactful than the Bavarian Count Armansperg. But there were compensating advantages on the young king's side. One was that the generation of leaders of the war of independence, and even the philhellenes, was passing away. Another was the remarkable tact and political flair shown by King George himself. One of his earliest personal acts was to insist that the dilatory proceedings of the National Assembly, engaged on preparing a new constitution, should be brought to a speedy completion. It was not the last time that he exercised the royal prerogative in a peremptory (but never an arbitrary) manner. Usually when he did so, he found public opinion on his side, whatever might be the feelings of the politicians. So it was in 1864: on 28th November he was able to take his oath to the new constitution. On paper, it was one of the most democratic constitutions in Europe.

From that date Greece became in fact as well as name a 'democracy under a king' (*vasilevoméni dimokratía*). The new constitution strengthened the rights and liberties of the people, and curtailed the irresponsibility of parliament. The powers of the king were considerable but strictly defined. They went far beyond those implied in the phrase that 'the sovereign reigns but does not rule'; but he could not act without the advice and signature of his ministers. Parliament was limited to one house, the senate (*gerousía*) being abolished. (It was replaced by a Council of State nominated by the Crown, but that in turn was abolished in 1865.) The single house of parliament (*vouli*) was to be elected by direct, secret and universal male suffrage. It was expressly stated that the deputies were to represent the nation and not their constituencies: hence the preference which the Greeks have usually shown for election by proportional representation, which relates deputies to constituencies less directly than the system of a majority vote. There was also provision for local government, which had been neglected since the days of Capodistria.

A particular source of strength to the new democracy was the homogeneity of the Greek people. Almost all of them belonged to the Orthodox Church: the only exceptions were the Roman

Catholics on a few of the islands, and a handful of Albanian Muslims. There was virtually no such thing as social class after the Ottoman system was swept away. Hereditary titles were neither conferred nor recognized where they had once existed. Large estates were compulsorily broken up, and the same practice was applied in each of the new territories as it was acquired. Many of the hundreds of monasteries, which were large land-owners, were closed and their lands sold by the state. Greece became a country of peasant small-holders, where great wealth was rare. There were nevertheless certain families which established a sort of aristocracy of talent, whose names reappear again and again in prominent positions: Koundouriotis, Zaïmis, Metaxas, Voulgaris, Mavromikhalis, Theotokis, Rallis, Trikoupis, are names which recur more than once in the century and a half of Greece's independence. But they owed their dignity only to their public service, generally beginning in the war of independence.

The Greeks were naturally proud of their democracy as well as their country's fame as the cradle of the concept. But they showed little skill at first in operating it. Elections were frequently corrupt, governments seldom lasted long, and the fate of both was often threatened by violence and bloodshed. Between 1864 and 1880 there were nine general elections and thirty-one distinct administrations; between 1881 and 1910 there were another twelve general elections and thirty-nine administrations. Great difficulty was experienced in evolving a party system. After the foreign-oriented parties had been eliminated by the crisis of the Crimean War (which ranged the protecting powers against each other), purely personal politics supervened, apart from a brief phase in 1862 when the parties of Kanaris and Voulgaris assumed the titles of the Mountain and the Plain, in imitation of the French revolutionaries (who had themselves been imitating the Athenians of the 6th century B.C.) It was only after 1872, when Kharilaos Trikoupis began to dominate the scene, followed and rivalled by Theodore Deligiannis, that a two-party system began to emerge.

A crucial moment in the new evolution was the success of Trikoupis in 1875 in imposing on the king recognition of the constitutional principle (never embodied in statutory form) that the king was obliged to entrust the formation of a government to the parliamentary leader who could command the largest following in the *vouli*. So simple a principle seems hardly to need stating, but almost every dispute between the crown and the politicians in the last hundred years has originated from an attempt to disregard it. There have been minority governments since 1875 (though usually only in anticipation of a general election) and there have been constitutional clashes; but the principle has never been formally denounced, nor could it be in a democracy. To Trikoupis belongs the credit of formulating the principle, even though it led immediately to his own downfall, when Koumoundouros succeeded in combining all the other parties in parliament against him in 1875. Trikoupis also has the credit of being the first party leader whose party survived his death (in 1896). His ascendancy was helped by a succession of deaths among his older rivals within a few years: Voulgaris in 1877, Deligiorgis in 1879, Thrasyvoulos Zaïmis in 1880, Koumoundouros in 1883. But above all it was due to his own personality—the first great statesman of modern Greek history.

Trikoupis' ascendancy during the last quarter of the century was persistently challenged by Deligiannis, a passionate nationalist whose policies, apart from pursuing the Great Idea, were limited to championing the exact opposite of whatever Trikoupis proposed. Thus Greece went through alternate bouts of economy and profligacy at home, caution and adventure abroad. To Trikoupis the country owed its system of protective tariffs, the passage of social and industrial legislation, the development of communications by land and sea, and the establishment of limited companies. To Deligiannis it owed a succession of ill-considered attempts to expand the national boundaries, almost all of them unsuccessful. Unfortunately the cautious statesmanship of Trikoupis had less appeal to the voters than the flamboyant nationalism of Deligiannis. Whenever foreign policy was at issue in an election, Deligiannis was sure to win. When his opportunism ended in an expensive rebuff, the voters would turn back to Trikoupis; but by then it was generally too late to do anything but acknowledge bankruptcy.

The national economy was simply unable to bear the cost of the adventures launched in the name of the Great Idea. Industry was still primitive, so the peasant had to meet most of the demands of taxation. The peasants were mostly poor: 25 acres

THE GROWTH OF THE GREEK KINGDOM 1832–1947

was a large property, even in the lowland plains. Before the development of tobacco-farming, the main agricultural products for export were highly vulnerable to conditions abroad: the sale of currants, for instance, depended on the state of the French wine-trade, and the cotton-dyeing industry of Thessaly was almost destroyed by competition from Lancashire. Greece became heavily dependent on foreign loans, with disastrous results. Between 1879 and 1890 six foreign loans were contracted, all at a heavy discount. By 1893, debt-service amounted to one-third of the national budget. Interest rates on mortgages and personal loans reached prohibitive heights. Unemployment or disguised under-employment presented an intractable problem, which only began to be alleviated after the turn of the century by large-scale emigration, chiefly to the USA. No wonder Trikoupis spoke bluntly of 'national bankruptcy' in 1893.

The auspicious beginning of the new reign was thus soon followed by disappointments. But if it is looked at as a whole over the half-century it lasted (1864–1913), there were notable improvements on balance in the state of Greece, both at home and abroad. The national economy, which could barely be said to exist in 1832, was greatly strengthened. Maritime trade was its basis: it multiplied five times over during the new reign, and Piraeus grew to be the fourth port in the Mediterranean. Production of currants, olives, figs and other crops was more than doubled. Mining was developed and steam-power introduced. Nearly four thousand miles of roads and 750 miles of railway were constructed, though Turkish obstruction made it impossible to connect Greece by land with western Europe. The principal towns, which continued (with the exception of Athens) to be sea-ports, grew apace; and allowing for the increase of territory as well as population, the density of population was trebled. The era of post-revolutionary stagnation was over. The new era could not be one of self-sufficiency, but it was marked by an approach to national maturity.

The new reign also saw the beginning of a new era in the cultural life of Greece. The revolutionary period could not, of course, be called one of cultural stagnation. By common consent, it was in part at least the poets and scholars who stimulated the revival of national consciousness which led to the war of independence. Koraïs and Rhigas Pheraios played the same role in Greece that Voltaire, Byron and Schiller played in western Europe. Nor were they without followers. In 1824 Dionysios Solomos wrote the 'Hymn to Liberty', part of which now forms the national anthem. Other major poets of the same generation were Andreas Kalvos and Aristotelis Valaoritis. Both, like Solomos, were born in the Ionian Islands; and the fact is significant. Outside the borders of mainland Greece, western influences were strong. They flowed from a tradition which looked upon the Greeks as the heirs of a classical tradition, which was in reality only a faint memory. To western Europeans, Greek meant the language of Sophocles and Plato. The spoken language of the people was distinguished as 'Romaic' and regarded as of no literary account.

Although the poets of the revolutionary era wrote a simple and intelligible Greek, it was not the language of the people. They felt compelled to conform to the expectations of their readers. Self-consciously dominated at first by the high-minded archaism of Koraïs, the Greeks had been taught to suppose that to be educated was to talk and write in the pseudo-classical language known as 'purist' (*katharévousa*). The people in general never had spoken this language, but they were compelled to write it if they wrote at all. In the latter half of the 19th century a revolution against this intellectual tyranny began. At first it went unnoticed. One or two almost uneducated heroes of the war of independence, notably Kasomoulis and Makrigiannis, recorded their memoirs in popular Greek (*dimotikí*). A translation of the Old Testament into modern Greek was published in 1834, followed by the Gospels and Acts of the Apostles in 1838, by a Greek scholar under the auspices of the British and Foreign Bible Society. Later there were other more self-conscious and ostentatious reformers, of whom the leading spirit was John Psykharis, who began publishing a series of controversial works in and about the colloquial language in 1888. His publications launched not only a literary but a political battle.

A notable figure in the battle which Psykharis launched was Alexander Pallis, who is chiefly known today from his translation of the *Iliad* into demotic Greek. This simple and welcome enterprise caused a great sensation when it was first published. Far more sensational, however, was the project of applying the same treatment to the New Testament, even though not for the first time. On this issue, at the turn of the century, Athens rioted and a government fell (1901). The language question continued for more than a generation thereafter to stir deep emotions, which regularly found political expression. It was one of the issues between Venizelos and his opponents during the first world war, and between the Communists and their opponents in the second. This is an important illustration of the fact that national identity, of which language is the most obvious symbol, continued for a long time to preoccupy the domestic as well as the external politics of the Greeks. It forms an essential background to the historical developments of the half-century of King George I's reign.

A large majority of those who thought of themselves as Greeks were still outside Greece's national boundaries. But King George I was 'King of the Hellenes', and that was taken to mean all of them. The Great Idea had certainly not died with Otho and Amalia. The new king was expected to assert Greece's national claims just as enthusiastically, only more effectively. His marriage in 1867 to the Russian Grand Duchess Olga was taken as a satisfactory sign that the Tsar's support for Greek expansion would be renewed. When their son and heir was born in 1868, popular clamour demanded that he should be christened Constantine (as he was), with the implication that he would one day reign in the capital which shared his name. Constantinople was still a long way off. But there were much nearer territories with a predominantly Greek population— Thessaly, Epirus, Crete and other islands. The only question was, which would claim *énosis* first? The answer came when King George had been on the throne less than three years. It came, as might have been expected, in Crete.

The Cretans rose regularly in revolt, for which they had ample provocation in the Turks' fiscal oppression and the denial of judicial equality and educational opportunity. They rose in 1841, soon after the island was transferred back from the Egyptian *pashalik* to direct Turkish rule, and again in 1858, when they secured the removal of the governor and the promise of a degree of self-government. The promise was not fulfilled, and in 1866 came another rising. The Sultan sent Egyptian troops to suppress it, again promising reforms if the islanders would agree to a restoration of the union with Egypt. The islanders convened an Assembly at Sphakia, rejected the Turkish offer, proclaimed their union with Greece, and appealed to the powers for protection. Volunteers flowed into the island from Greece, but the king and his government under Koumoundouros prudently maintained neutrality until the powers had decided. France and Russia both favoured a plebiscite on union with Greece, but the British government, having heard unfavourable reports of Greek mis-government in the Ionian Islands since *énosis*, alone opposed it.

There followed two years of violence and disorder, in which the most dramatic episode was the destruction of the monastery of Arkadi by its own Abbot, who blew up the powder-magazine rather than surrender (November 1866). A settlement was finally reached in the terms of what was known as the Organic Statute (1868). By this Statute, the Sultan conferred limited but equal rights of representative government on both Greeks and Turks in the island. The settlement lasted on paper for ten years, though it was never fully effective. Meanwhile it became plain to the Greeks that they had again lost the sympathy of the powers. In February 1869 they were obliged to accept a declaration of the powers on the initiative of Bismarck, requiring them to prevent the arming of frontier-crossers or blockade-runners into Turkish territory. In the following year the creation by the Turks of the Bulgarian Exarchate—in other words, an independent national Church, not subject to the Patriarch of Constantinople—found the Greeks without support for their resentment from either Britain or Russia.

British sympathy for the Greeks had long passed away with the philhellenes, but in 1870 there was a special cause for bitterness. In April of that year a band of brigands captured a party of British tourists near Marathon. Several of them bore aristocratic names: indeed, the brigands wrongly believed that one of them was related to Queen Victoria, and therefore expected a prince's ransom. Some were released to negotiate. But the episode was badly mishandled; there was suspicion that the court or the government was implicated in the brigands' activities; and the despatch of a rescue expedition led only to the murder of the remaining captives. British indignation was aggravated by a belief that Russian intrigues were instigating brigandage. Yet at the same time the Russians were behaving with almost equal hostility towards Greece, because they were becoming persuaded that pan-slavism was a more useful vehicle than Orthodoxy for extending their influence in eastern Europe. Hence their support of the movement for the autonomy of the Bulgarian Church.

A few years later the pan-slav movement led to yet another crisis in Russo-Turkish relations, from which the Greeks were eventually to derive incidental benefits. The crisis began with a series of disturbances in the Balkan provinces of the Ottoman Empire, inspired by the belief that Russia would come to the rescue. A revolt in Bosnia-Herzegovina (1875) was followed by another in Bulgaria (1876), which led to Gladstone's famous denunciation of the 'Bulgarian horrors' committed by the Turks in reprisal. Later in the summer of 1876 both Serbia and Montenegro declared war on the Sultan. Russia was unable, and not particularly willing, to help them effectively, and an armistice was soon signed. But these episodes convinced the Russian government that sooner or later they would have to intervene to end Turkish misrule in Europe, and that the Bulgars were probably the most effective instrument for the purpose. In 1876 there was renewed talk among European ministers of the partition of the Ottoman Empire. But being unable to achieve concerted action, the Tsar declared war against Turkey on his own in April 1877.

Of the existing national states, only Rumania came into the war on Russia's side. The Russians did not assign a serious role to the Rumanians, being confident of an easy victory. However, a stout Turkish defence at Plevna not only delayed their advance on Constantinople but also compelled them to seek allies. Their appeals to the Serbs and Greeks were met with circumspect evasiveness, under pressure from the British and Austrian governments. The Greeks went so far as to pass a resolution in February 1878 'to occupy the Greek provinces of Turkey', but it was too late to do anything effective. Plevna had fallen by then, and the Russians were at the gates of Constantinople. Britain threatened war on Russia if the Ottoman capital were captured. But divided counsels in the government and naval weakness made it impossible to intervene decisively. The Turks therefore accepted the Tsar's terms for an armistice, which were humiliating. Russia was able to conduct a peace conference at San Stefano in March 1878 unencumbered by allies or interfering neutrals.

The treaty of San Stefano provided for the independence of Rumania, Serbia and Montenegro from their remaining links with the Ottoman government, and for the creation of a Great Bulgaria with a considerable coast-line on the Aegean Sea. It also required that the Organic Statue of 1868 should be effectively enforced in Crete and that similar legislation should be introduced in Thessaly and Epirus. But these provisions were shortlived. So alarmed was the British government at the proposed enlargement and independence of Bulgaria that they insisted, under threat of war, that all the terms of the treaty of San Stefano should be submitted to a conference of the powers. At the same time they negotiated a separate convention with the Sultan by which Cyprus was to be occupied as a *place d'armes* from which Britain could, in certain circumstances, help to defend Turkey's possessions in Asia against Russian attack. With these preliminaries, the Congress of Berlin was convened in June 1878 to re-draw the boundaries of eastern Europe. A Greek delegate was admitted to the Congress, but allowed to play no effective part.

The Congress confirmed the independence of Rumania, Serbia and Montenegro; and Bosnia and Herzegovina were to be occupied and administered by Austria. The Bulgars were deprived of their outlet to the Aegean Sea and divided into two autonomous provinces called Bulgaria and Eastern Rumelia. Greece gained nothing directly from the Congress, except an undertaking forced upon the Sultan to enlarge her northern frontiers in later negotiation and to reform the administration of Crete. The latter proved the easier problem to agree upon, although the union of Crete with Greece was once again frustrated. By the Pact of Khalepa (October 1878), the Sultan not only agreed to carry out the Organic Statute of 1868, by establishing a form of parliamentary government with a General Assembly, but also appointed as governor of the island a Greek Christian who was a Turkish subject and an experienced administrator. His period of office was disturbed by less than the usual frequency of Cretan insurrections, and the Greek islanders were for the time being moderately content.

It proved more difficult to bring the Turks to agreement, or even to a meeting for discussion, on the subject of Greece's northern frontiers. Britain and France took the lead in trying to bring about a settlement. They arranged a meeting of a Greco-Turkish frontier commission at Preveza in March 1879 and again at Constantinople in August, but without result. In June 1880 a further meeting of the powers at Berlin agreed upon a frontier very favourable to the Greeks, including Ioannina, Metsovo and Mount Olympus. But the Turks refused, and the Greek government under Kharilaos Trikoupis made the mistake of ordering a threatening mobilization. The irritation of the powers led to a re-opening of the whole question, and it was not until May 1881 that a settlement was reached. It gave Greece Thessaly, which the Turks no longer wanted, but in Epirus only the area round Arta, leaving Ioannina and Preveza to the Turks. A new Greek Government under Koumoundouros reluctantly accepted it. Indeed, they had no alternative.

Greece's nationalist ambitions were naturally still far from satisfied. Trikoupis had learned his lesson, and concentrated on domestic and economic reforms rather than foreign adventures. But the rival National Party under Deligiannis took every opportunity to inflame public opinion against Turkey. Such an opportunity arose in 1885, when the Bulgars declared their independence and the union of their two provinces. Deligiannis swept Trikoupis out of office on a wave of public emotion, arguing that if the Bulgars could defy the treaty of Berlin, so could the Greeks. It required an ultimatum from the powers (from which France abstained) and a three-week blockade of Greece by a British naval squadron (commanded, ironically enough, by Prince Alfred, whom the Greeks had tried to elect as their king in 1863) to force the Greek government to submit and and demobilize. A similar outburst was caused in 1889 over Crete, when the Sultan took advantage of communal violence to suspend many of the provisions of the Pact of Khalepa. Once again Deligiannis used the agitation to defeat Trikoupis in a general election.

So long as the powers were determined to maintain the *status quo*, such ebullitions of Greek irredentism were invariably costly and ineffective. But they continued nonetheless, supported by a strong instinct that eventually, as constant dripping wears away a stone, the powers would be forced to recognize the validity of the Greek case. The most dramatic outburst of nationalist fervour, which was disastrous in the short run but probably decisive in the end, came in 1896. Once again the cause was Crete, where the Turkish administration proved itself incompetent to restrain the intolerance of the Muslim minority. In May there were riots in Khania. Britain opposed the wish of the other powers to blockade the island in order to prevent Turkish reinforcements from reaching it. The Sultan hastily agreed to restore the Pact of Khalepa and to re-appoint a Christian governor. But in the following year the riots broke out again on a far more serious scale, and the leaders of the Greeks (prominent among them the young Eleftherios Venizelos) withdrew from Khania to declare an independent government on the neighbouring peninsula (Akrotíri).

This time Deligiannis was able to carry with him not only the Assembly but the king in proclaiming a virtual crusade. War was declared on Turkey in April 1897. The Greek army was sent across the northern frontiers, under the Crown Prince Constantine. A flotilla under the king's younger son, Prince George, sailed to Crete to cut off Turkish reinforcements, and a force of Greek volunteers under Colonel Vassos was landed on the island. Once again the powers felt compelled to intervene. In Crete their object was simply to end the bloodshed. Six governments—the British, French, Russian, Italian, German and Austrian—combined forces to occupy Khania and to bombard the insurgents on Akrotíri. They promised to exclude Turkish reinforcements, blockaded the island, and proclaimed its autonomy under their own protection. In the following year the arrangement was regularized by the appointment of Prince George as High Commissioner, under Turkish suzerainty but subject to the removal of all Turkish troops (November 1898). Forces of four of the powers (Austria and Germany having withdrawn) remained in occupation to ensure peace and order. It was clear to the Greeks that *énosis* was now only one step away, and for the time being they were content.

Things developed very differently in the north, where the intervention of the powers was needed to rescue the Greeks from the consequences of their own folly. The attempt to invade Turkish territory was a disastrous failure. The Crown Prince's forces were driven back into Thessaly and his headquarters at

Larisa were overrun by the Turks. Two sharp battles ended the campaign in May 1897. Much the same happened in Epirus. Constantine was personally held to blame for the humiliating defeat, which nearly cost his father the throne. It was the one severe setback of George I's reign, as well as the only occasion in the history of Greece's progressive expansion when she had to cede territory already legally hers. At about a dozen points along the northern frontier, rectifications were made to Greece's disadvantage in order to give the Turks a more defensible line. An indemnity was also imposed on Greece, and a Commission of Control was instituted by the powers over Greek revenue until it was paid. For the Greeks it was a moment of despair.

For the Turks, the crisis of 1897 served as a warning that new policies were required if the Ottoman Empire was not to be continually eroded. They found a temporary solution in the principle to which the Balkans were peculiarly well adapted: *divide et impera*. In a sense, it could be argued that the same principle had underlain the structure of the Empire ever since the *millet* system was first devised, and that it had proved a beneficent system. But in the past the criteria of division in the *millet* system had been strictly religious. All Orthodox Christians, regardless of ethnic origin, belonged to the *millet-i-Rûm*, which thus included Serbs, Bulgars, Rumanians and Albanians as well as Greeks. Since nationalism had begun to emerge, however, the subject Christians had ceased to think of themselves as simply members of the Orthodox Church. They thought of themselves primarily in national or linguistic terms. Now their Ottoman rulers proposed to exploit their national separatism for their own ends. Balkanisation thus became a calculated policy.

The first deliberate step had been the creation of the Bulgarian Exarchate in 1870. After offering this sop to Bulgarian nationalism, the Sultan tried variants of the same policy with the Albanians, the Serbs and the Vlakhs. An Albanian League was formed by the Turks to help them delay the cession of territory to Montenegro in 1879, under the treaty of Berlin. The Serbs were allowed to establish an independent bishopric at Uskub (Skoplje), a concession already made to the Bulgars. The Vlakhs in the Greek border areas were encouraged to identify themselves with the Rumanians of Vallachia. Most of these tempting incitements were offered in the great undefined area known as Macedonia, where the mixture of populations is so inextricable that the territory has provided the French language with its equivalent (*macédoine*) of 'fruit salad'. Turkish policy had no reason to regret or oppose the creation about 1893 of a Macedonian Committee based on Sofia, whose purpose was ostensibly to promote the formation of an autonomous Macedonia with its capital at Salonika. Since this was clearly a new device for Bulgarian expansion, it was certain to annoy the Greeks.

The Macedonian Committee was only the visible part of the Bulgarian nationalist movement. More important was the Internal Macedonian Revolutionary Organization (IMRO), which deliberately set out to organize violence and terrorism. The raids of IMRO into Macedonia began in 1895. In 1894 a rival Greek organization was founded called the National Society (*Ethnikí Etairía*), whose purpose was to conduct anti-Bulgarian propaganda in Macedonia. Clearly it was only a matter of time before the rival organizations came to blows. The Turks were unmoved by the consequent disorders, which gave them an excuse for severe reprisals against both nationalities. From 1897 onwards, public order began to disintegrate in Macedonia. The Bulgar terrorists, known as *comitadjis*, or 'men of the (Macedonian) Committee', were opposed by Greek bands organized on the model of the *kléphtes* and officered by volunteers from the army. One of these officers, Paul Melas, became a national hero when he was killed in action.

By the turn of the century the disorders in Macedonia had become an international scandal. In 1901 an American woman missionary was kidnapped by IMRO, and had to be ransomed by her government. In 1903 there were serious bomb outrages in Salonika, caused by the same organization. The powers began to consider an intervention similar to that in Crete. Early in 1903 the Russian and Austrian governments proposed a limited scheme of reform to the Sultan. The British government went further and proposed that Macedonia should have a Christian governor and that the police should have Christian officers. Shortly afterwards (October 1903) the Emperor of Austria and the Tsar met near Vienna and proposed what was known as the Mürzsteg Programme of reforms. The programme was less far-reaching than the British proposals, but it provided for Austrian and Russian agents to advise the Turkish governor and for Europeans to control the police. It did not provide, however, for the withdrawal of Turkish troops from Macedonia.

Although the Mürzsteg programme was accepted by the Sultan within a few weeks, it was never fully put into force. There were sufficient loose ends to give the Turks ample scope for their usual tactics of evasion and delay. But European police officers did begin to arrive in 1904, and were assigned to different districts: the British to Drama, the French to Serres, the Italians to Monastir, the Russians to Salonika, the Austrians to Skoplje. For various reasons, however, the powers were still half-hearted in their intervention. Austria, along with Germany, was moving towards a pro-Turkish policy, of which the Kaiser's Baghdad railway was the dramatic symbol. France was deeply involved in Morocco, Russia in war with Japan. Only the British government was seriously concerned with the problems of Macedonia. It was on British initiative that a naval blockade of the Turkish islands of Mytilini and Lemnos was instituted in December 1905, with the object of coercing the Sultan into agreeing to admit an international commission to Salonika to supervise the finances of Macedonia.

Still Macedonia was not to be pacified. Greek, Bulgar and Serb irregulars continued to fight each other, and the Turks to fight all comers. By the beginning of 1908 the British government had reached the conclusion that another determined effort at pacification and reform must be made. The *ententes* which had been reached with France in April 1904 and with Russia in August 1907 made the chances of success greater than before. A proposal was put to the other powers that they should insist on having a right to approve the choice of the governor of Macedonia, though he might be a Turk; and that he should have European officials under him. Both the Russians and the French agreed to these proposals, which were strenuously resisted by the Germans and Austrians. They were finally formulated at a meeting between the Tsar and King Edward VII at Reval in 1908. But their only effect was to alarm the more progressive and patriotic elements in the Turkish army, who were already thinking of overthrowing the Sultan. The outcome of all the projects of reform was therefore a revolution, but one which began unexpectedly among the Turks, instead of among the oppressed nationalities.

The Emergence of the Greek Kingdom (1833–1908)

It did not make much difference where the revolution began or by whom it was initiated. It was bound to run through the whole Balkan peninsula. The Greeks had been awaiting it for a generation: indeed, they had repeatedly tried to set it off, without success. Macedonia and Crete were the focal points of the Greeks' nationalist enthusiasm, and were to be the decisive areas of the revolution when it came. Macedonia was in a state of chronic disorder. Crete was superficially more peaceful, because the forces of the powers remained in occupation. But below the surface emotions still seethed. Prince George served for eight years as High Commissioner without bringing *énosis* any nearer, and finally resigned in 1906 after a quarrel with Eleftherios Venizelos, who had set up a rival government and proclaimed the union of the island with Greece. The successor to Prince George as High Commissioner was Alexander Zaïmis, already well on his way to becoming an elder statesman. He showed tact in handling Venizelos, whose reputation grew year by year; but it was clear that in Crete, as in Macedonia, a crisis could not be long delayed.

These two provinces were, in Greek eyes, only the starting-point in the next stage of advance towards the absorption of all the unredeemed territories within the Greek kingdom. The expansion of their boundaries had been steady and almost uninterrupted since the war of independence. Other territories, which adjoined them or shared a historical connexion with them, could be expected to fall into place of their own accord once Macedonia and Crete were gained. These included Northern Epirus, Thrace, the rest of the Aegean islands, perhaps eventually even Cyprus, Smyrna, and Constantinople itself. Thus did the whole future of the Great Idea turn upon Macedonia and Crete. But during most of George I's long reign, Greece had never succeeded in exercising an initiative in foreign policy: her gains were the by-product of greater events elsewhere. In this respect the events of the year 1908 were to prove not merely a crisis but a turning-point. Thereafter, whether she won or lost, Greece had come of age.

CHAPTER VII

The First National Crisis
(1908–1923)

Greece's first great crisis of the 20th century ended with the Treaty of Lausanne in 1923. It is more difficult to say exactly when it began. In choosing the year 1908 as the starting date, it needs to be emphasized that the events of that year, which made the Balkan countries a powder-keg once more, were largely outside the control of the Greeks. They deeply affected Greece, but they took place mainly elsewhere: in the nominally Turkish provinces of Bulgaria, Bosnia and Herzegovina; in Macedonia and Constantinople; and elsewhere in the Ottoman Empire. There were consequential reactions both in Crete and Greece, but the initiative did not lie with them. One of the unmistakeable changes, however, which mark the year 1908 in retrospect as a watershed, was that from these events begins the emergence into public prominence of the most dynamic figure in modern Greek history, the Cretan statesman Eleftherios Venizelos. With his emergence, Greece could be said for the first time to become an initiative force in Balkan politics, instead of simply a plaything, a victim, or a spectator.

The decisive event of the year 1908 was the outbreak of the revolution of the Young Turks, whose official name was the Committee of Union and Progress, in Macedonia early in July. This was the beginning of Turkish nationalism in the European sense. It was in fact a reaction to the nationalist movements which had plagued the Ottoman Empire for a century: first the Serbs, the Greeks and the Bulgars; later the Arabs, the Armenians, the Kurds and even the Albanians. Like most of the reformist movements of the Near East, its leaders were intellectuals and officers. There was, however, no united ideology among them. Some wanted to reform and strengthen Ottoman control of the empire, some to diffuse it among the component nationalities in a federal system. Of the leaders of the Young Turks, Enver Pasha, the first to win prominence, was later to become an expansionist and imperialist. A much less important figure in the early days, Mustapha Kemal, was later to be responsible for reconstructing Turkey as a purely national state with no more than an unavoidable minimum of subject peoples. In 1908 they were agreed only in demanding a constitution from the Sultan.

The revolution began as a mutiny in the army. The rebels quickly gained control of European Turkey from their base in Salonika, and threatened to march on Constantinople. By the end of July 1908 the Sultan had capitulated and promised a constitution. Elections were held in November, resulting in a large majority for the Young Turks. They found power harder to exercise than to win. Five months later a counter-revolution took place in Constantinople (April 1909) under the inspiration of conservative religious leaders loyal to the Sultan. The army at once moved on the capital in defence of the revolution. The Sultan was deposed and replaced by a nonentity; and the Committee of Union and Progress resumed control. Meanwhile the Balkan nations and their neighbours were quick to take advantage of the confusion in the empire. In October 1908 the Austrian government annexed Bosnia and Herzegovina. Simultaneously King Ferdinand of Bulgaria proclaimed his country's independence. Less dramatically, the Slavonic peoples met in conference in Prague and the Albanians in Monastir; but there could be no doubt that independence was their theme.

Among the Greeks, the first reactions to the Young Turks' revolution were confined to Crete. At the end of July 1908 the powers still in occupation of the island began to withdraw their troops. Three months later, on 12th October, the Cretan Assembly proclaimed its union with Greece. A committee of five, including Venizelos (who was technically a Greek subject by birth), was formed to carry on the government in the name of King George. The Greek government was put in the unenviable position of having to choose between offending Greek nationalist opinion and offending the Turkish government, and perhaps also the powers. The prime minister, George Theotokis, who had succeeded to the leadership of Trikoupis' party, declared that he could take no official cognizance of the Cretan proclamation, but resigned in July 1909 under nationalist pressure. His successor, Dimitrios Rallis, found an alternative escape in a formula disavowing the Cretan action, but placing the future of Crete, Macedonia and Epirus in the hands of the powers. The powers, however, had in the meantime completed their withdrawal from Crete, and the Cretans promptly ran up the Greek flag.

The pusillanimity of two successive prime ministers had by this time so exasperated the Greek nationalists that a rebellion broke out in Athens, in a form not unlike that of the Committee of Union and Progress in Turkey a year earlier. The Military League had been formed by a group of dissident officers in May 1909. In July it rose against the government of Dimitrios Rallis and forced his resignation. The army officers concerned, joined by mutineers in the Navy, then forced the king and parliament to accept a number of measures under the threat of force, including the dismissal of all the king's sons from their service posts and the removal of members of the cabinet. Fortunately, before they could reduce the country to total chaos, the idea occurred to them and their opponents alike that the solution to the crisis lay in summoning Venizelos from Crete. On his arrival, he persuaded the king to summon a National Assembly to revise the constitution, which met in September 1910. The Military League agreed to its own dissolution, and Venizelos became prime minister for the first time in October.

Even so, Venizelos' task was not easy; but he was seldom at a loss for satisfactory expedients. He had no majority in parliament, which was still dominated by the old party-leaders. Failing to win a vote of confidence in the Assembly, he at once resigned. The king dissolved the Assembly; Venizelos won the ensuing elections by a substantial majority; and a second Constituent Assembly, sitting from January to June 1911, produced the revised constitution that he desired. The changes were not revolutionary: they were no more than had been shown to be required for practical convenience by nearly half a century of experience. The Council of State was revived as a Crown Council; the quorum of the Chamber was reduced; officers were declared ineligible for election; civil servants were guaranteed security of tenure; education was made free and compulsory. A new military post was created for the Crown Prince Constantine as a gesture of compensation for his dismissal two years earlier. Once the new constitution was in operation, new elections were held in March 1912, which gave Venizelos an even greater majority. A new era of stability and harmony appeared to have been inaugurated.

It could not, however, be an era of peace. The personal ascendancy of Venizelos was such that he succeeded in refusing to admit to the Chamber the deputies whom his fellow-Cretans duly returned at each of the elections. He did so in order to avoid involving Greece in a war before the national forces were capable of holding their own. But neither nationalist emotion nor his own past history and associations could allow such a passive attitude towards Crete to continue. It was imperative to prepare the Greek army and navy for war, and to create the necessary alliances without which it could not be won. Venizelos invited a French military mission and a British naval mission for the first purpose. For the second, he set about establishing a Balkan alliance. He had to work fast, for the Ottoman Empire was once more on the brink of dissolution, and there were rivals for the spoils. Italy had declared war on Turkey in 1911, principally to secure control of Libya, but in the course of operations the Italians had also bombarded the forts of the Dardanelles and occupied the Greek-inhabited islands of the Dodecanese. The Turks made peace with Italy, accepting the temporary occupation of the islands, in October 1912, the very month in which Venizelos' plans for the first Balkan War matured.

The Balkan League of 1912 was a remarkable but precarious achievement. It linked four countries—Greece, Serbia, Montenegro and Bulgaria—in a network of bilateral agreements, not all of them formulated on paper. Serbia and Bulgaria reached agreement on their conflicting claims through the good offices of Russia. Montenegro entered into written conventions with both Serbia and Bulgaria. Greece had unwritten agreements with both Serbia and Montenegro, which caused no difficulty because their claims did not conflict. The last link, which was an understanding between Greece and Bulgaria, presented the greatest difficulty because of the inextricable conflict of their claims in Macedonia. Venizelos persuaded the Bulgarian government that the only solution was to postpone discussion of the spoils until after victory was won. On this basis the alliance was completed. There were only two omissions from it: the Rumanians, who had unacceptable claims against Bulgaria as well as Turkey; and the Albanians, who were not yet recognized as a nation, though the Austrian government at least was determined that they should be. Both were to make themselves felt before the Balkan Wars were over.

The first shots were fired by the Montenegrins on 8th October 1912. Serbia and Bulgaria declared war on the 17th. The Greek government followed suit next day, after proclaiming the annexation of Crete and admitting the island's deputies to the Chamber. The Balkan allies were quickly and overwhelmingly successful, to such an extent that the powers felt compelled to intervene. The British and French governments were unwilling to allow the Aegean islands covering the Dardanelles to fall to the Greeks, whose navy under Admiral Paul Koundouriotis had complete control of the sea throughout the war. The Austrians were determined that the Serbs should not obtain an outlet to the Adriatic. They therefore pressed urgently forward their scheme for establishing an independent Albania. The Russians were also determined that the Ottoman Empire should not be finally destroyed, and in particular that no rival power should gain possession of Constantinople. This the Bulgarian army seemed to be on the brink of achieving, having overrun Thrace, invested Adrianople, and approached the last line of defence before the Ottoman capital. If the Bulgars had succeeded, they would have found themselves immediately in conflict with the Greeks, who looked upon the city as their natural capital. Such a conflict was barely avoided when the Greeks captured Salonika in November, only a few hours ahead of the Bulgars.

The Turks needed little persuading to accept an armistice after two disastrous months. It was signed on 3rd December 1912, though the Greeks refused to be a party to it. There followed ten days later a meeting in London of the Ambassadors of the belligerent powers to decide on the terms of peace. But the war was still far from finished. In January 1913 Enver

Pasha, at the head of a group of Young Turks, overthrew the government which had signed the armistice, and renewed the war. Once again the outcome was disastrous. The Serbs joined the Bulgars in a final assault on Adrianople, which fell to them in March. The Greeks took Ioannina, the chief city of Epirus. In Albania and Macedonia the forts still remaining in Turkish hands fell to the allies. By the end of May the Turks had surrendered again and the peace conference was resumed. The Russians threatened to send a naval force to protect Constantinople if the Bulgars attacked the city. The Serbs and Montenegrins were held back by threats of action from the Austrians; and the new state of Albania was formally created in July 1913, under a German prince, William of Wied, who barely dared to set foot there.

Despite the pressures of the great powers, all the Balkan allies had made substantial gains at Turkey's expense. Unfortunately they were not all satisfied with what they had won. The Bulgarian government disputed possession of Salonika with the Greeks, and of the rest of Macedonia with both the Greeks and the Serbs. The Serbs were disappointed at the loss of an outlet to the Adriatic, and both they, the Montenegrins and the Greeks resented the creation of Albania. The Greeks, though gratified by the acquisition of Ioannina, Salonika and Crete, had much also to resent. They were deprived of a large part of what they called northern Epirus (incorporated in Albania); of a coastal strip of eastern Macedonia, which was to provide Bulgaria with an outlet to the Aegean Sea; and of a number of islands, including Imbros and Tenedos, which were reserved for assignment by the great powers because of their strategic situation covering the Dardanelles. Quite apart from all these disappointments to the allies, Rumania began to claim 'compensation' for Bulgaria's victories by an occupation of the Dobrudja, for which there was at least some ethnic justification.

Inherent in the multilateral conflict was a natural tendency for the Greeks, the Serbs, and the Rumanians to ally themselves against the Bulgars. A treaty was signed between Greece and Serbia at the beginning of June 1913. Its provisions governed not only the operations which immediately followed, but also the relations of the two countries in the First World War and after. In particular each undertook to assist the other, if attacked, and not to make a separate peace with Bulgaria. The *casus foederis* arose for the first time within the month, when the Bulgars attacked the Serbian army in Macedonia. The attack was a complete failure. The Serbs repelled the attack, the Greeks drove the Bulgars out of Thrace, the Rumanians advanced on Sofia from the North, and the Turks took advantage of their enemies' disarray to recover Adrianople. Within two weeks of starting the second Balkan War, Bulgaria appealed to the Tsar for mediation. An armistice was followed by a peace treaty signed at Bucharest in August. Bulgaria lost territory to all her antagonists, but retained an outlet to the Aegean Sea at Dedeagatch.

Greece's gains from the two Balkan Wars were considerable. The territorial additions—southern Epirus and Macedonia, the islands of Crete and Samos—nearly doubled the size of Greece, and they included the important towns of Ioannina, Salonika and Kavalla. These were also rich areas: the tobacco industry, for example, which has long been Greece's major export, was concentrated in Macedonia. At the same time, there were disappointments. Two of the indisputably Greek islands of the Aegean, Imbros and Tenedos, were reserved for the disposition of the powers. The Dodecanese, no less indisputably Greek in population, remained in the 'temporary' possession of Italy. Parts of Macedonia remained in Bulgarian possession, though the composition of their population was at least disputable. The creation of a Bulgarian outlet to the sea was also a cause of Greek resentment. So, above all, was the establishment of Albania, including the Greek-speaking area of northern Epirus, which the Greeks had actually occupied during the war.

The disappointments did not diminish the fact that Greece's national pride was amply satisfied. The dishonour of the war of 1897 was redeemed. Among those who could take special pride in the national revival was the Crown Prince Constantine, who had been blamed for the defeat of 1897 and deprived of his military rank by the Military League in 1909. As Commander-in-Chief in 1912–13, he had played an honourable part in the capture both of Salonika and of Ioannina. But even before the second war broke out, tragic circumstances had brought him to the throne as Constantine I. On 18th March 1913 a madman assassinated King George I in Salonika, in the fiftieth year of his reign. The loss of one of Europe's outstanding constitutional monarchs at such a critical moment was a bitter blow. Yet the circumstances contributed to the assurance of a peculiarly warm welcome for his successor. He bore the name of the founder and the last Emperor of Byzantium, and many wished to call him Constantine XII in succession to the latter. Few doubted that he would one day reign in the city whose name he shared.

The new reign thus began under not unhappy auspices. Despite some friction in the past, Venizelos and the king were reconciled by the triumphs of the war and the circumstances of the succession. Venizelos was the dominant figure of south-east Europe. A master of compromise, he had succeeded not only in establishing a genuine friendship with the Serbs, but also in making peace with Bulgaria and Turkey on terms which avoided humiliating the enemy without exacerbating nationalist feeling in Greece. It was an achievement that would have been beyond the grasp of any Greek who was not at the same time a genius in diplomacy, a humane and far-seeing statesman, and an unchallenged leader of his fellow-countrymen. The disasters which were to follow within a year or two, and the errors of judgment which Venizelos committed later in his life, should not be allowed to diminish the brilliant reputation which he rightly enjoyed in the fiftieth year of his life. Another forty years were to pass before Greece enjoyed such a harmony of monarch and prime minister again.

It was too good to last. In the summer of 1914, while Venizelos was actually on his way to Brussels to negotiate an improvement in relations with the Turkish government, the First World War broke out. At first none of the Balkan states except Serbia were involved, and it was arguable that no *casus foederis* had arisen under the Greco-Serb treaty of June 1913, since it was not Bulgaria but Austria which had attacked Serbia. Venizelos at once confirmed to the Serbs that Greece would declare war if Bulgaria attacked them; but he also went further. He offered Greek support to the western allies against Turkey if they could guarantee Greece against Bulgarian attack. The offer was not accepted by the allies, who were anxious to limit the war so far as possible and did not wish to risk drawing in either Bulgaria or Turkey against them. Venizelos' offer was also unwelcome to King Constantine, who was married to the sister of the Kaiser and was impressed by the strength of Germany's army. This was a strong argument for not entering the war against Germany. On the other hand, it was counter-balanced by the strength of the British and French navies in the Mediterranean, which argued against entering the war on Germany's side.

At the same time that Venizelos was giving assurances to the Serbs and making his offer to the western allies, the king was in communication with his brother-in-law through the Greek Minister in Berlin, who was persuasively supporting the German cause. The Kaiser impressed on Constantine the growing strength of the central powers. He claimed that Turkey, Rumania and Bulgaria were all aligned with Germany; and Turkey had been reinforced by the arrival of two German warships (*Goeben* and *Breslau*) at Constantinople, which had escaped the surveillance and pursuit of the British Mediterranean Fleet on the outbreak of war. The Greek Minister added his own opinion that, if Greece did not join Germany, Bulgaria would be rewarded for doing so at the expense of Greek Macedonia; if Greece did join Germany, then she would be able to claim a reward at the expense of Serbian Macedonia. These sordid calculations were not accepted by Constantine. But his personal decision in favour of neutrality contrasted sharply with the bold attitude of his prime minister. It also made a mockery of constitutional government.

The first rift between the king and his prime minister thus appeared in the opening weeks of the war. Constantine's enemies labelled him pro-German and anti-British, and it is true that later in the war he surrounded himself with ministers and courtiers who were at best defeatist. But Constantine himself was rather pro-Greek than for or against any foreign power. He believed that neutrality would best serve his country's interests. It was not an unreasonable calculation, even if it was also not a courageous one. Constantine already knew that the Kaiser had committed German policy to the support of Turkey. His brother-in-law had told him in so many words that for this reason 'unfortunately Germany can do nothing for Greece'. There was therefore no incentive to enter the war on Germany's side. The only alternative to neutrality was to run the risk of fighting three powerful enemies simultaneously: Germany, Austria and Turkey. In rejecting this perilous prospect, Constantine had the support of his Chief of the General Staff, Colonel Metaxas.

The first appearance in these circumstances of John Metaxas, later prime minister and dictator (1936–41), naturally gives rise to a momentary suspicion; but it cannot reasonably be more than superficial. It is true that Metaxas was trained in Germany. So were many other Greeks, including a Liberal prime minister, George Papandreou, who was a whole-hearted ally of the western powers in both World Wars. It is equally true, on the other hand, that Metaxas committed his country to war against the Axis in 1940, and would (had he lived) have resisted Hitler as ferociously as he resisted Mussolini. Like his sovereign, Metaxas was simply pro-Greek. He happened to be a particularly able staff officer and to have first-hand experience of the German army. That is why his opinion carried weight. His judgment may have been wrong, though it was not always so. The tragedy of the First World War for Greece was that two such brilliant men as Metaxas and Venizelos were seldom in agreement and never both right together. But neither was any the less a patriot for that.

The dilemma of Greek policy was that there was reason behind the opposite calculations of both Constantine and Venizelos. There was greater force in the king's arguments so long as Turkey and Bulgaria both remained neutral. That condition was to change, but it did not change all at once. Turkey entered the war on the side of the central powers in November 1914, but Bulgaria did not do so for another year. The entry of Turkey into the war immediately made the support of Greece much more desirable to the western allies, but it did not decisively alter the calculation on the side of the Greeks, who still looked on Bulgaria as the more formidable enemy. The western allies set about wooing the Greeks, but with less success than they might have achieved three months earlier. They allowed the Greeks to occupy northern Epirus; they promised important gains in Asia Minor; and they undertook to discuss the future of Cyprus. In the haggling which ensued at the turn of the year 1914–15, Venizelos was naturally more ready than the king to come to terms with the allies, but he was nonetheless determined not to sell Greece's services cheaply.

Venizelos was chiefly concerned to secure Greece against attack by Bulgaria. He went so far as to agree to cede further territory to Bulgaria in Macedonia (including the port of Kavalla) as the price of neutrality. Bulgaria, however, preferred to accept a loan from the central powers, which virtually assured her alignment with them. Regarding Bulgaria now as a potential enemy, Venizelos sought two fresh commitments from the western allies: an Anglo-French expeditionary force to be landed at Salonika, and a Rumanian intervention in the rear if Bulgaria should attack Greece. In return he offered a Greek army corps to support the allied attack on the Dardanelles, which was already being planned at the end of 1914. This combination met with insuperable difficulties. The Rumanians were unwilling to move. The Russians objected that the plan might lead to a Greek occupation of Constantinople, though they were persuaded to withdraw this objection. The British government preferred to concentrate its resources against the Dardanelles rather than detach part of them to Salonika. Above all, Venizelos' plan separated him irrevocably from Constantine.

Constantine had reluctantly consented to the plan at first when it was presented to the Crown Council. He changed his mind when his Chief of Staff, Metaxas, carried his opposition to the use of Greek troops against the Dardanelles to the point of submitting and publishing his resignation. Venizelos tried to regain his consent by reducing the commitment from an army corps to a single division. The king absolutely refused. Venizelos resigned, and the king called on Dimitrios Gounaris, an old opponent of Venizelos who had the reputation of being pro-German, to form a government. Constantine was now committed to a losing battle with democracy. Venizelos retained a majority in parliament, which was not substantially reduced in the general election held in June 1915. Yet the king kept Gounaris in office until August, when he could no longer refuse to recall Venizelos. Meanwhile in March the western allies had undertaken their fateful attack on the Dardanelles, which was clearly not proving a success. The temptations to Bulgaria to enter the war on the opposite side were growing stronger.

Venizelos hastened to assure the allies again that Greece would carry out her obligations to Serbia in the event of a Bulgarian attack. He also persuaded the Serbs to offer concessions to Bulgaria to avert such an attack. But Constantine was known to be talking in a quite different sense. It was believed that he had assured the Kaiser of Greece's continuing neutrality. The pressure of the allies on both Serbia and Greece to make still more concessions to Bulgaria also had an adverse effect on Venizelos' policy of delicate compromise, and encouraged the Bulgars to be intransigeant. In September 1915 a general mobilization was proclaimed in Bulgaria. Venizelos at once called on the king to proclaim a general mobilization in Greece, which at first he refused to do. Under the threat of Venizelos' resignation, he finally signed the decree, but encouraged his General Staff to treat it as a purely defensive measure involving no commitment to Serbia. Venizelos retaliated by renewing his invitation to Britain and France to send troops to Salonika in support of Serbia. This time the invitation was accepted.

The point was now past at which the dispute between Constantine and Venizelos could be treated as a legitimate difference of judgment. Even if Constantine's judgment were right, he was straining at the constitution and seeking to impose extremely doubtful interpretations on it. Unfortunately, as Commander-in-Chief of the armed forces, surrounded by able staff officers who were convinced that the central powers were invincible, he was still in a strong position to undermine his prime minister's policies. That he did so for more than two years was inexcusable. Even after the Greek mobilization and the Bulgarian declaration of war on 4th October, the king refused to allow Greek troops to move. On the same day Venizelos won a vote in the Chamber in support of his policy of fulfilling the letter of the treaty with Serbia. On the following day the king dismissed him, just as the Anglo-French forces were beginning to land at Salonika. His successor, Alexander Zaïmis, lasted barely a month, during which he was responsible for the fateful decision to ignore an offer from the British government to cede Cyprus to Greece in return for supporting Serbia.

There followed one of the unhappiest years in modern Greek history. Relations between Greece and her nominal allies— Britain, France, Russia and Serbia—were exceedingly bad; between Constantine and Venizelos they were totally severed. The allies could not, and Greece would not, help to prevent Austria and Bulgaria overunning Serbia, the remnants of whose army escaped across the mountains to take refuge in Corfu.

Confidence was further shaken by the emergence of accurate reports about the treaty of London (April 1915), which assigned the Dodecanese definitively to Italy, promised Italy an 'equitable share' in the eventual division of Anatolia, and arranged a partition of Albania more favourable to Italy than to Greece. In anticipation, the Italians were allowed to take over the occupation of northern Epirus from the Greeks as soon as they entered the war in May 1915. To emphasize their displeasure, the allies demanded the demobilization of the Greek army (which was not carried out), instituted a partial blockade of Greece, and declared military law at Salonika. The last measure was justified by a genuine fear that the Austro-German and Bulgarian forces would attack Salonika once they had disposed of Serbia. But this they never attempted.

The month of December 1915 was the most melancholy period of the war. The British government finally recognized the failure of the attack on the Dardanelles, and withdrew the troops engaged. The withdrawal still further shook Greek confidence, even though it enabled the allies to strengthen their hold on Salonika. Constantine judged the time ripe to dissolve parliament, although there was no question that Venizelos held a clear majority. The pro-German faction at court believed that the failure of the allies, who had shown themselves both interfering and ineffective, would contribute to the emergence of an anti-Venizelist majority. They also believed that the army, which was still mobilized, would help to achieve the same result. Venizelos had no doubt that the electors would be subject to pressure and threats. He advised his followers to abstain from the election, in which as a result the poll was barely a quarter of the poll by which his party had been elected to power only six months earlier. The new prime minister, a wealthy nonentity called Skouloudis, remained in office although he lost his seat. Constantine had treated with undisguised contempt the constitutional principle of the parliamentary mandate, which Trikoupis had obliged his father to accept in 1875.

The king's government now felt justified in pursuing an active collaboration with the central powers. Secret staff talks took place, and orders were given to senior commanders in Macedonia not to oppose a Bulgarian advance if it should take place. An official protest was lodged against the help provided by the allies to the remnants of the Serbian army, first in landing them on Corfu and then in transferring them to Salonika. To emphasize the hostile action of the allies in admitting the Italians to northern Epirus, Constantine proclaimed the annexation of the area in April 1916, though naturally he was unable to make it effective. By far the gravest of the acts committed by the Skouloudis government to the detriment of the allies was the surrender to the Bulgarians in May of the frontier fort of Rupel on the River Struma, which risked the exposure of the whole of eastern Macedonia to attack. The Greek people has ever since felt the same sense of shame at this act of treachery as they think the British people ought to feel over the surrender of Parga to Ali Pasha in 1819.

In other theatres the allies won some successes in the first half of 1916. These came too late to deter Constantine from his fatal course, but the Russian offensive in particular stirred Rumania into joining the allies in August. It was hoped that the Balkan deadlock would be in some way broken as a result, but after some early victories the Rumanians were disastrously defeated. A limited offensive by the allies with the help of Serb troops captured Monastir, thus giving the Serbs a small foothold again on their native soil; but the Bulgars gained even more by over-running eastern Macedonia. By the end of the year Bucharest was also in enemy occupation and Rumania was finished as a combatant power. Constantine may well have congratulated himself once more that he had chosen the right side. The western allies, however, had already been stirred to firmer action. In June they presented an ultimatum demanding the total demobilization of the Greek army, the dismissal of Skouloudis' government, and the dissolution of parliament. Reluctantly, the king gave way, though his General Staff effectively evaded the decree of demobilization and the elections were repeatedly postponed. Venizelos declared that it was no longer possible for his party to co-operate in the government of the country.

In the last week of September 1916 Venizelos left Athens for his native Crete, accompanied by Admiral Koundouriotis, Commander-in-Chief of the navy. At Khania he proclaimed a revolutionary movement, calling on the Greek people to return to their alliance with Serbia, to enter the war against the central powers and Bulgaria, and 'to save what may still be saved'. After an enthusiastic reception in Crete, he proceeded to Salonika, where he landed on 5th October 1916, to establish a 'provisional government'. Large numbers of supporters joined him there, including officers, politicians and officials. But he was unable yet to obtain the recognition of the allies. The Russian and Italian governments, both of whom now had troops on the Salonika front, were implacably hostile to Venizelos. The Russians objected to the anti-monarchical character of his movement, especially as Constantine's mother was a Romanov. The Italians looked on Venizelos as a potential rival to their claims in Asia Minor. The British and French, although they supported the cost of Venizelos' armed forces, still feared that recognition would precipitate a civil war and thus draw off allied troops from their main task.

The Anglo-French authorities nevertheless found the new situation useful for putting pressure on the king and his government. They demanded control over the railway to the north, the surrender of certain warships, the disarmament of the land-batteries at Salamis and Piraeus, and the departure of the enemy legations. The king, attempting to regain the allies' good graces, himself suggested the surrender of a quantity of guns and other equipment and the withdrawal of his troops to the Peloponnese. The allies agreed to accept a smaller quantity of arms, but as soon as they had done so, the pro-German faction in Athens launched such a campaign of propaganda against the allies that Constantine felt impelled to withdraw his offer, and issued a protest against the actions already taken by the allies. The French Admiral in command at Piraeus, believing that a show of force would bring the king to reason, landed a small Anglo-French force to march on Athens. On 1st December 1916, they came under fire as they approached the capital, and substantial casualties were inflicted on both sides.

This disastrous incident was the last straw. While the allied troops withdrew and a reign of terror against Venizelos' supporters broke out in Athens, the allies retaliated by conferring official recognition on Venizelos' provisional government, to which French and British diplomatic representatives were accredited at Salonika. They declared a blockade of Greece and demanded reparation from Constantine's government. Not being satisfied with the response, they presented fresh and very severe demands to Constantine at the end of December, including the reduction of the Greek army to the bare minimum necessary to maintain order. But they were careful not to sever relations with him altogether: they continued in fact to recognize both rival governments of Greece, partly because the British and French governments were still unable to carry the Russian and Italian governments with them. By the end of January 1917 the government in Athens had sufficiently complied with the allies' conditions to justify a return to normality. But it was a most unsatisfactory relationship, and the pro-German faction continued to intrigue with the central powers.

Meanwhile Venizelos' movement was growing in strength. Most of the diplomatic and consular representatives of Greece abroad declared in his favour. So did all the more important islands. Officers and men continued to flock to his forces, up to a total of some 60,000. Even the hostility of the Russians and Italians began to wane. In Russia, everything was changed by the revolution which overthrew the Tsar in March 1917. The Italian government's attitude was greatly modified as a result of the treaty of St. Jean de Maurienne in April, which gave Italy considerable freedom of action on the Adriatic seaboard and the prospect of a sphere of influence in Anatolia after the destruction of the Ottoman Empire. Both countries were therefore less antagonistically disposed towards Venizelos. In May his supporters held a vast demonstration in Salonika demanding that the allies repudiate and depose Constantine. In Athens it was recognized as probable that they would soon do so.

Alexander Zaïmis was recalled to form a more conciliatory government, and he did his utmost to oblige the allies. But their tolerance was exhausted. On 10th June the French diplomatic representative informed Zaïmis that the allies required the abdication of Constantine on the ground that he had violated his oath to rule as a constitutional monarch. The ground was incontestable; so was the allies' right to act upon it, since they were still by treaty the protecting powers. Constantine contrived one last evasion. He replied that he had decided to leave the country with the Crown Prince George (who declined to take his place, and would in any case have been unacceptable to the allies), leaving his second son Prince Alexander to succeed him. In other words, he never explicitly abdicated. This subterfuge was to prove unexpectedly important three years later. Meanwhile in the general relief at Constantine's departure, it passed unnoticed. Alexander gave promise of being a more docile and popular successor.

Venizelos returned to Athens on 27th June 1917 with his government, Zaïmis having already resigned. War was declared on the central powers on 2nd July. Venizelos insisted on recalling the parliament of June 1915, since he regarded its successor as invalid. From it he obtained a unanimous vote of confidence after a speech lasting nearly nine hours. His triumph was complete, but his difficulties were only just beginning. Greece was in poor condition to make a substantial contribution to the war. The army was full of officers who were at best defeatist, at worst pro-German. Many were sent into exile, including Metaxas. The Italians took advantage of Greece's weakness and confusion to enlarge their foothold in the north-west. They declared the independence of Albania, which they intended to make an Italian protectorate, and they occupied Ioannina. It was not until the middle of 1918 that the Greek army was ready for action again. There could be no question of resisting the pressure of jealous allies in the meantime.

By the spring of 1918, a quarter of a million Greeks were mobilized. They were in action for the first time at the end of May. When the final assault of the allies took place in September, the Greeks were able to make an honourable contribution to it. In conjunction with British, French and Italian troops they cleared Macedonia of the enemy and advanced into Serbia and Bulgaria. At the end of September, after only a fortnight's fighting, the campaign for which the allies had waited three years in and around Salonika was over. The Bulgars asked for an armistice on 30th September, thus cutting off Turkey from her allies in Europe. A month later the Turks in their turn capitulated, and by 11th November the war was over on all fronts. Greek troops took part in the allied entry into Constantinople, and Greek warships anchored in the Bosporus. It was a triumph of which Venizelos had every right to be proud. But it would also have been well for him to remember what his ancestors had to say about pride that overreaches itself.

The peace conference added to his personal laurels. His intellectual brilliance, his wit and tact, his statesmanlike manner, and not least his unquestioned and heroic loyalty to the allied cause, all combined to captivate the other participants, particularly Lloyd George. Unfortunately Venizelos placed too great a reliance on the influence of Lloyd George, who did not command a united country any more than did President Wilson. Venizelos allowed himself to be seduced into sending Greek troops to take part in the expedition against the Communists in Russia, where they suffered heavily. Both men also failed to detect the Turkish revival, which was sparked off by the impact of defeat. In contrast with his prudence after the Balkan Wars, Venizelos put forward claims which were bound to be considered potentially just as dangerous as had been the Great Bulgaria briefly created by the treaty of San Stefano in 1878. His claims included northern Epirus, Thrace, Smyrna with its surrounding district, and the Dodecanese. He also sought to keep the future of Constantinople open by making it an international city.

All of Greece's claims presented difficulties with at least one of the allies, who were deeply divided among themselves about the disposal of the former Ottoman Empire. In the case of both northern Epirus and Thrace the opposition to Greece's claims came from President Wilson, since the former would involve the partition of the new state of Albania (created only in 1913), and the latter would again cut off Bulgaria (with which the USA had never been at war) from the sea. The Greek claims to Smyrna and the Dodecanese naturally evoked the opposition of the Italians, who had occupied the latter since 1911 and had been virtually promised the former in 1916. Nevertheless, with the strong support of Lloyd George, Venizelos was authorized to occupy Smyrna in May 1919 and northern Epirus in December. Already, however, a far more formidable antagonist than Italy or even President Wilson was coming into view. In the middle of 1919 Mustapha Kemal, who had helped to create the Committee of Union and Progress in 1908 and fought valiantly at the Dardanelles in 1915, was beginning to lead a national reaction against Turkey's humiliation.

While Kemal was mustering his forces in central Anatolia, and a nonentity on the throne of Constantinople was purporting to dismiss him from his military command, the allies pursued their leisurely and quarrelsome course of peace-making. It was not too difficult to frame treaties to be imposed on Germany,

Austria and Bulgaria, all of which were completed within 1919. But the intractable problems of the Near East delayed a settlement until August 1920, when the Treaty of Sèvres was at last signed. It fulfilled almost all the fondest hopes of Greek nationalism. Greece was to receive the whole of Thrace, including Adrianople; the Gallipoli peninsula and the northern coast of the Sea of Marmora, subject to an International Commission for the Straits; all the Aegean islands, including Imbros and Tenedos, but excluding the Dodecanese (which were subject to a separate convention with Italy); and Smyrna with its hinterland, for an initial period of five years, after which a local assembly might opt for either Greek or Turkish sovereignty.

It may well have seemed to the Greeks too good to be true; and so it proved. The Treaty of Sèvres was never ratified. The convention with Italy, by which the Dodecanese was eventually to be transferred to Greece, lapsed with it. The allies decided to retain the Sultan in nominal control at Constantinople. At all these points Venizelos' dream began to dissolve, chiefly because of the growing power of Mustapha Kemal. With the unwise encouragement of Lloyd George, he decided in October 1920 to restore the situation by ordering the Greek troops at Smyrna to advance against Kemal's still ill-organized national army. It was a disastrous blunder. Nemesis was already at hand. On 25th October the still youthful King Alexander died of a monkey-bite, thus re-opening the question of the monarchy. Venizelos tried to persuade his youngest brother, Prince Paul, to accept the crown he refused. Three weeks later Venizelos was severely defeated at a general election. In December, despite allied warnings, the Greeks voted in a plebiscite to restore King Constantine by an overwhelming majority.

Since Constantine was later to be blamed for the coming fiasco in Anatolia, it is well to record that the first steps towards disaster were taken by Venizelos before he fell. It was on his orders that the Greek army began to advance to the interior. Conceivably it was the prospect of endless warfare, which had now kept the Greeks mobilized for the best part of ten years, that helped to bring about Venizelos' defeat. Otherwise it is difficult to explain, though it is clear that, like other national leaders of other countries, he had lost touch with the feelings of his own people while playing a greater role on the international stage. If this were so, the wisest thing Constantine could have done on his restoration would have been to liquidate the military expedition against Mustapha Kemal. Instead, he allowed his military advisers (no longer, unfortunately, including Metaxas) to proceed with it. The new Chamber, full of royalist adherents, occupied itself with such relative trivialities as increasing the king's Civil List, voting compensation to the alleged victims of the Venizelist regime, and substituting demotic Greek for the neo-classical *katharévousa* language in the schools.

The army in Anatolia, inadequately equipped and led by inexperienced officers newly appointed for their monarchist loyalties, marched on to its destruction. In January 1921 its advance was momentarily checked, but soon resumed. At the beginning of April, very nearly one hundred years to the day from the outbreak of the War of Independence, it suffered a serious defeat. Still the advance went on. In June Constantine personally installed himself at G.H.Q. in Smyrna with his prime minister, Gounaris, in readiness for a triumphal entry into Ankara, which was Mustapha Kemal's new capital and the objective of the campaign. The last Greek offensive began on 15th June, and reached the River Sakaria. It was the last obstacle between the Greeks and Ankara, and the line on which Kemal had chosen to fight. In August, he counter-attacked and won a brilliant victory. Throughout August and September the Greeks retreated, still in good order and capable of holding a reduced line within 150 miles of Ankara. But it was clear that the possibility of outright victory was lost for good.

There seemed no alternative but an appeal to the powers for mediation. It was a discouraging prospect. Meeting in London earlier in the year 1921, the British, French and Italian governments had already decided to revise the unratified Treaty of Sèvres in favour of Turkey, whose revival under Mustapha Kemal was a fact that could not be ignored. The French had virtually changed sides by October, when they signed an agreement with Kemal settling their differences and undertaking to supply him with arms and ammunition. The Italians reverted to their customary anti-Greek position at the same time: their foreign policy had already been summed up by one of their own prime ministers as '*sacro egoismo*' well before the emergence of Mussolini. When Constantine, turning to the only remaining ally, placed the fate of Greece unconditionally in the hands of the powers through the good offices of the British government (December 1921), Curzon replied that nothing could be done until a new conference could be convened, and meanwhile the Greeks must hold on.

The Greeks held on through the winter of 1921–22. So did Gounaris, in spite of a defeat in the Chamber in March 1922. In the same month a conference of the powers in Paris proposed an armistice, which Greece accepted but Kemal made conditional on the prior evacuation of Asia Minor. As a final and fatal disservice to the Greeks, the powers rejected Kemal's condition. He thereupon prepared to enforce it willy-nilly. While Constantine desperately shuffled prime ministers and commanders-in-chief, the Turks mounted an overwhelming offensive against Smyrna. It began at the end of August 1922 and ended in complete victory within ten days. Smyrna was sacked and looted; every Greek inhabitant who could escape took to the sea; the Greek government ordered the demobilization of the army and resigned; Constantine abdicated and retired to Sicily, where he died four months later. Thus the Crown Prince at last came to the throne, as George II, in circumstances of indescribable chaos. The Turkish triumph also destroyed Lloyd George, whose coalition broke up over the confrontation with Mustapha Kemal at Chanak in October; and finally it destroyed the remains of the Sultanate, which Kemal abolished as the last Sultan fled from Constantinople in November.

Greece's fortunes were now at their lowest ebb. Her position in Asia Minor was irretrievably lost. Kemal also successfully insisted, in the confrontation at Chanak, that eastern Thrace and Adrianople should be handed over to Turkey by the Greeks and that the straits and Constantinople, still occupied by the British, should be restored to Turkish sovereignty. In November 1922 a peace conference was convened at Lausanne, which was bound to recognize the strength of the Turkish position. Meanwhile the Greeks were left to put their house in order, which they started to do in the most unseemly way. A group of officers under Colonel Nicholas Plastiras had taken refuge from Smyrna on the island of Chios, where they formed a Revolutionary Committee and prepared to seize power in Athens. Venizelos refused their invitation to return, and Zaïmis also refused to form a government until the Committee was dissolved. Accordingly the revolutionary officers formed their own cabinet under Plastiras.

No force existed which could dispute their control in the capital. They therefore took on themselves responsibility for one of the most lamentable and uncharacteristic acts of modern Greek history. Five senior ex-ministers and the former commander-in-chief were put on trial for their lives before a military court of eleven officers. Despite protests from the allies, all were shot at the end of November 1922. Constantine's brother, Prince Andrew, the father of the Duke of Edinburgh, narrowly escaped the same fate. Venizelos, who had already announced his retirement from public life, made only a feeble effort to intervene. His ambiguous position was made all the more false by the fact that two members of the court martial (it is customary to say 'only two', as if that made it better) were known Venizelists. But he had offered to represent Greece at Lausanne, and he knew that the executions would damage his standing there. His failure to protest more vigorously was therefore ill-judged as well as feeble. The giant among modern Greeks was beginning to show human frailty.

He was, nevertheless, at his ingenious best at Lausanne. The Treaty of Lausanne, under the guidance of Curzon, was eventually completed in July 1923. It was not, as it turned out, an unmitigated disaster for Greece, though it must have seemed so at the time. While the conference was in progress, the revolutionary government slightly improved Greece's bargaining position by sending a force to Thrace under General Theodore Pangalos, thus threatening Turkey on the European side and ensuring at least that there would be no question of restoring Bulgaria's access to the sea. Elsewhere Greece lost most of her prospective gains under the Treaty of Sèvres and its predecessors: Smyrna and its hinterland returned to Turkey, as did Tenedos and Imbros; northern Epirus was restored to Albania; Italy retained the Dodecanese, and Turkey renounced her claims to Cyprus in favour of Britain. An international convention was signed to control the Straits, but Turkish sovereignty over Constantinople was no longer at issue. To avert future claims of an irredentist character based on population, a vast exchange of populations was compulsorily carried out between

The First National Crisis (1908–1923)

Turkey and Greece, as had already occurred on a smaller scale between Greece and Bulgaria.

With the exception of the acquisition of the Dodecanese by Greece in 1947 and the independence of Cyprus in 1960, the territorial settlement of 1923 has remained intact to the present day. Considering the disastrous character of the campaign against Turkey in 1920–22, the most remarkable fact about it is that Greece lost so little territory and actually emerged with an addition (western Thrace) to the gains made in the Balkan Wars. The most bitter disappointment was probably the failure of the Greek claim to the Dodecanese, and by implication to Cyprus too, rather than the loss of Smyrna, which would have been a useless acquisition and a perpetual source of friction with Turkey. The most important consequence of the treaty of Lausanne, painful at the time but salutary in the long run, was probably the enforced exchange of populations. Greece had to absorb about a million refugees, among whom discontent was naturally slow to disappear. But the increased homogeneity of the Greek population was an undoubted benefit. It was not complete, however, since the exchange of population did not apply to the Turks of western Thrace nor to the Greeks of Constantinople; and of course—more ominous still in the long run—it did not apply to Cyprus either.

The influx of the refugees was important also in other respects, both advantageous and disadvantageous. They contained a complete cross-section of the population of Smyrna and the surrounding country, whose general level of culture and material prosperity under Turkish rule had been distinctly higher than that of mainland Greece. They brought with them agricultural and industrial skills which were of great value to their compatriots, particularly in developing the production of tobacco. They also brought more sophisticated novelties. Greece's first winner of a Nobel prize for literature, George Sepheriadis, was born in Anatolia. So were a number of the leading figures in the Greek Communist Party (KKE). The suburb of Athens known as New Smyrna (*Néa Smýrni*), where thousands of refugees lived for many years in poverty-stricken discontent, became notorious as a breeding-ground of Communism. The exchange of populations thus generated new experiences for Greece even while it disposed of old problems.

The First National Crisis (1908–1923)

It would be idle to pretend that the dream of the Great Idea (*Megáli Idéa*) was finally laid to rest at Lausanne. To most Greeks some fragments of the old dream remained vivid, and one or two of them to almost all. Constantinople became increasingly remote after the momentary flash of hope in 1917. Macedonia and northern Epirus were less remote, but still very improbable acquisitions except in the circumstances of another war, which was to prove delusive yet once more. The Dodecanese and Cyprus, and even Imbros and Tenedos, were less unrealistic aspirations, though only that for the Dodecanese was to be fulfilled. Cyprus also was to be had for the exercise of a little diplomatic skill, but the opportunity was thrown away at least twice in Greek history by a combination of cupidity and stupidity. But the year 1923 was clearly not a year of opportunity for any kind of assertion of Greek nationalism. The Greek people was exhausted, confused, defeated and demoralized. There were to be no more foreign adventures.

The day of foreign adventures had ended for other countries as well. For the Ottoman Empire, indeed, it had ended a century and a half earlier at Kütchük Kainardji (1774). But Mustapha Kemal went much further. He converted his country into a secular, national state, as nearly as possible confined to ethnic Turks (though Kurds and Armenians presented an insuperable difficulty) and shorn of foreign accretions and imperial ambitions. It is only since Kemal's day that Turkey has properly been the name of a sovereign state. This made it easier for his government to settle down to peaceful co-existence with Greece. He even cultivated friendly relations with Soviet Russia, and acquiesced in the cession of Mosul (a valuable source of oil) to the British-mandated territory of Iraq. So dedicated was he to the idea of a Turkish national state within self-contained frontiers that he encouraged the Turkish minority in Cyprus to emigrate to the mainland. But in this case there was no compulsory exchange, and a later generation of Turks was to reverse and deplore the policy.

Britain too lost interest in foreign adventures after the Chanak crisis in 1922 had broken up the Lloyd George coalition. The prime ministers who followed Lloyd George were more interested in domestic and imperial affairs. When they looked to Europe at all, Greece fell within their blind spot. The Near

East was insensibly superseded by the Middle East, which meant the Arab states and the problem of carrying out the Balfour Declaration on Palestine, made in November 1917. Only a naval mission and occasional visits of the Mediterranean fleet to play cricket on Corfu or to show the flag at Piraeus helped to maintain the traditional connexion. But unfortunately the same indifference did not apply to other powers. Hitler was still a decade from power, but the Comintern had seen to the creation of a Communist Party in Greece (KKE), in the early 1920's. An even more immediate menace was Mussolini, who had seized power in Italy in October 1922. His first act of aggression was in fact committed against Greece almost as soon as the Treaty of Lausanne was signed.

Towards the end of August 1923, while an international commission was settling the frontier between Greece and Albania, the chief Italian delegate was murdered with four members of his staff on Greek soil. Before the Greek government could take action, Mussolini presented an impossibly unacceptable ultimatum. It was followed within a few days by a naval bombardment of Corfu, and an occupation of Corfu and other islands by Italian troops. The Greek government appealed to the League of Nations, which was thus confronted with its first serious crisis. The protests expressed in Geneva against Italy's action compelled Mussolini to withdraw his forces of occupation at the end of September. A conference of Ambassadors in Paris then awarded an indemnity to Italy on account of Greek negligence, which was duly paid. The incident ended in mutual congratulation among the powers. But Mussolini had learned a lesson about frontier incidents, which was to be applied again in 1940; and Greece had learned what it meant to be small and friendless in the post-war world. As the first great crisis of the 20th century came to a close, the second was already casting a shadow before it.

CHAPTER VIII

The Republic and Dictatorship
(1924–1940)

The crisis in Greek history which ended in 1923 had been a traumatic shock. Reaction was natural, and almost as naturally it was irrational. A scapegoat was wanted and found; a total break with the past was also wanted, but harder to achieve. The fumbling, agonized quest for both involved the Greeks deeply in unconscious contradictions. King Constantine was an obvious scapegoat: he was antipathetic to Greece's traditional allies, Britain and France, and he was nominally in command of the defeated armies. But it was not he who had launched Greece upon the fatal adventure in Anatolia. Venizelos had done so, yet his reputation was hardly tarnished and his voluntary exile could be ended whenever he chose. Even more perversely, because of his quarrel with Constantine, Venizelos was associated in the minds of the Greeks with the republican movement among the officers of the army and navy, which seized power after the disaster in Asia Minor. Yet Venizelos was never a republican by conviction, and his quarrel with Constantine, though constitutional in substance, was purely personal and did not involve the monarchy as such.

Legends are often more powerful than realities. For a generation after 1923, the debate over Greece's constitution was conducted in terms of personalities and their following, regardless of the underlying facts. There was, or was thought to be, a pro-monarchist movement, which came to be identified with the so-called Populist Party (*Laikón Kómma*); and an anti-monarchist movement, identified with the Liberal Party (*Phileléftheron Kómma*), whose father-figure was Venizelos even when he was not its titular leader. The two trends of opinion thus seemed to be personified in two men, who were indeed irreconcilable antagonists: the ex-King Constantine and Eleftherios Venizelos. Their schism was even transmitted to the following generation, for at least one of the sons of each man inherited his father's stance. It was not until the greater menace of Communism began to overshadow Greece that the comparative insignificance of the constitutional dispute became apparent and the protagonists became superficially reconciled. But in the intervening generation great harm was done to Greece by the unresolved and unforgotten quarrel over the constitutional question.

The question came to a head for the first time at the end of 1923. It was unavoidable that it should do so: there could be no stable equilibrium between the revolutionary government of republican colonels under Plastiras and the precarious throne now occupied by the young King George II. The revolutionaries were not by nature extremists. They wanted to return to constitutional government if they could find a way of doing so; but both Venizelos and Zaïmis refused to help them. In the meantime, once the shock of the executions had worked itself out, the limited measures which they initiated were moderate and progressive. They decreed an amnesty for political offences in January 1923. It was also under this irregular and self-consciously temporary regime that Greece first adopted the Gregorian calendar (March 1923) and signed the concession of a free zone for Yugoslavia at Salonika (May 1923). But the path back to legality was hard to find, and it was made harder by the activities of the irreconcilable monarchists, led by General Metaxas.

While negotiations were in progress towards the end of 1923 for a coalition government including both Venizelists and moderate monarchists, Metaxas organized an attempt to seize power. It failed, but it did great damage to the young king's position, although there was no evidence to connect him with the plot. At the general election in December 1923, the Populist Party, which favoured a constitutional monarchy, abstained from taking part. The supporters of Venizelos won nearly two-thirds of the seats, but the Republicans, who won the remainder, were strongly backed by the high command of both the army, under General Pangalos, and the navy, under Captain

Khadjikyriakos. The revolutionary government thought it wise to ask King George to leave the country for three months while the constitutional question was settled. He agreed to go, but without abdicating. Admiral Koundouriotis was appointed Regent, Venizelos was recalled as the victor of the elections, and the revolutionary committee dissolved itself in January 1924.

Venizelos held office for less than a month. He proposed that a plebiscite on the constitution should be held in two months' time, but his republican opponents insisted that a Republic should be declared at once and retrospectively ratified by a plebiscite. After a violent controversy in parliament, Venizelos resigned in February 1924 and was followed within the year by a succession of republican Prime Ministers—Kaphandaris, Papanastasiou, Sophoulis, Mikhalakopoulos—some of them nominally adherents of his own party, but none of them capable of holding together a stable majority. They were at least able, however, to carry out their determination to establish a Republic, which was proclaimed on 25th March 1924 under the presidency of Admiral Koundouriotis. It was confirmed by a subsequent plebiscite in which over two-thirds of the votes were cast for the Republic; but the minority in favour of the monarchy was at least sufficiently large to show that there was no question of tampering with the votes. It also showed that there was still so strong a monarchist sentiment that the Republic could not be regarded as firmly based.

The Republic was nevertheless recognized by Britain and the other powers without delay. It lasted less than twelve years, and its history was chequered and uneasy. A confusing succession of coups and counter-coups was interspersed with periods of more constitutional government, usually associated with the re-emergence of Venizelos. But the truly democratic forces were throughout fighting a losing battle with revolutionary extremists, among whom the best-known names were generally the holders of high rank in the army or navy: Generals Plastiras, Pangalos, Kondylis, Gonatas, Metaxas; Admiral Khadjikyriakos; Colonels Zervas, Saraphis, Bakirdzis, and Psaros (all later to be prominent in the resistance to German occupation). So pervasive and infectious was the spirit of anti-constitutional rebellion in the armed forces, both for and against the Republic, that in the last years of his life even Venizelos allowed himself to be seduced into lending his name to a military revolt (1935). In the background there loomed throughout the still more ominous threat of the Greek Communist Party (KKE).

Inherently unstable though the republican constitution was, it was preserved for a time by the force of external events, which distracted the Greeks from their internal troubles and imposed a semblance of national unity. With all her territorial neighbours, Greece's problems and disputes arose inevitably from the impossibility of demarcating natural frontiers. Neither the conformation of the Balkan peninsula nor the distribution of populations would permit any simple demarcation. The mountain ranges and their intervening valleys ran at right angles to the direction of the frontiers. Mutually incompatible nationalities lay on both sides of any conceivable lines. Valleys that ran across the frontiers down to ports on the Aegean Sea often provided the natural outlet for the trade of a landlocked hinterland across national frontiers, as in the case of Salonika and Kavalla. The survival of Turkey in Europe aggravated the problem. The same fundamental anomaly which had produced the crisis with Italy over Albania in 1923 also underlay the renewed friction with Turkey, Bulgaria and Yugoslavia a year later.

In the case of Turkey, the friction was caused by the aftermath of the exchange of populations imposed by the Treaty of Lausanne. The exchange should have resulted in a purely ethnic frontier between the two countries, and it almost did so. But an exemption had been granted to the Greeks 'established' in Constantinople before the end of October 1918. The meaning of the phrase was disputed. After much wrangling, the matter was settled by a Mixed Commission of the League of Nations in a sense favourable to the Greeks, and diplomatic relations were finally resumed between Greece and Turkey in June 1925. But just because such large numbers of Greeks were allowed to remain in Turkey, a running sore was perpetuated in Greco-Turkish relations, which was to burst out again a generation later. The same was true of the position of the Patriarch of Constantinople, who was required to be a Turkish national. A series of contentious appointments culminated in an attempt by the Turks to evict a new Patriarch in December 1924 on the ground that he was not 'established' before 1918. Despite the intervention of the League of Nations, he felt obliged to abdicate. His successor survived by a policy of conciliatory inactivity; but the latent source of friction remained.

With the Yugoslavs, though the underlying anomaly was the same, the immediate source of friction was geography rather than population. The Yugoslav government, inheriting the commitments of Serbia as one of its component states, denounced the treaty of alliance with Greece in November 1924 on the ground of the Greeks' failure to honour it in 1915. Although the revolutionary government under Plastiras had conceded a free zone to Yugoslavia at Salonika, the Yugoslavs were dissatisfied with the terms, particularly because their only access to the port was over the Greek railway-line. Further concessions were offered by the republican government, but the Yugoslavs would accept nothing less than an enlargement of the free zone and its complete cession to Yugoslavia. More significantly in the long run, they demanded that Greece should recognize the Slav population of Greek Macedonia as being not Bulgars but Serbs. Clearly the Macedonian question was not closed. Although the negotiations broke down in 1925, they were brought to a temporarily satisfactory conclusion a few years later; but Macedonia has never ceased to bedevil Balkan relations.

In the case of Bulgaria, the sources of friction were even more obvious and predictable. The exchange of populations under the Treaty of Lausanne proceeded uneasily, and was complicated by external factors. A straightforward movement of Bulgars out of Greece and of Greeks out of Bulgaria might have been manageable, even though the Greeks were more willing to move than the Bulgars. But at the same time there were Greeks moving into Macedonia from Turkey; and there was strong pressure from Yugoslavia to resist the assumption that all the Slavs in Greek Macedonia were Bulgars. Greece's relations with Yugoslavia were severely strained by this pressure. So were her relations with Bulgaria by a number of ugly incidents on the frontier, the most serious of which culminated in an actual invasion of Bulgarian territory by a Greek army corps (October 1925). On the intervention of the League of Nations, the Greeks were obliged to withdraw and to pay an indemnity, which they greatly resented. Once again the symptoms of friction were temporarily stifled without removing their underlying causes.

The Republic and Dictatorship (1924–1940)

The violence of the Greek action against Bulgaria in 1925 was attributable to an equally violent change of course which had taken place in the Republic a few months earlier. On 16th June the military and naval leaders, General Pangalos and Admiral Khadjikyriakos, lost patience with the government under Mikhalakopoulos and overthrew it in a bloodless *coup d'état*. Pangalos formed a new government, dissolved parliament, and proclaimed a new constitution which he proposed to submit for ratification to a new parliament, to be elected in January 1926. Once the Bulgarian crisis was over, however, he changed his mind. He announced that the elections would be indefinitely postponed, and that all power was to be vested in himself. Having seized absolute power, with none to challenge him, he had no further ideas for constructive action. He imposed censorship on the press, devalued the currency by cutting all banknotes in half, decreed a minimum length for women's skirts, and exiled most of his opponents. When he announced that a new constitution would be promulgated in April 1926, under which he proposed to stand for election to the presidency, the much respected President, Admiral Koundouriotis, could stand no more and resigned.

Pangalos was not at heart anti-democratic, but he preferred action—any action—to argument, and he was irritated by opposition. When his opponents of all parties combined to put up a compromise candidate, Constantine Demertzis, against him for the presidency, he resorted to a series of manoeuvres to force his rival's withdrawal. In this he was finally successful. As the only candidate he was then duly elected President in April 1926, but had difficulty in finding anyone to serve as Prime Minister under him. It did not greatly matter, for four months later Pangalos' former military colleagues turned against him. With the help of a para-military formation known as the Republican Guard, under Colonel Napoleon Zervas, originally created by Pangalos himself, he was overthrown in another bloodless coup by General Kondylis (August 1926). Kondylis then forcibly disbanded the Republican Guard, whose leaders were sentenced to life imprisonment, and invited Admiral Koundouriotis to resume the presidency. The first period of dictatorship thus came to a more or less peaceful end.

It is not surprising that it was wholly abortive. Pangalos left everything undone, even if some of his intentions were good. He rightly saw, for instance, that Greece must come to terms with her neighbours on a more permanent basis. It was under his presidency that negotiations were re-opened with Italy for the first time since the seizure of Corfu, and a commercial treaty was eventually signed in November 1926; but the Italians' condition, that the British Naval Mission in Greece should be dismissed, was fortunately evaded. It was also under Pangalos' presidency that a new treaty of friendship was negotiated with Yugoslavia, though his downfall a few days after it was signed had the result that it was never ratified. No permanent achievement remained to mark his year of power, nor was there any trace left of support for him when a general election was held in November. The result of the election was to give the republican parties a small majority, but the monarchists were strong enough to secure participation in a coalition government. The most notable feature of the new parliament was the election for the first time of ten Communist deputies.

General Kondylis duly retired from public life, as General Plastiras had done before him, though neither of them for the last time. The new Prime Minister was the respected and uncontentious Alexander Zaïmis, but his colleagues included strong partisans of both sides, all of them past or future Prime Ministers: the republicans Kaphandaris, Mikhalakopoulos, and Papanastasiou; and the monarchists Panagiotis Tsaldaris and Metaxas. It was not to be expected that so incompatible a team would last long, but the coalition nevertheless survived several reconstructions. Zaïmis in fact remained Prime Minister from November 1926 to July 1928, though the monarchist Tsaldaris resigned in August 1927 and the republican Papanastasiou in February 1928. In neither resignation was the constitution an issue, nor was the Republic to be seriously questioned for several years. But there were many intractable problems left behind by the chaotic autocracy of Pangalos, on which differences of opinion were not dictated by party lines. The issue in Tsaldaris' resignation was the gold reserve of the National Bank; and in Papanastasiou's case it was the acceptance of a tender for road construction.

Weakened as it was by these resignations, the coalition could not be expected to survive the even greater shock of the return to politics of Eleftherios Venizelos. After living abroad for four years, during which he married a wealthy wife from the Greek colony in England, he came back by way of Crete to Athens in March 1928. Once he had resumed the leadership of the Liberal Party, it was clear that he alone could form a stable government. Zaïmis reconstructed his government once more in May, but finally resigned at the beginning of July. Venizelos immediately took office and dissolved parliament. He obtained a decree from the President for the general election replacing the system of proportional representation by the majority vote, which resulted in an overwhelming victory for his party. From August 1928 he enjoyed his longest period of office—four and a half years, with brief interruptions. His parliamentary majority survived two more elections (September 1932 and February 1933), though it was reduced each time, and eventually his opponents succeeded in forming a coalition against him. During this last period of Venizelist rule, he showed his accustomed mastery of foreign diplomacy, but was unable to overcome his country's domestic problems.

Among Venizelos' early problems were several affecting the constitution. A new republican constitution had been passed into law in June 1927, to put right the chaos created by Pangalos' dictatorship. Although pro-monarchist feeling was already growing against the Republic, and although Venizelos himself was at heart a constitutional monarchist, he was determined to respect the constitution. One problem which immediately presented itself was to re-create the Senate, or upper house of parliament, for which the 1927 constitution provided. A bill for this purpose was passed with some difficulty in 1928, and the first elections to the new Senate were held in April 1929. The outcome was naturally a Venizelist majority, which was to outlast his majority in the lower house and thus cause bitter complications after 1933. Another delicate question was the election of a successor to Admiral Koundouriotis as President when his five-year term expired in 1929. Fortunately an equally popular figurehead was available in Alexander Zaïmis, who was elected by a huge majority. Constitutional stability was thus temporarily assured. It was almost the last success for Venizelos on the domestic scene.

Abroad, his outstanding achievement was a linked series of

The Republic and Dictatorship (1924–1940)

pacts with Greece's neighbours, including Italy and Turkey as well as the Balkan countries. The credit does not belong exclusively to Venizelos, since the series began with Rumania (March 1928) before he returned to office, and the momentum of reconciliation in south-east Europe continued after his final resignation. But all the most difficult and delicate steps were taken under his premiership. With Rumania there were no territorial claims outstanding; with Italy, Albania, and Yugoslavia, all of whom Venizelos approached before the end of 1928, the position was very different. In announcing the pact with Italy (September 1928), Venizelos declared that the question of the Dodecanese was closed. The settlement with Albania (November 1928) involved recognizing a virtual Italian protectorate and resigning Greek claims to northern Epirus. The negotiations with Yugoslavia, from October 1928 to March 1929, involved concessions at Salonika and on the railway connecting the port with the hinterland. No Greek leader other than Venizelos could have persuaded the Greeks to concede all these delicate points.

With Turkey and Bulgaria the problems to be settled were more intractable. In both cases they arose from the aftermath of the war, and in particular from the exchange of populations and related territorial claims. With Turkey there was the further anxiety caused by the naval preponderance gained by the Turks through the acquisition of the German battle-cruiser *Goeben*, in 1914. Nevertheless, Venizelos succeeded in negotiating a convention settling current disputes with Turkey in June 1930. It was followed by a personal visit to Constantinople and Ankara which was perhaps Venizelos' most spectacular triumph. Within the same year the preliminary convention was succeeded by a far-ranging treaty, with additional provisions governing trade and naval armaments. To the Turkish President, Mustapha Kemal, now known as Atatürk, Venizelos said: 'We have agreed on the future of the Near East.' However optimistic those words may have been, it is beyond doubt that no two men could have done more to reconcile their peoples. That they were contemporaries was a fortunate conjunction for Greece and Turkey.

The *annus mirabilis* of 1930 also witnessed the beginning of the next stage in Balkan reconciliation. On the invitation of the republican leader, Papanastasiou, and with Venizelos' approval, an unofficial Balkan Conference was convened in Athens. It was attended by delegates from Greece, Turkey, Yugoslavia, Rumania, Albania, and even Bulgaria, although the Bulgars were still dissatisfied by the territorial settlement imposed at the end of the first World War. There followed a second, third and fourth such conference in the next three years; but the fifth in 1934 had to be cancelled because of uneasy relations between Bulgaria and her neighbours. The unsettled questions concerned war debts, minorities, and even the terms of the peace treaties, whose revision was demanded by the Bulgars and rejected by both the Greeks and the Yugoslavs. As the other Balkan countries moved towards the Balkan Pact of 1934, Bulgaria became increasingly isolated as the one dissatisfied power. But before events reached this point, Venizelos' long supremacy had come to an end.

One last problem in international diplomacy arose to tax his special powers before his final resignation, when the nationalist movement in Cyprus came to a head in open violence (October 1931). The Greeks of Cyprus had never ceased to aspire for union with Greece (*énosis*), and public opinion in Greece naturally supported them: this was the last practicable remnant of the *Megáli Idéa*. Successive Greek governments found it difficult to oppose the movement. British governments also from time to time made gestures which unwittingly encouraged it. In 1907 Winston Churchill, as Under Secretary of State for the Colonies, made a speech in Cyprus in which he said he thought it[1] 'only natural that the Cypriot people, who are of Greek descent, should regard their incorporation with what may be called their mother-country as an ideal to be earnestly, devoutly, and fervently cherished'. In 1915 the British government had actually offered Cyprus to Greece as a condition of entering the war. But these gestures had been nullified by the formal annexation of the island from Turkey and its establishment as a Crown Colony in 1925.

The agitation for *énosis* nevertheless continued. In 1929 a Cypriot delegation went to London with a petition to this effect, and was rebuffed. In 1931 the crisis was precipitated by a vote in the Legislative Council on the budget, in which the Greek majority was defeated by the combined votes of the Turkish

[1] These words are misquoted with misleading effect, in Sir George Hill's *History of Cyprus*, Vol. IV, p. 515.

minority and the British official members. The Greek nationalists declared a boycott of British goods and called on the Greeks to refuse to pay taxes. One of the leading bishops (not on this occasion the Archbishop) issued inflammatory proclamations. A demonstration on 21st October in Nicosia, the capital, turned into an attack on Government House, which was burned to the ground. The rising spread throughout the island, but was quickly put down by British forces. The Legislative Council was abolished, the ringleaders were deported, and an uneasy peace was restored. Cyprus remained superficially quiet for more than a decade, but the seeds of future trouble were unmistakeably sown.

It is noteworthy how little part in these events was played by Turkish nationalism. Turkish Cypriots, who numbered about one-fifth of the population, were content under British rule. The Turkish government in Ankara did nothing to inflame them. This disinterest was a matter of policy for Atatürk. He wished to confine Turkey to its national homeland in Anatolia, without peripheral commitments. When he signed the Treaty of Lausanne, he thereby renounced to Britain all rights over Cyprus, so that his government would have had no standing in law to object, or even to insist on consultation, if the British government decided to cede Cyprus to Greece or to dispose of the island in any other way. (Only the French government had such a right, by virtue of an Anglo-French agreement in 1916, made in view of the close proximity of Cyprus to the future French mandate of Syria.) Moreover, in the 1920's the Turkish government had actually encouraged Turkish Cypriots to emigrate to the mainland, in pursuance of Atatürk's policy of national homogeneity.

Only one tenuous relic of the Ottoman regime remained in Cyprus. This was the annual tribute of slightly less than £100,000 a year, which had been paid to the Sultan up to 1878. The British government had continued to collect the tribute on behalf of the Sultan, but the proceeds were applied to service the Ottoman debt and not paid to the treasury at Constantinople. The tribute was gradually reduced by means of grants to the island from the British Treasury, and finally abolished altogether in 1928, largely thanks to the good offices of the same Governor (Sir Ronald Storrs) whose house was burned down by the Greek nationalists in 1931. The upshot of the melancholy story was that the island was neglected by the British government and ignored by the Turks. The Greek Cypriots thus had free rein to foster their nationalist aspirations. They did so largely through their schools and their Church, whose Archbishop was popularly elected and known (like the Patriarch of Constantinople before him) as the *Ethnárkhis* or 'leader of the nation'. The troubles of 1931 were only the harbinger of more serious events a generation later.

Naturally there was strong sympathy in mainland Greece for their unredeemed brethren. But Venizelos adopted a firm and discouraging attitude. He declared that there was no Cypriot question between the Greek and British governments, only between the latter government and its Cypriot subjects. Agitation was useless; nothing could alter the determination of the powers (including, by implication, the Italians in the Dodecanese); and it was essential that Anglo-Greek friendship should not be impaired. He nevertheless hoped personally that the idea of *énosis* need not be abandoned for ever. His attitude was in fact the same as he had adopted in the case of his native Crete up to 1912. Once again it was an attitude which could have been maintained only by a man with Venizelos' exceptional command over Greek public opinion. It was, however, his last successful act of international statesmanship, for the internal problems of his country were already on the brink of overwhelming him.

Venizelos was unequipped by training or past experience to handle the domestic problems of Greece in the decade after the Treaty of Lausanne. He was a romantic nationalist, not a political economist. Greece's development during this period was dominated by the consequences, which he never fully grasped, of two great upheavals: the influx of over a million refugees, and the incorporation of relatively huge new territories into northern Greece. Advantage as well as disturbance came out of these events. A re-distribution of land was necessitated by the addition of the new territories, where the old Turkish *chifliks* still survived on a large scale; and nearly 40 per cent of the agricultural land of Greece was re-distributed in these years, to the great benefit of the peasants. The refugees also brought with them new skills which helped to promote the growth of industry, with the help of high tariffs. Tobacco production, particularly in the new territories of Macedonia and Thrace, became Greece's major export industry, outstripping the currant production of the Peloponnese. But in these healthy developments Venizelos played relatively little part.

The economic disadvantages of the new situation, on the other hand, found him quite unable to hold his own. Even after the re-distribution of the *chifliks* Greece's peasants remained very poor. Those who lived in the mountains and took seasonal employment in the plains and cities found that the influx of refugees cut off their main source of income. Rural over-population and low productivity interacted upon each other in a vicious spiral. Under-employment in the countryside was not compensated by the slow growth of urban industry. The regressive system of taxation, which drew more than three-quarters of the state's revenue from indirect taxes, hit the peasants more hardly than industrial workers in the towns. Even so, industry could not cover the deficit on foreign trade. Greece has always had to import nearly half her grain supplies; and in the years between the wars her agricultural exports, which were largely in the category of luxuries, were hampered by protectionism in western Europe. Her industrial production, on the other hand, was chiefly confined to consumer goods for the home market. The country's minerals, which were potentially of high value, were exploited by foreign capitalists, since Greece could not generate the necessary capital from her own resources.

The obligations of rich nations towards the under-developed were not yet recognized between the wars. Like the other Balkan countries, Greece was left to fend for herself in most unfavourable circumstances. Part of the deficit on balance of payments was met by remittances from Greek emigrants to the USA, who had been seeking their fortunes there in large numbers since the turn of the century. In the decade before the first World War, some 300,000 Greeks went to America, and in 1921 their remittances reached a peak of over 120 million dollars. But in the same year the American government imposed its quota-system, which admitted no more than 100 Greek immigrants a year. Similar restrictions were imposed in the British colonies. The European powers were equally short-sighted and unfeeling as the great depression moved across the world after 1929. The doctrines of Keynes were scarcely yet formulated, let alone understood; and the under-developed countries, like Greece, were the principal victims of international policies which sought salvation from depression in the most savagely depressive measures that could be devised.

The depression came at a time when Greece had once again just sought revival in foreign loans. A series of loans were raised in Washington and London in the years 1928–30, principally for essential public works such as water-supply, land drainage and road construction. The service of these debts, which amounted in some years to one-third of Greece's budget, began to fall due in the years when the depression was beginning to make its maximum impact. Little sympathy was shown towards Greece's predicament by the creditor governments, which were themselves in a desperate situation. The British government abandoned the gold standard in 1931 without considering the consequences for countries like Greece, whose currency was linked with sterling and supported by reserves of which a quarter was held in London. Similarly, the moratorium on war debts and reparations, adopted by President Hoover, severely affected Greece, since she was a net creditor to the extent of half a million pounds a year. It is a curious irony that the only country whose government showed a sympathetic understanding of Greece's economic problems between the wars was Germany.

In this sea of troubles, Venizelos floundered and lost his grip. Early in 1932, he toured the European capitals to seek loans, with little success. The financial committee of the League of Nations offered help only on terms which Venizelos found unacceptable. He offered to resign in favour of a coalition government, but the leader of the Populist Party, Panagiotis Tsaldaris, refused to join him. After a further plea to the League of Nations, Venizelos found himself forced to a partial default on payments to foreign bondholders, with disastrous results to Greece's long-term credit. At the same time there was bitter controversy in parliament over two of Venizelos' domestic measures: one to re-introduce proportional representation, and the other to restrict the freedom of the press. Both were symptoms of Venizelos' awareness of the weakness of his own position. Although he eventually gained his bill for proportional representation, the opposition to his restriction of the press was so intense that in May 1932 he felt compelled to resign. It was the beginning of a new period of instability such as had once been normal in Greek politics.

Venizelos was succeeded briefly by the Republican leader Papanastasiou and the Monarchist leader Tsaldaris in succession, but neither could command a majority. Within three weeks Venizelos was back in office, if only precariously. A military league of officers, pledged to preserve the Republic, intervened to demand an undertaking from all political parties that they would not raise the constitutional question for ten years. It was suspected that this move was instigated by Venizelos. If so, it was another sign of his waning powers, for the intervention was not only improper but was indignantly repudiated. He thereupon dissolved parliament (August 1932). In the general election the Populists won seats but Venizelos' Liberals remained the strongest single party by a narrow margin. A coalition was formed under the Populist leader, Tsaldaris, who still had only a minority of supporters against the Venizelists and their republican allies. Despite the tolerance of this anomaly by Venizelos, the coalition fell on issues of financial policy in January 1933, and Venizelos resumed office.

His tenure was brief, and it was his last premiership. The balance of power in parliament was so even that stable government was impossible. Venizelos therefore obtained a dissolution from the President, and another general election was held in March 1933. The result was a Populist majority in the Chamber, though the Liberals retained a majority in the Senate and could thus block legislation. The extreme republicans concluded that the Republic was now in danger of liquidation. Led by General Plastiras, they attempted a military *coup d'état* on election day as soon as the results indicated a Populist victory. But the rising collapsed for want of public support, and Plastiras was forced to flee the country. Venizelos made no attempt to encourage it: indeed, at the President's request, he participated in a triumvirate appointed to restore order and then to hand over power to Tsaldaris. This did not prevent him from later publicly defending Plastiras in parliament, and thus exacerbating the growing controversy over the constitutional question.

It was clear that the days of the Republic were in fact numbered. Tsaldaris brought back into office a number of extreme

Monarchists, including Metaxas and Kondylis, the latter of whom had been converted from republicanism though without abandoning his dictatorial tendencies. These men strongly resented the fact that a Venizelist majority in the Senate restrained the government's freedom of action. They wished to suspend the constitution on the ground that the opposition's tactics made government impossible. The opposition justified their tactics on the ground that the Populists were themselves undermining the Republic. During these uneasy years there was an attempt to assassinate Venizelos (June 1933) by men whom the police were less than assiduous in seeking to arrest; and there were many scenes of violence in the Chamber. The battle came to a climax in 1934 over the related issues of the electoral system (proportional representation or majority vote) and the election of a President of the Republic when Zaïmis' five-year term expired. Upon the resolution of these issues depended the fate of the Republic.

The Liberals, being electorally weak, wished to retain the system of proportional representation. The Populists, as the stronger party, wished to revert to the majority vote, as strong parties usually do. At the same time the re-election of Zaïmis as President, which the government desired, could only be achieved with the support of the Liberals, since they still controlled the Senate. Venizelos offered a bargain to Tsaldaris, that he would support Zaïmis' candidature if the government would yield on the issue of the electoral system. Tsaldaris attempted a compromise, but he and Venizelos could not reach agreement. The government therefore introduced its own electoral bill, which the Chamber passed and the Senate rejected. At the last minute, however, a group of Liberal Senators offered to support Zaïmis' candidature if the bill was dropped. Tsaldaris accepted, and Zaïmis was duly re-elected (October 1934) by a joint session of both houses. Venizelos retired to Crete, protesting indignantly that the men who had attempted to assassinate him more than a year earlier had still not been brought to trial.

The tide was now set in favour of a restoration of the monarchy. Apart from the steady trend in that direction, only one significant event marked the two and a half years of Tsaldaris' administration. This was the signature in February 1934 of the Balkan Pact, comprising Greece, Turkey, Yugoslavia and Rumania, but not Bulgaria and Albania. Bulgaria refused to accede on the grounds that to do so would imply renunciation of her claims to revision of the post-war treaties. Albania was in dispute with Greece over the status of the Greeks under Albanian rule in northern Epirus; but a more decisive reason for Albania's exclusion was the growing subjection of the country to Italian influence. For the rest, the pact was one of mutual defence against aggression, though a number of qualifications limited its efficacy. With the growth of Italian and German aggressiveness in the following years, it needed to be supplemented by a number of bilateral arrangements. The pact itself aroused no great enthusiasm in Greece, where a deep sense of insecurity pervaded both domestic and external relations.

It was this sense of insecurity which led to the restoration of the monarchy in 1935. The Republic had manifestly failed to make good, even under the guidance of Venizelos. There was a feeling, too, that the dangerous situation in central Europe, which was leading to both German and Italian pressure on Greece, required the restoration of a kind of government which· would be not only stable but also acceptable to Greece's traditional and pre-eminent ally, Great Britain. Although the British government had insisted on deposing King Constantine, Britain had provided asylum to his son and successor, George II. It was assumed, rightly or wrongly, that Britain would welcome his restoration. By the beginning of 1935 it was evident that all these factors combined to favour the monarchist cause. A last attempt was made to frustrate the trend by a military rising, again inspired by General Plastiras, in March 1935. Venizelos, still in Crete, was persuaded momentarily to put himself at the head of the movement, but it collapsed ignominiously. He never returned to Greece; nor did Plastiras for another twelve years.

The leading role in suppressing the last republican *coup* was played by General Kondylis, as Minister of War. He now became the dominant figure in Greece, and virtually the king-maker. Severe sentences were passed on the rebels, though only one general was executed. Venizelos and Plastiras were comdemned to death *in absentia*; General Gonatas and other senior officers were sentenced to long terms of imprisonment; and many officers of middle rank who were later to play a prominent part in the resistance to German occupation (including Colonels

Bakirdzis, Saraphis and Psaros) were cashiered. Kondylis also took advantage of the rout of the rebels to ensure the abolition of the Republic. Acting on behalf of the government as Deputy Prime Minister, he secured the abolition of the Senate and the dissolution of parliament. He further announced that after the general election, to be held in June, if the results indicated that public opinion so wished, the government would submit the constitution to the test of a plebiscite.

The outcome of the elections showed an undeniable swing towards the monarchists, which was not disguised by the refusal of the Liberals and Republicans to take part. But Tsaldaris' followers greatly outnumbered the more extreme monarchists who supported Kondylis and Metaxas; and Tsaldaris was a cautious man who was by no means in a hurry to abolish the Republic. The new Chamber duly voted in favour of a plebiscite, but Tsaldaris at first resisted Kondylis' pressure to declare the government in favour of the monarchy. First Kondylis and then Tsaldaris resigned; and finally Kondylis had his own way when he was able, as Prime Minister himself, to obtain a vote in the Chamber (October 1935) proclaiming Greece to be a constitutional monarchy, subject to ratification by a plebiscite in the following month. Kondylis then proclaimed himself Regent, and President Zaïmis retired into private life. The plebiscite on 3rd November 1935 produced a vote of 97 per cent in favour of the restoration of King George II; but it was generally believed to have been manipulated by intervention of the army.

Whatever the facts about the plebiscite, there could be no doubt that the tide of opinion was emphatically against the Republic. At the same time it was doubtful whether it would long favour the constitutional aspect of the restored monarchy. As soon as King George returned to Athens in the last week of of November 1935, friction began between him and his dictatorial Prime Minister, at first over the question of a political amnesty. The king wished it to be total and unconditional. Refusing to agree, Kondylis and his government resigned. The king appointed Constantine Demertzis as Prime Minister, proclaimed the amnesty, and dissolved parliament. Venizelos, who was included in the amnesty, endorsed the king's wisdom from his exile abroad and urged his fellow-countrymen to accept the restoration. It was his last public act before his death in March

1936, and it showed that his natural good sense and magnanimity had returned to him. But his hope that the constitutional feud might at last be put to rest was to be frustrated.

After the wise inauguration of his resumed reign, King George II soon found himself plunged again into an atmosphere of crisis. The general election held in January 1936 was inconclusive. The Liberals, now led by Themistoklis Sophoulis, won the largest number of seats, but when the allies of the two principal parties were ranged on their respective sides, the result was very near deadlock. The balance of power between the Liberal alliance and the Populist alliance was in fact held by 15 Communists, a situation clearly pregnant with danger for what remained of Greek democracy. It seemed probably only a matter of time before one or another of Greece's stronger leaders would again seize dictatorial power to combat the danger. By a strange coincidence, however, a number of leading figures died in rapid succession within a few months: Venizelos, Kondylis, Tsaldaris, Demertzis. So did the two father-figures of the Republic, Koundouriotis and Zaïmis. By a process of elimination, General Metaxas found himself promoted from Deputy Prime Minister to the premiership in April 1936, although he had only six followers in parliament.

The king now faced a very grave crisis without the benefit of any elder statesman to advise him. Both at home and abroad the prospects for Greece were menacing. Abroad, the dictatorships of Hitler and Mussolini threatened the peace of Europe, and Greece was a target of both. Germany's threat at this stage was primarily economic. By an astute commercial policy, Germany dominated the trade of south-east Europe, evidently with the object of establishing a source of food and raw materials which would be safe from blockade in the event of war. In the case of Greece, the policy took the form of buying most of the tobacco crop at high prices, so that Greece was compelled to draw most of her imports from Germany. The growth of German trade was, as it happens, largely at the expense of Italy. But Italy was seeking compensation elsewhere, chiefly in Africa. The Abyssinian war (1935–37) sharpened the antagonism between Mussolini and Greece. The Greek government not only supported the League of Nations in sanctions against Italy, but assured Britain that Greece would go to war if Italy retaliated by military action. Albania also continued to be a bone of contention between Italy and Greece.

The deterioration in international relations from the mid-1930's was serious enough, but less serious in the eyes of politicians in Athens than the internal situation. Metaxas had never had much sympathy with parliamentary government, still less when parliament was virtually at the mercy of fifteen Communists. The king could hardly dissolve parliament for a third general election within twelve months, nor was there any reason to expect a substantially different outcome. He gradually became more and more dependent on Metaxas, who had the undeniable merit of having faithfully supported the monarchist cause through bad times and good for over twenty years. Metaxas was further helped by the unwise tactics of the official opposition, led by Sophoulis. To avert the possibility of a *coup d'état*, Sophoulis proposed the adjournment of parliament for five months, allowing Metaxas to govern by decree, subject to a parliamentary committee of forty members (April 1936). The proposal was accepted; but it was unworkable in practice, since the committee naturally reproduced the proportions of parliament itself. The Chamber did not meet again for ten years.

Metaxas immediately took advantage of his new powers to arrest labour leaders, dissolve the most militant Trade Unions, and declare strikes illegal. The Communists reacted by organizing a series of strikes, including a preliminary general strike in Salonika on 9th May, which resulted in bloodshed and some thirty deaths. A nation-wide general strike was proclaimed for 5th August. Two days earlier, Sophoulis approached the king with the new leader of the Populists, John Theotokis, offering to form a coalition government, which would have commanded a huge majority in parliament. But the king was now too deeply imbued with the alarmist propaganda of his Prime Minister. He rejected Sophoulis' offer, and signed decrees on the following day declaring a state of emergency, suspending the provisions of the constitution for personal liberties, and dissolving parliament without fixing a date for new elections. (The last of these acts was certainly unconstitutional.) Metaxas was now master of Greece with unlimited powers, which he used at once to forestall the general strike by military force. The dictatorship of the

Fourth of August had begun; the restoration of constitutional monarchy had lasted barely eight months.

Metaxas remained in power until his death in January 1941. During those four and a half years he did much that was tyrannical, still more that was absurd, and little that lasted beyond his death. But none of these criticisms should be exaggerated. His tyranny was not to be compared with that of Hitler or even Mussolini. Although there was no freedom of political action under the regime of the Fourth of August, there were also no political executions. Left-wing politicians and Trade Union leaders were exiled or imprisoned, but not tortured. The Communist Party of Greece (KKE) was disrupted more by the ingenuity of Metaxas' secret police under Constantine Maniadakis than by systematic brutality; and the political opposition was neutralized chiefly by its own divisions and ineptitude. Freedom of speech was suppressed by means that were often ridiculous, such as the decree censoring Pericles' funeral oration in Thucydides. A youth organization (EON) was created on the Nazi model. But public opinion had little difficulty in treating all these manifestations of dictatorship with the mockery of which the Greeks are masters.

The main object of Metaxas' dictatorship was to create a modern and efficient state. For this reason he was more unpopular in the towns than among the peasants, whose way of life was remoter from the twentieth century and who had scarcely begun to feel the impact of the new regime before it ended. The one criticism of Metaxas constantly reiterated in the countryside was that he had tried to restrict the number of goats, because they hindered his schemes of re-afforestation by nibbling the young shoots. In the towns there were much deeper feelings, provoked principally by the suppression of free Trade Unions. The labour and social legislation which he imposed was by no means inhumane or ineffective; but its defect was that it was not freely negotiated or democratically debated. Metaxas' case was that the Greeks had shown themselves incapable of effective administration under a democratic constitution. The case against him was that free institutions could not be abolished for ever, and as soon as they were restored his edifice was bound to collapse. Collapse it did, though under other pressures before free institutions could be restored.

The Republic and Dictatorship (1924–1940)

Metaxas deserves credit for having foreseen the coming catastrophe and for doing all that was humanly possible to prepare
his country for it. A new European war can be seen in retrospect
to have been inevitable from 1936 onwards. Metaxas saw its
inevitability at the time, which is more than can be said for
many ministers in western Europe. His enemies have always had
difficulty in reconciling their criticisms of him as a fascist and a
Germanophile with the fact that his country was, within its
limits, better prepared for the shock of enemy attack when it
came than any other in Europe. The explanation of the paradox
lies partly in the fact that the primary enemy of Greece was not
Hitler but Mussolini, for whom neither Metaxas nor any other
Greek had any sympathy or admiration. It lies partly also in
the nature of Metaxas' personal orientation, which was neither
pro-German nor pro-allied but pro-Greek. The one solid benefit of his years of rule was thus to establish the military, material
and psychological foundations on which Greece could face the
calamity of 1940.

At home the preparations were twofold. The modernization
of the armed forces was hastened and plans for mobilization
were brought to a high state of readiness. In this work Metaxas
was ably seconded by the Chief of the General Staff of the army,
General Alexander Papagos, who was later to be a successful
Commander-in-Chief and Prime Minister. In support of the
military preparations, the extensive programme of public works
was concentrated especially on strategic requirements: new
roads in the frontier areas, new rolling-stock on the railways,
improved fortifications. Unfortunately the Greek government
was too often compelled, by the German domination of the
country's foreign trade, to purchase German equipment for both
military and civil purposes. Metaxas tried to reduce his dependence on Germany by offering to buy equipment from Britain
in return for specified purchases of Greek tobacco or currants,
but results were slow in coming. He was also glad to retain the
British Naval Mission; and against his reputation for sympathy
with Germany should be set the fact that no German mission
of any kind ever set foot in Greece under his government.

Abroad, Metaxas had to take account of certain existing facts
in developing safeguards for Greece's security. There was the
militant strength of Germany and Italy, but there was also the

British Mediterranean Fleet to set against them. There was the general timidity of the democratic powers in confronting the dictators, which communicated itself to the Balkans in an atmosphere of isolationism and *sauve qui peut*. Metaxas was no more inclined than his neighbours to place unqualified reliance on the Balkan Pact of 1934. The outcome was that Greece, like the other Balkan countries, began to make cautiously pragmatic arrangements of a kind designed to secure her freedom of action. A small power could not be bound by the doctrine of collective security when the great powers were progressively abandoning it. The pattern of international negotiations both within and outside the Balkans from 1936 onwards shows the impact of fear and desperation rather than any consistency of policy. It is to the credit of the Greeks, however, that they alone of the peoples of south-east Europe presented an effective opposition to aggression when it came. Metaxas cannot be denied his share of the credit.

The first major move after the Balkan Pact of 1934 was the modification of the Treaty of Lausanne by the Montreux Convention in July 1936. By its terms Turkey recovered full control over the Dardanelles, and Greece incidentally regained the right to fortify the islands of Lemnos and Samothrace. There now remained virtually no obstacles to Greco-Turkish friendship, since the issue of Cyprus was not yet back on the horizon. With the gradual loss of confidence in the Balkan Pact, however, all its members were looking for new safeguards. This became obvious at the Balkan Conference at Belgrade in May 1936. Yugoslavia made separate treaties with both Bulgaria and Italy in 1937; and a Greco-Turkish treaty of friendship and neutrality was signed in 1938. In the same year an attempt was made to enlarge and reinforce the Balkan Pact by accommodating Bulgaria, but this was achieved only at a high price. By the Pact of Salonika (July 1938), the four members of the Balkan Pact admitted Bulgaria to membership and released her from the restrictions on armaments imposed by the Treaty of Neuilly (1919) in return for no more than a promise not to seek frontier revision by force.

All these manoeuvres were motivated by fear, and the fear was justified; for before the end of 1938 the Munich Agreement had shown that the only alternatives to frontier revision by force were war or surrender. In April 1939, while Hitler completed the destruction of Czechoslovakia, Mussolini extended the evil doctrine to the Balkans by occupying Albania on Easter Monday. Greece now had a fascist power on her borders for the first time: an alarming situation which Metaxas handled with his habitual coolness. He accepted a guarantee offered by Britain and France of Greece's territorial integrity, which was also extended to Rumania. The Italian government tried to lay the Greeks' natural fears to rest by denying that they had any aggressive intentions against Greece, by withdrawing troops from the frontier area of Albania in September, and by reaffirming the pact of friendship signed with Greece in 1928. Metaxas accepted these gestures for what they were worth and continued his quiet preparations. His most fruitful diplomatic contacts were now with Turkey, France and Britain.

With Britain he negotiated a financial agreement which went some way towards offsetting the German grip on Greece's economy, though there continued to be resentment in London at Greece's default on past loans. Much more important were the Anglo-Turkish and Franco-Turkish agreements on mutual aid against aggression in May–June 1939, which were merged in a tripartite treaty later in the year. In the meantime, however, war had broken out in Europe (September 1939). Both Greece and Turkey declared their neutrality, and so did Italy. For the time being no threat to the Mediterranean area arose; but few Greeks doubted that it would come. They were deeply confused and disturbed in particular by the Nazi-Soviet pact which immediately preceded the outbreak of war. It seemed to threaten south-east Europe with the equally dread alternatives of domination by the fascists or the communists. Greek sympathies were in consequence even more strongly attached than before to the western democracies, but they had the gravest doubts whether Britain or France could do anything to protect them.

After the fall of France and the declaration of war by Italy in the summer of 1940, no doubt could remain that the involvement of Greece in the war was only a matter of time. Metaxas began to call up certain reservists as early as May 1940, and spoke in public of the national danger in the following month. A barrage of Italian protests that Greece was permitting Britain to infringe her neutrality led Metaxas to re-affirm it early in August. But Italian aircraft began to harass Greek ships at sea, and on 15th August an 'unidentified' submarine, which was always known to be Italian, torpedoed and sank the Greek cruiser *Elli* in the harbour of Tinos during a religious festival. At about the same time Mussolini began to accuse the Greeks of official responsibility for the murder of an Albanian patriot called Daut Hodja, who was in fact a brigand killed in a frontier brawl. Mussolini was building up a case to justify an attack on Greece, largely inspired by childish annoyance at the way in which Hitler launched aggression after aggression without telling him in advance.

Mussolini assumed that he would have a walk-over through Greece. But his military preparations were conducted with an incompetence which showed that he was a fool as well as a scoundrel. The Greeks on the other hand pursued their calm mobilization with efficiency and a heroic confidence in their still unwritten alliance with Britain. Although Metaxas continued negotiations for a commercial treaty with Germany and urged Hitler to restrain his Italian colleague, he sensed after the meeting between Hitler and Mussolini at the Brenner Pass in October 1940 that all hope of peace was gone. The crisis came at the end of the same month. On 26th October, Mussolini fabricated a frontier incident; on the 27th a reception was held at the Italian Legation in Athens, which Metaxas attended; early in the morning of the 28th the Italian Minister presented an ultimatum to Metaxas, which was instantly rejected, while Italian troops were already crossing the Albanian border. No Italian today would deny that this was the most shameful moment in the history of an honourable nation.

For the Greeks it was, in Churchill's phrase, their 'finest hour'. Legend has refined Metaxas' brave retort to the single word: 'No!' History cannot forget that in 1940 Greece was the only country to enter the war voluntarily on the allied side when Britain stood alone. It was the first moment for many years which found the Greek people and their government wholly united. Nor was the prospect as forlorn as it might seem. Material help from Britain was relatively slight, but the existence of the Mediterranean Fleet was a strong support. The efficiency of Metaxas' mobilization, matched by the incompetence of Mussolini's planning, enabled the Greeks to take the offensive within a few days. Not only did they drive the Italians back into Albania: they occupied the major towns of what they called northern Epirus—Koritsa and Argyrocastro, both predominantly Greek in population—before the end of the year. At the same time British offensives in Africa were driving the Italians out of Libya, Eritrea and Abyssinia. The New Year of 1941 was a season of almost unbridled optimism. But on both sides of the Mediterranean it was too good to last.

The Italian forces recovered courageously from the criminal follies of Mussolini and his contemptible entourage. After the first shock of defeat, they succeeded in holding a line in the wintry mountains of Albania, and prevented the Greeks from capturing Valona, the principal port in the south, which would have enabled the Greek forces to be supplied by sea. The Albanian war was thus reduced to deadlock, from which neither side could break out. In this impasse, Hitler decided that he must intervene: not indeed to rescue Mussolini from the consequences of his idiocy, but to secure his own southern flank in the Balkans in readiness for the projected invasion of Russia. The British government had also foreseen Hitler's intervention in the Balkans, and urged Metaxas to allow a British Expeditionary force to land in Greece. Metaxas resisted the proposal because the force offered seemed to him too small to hold a front, and therefore likely only to be provocative. But at the end of January 1941 the drama took a new turn. Metaxas died after a short illness, leaving the fate of his country in weaker hands. Greece's second great crisis of the 20th century was upon her.

CHAPTER IX

The Second National Crisis
(1941–1952)

In a state of war it was hard to appreciate the fact that the death of Metaxas had ended the dictatorship and all its works, but without restoring constitutional government. The position of the king was anomalous and would have been embarrassing in time of peace. If Greece had not been at war, it would have been impossible for him simply to appoint a new Prime Minister in Metaxas' place without reference to popular will. There would have been vociferous demands for a return to parliamentary procedures. But as things were, the king was able to nominate a mild and blameless banker without political experience, Alexander Koryzis, and no questions were asked. The general acquiescence was not merely due to the fact that most of the Communist leaders were in gaol and most of the republican opposition in exile. It was also because the Greek people were psychologically united as never before by the Albanian war; and the king himself, for all his faults, was the only possible symbol of that unity, so that all power fell naturally into his hands. Unfortunately he was in no position to use it effectively, and had forfeited the right to do so.

The British government soon renewed to Koryzis the proposals for an expeditionary force which Metaxas had rejected. There were good grounds for proposing such an intervention provided that an adequate force could be found. German troops were already moving, or about to move, into three of the neighbouring Balkan countries—Hungary, Rumania and Bulgaria—to safeguard their southern flank in anticipation of the attack on Russia. Only Yugoslavia held out for the time being against Hitler's threats and promises. If British forces could help the Greeks to hold a front and stiffen Yugoslav resistance against Hitler, than not only would the guarantee of April 1939 be honourably fulfilled, but also the German attack on Russia might be delayed or even forestalled. It may be doubted how far sympathy for the USSR entered into the British calculations, but there is no doubt that the necessity of a Balkan campaign, forced on Hitler by the concatenation of events, decisively affected the Russian campaign by disrupting its time-table. But these retrospective arguments could not have been foreseen by Koryzis in February 1941, when the British proposals were renewed.

Koryzis reaffirmed his predecessor's requirements to the British government, and asked if they could be met. Essentially what was required was a force of ground-troops, with naval and air support, sufficient to ensure that a front could be held against the Germans in northern Greece, preferably north of Salonika, in the hope that Yugoslavia would also stand firm. A high-ranking British mission, including Anthony Eden (the Foreign Secretary) and Generals Dill and Wavell (respectively Chief of the Imperial General Staff and Commander-in-Chief of the Middle East Command) visited Athens in February 1941 to concert plans. Since Wavell's army in the North African desert had virtually cleared the Italians out of Egypt and Libya a few weeks before, it seemed possible to release a sufficient force for Greece, including an army corps of Australian and New Zealand troops. The king and Koryzis allowed themselves to be persuaded that the proposed force was adequate. It began to move into Greece from Egypt in March, watched by officials of the German legation in Athens, which was still neutral in the war between Greece and Italy. At the same time German armoured divisions were moving through Rumania into Bulgaria.

Whether or not it might have been practicable to hold a front in the southern Balkans with the relatively inferior forces available, the prospect was soon obliterated by a succession of setbacks. First, there was a disastrous misunderstanding about the allied intentions between the Greek and British Commanders-in-Chief. Wavell and Eden believed that Papagos had agreed to withdraw his forward divisions from western Thrace and eastern Macedonia in order to hold a line on the River Aliakmon, south-west of Salonika, where the British Expeditionary Force would join them to form a front. The right flank of the Greek front in Albania would also be withdrawn to connect with the new line. A good deal of Greek territory (including Salonika) as well as conquered territory in Albania would be sacrificed. Papagos, however, believed it had been agreed that he should not make these withdrawals until the British government had first ascertained the Yugoslavs' intentions, since if they would fight it might be possible to save Salonika and even drive the Italians out of Albania. He waited in vain for a response throughout the latter part of February and early March.

How the misunderstanding occurred has never been explained. Because of it there was a fatal delay. When the British forces began to arrive, the Greeks had not yet begun their planned withdrawal. No word had been received of Yugoslav intentions because none had been sought. Meanwhile Hitler was exercising brutal pressure on the Yugoslav government and the Regent, Prince Paul, who was acting for his young nephew, King Peter. They eventually agreed in March to join the Italo-German Axis, but a popular revolution, initiated by the army, overthrew them a few days later. The boy-king's majority was declared to have arrived, and a new government took power under pro-British officers. Although they did not immediately denounce the German alliance, it was plain that they had no intention of allowing German troops to pass through Yugoslavia without resistance. They appealed for help from Britain and agreed to hold staff talks with the Greeks. Unfortunately it was already too late to frustrate Hitler's revenge.

On 5th April 1941, the German attack on Yugoslavia and Greece began. Belgrade was savagely bombed, and Yugoslav resistance collapsed within a few days. The Greeks were better prepared to resist, and had the benefit of support by a small but well-equipped British, Australian and New Zealand force. The determination of Greece to fight to the last had never been in doubt. It was eloquently expressed by a leading newspaper editor, Vlakhos of the *Kathimerini*, in an open letter to Hitler during March, which has long been remembered as one of the great declarations of national independence. But the will and the spirit were not enough in confrontation with overwhelming force. The misunderstanding between the Greek and British high commands resulted in an ill-organized formation of the new front on the Aliakmon line, and the loss of good Greek divisions in the north-east of the country. The defenders of the Rupel fort, on the Bulgarian frontier, amply avenged the dishonour of its surrender in 1915 by dying at their posts. But the German armoured divisions flowing through the Vardar gap from Yugoslavia outflanked the Greek defences and quickly captured Salonika. The fall of Greece was clearly only a matter of weeks at the outside.

As the expeditionary force fought a series of rearguard actions from the Aliakmon line back to the Bralo range and eventually to the isthmus of Corinth, signs of demoralization set in. On 18th April Koryzis committed suicide and the King replaced him (after briefly acting as Prime Minister himself) with another banker, Emmanuel Tsouderos. The fact that Tsouderos was a Cretan, and that he appointed another Cretan as his Minister for War, was significant. It was becoming clear that Crete was the only considerable part of Greece that might still be held, and preparations were made to withdraw the court and government to the island. Simultaneously, but independently and without authority, one of the army corps commanders on the Albanian front, General Tsolakoglou, signed an armistice with the Germans in Salonika. Papagos at once repudiated his action, but proposed to the British commander, General Maitland Wilson, that the British Expeditionary Force should be withdrawn from Greece. The evacuation took place, notably without inter-allied recriminations, during the last week of April and the first of May. On 30th April the Germans appointed Tsolakoglou Prime Minister.

The King and his government under Tsouderos, still the sole legitimate authority recognized by the allies, established themselves on Crete, where British and New Zealand forces under General Freyberg set about strengthening the defences of the island. Once again it was too late. Probably the island could have been saved from the Germans, even though it was almost impossible to operate aircraft from its aerodromes with the Greek mainland in enemy hands. When the Germans launched their attack by air-borne forces on 20th May, the defending forces nearly succeeded in defeating it, and might have done so but for a few crucial errors of judgment and failures of nerve. In the end the Germans succeeded by a narrow margin in this unique and costly operation. By the end of May 1941 Crete was in their hands and the conquest of Greece was completed. The king and his government again narrowly escaped, and established themselves in Egypt. For the next five years the king lived in exile, moving between Egypt, South Africa and London. His government enjoyed recognition without power.

A constitutional crisis was now in being as grave as that of 1917, but it was concealed by the enemy occupation of Greece. The appointment of Metaxas as Prime Minister had not been unconstitutional, though the failure to hold elections within the prescribed period after dissolving parliament undoubtedly was so. Even more serious was the appointment of a succession of Prime Ministers after the death of Metaxas without any possible basis of parliamentary support. In the circumstances the king had no alternative, but the origins of the situation which left him no alternative lay in his own weakness in the summer of 1936. The German occupation of Greece aggravated the situation, but did not create it. It is not surprising therefore that one of the consequences of the tragic events of 1941 was to call in question the constitutional position of the king and of the monarchy itself. Bitter feeling on the subject was not confined to the Communists and other professed republicans. It was shared by Venizelists and others who had once been loyal to the monarchy, at least until the excesses of the KKE (Communist Party of Greece) made them even more odious than the king.

So it happened that the agony of enemy occupation was compounded by a deep division of loyalties among the Greeks, such as other occupied countries (like Norway and the Netherlands, where the status of the exiled monarch was unchallenged) never had to suffer. Events divided the story of Greece for the next four years into two streams, which flowed almost independently of each other. In Egypt, where there was already a large Greek colony, the exiled authorities established themselves and recruited such forces as they could muster to re-form an army, navy and air force under British command. In Greece a succession of puppet governments was established under German control. Outside Athens and the major towns, the writ of the collaborating governments soon ceased to run effectively. The lines of communication through Greece, consisting essentially of a single railway and two inadequate roads from north to south, were controlled at first by the Italians and later by the Germans. Macedonia was divided between the Germans and the Bulgars, Crete and other islands between Germans and Italians. But the hinterland, consisting largely of mountains accessible only on foot, was left to its own fate, just as it formerly had been by the Turks.

Between the Greeks in exile, the Greeks under effective enemy occupation, and the Greeks in the mountain provinces, there was imperfect communication. Small boats (*caiques*) crossed the Aegean Sea, often carrying couriers or more important figures out of Greece through Turkey. A few clandestine wireless-sets operated from Athens, mostly under British control. Black marketers travelled between Athens and the mountains, though they had to evade enemy check-points to do so. Since Greece had normally imported a large proportion of its food, the British blockade and enemy indifference caused great hardship, which the neutral and international Red Cross tried to relieve; and this too provided some communication between the separated Greeks. But in the main the separation was nearly absolute, and great misunderstandings resulted from it. The most serious was the failure of the exiled government to appreciate the strength of anti-monarchist feeling among the politically conscious Greeks—which means almost all Greeks—under the enemy occupation. It was this feeling that enabled the Communists to become so powerful between 1941 and 1944.

Many of the Communist leaders were in prison when the German occupation began. The Germans released most of them (with the notable exception of the Secretary General of the KKE, Nikos Zakhariadis, who spent the years of occupation in German concentration-camps), and they immediately set about organizing a resistance movement under the name of the National Liberation Front (*Ethnikón Apeleftherotikón Métopon*—EAM). The German attack on the Soviet Union in June 1941 came at the critical moment to give impetus to the notion of resistance, though the crushing weight of defeat, occupation and famine prevented any development of armed activity in the first winter. One of the first gestures of resistance was the work of a young boy, Manolis Glezos, later identified as a Communist, who tore down the Nazi flag from the Acropolis. British agents were soon active in Greece, particularly in Crete, but their activity was at first mainly directed to espionage and the evacuation of the thousands of British and Commonwealth troops at large in the country, who had been left behind in the retreat but evaded capture by the enemy. During the first year of the occupation, it was still hard to see what form resistance would take.

A large number of organizations came into existence in the first winter of the occupation. Most of them had in common a political bias against the Metaxist regime and therefore against the king. But as the Communists pushed their natural advantages to extremes, there gradually developed a contrary sense that perhaps the monarchy would be a lesser evil than Soviet imperialism. The traditional Venizelists were particularly torn by such strains of political conscience. They shared with the Communists the common experience of repression under Metaxas, and many of them joined EAM. But it was not long before the pretensions of EAM to be a truly national coalition began to seem transparent. In name, it included many different parties— socialist, agrarian, liberal, and even purportedly monarchist, as well as Communist—but in practice most of them appeared to be different incarnations of the KKE, which held all effective control in its own hands. Other groups therefore began to form themselves outside EAM, always with the primary object of helping the allies, but with a strongly pro-British bias.

Such independent organizations were invariably a target for the KKE, either to infiltrate and take them over or to destroy them. Several were effectively eliminated in Athens during the first winter of the war. The Communist organization in the major cities was strong and experienced. No other group had the same tradition of organized conspiracy behind it. The only rivals to the KKE which survived in Athens were the intelligence networks under British control and the escape organizations, largely manned by patriotic amateurs, though both suffered severe casualties from the German and Italian secret police. Outside Athens, it was rather easier to work freely. In 1942, when armed bands began to emerge in the mountains, a number of rival forces took the field. First came the National Popular Liberation Army (*Ellinikós Laikós Apeleftherotikós Stratós* —ELAS), under the control of EAM; next, the National Republican Greek League (*Ethnikós Dimokratikós Ellinikós Sýndesmos* —EDES), under the former republican colonel, Napoleon Zervas; and later others of less permanent significance. All were at various times violently attacked by ELAS.

The adherents of the monarchy played little part in these first stirrings of resistance to the occupation. Their reasons were various. The armed forces in the Albanian war were largely under officers loyal to the king. While they were occupied at the front, their left-wing or Venizelist predecessors were unemployed in Athens, where they were readily available for recruitment and preparation for post-occupational activities. When the collapse came in April 1941, some senior officers on active service escaped with the king; others returned home, demoralized by the surrender and discredited by failure, however undeservedly. The absence of the king left them without a rallying-point or political guidance, and their association with the Metaxist regime damaged their prestige. A small group of monarchist officers, known as the Six Colonels, established a link by wireless with the government in exile and acted as a liaison with the officer corps in Athens. But their instructions were not to engage in premature activities of a provocative character, and few officers above the rank of captain disobeyed them.

One who deserves mention, though his active role was minor and obscure at this time, was Colonel George Grivas, a Cypriot by birth who later gained notoriety in his native island. Grivas was sometimes said in later years to have been a leader of resistance under the occupation, and to have enjoyed official support from the British as such. His case was typical of many. Agents on behalf of the British clandestine services made contact with many unemployed officers in Athens, offering them inducements to take to the mountains; but Grivas was not among those who responded. Instead, he remained inactive until the closing months of the occupation, when he formed a gang of thugs under the name of *Khi* (the Greek letter X) to fight the similar gangs of Communists in the streets of Athens. His was an extreme form of the reaction among army officers of monarchist loyalties, who saw Communism as a greater danger than the German occupation. Most of his colleagues were content to follow the example of the Six Colonels and bide their time.

Meanwhile resistance to the occupation grew, by-passing the elements which remained loyal to the King, and largely ignored by the legitimate authorities in exile. An important turning-point came in the autumn of 1942, when GHQ of the Middle East Command required a major military operation in Greece in support of the impending offensive of the Eighth Army in North Africa. Since most of the German supplies in North Africa travelled over the single railway-line through Greece, it was necessary to cut the line for several weeks, which could only be done by destroying one of the major viaducts north of Athens. A party of British parachutists was dropped in Greece at the end of September 1942 to co-operate with such armed bands as it could find in the mountains for this purpose. Both ELAS and EDES were already active, though on a small scale; and a force of about 150 men was mustered from their combined bands under the command of Zervas, which successfully attacked and destroyed the Gorgopotamos railway-viaduct on the night of 25th–26th November. This dramatic event raised resistance to a new level, and set in train a political drama as well.

The British parachutists remained in Greece (some of them reluctantly) as liaison officers with the resistance organizations, which quickly grew in numbers. They were supplied, though never lavishly, with arms, ammunition and money, by the British Military Mission (BMM), as the liaison officers were called. Much the largest organization, and the only one with a nation-wide extent, was the Communist-controlled ELAS. Next in importance, particularly in the north-west of Greece (which was remote from the main towns and lines of communication), was EDES under Zervas, who recognized the old revolutionary, General Plastiras (then living in France), as titular head of his organization. New forces sprang into action under the impetus of the triumph at the Gorgopotamos. Colonel Psaros came to re-form his old regiment in his native area of Mount Parnassus, supported by a political organization known as National and Social Liberation (*Ethniki kai Koinoniki Apelefthérosis*—EKKA), whose politics were liberal republican. Colonel Saraphis arrived in Thessaly to recruit another nationalist, anti-Communist force, supported in Athens by a somewhat perplexing range of political figures who were said to include both General Pangalos, the former republican dictator, and George Papandreou, a future Liberal Prime Minister.

The kaleidoscopic shifts of personal loyalties in the first year of the occupation are interesting but not surprising. Zervas, once an ardent republican, veered round towards the monarchy as a lesser evil than Communism. His officers included both monarchists and ex-Communists, some of whom later reverted to their left-wing sympathies. His organization in Athens even included men suspected of collaborating with the Germans. Psaros and Saraphis were both republicans, who had been cashiered after the abortive *coup* of 1935. But Saraphis, whose force was twice attacked and dispersed by the Communists, later joined his enemies and emerged as Commander-in-Chief of ELAS: whereas Psaros, who resisted the violent pressure of ELAS to the bitter end, was murdered by the thugs of the fanatical Communist, Athanasios Klaras (usually known by his pseudonym, Aris Veloukhiotis), who had played a distinguished role under Zervas in the attack on the Gorgopotamos viaduct. Psaros never ceased to be a republican; but his chief political adviser, George Kartalis, was a former minister in more than one Populist government under the monarchy. Such mutations were characteristic of the political confusion created by the occupation.

The confusion grew as it gradually became clear that EAM differed from all other organizations in the nature of its aims, which included not simply the expulsion of the Germans but the total transformation of Greek society on Soviet lines. Not content with organizing a resistance army (ELAS) and even a navy (ELAN), the Communists had a trade union organization (EEAM), and youth movement (EPON), a co-operative society (EA), a secret police (OPLA), and a civil guard (EP). They also had their own system of foreign relations, not merely with the allies through the British Military Mission but also with the Communist parties of the neighbouring countries, Yugoslavia, Albania and Bulgaria. They also collaborated, though by no means always amicably, with a Communist-controlled organization of Slavophone Macedonians known as SNOF. These relations enabled their opponents to accuse them, not without justice, of being unpatriotic on the subject of the northern frontiers and willing to cede Greek territory to an independent Macedonia. Finally, through Tito in Yugoslavia, they had communication with the Soviet Union, which eventually sent a small military mission to Greece in July 1944.

The dangers were little understood by the Greek authorities in exile, who did not wish to believe what they were told. British reports on the climate of opinion in Greece were difficult to ignore as entirely tendentious, but even the British authorities were divided. Churchill and the Foreign Office never wavered in their loyalty to the king, but the BMM presented a disturbing picture of pro-republican sentiment; and the British military authorities were in no doubt that ELAS was the most effective armed force in the country, if it could be harnessed to allied strategy. On the other hand, it was equally clear that the Communists would only support the allied strategy so far as it suited their primary object, which was to take control of Greece after the war. All these tensions boded ill for the future. In retrospect, it can be seen that as early as 1942 one of two consequences was already inevitable: either a civil war or an unopposed Communist take-over. Some people believed that, if the controversial personality of the king were removed from the arena, a more acceptable outcome could be peacefully achieved; and some held the same belief about the British Military Mission in the mountains. But it is hard to see any real evidence for either belief.

A first opportunity for the Greek and British authorities to become aware of the nature of the threat came in the late summer of 1942, when a number of influential and well-informed personalities arrived in Egypt from Greece by way of Turkey: among them Panagiotis Kanellopoulos, who shortly joined the government in exile, and Colonel Bakirdzis, who had been cashiered in 1935 and later became a leading agent of the British clandestine services. Their information was later corroborated by British liaison officers in the mountains and by further informants escaping from Greece. For a long time the Greek authorities ignored the warnings, in spite of politically inspired disturbances in the armed forces in Egypt and violent attacks by ELAS on most of its rivals in the mountains. A *modus vivendi* was reached between ELAS, EDES and EKKA with the help of the British Military Mission during 1943. It was embodied in an agreement constituting them 'National Bands of Greek Guerillas', under allied command through a joint GHQ. Although soon a dead letter, the agreement again made possible effective operations against the Germans for a short time. But these very operations served to bring to the surface again the latent disputes, which burst out in a major crisis in August 1943.

The object of the guerilla operations in June and July 1943 was to convince the Germans that Greece was about to be invaded by the allies, whereas in fact the real target was Sicily. The deception was successful, but it also deceived most of the Greeks, in particular the KKE. Believing that Greece would shortly be liberated, the Communists concerted a series of plans aimed at seizing power, in which chances of timing at first appeared to give them every hope of success. First, the construction of a landing-strip for aircraft in the mountains of Thessaly made it possible for a deputation of resistance leaders to be flown to Egypt, along with the commander of the British Military Mission, in August 1943. The deputation was dominated by EAM with four out of six representatives, the other two being from EDES and EKKA. In Cairo the Communists precipitated an immediate crisis by demanding the formation of a coalition government, including representation of the resistance, and a statement by the king that he would not return to Greece until after a plebiscite in his favour. The EDES and EKKA representatives supported the Communists, though less violently. The Greek and British authorities refused to consider their proposals, and sent the deputation back to Greece empty-handed.

The mood in which the resistance leaders returned to Greece, by aircraft to the same landing-point from which they had left, was naturally one of extreme disappointment. It is not possible to analyse their motives with certainty, but it is reasonable to suppose that there were divided opinions within the leadership of EAM and even within the KKE at this time, which persisted throughout the next few years of intermittent crisis. On the one hand were those who believed in tactics of peaceful penetration and subversion from within. These, whom their opponents would call adherents of a 'soft line', included George Siantos, the acting Secretary General of the KKE (in the absence of Nikos Zakhariadis, who was in a German concentration-camp); and they must also have included the non-Communist members of EAM, such as the Socialist Elias Tsirimokos, who were not widely separated from some of the political leaders of EDES and EKKA. Other adherents of a 'soft line' were no doubt the military leaders of ELAS, such as Colonel Saraphis, the titular Commander-in-Chief, and Colonel Bakirdzis, who had left Greece in 1942 after operating as the leading British agent in Athens, and returned to Greece in 1943 in the same aircraft as the resistance delegation.

On the other side were the advocates of a 'hard line', who included most of the Moscow-trained Communists and also the popular guerilla leaders known as *capetánioi*. The most notorious of these was Aris Veloukhiotis (Athanasios Klaras). There were several others, including Markos Vaphiadis, who held an important command in Macedonia and later became leader of the post-war rebellion in 1947. Macedonians were particularly prominent among advocates of the 'hard line', among them some who were at least in part of Slav rather than Greek origin; and there were others who, although Greeks in the ethnic sense, were born outside Greece, particularly in Asia Minor. One of the most intractable tasks of the KKE was, in consequence, to live down the reputation of being an unpatriotic party dominated by semi-aliens. Strenuous attempts were made in the summer of 1943 to live down this reputation, particularly in the composition of ELAS GHQ (which consisted of Siantos, Saraphis and Aris Veloukhiotis) and in all dealings with the British Military Mission. But the sharp rebuff in Cairo gave a fresh impetus to the extremists. Events now played into their hands.

At almost the same time, with the allied invasion of Italy imminent, Mussolini fell and Italy surrendered soon afterwards. About 15,000 Italian troops in Greece transferred their allegiance to the allies through the British Military Mission.[1] By the end of September ELAS had succeeded in disarming most of the Italians, contrary to the armistice agreement. The Communists now had an overwhelming material superiority over all their rivals. They also believed that the time was ripe to seize power, since they assumed that Greece was about to be liberated and that the British would try to re-impose the monarchy. In October 1943 ELAS launched an attack on all the other resis-

[1] American officers joined the Mission at about the same date, whereupon its name was changed to the Allied Military Mission.

tance forces, with one exception—EKKA, which remained neutral until the following year, when it was also attacked. Only EDES survived, under the vigorous leadership of Zervas, and that only in a reduced area of north-west Greece. The civil war between ELAS and EDES continued until February 1944, when an armistice was arranged by the Allied Military Mission, as it was now called. An inducement to ELAS to accept the armistice, apart from its manifest failure to destroy EDES, was the offer to renew military supplies, which had been cut off at the beginning of the civil war.

The Allied Military Mission now sought to direct the energies of the resistance to preparations for the final operations which would eventually lead up to the liberation of Greece. It was likely—as indeed happened—that the Germans would withdraw without a fight; but it was desirable to find any expedient that would distract the resistance leaders from internecine feuds, however momentarily. In particular it was important to ensure that ELAS should not take over the country unhindered on the day the Germans left. Small British and American units were infiltrated into Greece, partly to harass the retreating Germans and partly to ensure an allied presence as soon as the country was liberated. Many efforts were made to persuade the resistance leaders, particularly the Communists, to pursue reasonable policies in the last months of enemy occupation, while at the same time the Germans did everything possible to create dissension among them. The Germans succeeded in convincing both ELAS and EDES (in both cases probably with some degree of justification) that they were in secret collaboration with the other organization. They also established a force of anti-Communist armed Greeks known as the Security Battalions.

The danger of a fresh and bitterer civil war grew daily as the liberation drew nearer. Much depended on the reactions of the Greek and British authorities abroad, which were still based on imperfect understanding. The difficult task of regularizing the position of the king, on which so much depended, was tentatively approached by a number of cautious steps, all of which seemed inadequate to the resistance leaders. Late in 1942, the Prime Minister, Tsouderos, stated publicly on behalf of the king that after the war the Greek people would have the final say in determining their new conditions of life; but this was too vague to carry conviction. In April 1943 the king and Zervas exchanged friendly telegrams; but this did more to damage Zervias' prestige than to enhance the king's. In July 1943 the king promised a fully representative government upon the liberation and elections to a Constituent Assembly within six months; and in November he declared that 'when the hour of liberation struck, he would examine anew the date of his return'. But each stage of these concessions came too late, as was made clear when an anti-monarchist mutiny broke out early in 1944 among the Greek forces in Egypt.

One of the immediate causes of the outbreak was the establishment in the Greek mountains of a Political Committee of National Liberation (PEEA), under Communist domination but with a somewhat more widely representative character than EAM. The mutineers in Egypt wished to force the government of Tsouderos to come to terms with PEEA. Tsouderos resigned and was succeeded by Sophoklis Venizelos, son of the great Liberal leader, who attempted to suppress the mutiny but held office only a few days. He was followed by another Venizelist, George Papandreou, who had arrived from Greece only a few days before. With his approval, the mutiny was suppressed by British forces. Papandreou then convened a conference in the Lebanon with a view to forming a Government of National Unity. Most of the leading politicians in exile attended the conference; so did representatives of PEEA, EAM, ELAS, and the KKE, all still claiming to be distinct entities; and also representatives of EDES and EKKA. After vigorous attacks on the Communists by all the other representatives at the Lebanon Conference, a coalition government was duly formed.

Although the representatives of PEEA agreed to join the coalition and signed the document known as the Lebanon Charter, their agreement was at once denounced by their leaders in the mountains. Further months of negotiation followed before the Communists finally agreed to allow their various fronts to join Papandreou's coalition (at the price of five seats in a cabinet of fifteen) and to put their armed forces under the commander of the British forces preparing the liberation, General Scobie. The motives for their change of tactics are obscure, but they may have included pressure from a small Red Army mission, which arrived in Greece from Yugoslavia in July 1944. Presumably the

Communists believed in any case that they could take over the government from within, especially with the support of the Red Army, which was soon to be on the northern frontiers of Greece. If so, they miscalculated; but their miscalculation fortunately made possible an orderly and almost bloodless liberation of the country during September, as the Germans withdrew through Yugoslavia, leaving small garrisons in Crete, Rhodes and other islands, which surrendered only in May 1945.

The almost painless and wholly joyful process of liberation was soon followed by renewed tension, as the KKE began to appreciate its errors of judgment. With the liberating forces came not only Papandreou's government but also strong units of the Greek army—particularly the Rimini Brigade, which had earned that title by its valour in the Italian campaign, and the Sacred Company, a commando-type unit composed entirely of officers. Although the king did not return with them, he gave no indication of abandoning his claims; and the new influx of powerful and disciplined Greek and British units made it clear that there would be no unopposed take-over by the Communists. The tension between the KKE and its opponents grew through October and November 1944 to a point where violence awaited only a chance to break out. It came at the end of November when General Scobie ordered the dissolution of the guerilla forces. Zervas agreed on behalf of EDES (which was located entirely in Epirus, round Ioannina and Arta), but the ministers of EAM refused to disband ELAS and its ancillary organizations. They resigned from Papandreou's government, and prepared to fight.

Fighting broke out in Athens on Sunday 3rd December, as a result of a Communist-organised demonstration which the government had at first authorized and then banned. It is uncertain whether the first shots were fired by the police or by the demonstrators, who were probably not so harmless as they were intended to appear. But if it had not been this incident which started the revolution, it would have been another. The best units of ELAS were already concentrated round Athens, ready for immediate action; and their artillery was able to range on General Scobie's headquarters with its first shots. A bloody struggle ensued for nearly six weeks, during which Athens (but only Athens of the major towns in Greece) almost fell into Communist hands. Zervas' forces were rapidly cleared out of Epirus in the last week of the year, having no more stomach for civil war. But in Salonika, Volos and Patras the British forces were not attacked. Many of the rank and file of ELAS, and even some of its officers, were appalled by the situation in which they found themselves, but the hard core fought to the bitter end.

An attempt was made by Churchill and Eden to intervene. They arrived in Athens on Christmas Day, and held an all-party conference, including the Communists, under the chairmanship of Archbishop Damaskinos, the head of the Church in Greece; but it failed to stop the fighting. The one positive outcome was to convince Churchill at last that the king must declare his intention not to return to Greece without a plebiscite. The decision was forced on the king (who was in London), much against his will. He was able to claim, quite correctly, that less than a year ago, when Eden had pressed the same unpalatable concession on him, he had been urged to resist it by none other than President Roosevelt; but in December 1944 the Americans in Athens were osentatiously neutral, and the king could no longer expect support from the President. In the end he agreed to make the required declaration. At the same time, Archbishop Damaskinos was appointed Regent. Papandreou resigned, and was succeeded by General Plastiras, the titular head of EDES.

With the problem of the king out of the way, it was possible for ELAS, which had narrowly failed in its attempt to seize control of Athens, to give up the struggle without too much loss of face. A truce was negotiated on 13th January 1945, and followed by a political settlement at the Varkiza conference a month later. ELAS surrendered a surprisingly large quantity of arms, comparatively few of which had originally been supplied by the Allied Military Mission. In return, the government of General Plastiras agreed on a number of liberal reforms, an amnesty for political crimes, and a plebiscite to be held on the monarchy under international supervision. The terms were received with great relief by most Greeks, who had suffered intolerably during the past four years. They were repudiated only by the fanatical Communist guerilla-leader, Aris Veloukhiotis, who took to the hills with his personal followers in the spring of 1945, and was killed by security forces later in the year. His case apart, the one desire of the Greek people was to reconstruct their shattered country in peace.

The task of reconstruction was formidable, even if the Greeks had been left in peace. War and enemy occupation had ruined the country to an extent hardly paralleled in Europe. There was virtually no central or local administration. Many towns and villages were largely destroyed, their populations decimated by starvation, fighting, and deliberate reprisals. Roads, railways and ports had been put out of action, even if there had been vehicles, locomotives and ships to use them. Inflation was out of control, largely because of the influx of gold sovereigns through the Allied Military Mission. Foreign trade, on which Greece depended for purchases of essential food, was at a standstill. In particular, Greece's most important pre-war customers, the Germans, who took the bulk of the tobacco crop, were themselves ruined by Hitler's war. Clearly Greece could survive only with the help of massive aid, whether from Britain, the USA or UNRRA (the United Nations Relief and Rehabilitation Administration). The difficulties of reconstruction were further compounded by internal dissensions, and by the dangerous tensions in international relations which were concentrated upon Greece.

Political life had been gravely disrupted by the events of the past ten years. There were bitter feelings between those who had escaped abroad in 1941 and those who had endured the occupation; also between those who had resisted the occupation and those who had acquiesced or collaborated in it; and between monarchists and republicans, whose divisions were now overlaid by those between Communists, their fellow-travellers, and the rest. Parliamentary democracy had to be restored, having been in abeyance since 1936; and the personal position of the absent king had to be regulated. A fundamental revision of the constitution was inevitable, and the work of drafting it was protracted. All these tasks would have been hard enough even without the additional problems of international relations. Apart from their traditional allies, Britain and France, and their new ally, the USA, the Greeks had to consider their future relations with their ex-enemies, Germany and Italy; with the Soviet Union and their Communist-controlled neighbours, Albania, Yugoslavia and Bulgaria; and eventually with the newly emerging powers of the eastern Mediterranean, particularly Turkey and Egypt. These many problems at home and abroad interacted to aggravate each other during the early post-war years.

Greece did not enjoy the same period of respite for reconstruction as other countries of Europe. Crisis followed crisis almost as soon as the Varkiza Agreement had ended the first Communist rebellion in February 1945. In April, Plastiras was forced to resign after coming under attack for compromising remarks he was alleged to have made while living in occupied France. He was succeeded by Admiral Voulgaris at the head of a non-political or 'service' government, which lasted six months. It failed to carry out the economic reforms recommended by its most eminent member, Professor Varvaressos, who resigned in August. The government could not control inflation, and it was overwhelmed by the political problems. Chief among them were the congestion of the gaols with prisoners awaiting trial, both Communists and collaborators, and the impossibility of holding elections in the defective state of the register. A visit to London by the Regent, Archbishop Damaskinos, brought no relief or satisfaction, not even a promise of the long-expected cession of Cyprus to Greece. In October Voulgaris resigned, nominally on account of opposition provoked by his announcement of a general election in January 1946.

A prolonged crisis followed, the Regent being unable to find any government willing to take the responsibility of elections at so early a date. Sophoulis and Sophoklis Venizelos each failed to form a government, and one formed by Kanellopoulos lasted less than three weeks. The Archbishop himself assumed the premiership for a few days, and at least once threatened to resign the Regency. Finally the aged Sophoulis, the last of the great Venizelos' contemporaries, succeeded in forming a government of comparatively young politicians of the Centre, including several who had distinguished themselves in the resistance. It boldly declared a political amnesty, withdrew some 60,000 prosecutions, and announced the first general election in Greece for over ten years, to be held on 31st March 1946. Under the terms of the Varkiza Agreement, the British, French and US governments accepted invitations to send observers to supervise the elections; but the Soviet government declined, on the ground that it was an interference in Greece's internal affairs. The KKE boycotted the elections, which nevertheless produced a 60 per cent poll, of which the Populist party under Constantine Tsaldaris (nephew of the old Populist leader) won more than half.

The election of March 1946 marked a watershed in Greece's foreign relations. For the first time the government of the USA was directly involved in Greek affairs alongside Britain, through participation in the Allied Mission for observing the Greek elections (AMFOGE). It was a first step towards the Truman Doctrine. At the same time the Soviet Union had taken a decisively hostile step. Stalin had hitherto kept his word to Churchill, given at the Moscow and Yalta conferences, to allow Britain a free hand in Greece. Soviet influence had probably been used to persuade the KKE to join Papandreou's coalition in 1944, and almost certainly there had been no Soviet encouragement of the December rising. But in 1946 the atmosphere had changed. In January, the Soviet government used the first meeting of the UN Security Council to demand the withdrawal of British troops from Greece, without success. It also pressed for a revision of the Montreux Convention of 1936, in order to gain improved access through the Straits to the Aegean. It even claimed the cession to the USSR of the Dodecanese, which had already been promised to Greece. Still worse was to come after the Greek elections.

One of the first acts of Tsaldaris' government on taking office in April 1946 was to announce a plebiscite on the monarchy for 1st September. The British and American members of AMFOGE (from which the French now withdrew) declared that the register was in an adequate condition and that the elections had been fairly conducted. There was no reason to dispute the validity of the subsequent plebiscite, although the parliamentary opposition expressed indignation that the question posed was whether or not King George II should return to his throne, not whether Greece should be a monarchy or a republic. The electorate voted overwhelmingly in favour of the king, who was now looked upon as the one guarantee against a revival of Communism. He returned to his throne for the second time at the end of September, to confront a rapidly deteriorating situation. Fighting had broken out in northern Greece in May, and in the Peloponnese in November. Reconstruction was at a standstill; inflation continued and the black market flourished. The country was on the brink of civil war, and the grievances were not confined to the Communists.

It was already clear that Greece's northern neighbours were helping to promote disorder in Greece by infiltrating and supplying Communist guerillas. The public conduct of Soviet representatives strongly suggested their connivance. In December 1946 Tsaldaris brought a complaint to the U.N. Security Council, which agreed to send a commission of inquiry. In January 1947, when the United Nations Special Commission on the Balkans (UNSCOB) first arrived in Greece, even graver events were imminent. Tsaldaris resigned, and was succeeded by a right-wing elder statesman, Dimitrios Maximos, who included in his government General Zervas, the former leader of EDES, as Minister of Public Order. The signs that security was breaking down were followed by other signs that Britain could no longer sustain the burden of Greece's economic recovery. An economic mission from the USA arrived in January 1947 to investigate Greece's needs. Two months later, on 12th March, came the dramatic announcement of the Truman Doctrine, aimed at preventing Greece and Turkey from passing under Soviet control. In the same month King George II died suddenly and was succeeded by his younger brother, Paul.

The cold war was now joined in earnest, and Greece was its first battle-ground. When the first report of UNSCOB, which broadly supported the Greek complaint, was debated in the Security Council in July 1947, the Soviet delegate vetoed a motion for the continuation of its work. The Secretary General, Trygve Lie, nevertheless ruled that UNSCOB was still in being. Although it remained in Greece, it was never able to cross the northern frontiers to verify accusations that supply depots and training camps were maintained for the rebels in Albania, Yugoslavia and Bulgaria. Meanwhile the Communis rebellion grew to the scale of a civil war. Twice in 1947 the rebels tried unsuccessfully to seize Konitsa, near the Albanian border, in order to establish a seat of government on Greek soil. On Christmas Eve the Communist leader, Markos Vaphiadis, proclaimed an independent government; but it wa never recognized by any foreign power, nor even admitted to the Cominform, which had recently been established in Belgrade. Nevertheless very large areas of Greece were under Communist control, and even between the major towns movement was possible only in military conveys.

Desperate though the situation was becoming, the Greek government's hands were still tied by public and international opinion. Maximos was obliged to resign in August 1947 after complaints of the ruthless methods of General Zervas in preserving public order. He was succeeded by a coalition under Sophoulis and Tsaldaris, which in turn was succeeded by other governments of 'national unity' similarly based on co-operation between the two major groups in parliament. The new government offered the rebels an amnesty, which was ignored, and it released a number of men whom Zervas had arrested. (One of them celebrated his return to liberty by later murdering a senior Minister in the streets of Athens.) As the fighting grew bitterer and the threat of total collapse more imminent, the US government became more deeply committed. Apart from massive aid, much of it in the form of military supplies, a joint General Staff was formed by the Greek and US governments, and American 'military advisers' came close to combat action in the mountains. At the end of 1947 it was still doubtful whether an independent, pro-western Greece could survive.

The year 1948 was one of almost unrelieved gloom. Among the few items of encouragement was the re-establishment of friendly relations with Italy: the Dodecanese islands were formally ceded to Greece, agreement was reached on Italian reparations, and a treaty of Friendship, Commerce and Navigation was signed between the two counties. At home, the Corinth Canal was re-opened and the Gorgopotamos railway-viaduct rebuilt, both having been victims of the war. American aid also made possible the repair of many damaged roads at great speed, but they still served only military purposes. The civil war had rendered homeless nearly a quarter of a million Greeks, and nearly 30,000 children were carried off from their villages across the northern frontiers, to be brought up under Communist regimes. So grave was the threat to Greece that in October 1948 there was a general proclamation of martial law. The Communist guerillas now held an even larger extent of Greece than the resistance had held at its peak during the occupation, including much of the Peloponnese and even Attica. Coalition governments came and went, making little difference to the course of events. But in 1949 the tide began to turn.

Greece's allies had staunchly supported her, under President Truman's leadership. At the United Nations, the General Assembly condemned Albania, Yugoslavia and Bulgaria for aiding the rebels, on the basis of a report from UNSCOB in November 1948. But already Tito was on his way to changing sides. His breach with Stalin led to the expulsion of Yugoslavia from the Cominform in the summer of 1948. A year later came his decision to close the frontier with Greece. At the same time a rift developed within the leadership of the KKE. Markos Vaphiadis lost his command and disappeared. His place was taken by Nikos Zakhariadis, the pre-war Secretary General. The symptoms of collapse on the Communist side were accompanied by an improvement in morale on the side of the government. In January 1949 General Alexander Papagos was appointed Commander-in-Chief, bringing with him the prestige of victory over the Italians in Albania in 1940. A few weeks later the rebels were cleared out of the Peloponnese, and successful operations began in the north. By July 100,000 refugees were able to return home. In October the rebel leaders admitted defeat by proclaiming a 'temporary cessation' of hostilities.

The restoration of security left the Greeks again free to begin reconstruction, but it was soon followed by a reversion to political instability. Sophoulis died in office in June 1949, and was succeeded as Prime Minister by Alexander Diomedes, who resigned in January 1950 after a dispute with his Liberal colleague, Sophoklis Venizelos. It was the end of the Liberal-Populist coalition under which the Greeks had fought the civil war. A 'caretaker' government followed, with a mandate to hold a General Election in March 1950, the normal end of the four-year parliament elected in March 1946. So greatly had the state of security improved that martial law was lifted, and death sentences for treason passed by military courts were reviewed. Other signs of the changed atmosphere were the withdrawal of the British service missions and the renewal of friendly relations with Yugoslavia. The general election also marked the end of an era: the largest single party (though without an absolute majority) was neither the Populists nor the Liberals, but a new group called the National Progressive Union of the Centre (EPEK), led by General Plastiras and Emmanuel Tsouderos.

The result of the elections showed that no party commanded the full confidence of the people, and none could form a government except in a coalition. Several permutations were tried. Tsaldaris failed, and Venizelos lasted only two weeks; Plastiras formed a government with Liberal support, which was withdrawn a few weeks later; and Venizelos then formed a Liberal government in May. It lasted till September, when Venizelos formed a short-lived coalition with the Populists until November, followed by another coalition with a small party called the Democratic Socialists. This coalition was given general support by EPEK under Plastiras, and it lasted until the Democratic Socialists resigned in June 1951. Venizelos continued in office with the support of the Populists and EPEK in turn, but only for another month. Soon afterwards, EPEK broke up with the withdrawal of Tsouderos. The period of kaleidoscopic coalitions ended with another dissolution of parliament and a general election based on a new electoral law, aimed at promoting fewer and larger parties, and therefore more stable governments.

Electoral reform was clearly overdue, for it was impossible to carry out a planned reconstruction when governments were rotating at the rate of at least half a dozen a year, even if the differences between them were largely matters of personality rather than principle. Greece's difficulties at home were compounded in the course of 1950 by even more dramatic events abroad, which underlined the need for stable government. Two months after the general election of March 1950, the Korean War broke out. The Greek government at once offered an infantry brigade and an Air Force unit to serve under UN command. The fear that war would spread to Europe led to an extension of the military organization of NATO, which had been set up in 1949. Greece and Turkey were invited to be associated with it for Mediterranean affairs, and in 1951 to become full members. They were also admitted to the Council of Europe. American military aid was increased, but civil aid was cut, partly as a mark of disapproval of Greece's political instability. The need for firm government was imperative on all counts.

The Second National Crisis (1941–1952)

The most influential advocate of electoral reform was General Papagos, the victor over the Communist rebellion, who had been promoted Field-Marshal (a rank hitherto held only by the sovereign) and Commander-in-Chief of all the armed forces in 1950. Once public security was assured, he had no further interest in military rank, and determined to be the political saviour of his country. Sickened with the irresponsible confusion of party politics in a national crisis, he resigned all his appointments in May 1951 and announced two months later the formation of a new organization to fight the elections. In conscious imitation of de Gaulle's *Rassemblement du Peuple Français*, he called it not a political party but the 'Greek Rally' (*Ellinikós Synagermós*). With the support of many younger politicians, notable among them Spyros Markezinis and Constantine Karamanlis (though the latter was not at first prominent), Papagos contested the General Election of September 1951 for the first time. His hopes were only partially fulfilled.

Under a new electoral system known as 'modified proportional representation', the Greek Rally won 36 per cent of the votes and 114 seats out of 250. It was not enough for undivided rule, and Papagos refused to enter into any coalition. He demanded—but without success—that parliament should at once be dissolved and new elections held under the simple majority system. Instead, a government was formed by Plastiras with the Liberals: it was a coalition of the familiar kind. Baulked of his object, Papagos declared that he would support the foreign policy of the new government, which was one of loyalty to NATO and the western alliance, but not its domestic policy, which included a generous Pacification Bill intended to assuage the bitter feelings left by the civil war. Only the hard core of militant Communists, convicted (by military courts, in most cases) of treason and murder, were kept in prison, many of them for more than a decade longer. So quick were the Greeks to forget the savagery of the recent past that a crypto-Communist party, known as the Union of the Democratic—or Republican—Left (EDA), was allowed to contest the elections, and won ten seats.

Clearly the government could have no long life. Nor, in Papagos' belief, could the system which had produced it. But it lasted a year, and witnessed a number of important events.

The Second National Crisis (1941–1952)

Greece entered NATO, together with Turkey, in October 1951, and was elected to the Security Council of the UN in December. The opening of a new era in international relations was also marked by the development of friendly relations with Italy, Turkey and Yugoslavia, all enemies of the recent or earlier past. Closer relations with other Mediterranean powers were developed, particularly with Egypt, where the welfare of the Greek colony was an important interest. The Greek government recognized, at least by implication, Egyptian sovereignty over the Sudan in 1952. It also expressed interest in the Anglo-American proposal for a Middle East Defence Organization, modelled on NATO; but this project foundered upon Egyptian objections. In these ventures into a larger foreign policy, the Greek government enjoyed the support of all parties except the extreme Left.

It was quite otherwise at home. Papagos continued to oppose the government's domestic policy, particularly its tolerance of the extreme Left. He also insisted on further electoral reforms with a view to establishing stronger government. In January 1952 a new constitution was promulgated, but as usual it did not embody a specific electoral system. It was necessary for each parliament to legislate for the election of its successor, and constitutionally there was no obligation to do so for four years from September 1951. Nevertheless, the days of Plastiras' government were clearly numbered when not only the Greek public but also the US authorities became impatient with its incompetence to initiate the dynamic reconstruction which was needed. Under pressure from the American Embassy, the government resigned in the late summer of 1952, after passing an electoral law providing for majority voting and the enlargement of parliament from 250 to 300 seats. The outcome was an overwhelming victory for the Greek Rally in October.

Papagos won 239 seats, and was therefore able to form a strong government exclusively from his own following. The remaining 61 seats all went to a coalition of EPEK and the Liberals. The Communist-supported EDA lost all its seats. A few weeks later the police established the existence of links between EDA and a secret Communist cell detected in Athens. The danger of a Communist revival was therefore already real. Right-wing Greeks felt reassured that a strong government under the most powerful figure of modern times had emerged just in time. In fact the longest period of stable government by a single party in the whole history of modern Greece was about to begin. But Papagos was not a replica of Metaxas, greatly though he admired his former Commander-in-Chief. Although his personality inevitably dominated the government, he never deviated from parliamentary democracy. He had no need to do so, for he had achieved the whole of his ambition by entirely democratic means. The restoration of Greece's good name and prosperity was at last to be inaugurated after more than a decade of agony.

CHAPTER X

The Inheritance of Constantine (1952–1967)

The second great crisis of the 20th century ended for Greece in 1952. It was a crisis that had taken several successive forms—dictatorship, enemy occupation, civil war, political instability—but with a single persistent thread running through the agonizing years: the threat that the Greek people would lose their sovereign right to control their own destiny. From 1936 to 1952 there was no certainty of the outcome. The latter year, however, inaugurated a new era, in which Greece enjoyed a stability of government practically unexampled since the modern state was founded. For eleven years, the country had only two Prime Ministers (Field-Marshal Papagos and Constantine Karamanlis), in contrast to an average of half a dozen changes of government a year. The government was in the hands of a single party, though under a changed name after 1955. Most important of all, when it fell at the end of 1963, it was replaced in power after a constitutionally conducted general election by another single party—a rare event in Europe, outside Britain, since the second World War.

Stability was not the only advantage gained by Greece in these years. After centuries of separation, Greece had again become fully part of western civilization. Athens was no longer a remote Balkan capital but a major European city. Greece was a member not merely of the United Nations but of the Council of Europe, the North Atlantic Treaty Organization, and eventually (by a treaty of association) the European Economic Community. Other links with neighbours and friends were tentatively broached. All of them involved some diminution of total independence, but the diminution was voluntary and reciprocal. This was a different matter from the dependence that Greece had previously endured from the protecting powers, or the subservience imposed by the Nazis and unsuccessfully sought by the Communists. No country was totally independent in the second half of the 20th century, not even the USA or the Soviet Union. But outside the Iron Curtain (and even, gradually and progressively, inside it) it was at least possible to choose one's partners in inter-dependence, and the Greeks freely made their choice.

Nor was the emergence of Greece into an international role confined to the political context. Greek culture, having been profoundly influenced first from the east by the Arabs and Turks, and then from the west by the French, Italians and British, now began to assert an influence of its own. Before the second World War, the only Greeks known abroad were either ship-owners and other commercial magnates or the waiters and grocers and café proprietors of a dozen foreign cities. Gradually Greeks of another sort began to impose themselves on the consciousness of the western world: a poet, an opera-singer, a painter, an actress, a theatrical producer, a novelist, a composer—it is not even necessary to name them, partly because many of them are already famous, partly because they are in this context not so much individuals as typical of an historic evolution. Greece, from which the stream of European civilization originally flowed, had re-entered the mainstream. It did not happen overnight in 1952, any more than the Byzantine Empire fell instantly in 1453. But it was in the years after 1952 that the fact became unmistakable.

The great achievement of the years which began with Papagos' election was the restoration of national self-confidence. But there was still a long, hard road of economic recovery to be travelled, and Papagos was no expert in economic problems. He depended at first on his Minister of Co-ordination, Spyros Markezinis, who tried to revive the stern principles underlying the Varvaressos plan of 1945. His methods were orthodox and firm. The currency was devalued; the budget of 1953 showed a surplus for the first time since the war; a drastic reduction of government employees was started with some five thousand enforced retirements. Unpopularity was the inevitable price, but an attempt to organize a general strike in June 1953 was successfully resisted. Even so, the American authorities, on whom the government depended for both military and civil aid, were not easily satisfied. In the end Markezinis' economic policy proved too severe to be acceptable by the Greeks, and insufficiently severe to win the necessary measure of American support. After a personal dispute with Papagos, he resigned in April 1954.

Contentious though a particular programme might be, the underlying improvement in Greece's economy nevertheless gradually asserted itself as a fact during the next decade. The country was still very far from self-sufficiency, but some structural changes of a beneficial character were occurring. With the economic recovery of West Germany, the chief market for tobacco was restored, and a new outlet was created for underemployed labour. Germany became the main destination for Greek emigrants, whose remittances were a substantial contribution to the balance of payments. There was also a revival of remittances from the USA which had been cut off by the war. Another growing movement in the reverse direction added a further improvement to the balance of payments—the expenditure of tourists, which came to take second place only to agricultural products as a source of foreign exchange. The development of manufacturing industry and mining with indigenous capital, in place of foreign concessions, contributed further to the healthy trend. But the lack of any home-produced source of energy (other than rivers and some deposits of lignite) was a severe handicap. It remained true that Greece was still dependent for survival on foreign aid; and there was no end to this condition in sight.

Papagos' three years of office cannot be said to have made more than a marginal contribution to economic reconstruction. His personal contribution was no more than the indirect one of restoring security and confidence. The economic fruits of security and confidence only matured in later years, after Papagos' death. In foreign relations, on the other hand, his achievements were more immediately conspicuous, though not more lasting. There was a marked improvement in relations with Greece's northern neighbours. A partial settlement was reached with Bulgaria in 1953–54: frontier disputes were resolved, and prisoners were exchanged, but neither on reparations for the war nor on the restoration of diplomatic relations could agreement be reached. Much the same occurred with Albania, the restoration of diplomatic relations being frustrated by the Albanian refusal to accept the Greek stipulation that the status of northern Epirus (as the Greeks called southern Albania) should be left open to be settled at a peace conference. In practice it was already clear that Greece was to be disappointed of any substantial improvement of her northern frontiers as a result of the World War.

Such improvements as occurred in relations across the Iron Curtain were undoubtedly due to the changed atmosphere after the death of Stalin. Several East European countries to which Greek children had been carried off during the civil war agreed to repatriate them. Others signed trade agreements with Greece for the first time since the war. On the other hand, the most notable development in international relations in these years was one that owed its origin not to the death of Stalin but to the earlier threat which he had presented in his life-time, and which his death did much to remove. Turkey, Greece and Yugoslavia (after Tito's quarrel with Stalin in 1948) were all equally conscious of the threat to their independence from Soviet hostility. A common fear drew them together in Stalin's last years. Staff conversations between the military commanders of the three powers began in 1952. At the end of February 1953 a defence treaty was signed at Ankara, with the warm approval of the western allies. A few days later Stalin died, but it was too early yet to foresee the *détente* in south-east Europe which was to follow.

Papagos wished to carry the arrangements still further, on the lines of the North Atlantic Treaty. No one knew better than he, from experience in 1941, how easy it is for a reluctant ally to evade his obligations on the ground that the precise *casus foederis* has not arisen. The technique of NATO was to interlock the political as well as the military structures of the contracting parties in such a way that an attack on one must automatically, in reality and not simply on paper, entail an attack on the rest. Papagos sought to apply the same technique in the Balkans. There were precedents that could be quoted regionally as well as in western Europe. During the second

World War, the governments in exile of Greece and Yugoslavia had signed an agreement which was intended to form the basis of a Balkan union, open to other countries to join. But events had overtaken the good intention, which remained a dead letter. A new attempt was now to be made, beginning with a visit to Athens by Marshal Tito in June 1954, which set the seal on the restitution of the traditional friendship between Greece and Yugoslavia. A few weeks later the Balkan Pact was signed by the three powers at Bled in Yugoslavia (August 1954).

The Pact established a combined General Staff and a number of common institutions for co-operation in non-military fields. The first meeting of the Permanent Council was held in February 1955, and that of the General Staff two months later in Belgrade. But in the event nothing more came of these arrangements, which were to be formally pronounced a dead letter a few years later. The reasons were twofold. In the first place, changes in the foreign policy of the Soviet Union (which were already taking effect though not yet fully certain when the Pact was signed) made the precautions taken largely unnecessary. A partial reconciliation between Khrushchev and Tito was followed by a gradual normalization of relations between the Soviet government and both Greece and Turkey. The Pact was therefore no longer needed. In the second place, a far more serious problem arose to divide Greece and Turkey, which made the co-operation of the two countries in the Balkan Pact, or even in NATO, virtually impossible for several years. This was the dispute, also involving Britain, over the status of Cyprus, which came near to destroying the western orientation of Greek policy.

The Greeks' desire for the union of Cyprus with Greece (*énosis*) was strong, deep-rooted and virtually unanimous, especially among the four-fifths of the Cypriot population who were Greek in language, sentiment and religion. No kind of rational argument was of any value against it. It was no use pointing out that the Cypriots were better off under British rule, or that the Greek government in 1915 had itself failed to take advantage of a British offer to cede the island in return for nothing more than implementation of Greece's treaty obligations to Serbia. Being basically irrational, the Greek campaign for *énosis* naturally sparked off an equally irrational reaction on the part of the

Turks, who had shown complete indifference towards the one-fifth of the Cypriot population who were Turkish in language, sentiment and religion, ever since the island passed under British protection in 1878. The Turkish claim, for instance, that if Britain abandoned the island it must revert to Turkish sovereignty was without foundation in international law. But, just as in 1821, an outbreak of Greek nationalism stimulated an outbreak of Turkish nationalism, both being storms of emotion ineffectually disguised as reason.

The Greeks, however, could at least claim consistency. Hardly a year had passed since 1878 when the cry of *énosis* was not raised by the Cypriot Greeks. The contention that Cyprus was naturally Greek was self-evident to them. After all, four-fifths of them undeniably spoke Greek, belonged to the Orthodox Church, and thought of themselves as Greeks; and how is a Greek to be defined except as someone who thinks he is a Greek and wants to be one? In the complex of sentiments which went into the agitation, by far the most important was the religious element. The Archbishop of Cyprus, elected by his flock and hierarchically independent of any Patriarch, had always been known as the 'national leader' (*ethnárkhis* or *millet-bashi*) and was expected to act as such. It was the Church that had led the riots of 1931; it was the Church which organized the unofficial plebiscite of January 1950—conducted, indeed, generally in the churches, and therefore boycotted by the Turks—resulting naturally in an overwhelming vote for *énosis*; it was the energetic young Archbishop, Makarios III, who set himself at the head of the renewed agitation in 1954.

To this agitation the British government could only reply with arguments that were coldly rational. Cyprus never had been part of Greece—a blatant sophistry. Cyprus was better off under British rule—an insult, even if true. If the British left Cyprus, there would be civil war between Greeks and Turks; or even a major war between Greece and Turkey; or the Communists would take over. Cyprus was too close to the Turkish coast to be left in potentially unfriendly hands. So was Rhodes, of course, and Rhodes had become Greek in 1947; but Rhodes was at least closer to the main body of Greek territory than Cyprus; and in any case, the fact that Turkey was already hemmed in by Greek islands was not an argument for adding another to them.

So the futile dispute pursued its endless involutions—futile because the contest did not belong to the plane of reason at all. It was noticeable that the British seemed to argue the Turkish case before the Turks had even thought of it. The real British motive, it was suspected, was to retain a base in the eastern Mediterranean after the impending evacuation of the Suez Canal Zone.

Successive Greek governments were increasingly embarrassed by the campaign for *énosis*. They depended on British friendship; and when American influence replaced British, there was no sign of sympathy for *énosis* in Washington. All Greek governments, from the days of Eleftherios Venizelos, insisted that the aspiration for *énosis* must not interfere with Greece's traditional alliances. In 1950, when a Cypriot delegation passed through Athens on its way to New York, to report the result of the plebiscite to the United Nations, the Greek government of the day expressed the hope that Britain would respond favourably, but emphasized that it would handle the question in due time within the framework of the traditional friendship with Britain. The same policy was reiterated again and again, in particular by Papagos in March 1954. But new pressures were compelling a strengthened language with each reiteration. Most important among the pressures were those of the new Ethnarch, Archbishop Makarios, and the Cypriot-born army officer, Colonel George Grivas, who had played a minor and discreditable role in the closing stages of the German occupation of Greece.

Pressure from Makarios, riots in Athens, and a succession of rebuffs from the British government, were among the causes with finally made it impossible for Papagos to maintain a negative attitude towards the campaign for *énosis*. They were not the only reasons. The end of the civil war had not produced the expected benefits as soon as the Greeks had hoped. The national economy was improving only slowly. The Americans were proving difficult and were thought ungenerous over material aid, and refused to support the Greek claim to Cyprus. A disastrous series of earthquakes, first in the Ionian Islands in 1953, then near Volos in 1954, had a demoralizing effect which was even more harmful than the material damage done. There was almost universal sympathy in Greece for the Greek Cypriot nationalists, and a feeling of being deserted in the face of misfortune. In these circumstances, not only did Papagos feel obliged to take the problem of Cyprus to the United Nations in August 1954. There was also a marked deviation of Greek foreign policy away from its traditional alignment.

The United Nations added to Papagos' embarrassment by refusing to inscribe the Cyprus dispute on their agenda. Cyprus, it was argued by the British government, was a matter of exclusively domestic jurisdiction; the United States agreed; so did a majority of the other member-states, in the days before the great influx of new member-states began in 1955. The result was a renewed outbreak of riots in Athens and Salonika, directed particularly against American offices. Papagos severely repressed the riots. But he could do little—and perhaps tried even less than he could—against a far more serious phenomenon which emerged in Cyprus itself during April 1955. With a series of attacks on British installations and property (but not at first on human life) the campaign for *énosis* was launched into a new and dramatic phase by the National Organization of Cypriot Combatants (*Ethniki Orgánosis Kyprion Agonistón*—EOKA). It was led by Colonel George Grivas, who assumed the name of the legendary mediaeval hero, Dighenis Akritas. It was clandestinely blessed and encouraged, though openly disowned, by Archbishop Makarios.

By the latter half of 1955 the situation in Cyprus had become so bad that the British government tried to remedy it by inviting the Greek and Turkish governments to a conference in London on the problems of the eastern Mediterranean, from which Cyprus was not to be excluded. Although there was to be no question of a change of sovereignty, the proposal amounted to an admission that Cyprus was not, and could no longer be treated as, a matter of exclusively domestic jurisdiction. But the conference was not a success. While the Turks accepted with alacrity, the Greeks did so only after several days' hesitation, and Makarios protested against the Turks even being invited. Soon after the conference assembled at the end of August, the tension was aggravated by an outbreak of anti-Greek violence in Istanbul and Smyrna on 6th September. It was always suspected (and later proved, after the overthrow of the Menderes regime in Turkey in 1960) that the violence had been officially inspired and organized. Although the Turks offered apologies and amends, Greece withdrew from a number of inter-allied engagements, including the current NATO exercises in the eastern Mediterranean.

The abortive London conference of August-September 1955 resulted only in the re-affirmation of familiar positions. The Greeks would accept no settlement which excluded the possibility of *énosis*. The Turks would accept none which did not exclude that possibility. The British government would concede self-government to Cyprus if Greeks and Turks could agree on the terms, but would make no commitment on a change of sovereignty. The deadlock was absolute. Nor could the international organizations help. The North Atlantic Council considered the situation without result. This was not surprising, since Cyprus was excluded from the area covered by the Treaty, quite apart from the delicacy of an intractable dispute involving three of the members of NATO. Another appeal was addressed by the Greeks to the United Nations, which again refused to inscribe the dispute on their agenda in September 1955. Meanwhile Papagos was already on his deathbed. Events were slipping out of his control, and there was no acknowledged successor. He died on 4th October, universally respected for his services to Greece, but disappointed in his last great endeavour.

It had been expected that Papagos' successor would be his Foreign Minister, Stephanos Stephanopoulos. But instead King Paul summoned his Minister of Communications and Public Works, Constantine Karamanlis, a loyal adherent of Papagos but still relatively unknown. He was to astonish his people by holding office continuously for almost eight years—the longest uninterrupted tenure in the history of the Greek kingdom. During those years Greece achieved a new stability and prosperity, and made further progress towards international acceptance as an equal and responsible power. The national economy was steadily developed, security was preserved, communications improved, the foundations of modern industry laid, and external relations normalized. Even the long-drawn-out dispute over Cyprus was brought, if not to a final solution, at least to an interim settlement. These successes were not wholly attributable to Karamanlis and his government. They were built on earlier foundations, and not all of them proved permanent. But Greece was unmistakably a different, more confident and prosperous country at the end of Karamanlis' term of office than she had been at the beginning of Papagos'.

The succession was timely. Control of events had been visibly slipping from the hands of the dying Field-Marshal. He would probably have resisted, at the height of his powers, allowing the Cyprus dispute to cause a severe breach with Britain and a leftward incline of foreign policy in the direction of the neutralist and anti-colonialist powers. The attendance of Archbishop Makarios at the Afro-Asian Conference at Bandung in Indonesia in April 1955 was a startling symptom of this novel trend. Karamanlis took steps at once to restore the position. Secret conversations with the British government in November 1955 were followed by an announcement that the appeal to the United Nations would not be renewed. A Greek emissary was sent to Cyprus at the end of the year to confer with Makarios and with the new British governor, Field-Marshal Sir John Harding, formerly Chief of the Imperial General Staff. In an atmosphere of reviving hope, Karamanlis then dissolved parliament and held a general election early in February 1956. The new electoral law was complex, and produced a closely contested result.

Karamanlis' party fought the election under a new name— the National Radical Union (ERE) in place of the Greek Rally—but the personalities and policies were much the same. Since the electoral law distinctly favoured large parties, his opponents formed a single coalition, ranging from extreme Left to extreme Right, but with no intention of forming a coalition government if they had won. They very nearly did so; but although their share of votes touched 50 per cent, they had slightly under half the seats in parliament. Karamanlis, with less than half the votes, had a majority of 10 in a parliament of 300. He was therefore able to form a government drawn entirely from ERE. It was notable for being the first government to include a woman Minister—another sign that Greece was moving with the times. But it was clear that Karamanlis would not have an easy task. The electoral coalition formed against him, for all its diversity, had one characteristic in common—distrust of the western alliance; and this distrust had come near to prevailing with the electors.

During 1956 it appeared that the distrust might be justified.

The early optimism was soon dissipated. Negotiations between Makarios and the new governor of Cyprus (whose military background was itself a cause of unjustified suspicion) soon broke down, partly because Grivas declared from his secret HQ that he would not accept the settlement which Makarios appeared to be negotiating, and partly because the British terms were regarded as too severe. Early in March the negotiations ended. Makarios was deported to the Seychelles Islands as a presumed party to terrorism; the Greek Ambassador was recalled from London; and the Greek appeal to the United Nations was renewed. Karamanlis still struggled to contain the disaster. He rejected the anti-western neutralism of his opponents. Greece took part again in NATO manoeuvres. An offer of Soviet aid was rebuffed; but so was the British government's argument that a base in Cyprus was essential to safeguard supplies of oil from the Middle East. This argument was crucially tested when President Nasser nationalized the Suez Canal at the end of July.

The crisis over the Canal led to a sharp deterioration of an already strained situation. Apart from Egypt, Greece was the only country which refused to attend the international conference in London to discuss the crisis. In Cyprus itself there was a momentary respite when Grivas announced a truce in August; but when the governor misinterpreted it as indicating readiness to surrender, and dictated terms accordingly, there was a fierce revival of bloodshed, which grew still worse as the Anglo-French expedition against Egypt was mounted from the island. The terrorism of EOKA, which had originally been directed against unpatriotic Greeks, was now turned upon Turkish Cypriots and British troops. There was never any danger that the British authorities would lose control of the island, nor was the abortive operation against Egypt seriously hampered by EOKA. But the international unpopularity of Britain encouraged Greek hopes of action at the United Nations, which the violence in Cyprus helped to keep alive. By this time it was impossible for Karamanlis to swim against the tide of nationalist emotion.

The British government still sought a compromise short of the surrender of sovereignty. Lord Radcliffe was sent to Cyprus to draft a new constitution, which might well have led to *énosis* in the long run although it was designed to proclude it. But the

Greeks rejected it out of hand without scrutiny. They now relied heavily—however sceptical Karamanlis may have been personally—on the UN General Assembly, which had shown itself notably energetic on behalf of Egypt in the Suez Canal crisis. In February 1957 the Assembly passed a resolution urging the resumption of negotiations for a 'peaceful, democratic and just solution', which the British, Greeks and Turks all accepted. Shortly afterwards, as a conciliatory gesture, the British authorities released Makarios from the Seychelles, in return for an ambiguous statement deploring violence. But negotiations never were resumed, for whereas the Greeks envisaged negotiations between the British and 'the people of Cyprus', the British and Turks envisaged them between the three governments concerned. Despite a renewed offer of mediation by NATO, there was no breach in the deadlock.

Both the Greeks and the British were now entangled in ambiguous policies, swaying between hostility and reconciliation. So were all concerned except the Turks, who still would not agree to *énosis* at any price. The Turkish solutions to the problems were, in order of preference, that there should be no change at all, that Cyprus should revert to Turkish sovereignty, or that the island should be partitioned. The Conservative government in Britain sometimes inclined towards the last solution; but the Labour Party Conference in 1957 encouraged Greek hopes by voting in support of self-determination for the island without partition—a policy which it was too late to carry out when they came to power in 1964. The concept of self-determination was itself controversial and difficult to apply, since if interpreted as the Greeks wished, it would lead automatically to *énosis*; and if interpreted as the Turks wished, to partition. The dilemma facing all parties, which conditioned all their reactions, was that there was simply no acceptable solution, only a choice between more or less unacceptable alternatives. Even between Makarios and Grivas there was no harmony of policy.

The oscillations of Greek policy during the years of the Cyprus dispute are explicable only by the agony of mind which the dispute caused. In the Balkans, diplomatic relations were renewed with Rumania but a Rumanian proposal to enlarge the Balkan Pact by the admission of Rumania, Bulgaria and

Albania in September 1957 was rejected by Greece—although the Yugoslavs were willing to accept it. Relations with Yugoslavia remained friendly, but the Balkan Pact was clearly defunct. Even towards Turkey a friendly gesture was made by dismantling the fortifications of Leros, the nearest island of the Dodecanese to the Turkish coast, perhaps as a hint that Cyprus in Greek hands need not be regarded as a threat. Towards the USA Greek feelings were naturally ambiguous. Economic dependence dictated co-operation: hence an agreement was reached on American bases in Greece, and Greece endorsed the 'Eisenhower Doctrine' on the Middle East in 1958. But the American opposition to *énosis* in the United Nations, and the need to collect more votes there, dictated co-operation with the anti-colonial powers, including those of the Middle East. Hence the Greek refusal to allow American aircraft to land in Greece during the crisis in Lebanon and Jordon in 1957.

The Greek government's pursuit of new associations was an uneasy one, in which probably Karamanlis had little confidence. At the end of 1957, it enabled them to secure the inscription of the Cyprus problem on the UN agenda, and to carry their resolution calling for self-determination through the Political Committee and the General Assembly; but it did not give them the two-thirds majority in the Assembly needed to make the resolution effective. The quest for allies among the non-aligned states and even the Soviet bloc was therefore pressed further. During 1958 Greece undertook an unusually wide range of diplomatic initiatives in many fields, all having at least one object in common: to widen and shift the basis of Greece's international relations. Trade agreements with the USSR, Poland and Japan; commercial negotiations with Egypt and Yugoslavia; even a relaxation of controls on trade with Communist China, despite American discouragement—all had diplomatic as well as commercial significance. So did the interchanges of official visits with the Lebanon, Spain and the Sudan; and even an agreement with Albania on the clearing of mines from the Corfu strait, and another with Bulgaria on frontier questions. Only with Britain and the USA, as well as Turkey, were relations cool, even if not consistently so.

Karamanlis' position was made increasingly embarrassing by the necessity to pursue uncongenial policies, aggravated by the pressure of the opposition and the press to carry those policies to dangerous extremes. To make matters worse, Archbishop Makarios had installed himself in Athens after his release from the Seychelles, since he was debarred from returning to Cyprus. After the defection of two Ministers and a number of parliamentary supporters, Karamanlis resigned in March 1958, and parliament was dissolved. The general election was fought in May, on two issues forcefully pressed by the opposition: the government's weakness over Cyprus and its alleged willingness to allow US missile bases to be established in Greece But Karamanlis won a substantially increased majority, and was therefore able to pursue his cautious policy with more confidence. In the meantime there had been some signs of a change of mood in British policy, partly caused by an appreciation of the deficiencies of Cyprus, which had no deep-water harbour, in operations such as the Anglo-French expedition against Egypt. A new governor was appointed to Cyprus in October 1957— this time a Colonial civil servant (Sir Hugh Foot, who came from a well-known liberal family) in place of the Field-Marshal. The conciliatory implication of the change was confirmed by the announcement of a new British plan in August 1958.

The new plan was brought personally to Athens by the British Prime Minister, Harold Macmillan. It proposed a partnership in the administration of Cyprus between Britain, Greece and Turkey. Such an internationalization of the island, though it represented a considerable concession on the part of Britain, would have had fatal results from the Greek point of view, because what was conceded was the existence of a Turkish interest. Karamanlis therefore felt obliged to reject it. The British government nevertheless declared its intention to impose the partnership from the beginning of October 1958. Although the Greeks could not be compelled to participate, the British decision meant that representatives of the Turkish government would be allowed to establish themselves on the island. Such an unwelcome prospect called for drastic measures, which may have been the British government's intention in proposing it. Makarios made an unexpected statement in September that he would accept independence for Cyprus as an alternative to *énosis*. This was clearly a relief to the Greek government, though not to Grivas, who came near to repudiating Makarios on behalf of EOKA. But the gesture was decisive. Greek and Turkish Ministers were engaged in private talks before the end of the year.

A settlement of a kind—though it soon proved to be a very unsatisfactory kind—was reached with extraordinary rapidity in a series of negotiations which began in Paris (under the auspices of NATO), and continued in Zürich and London. The Prime Ministers of Greece and Turkey, with Archbishop Makarios and the Turkish Cypriot leader, Dr. Kütchük, agreed that Cyprus should become an independent Republic, under a Greek President and a Turkish Vice-President. Ministerial offices and government posts were to be shared by a complex range of formulae which invariably gave the Turkish Cypriots disproportionately high representation. There were to be communal chambers and a degree of local self-government. The British were to retain sovereignty over two military base-areas, and both Greece and Turkey were to have the right to station specified numbers of troops in the island. A treaty of guarantee safeguarded the constitution against any alteration entailing either *énosis* or partition. The island was to have the right, which it exercised when the Republic formally came into being in August 1960, to remain within the Commonwealth. The details took nearly a year to complete, chiefly because of the hard and elusive bargaining of Makarios.

Both Makarios and Karamanlis were in fact put under pressure to frustrate the Zürich-London agreements. Karamanlis secured ratification in parliament only after a bitter debate, though by a substantial majority. Grivas reluctantly accepted Makarios' policy, though he strongly criticized it. He came out of hiding to a hero's welcome; high decorations and the rank of Lieutenant-General were conferred on him by King Paul. But his subsequent behaviour was undignified, embarrassing and often apparently unbalanced. He repeatedly threatened to intervene in Greek politics, seeing himself in the same role as Papagos, but he commanded practically no following. He also attacked Makarios and quarrelled publicly with him on a number of occasions. He even declared himself a candidate for election as President of Cyprus against Makarios, but he was persuaded to stand down. Makarios was elected by a large majority over a respected lawyer, whose motives for entering the unequal contest were not clear. Dr. Kütchük was elected Vice-President unopposed. Cyprus was quietly launched on independence in August 1960; but the last had not been heard of either Grivas or *énosis*.

In Greece, it was possible at last to revert to normality after five years of intolerable tension. Public opinion had been almost exclusively preoccupied with Cyprus since 1954. Yet characteristically, very little bitterness was shown towards the British or Americans personally. In 1959, the sense of spontaneous relief was obvious when it ceased to be necessary to appear to be bitterly hostile towards Greece's natural friends. Representatives of the NATO powers were speedily welcomed again to Athens. An agreement on nuclear weapons was signed with the USA. The Royal Navy and RAF paid official visits for the first time in many years. A particularly rapturous reception was given to President Eisenhower (December 1959). Negotiations were opened in 1960 to secure a treaty of association with the European Economic Community or 'Common Market', established by the Treaty of Rome in 1957. The interrupted progress of Greece towards a closer integration with the western world was thus resumed. Even with Turkey there was a renewal of friendly exchanges. On the other hand, the Cypriot nationalist were no longer treated as heroes. Grivas cut a ludicrous figure in Greek politics, and Makarios was received with marked coolness on his first visit to Athens as President of Cyprus in 1962.

The Greek government's unnatural flirtation with the Communist, neutralist and ex-colonial states was also quickly terminated. A few typical episodes restored relations with the Soviet Union to their normal frigidity. In 1959, Khrushchev praised the KKE in a speech in Budapest which coincided with Eisenhower's visit to Athens. There was already fear of a Communist revival in Greece, typified by the sentence of five years' imprisonment imposed on a young Communist, Manolis Glezos, who had distinguished himself as a boy by tearing down the Nazi flag from the Acropolis. When the Hungarians issued a stamp with Glezos' portrait, the Greeks retaliated with a stamp bearing the portrait of Imre Nagy, the tragic Prime Minister of Hungary who was executed after the rising of 1956. Again in 1961, when NATO manoeuvres were held in Greek and

Turkish Thrace, Khrushchev threatened that Soviet rockets would spare 'neither olive-trees nor the Acropolis'. Karamanlis returned a curt and dignified reply. Such gestures marked the return to normality. It was characteristic that an attempt was even made to restore relations between Greece and Albania (still nominally in a state of war) when the Albanians supported the Chinese Communists in their quarrel with the Soviet Union.

The same spirit soon affected the Greeks' relations with other powers towards whom they had been attracted during the Cyprus dispute. President Nasser's government of Egypt proved a disappointment: Greek property there was confiscated with inadequate compensation; Greek nationals were expelled or accused of espionage; and the expectations of mutual support in international relations proved illusory. The same was true of Yugoslavia. Exchanges continued, but they became civil rather than friendly. The Balkan Pact was pronounced defunct in 1960. In the following years, the perennial disagreements over the status of Macedonia and revision of the frontier became active again, though the Greek government insisted that there was no question to discuss. The revival of Communism in Greece was also associated with the new atmosphere of coolness in Balkan relations, since most of the prominent leaders of the KKE were known to be in East European capitals, and their courier-lines to Greece ran through Yugoslavia and Bulgaria. In Athens it was taken for granted that the left-wing party, EDA, was scarcely more than a front for the illegal KKE, though in fact there were some real differences of policy between the two.

The fundamental danger to Greece, however, lay neither in foreign threats nor in internal subversion. It lay in the chronic weakness of the national economy and the tendency to political instability, which Karamanlis' long term of office diminished but could not wholly cure. Both weaknesses came to the surface in the early 1960's, once the overriding pre-occupation with Cyprus had ceased to disguise them. Public opinion was naturally grateful to Karamanlis for achieving a settlement in Cyprus and for the return to normality. Their gratitude was shown in the general election of October 1961, which improved his majority for the third successive time. He won almost exactly half the votes and an overall majority of more than fifty seats.

But there was extreme discontent on the side of the opposition, led by George Papandreou and Sophoklis Venizelos, who contended that the elections had been fraudulently conducted with the connivance of the army and even with the approval of the king. These accusations portended a return to historic feuds with tragic implications. Even more serious for the moment were the unsolved problems of the national economy.

Economic improvement under the Karamanlis government had been considerable. Inflation had been checked and the currency stabilized. People ceased to hoard sovereigns; shipowners returned to the national flag instead of registering their ships under flags of convenience; they even invested their profits in Greece. Industrial development followed, stimulated by an Industrial Development Corporation. A new ship-yard was built at Skaramanga; an oil refinery, an aluminium plant, an atomic reactor, and the beginning of an iron and steel industry were established. The tobacco industry recovered some of its export markets, though it had to supplement those in western Europe with new ones in the Soviet bloc. Tobacco was rivalled by tourism as the major contributor to the balance of payments. But, for all these improvements, the national economy still suffered from uncured weaknesses, chiefly the lack of indigenous facilities to exploit raw materials and the need to import a high proportion of the nation's food. Of the relatively backward industrial development, too high a proportion was still in the control of foreign capital.

The economy had now to take a number of new strains. During 1962, US civil aid came to an end (though military aid continued); the negotiations with the European Economic Community ended with the admission of Greece as an Associate; and partial settlement was reached of Greece's long-standing indebtedness to creditors in the USA and to private creditors in Britain. In each case the result was to add to the strain on the balance of payments. Efforts were made to correct the chronic imbalance by every kind of device. Western governments were encouraged to establish industries in Greece. Economic missions were sent by both NATO and the Organisation for European Co-operation and Development (OECD) to study Greece's problems. New trade agreements were signed with countries in the Soviet bloc, and even diplomatic relations were restored with Poland and Czechoslovakia. The international Trade Fair was revived at Salonika. It was nevertheless clear that the economic recovery which had begun in 1952 was slowing down a decade later. The fact that nearly one-third of the budget was still devoted to defence—without which under-employment would have been still more conspicuous—spoke for itself.

The stringency of the economic state of the country led to a number of ugly demonstrations. Strikes became increasingly frequent, by workers of all kinds—in agriculture, tobacco and horticulture, in building and transport—and also by public servants and teachers. Taxes went up, but salaries did not; and the opposition contended that the social services were deplorably neglected. An unlucky by-product of the bitterness over economic hardship was a new grievance against the royal family, whom republicans attacked as an expensive luxury. Queen Frederika, who had a reputation for autocracy not unconnected with her German descent, was accused of mishandling a royal fund raised during the civil war for relief of refugees. An increase of the civil list was opposed in parliament, and so was the dowry of Princess Sophia on her marriage to a Spanish prince. Attacks on members of the royal family, including King Paul himself, began to multiply ominously. They were encouraged by the leader of the opposition, George Papandreou, who repeatedly accused the king of involving himself in politics. At the same time, relations between the king and his govermnent were not easy.

After a number of trivial and exaggerated incidents, matters came to a head in 1963. King Paul and Queen Frederika were invited to make a state visit to London, which they accepted. Criticism of the visit was heard both in London and Athens. In London, left-wing organizations attacked the queen as a 'fascist' and held the crown responsible for the continued detention of so-called 'political prisoners', most of whom had been sentenced for crimes against the state during the civil war. Matters were made worse when the queen, on a private visit to London in April 1963, was molested by a hostile crowd of Greek and British demonstrators on behalf of the 'political prisoners'. An obscure apology by the Foreign Secretary in Parliament led to redoubled fury in both capitals. In Athens the opposition put down a motion of censure on the government, but found it difficult to force a vote over the 'political prisoners' because they had themselves been in office when most of the sentences were passed. Still worse was to come in May, when a left-wing deputy of EDA, Grigorios Lambrakis, was killed in a Salonika street by a motor vehicle after speaking at a meeting of the local Peace Committee.

Those responsible for Lambrakis' death, including senior police officers, were eventually convicted over three years later, though only of culpable homicide, not of murder. In the meantime Communist propaganda made the utmost of its opportunity. A monstrous picture was assembled and presented to the public of a fascist monarchy, a police state, a corrupt and incompetent government, and a systematic oppression of national heroes in concentration-camps. To this hotch-potch the protest organizers in London inconsequently added the issue of nuclear weapons. The inflammation of feeling in both capitals was such that Karamanlis advised the king to postpone his state visit. The king, and more particularly the queen, firmly refused the Prime Minister's advice. Karamanlis therefore resigned in June, after nearly eight years in office. It was widely believed that economic problems played a contributory part in his decision, but this he vigorously denied. Papandreou immediately claimed the right to form a government, but the king formed instead a government drawn exclusively from ERE under a former constitutional adviser to the crown, Panagiotis Pipinelis. The state visit to London duly took place in July. Despite some ugly demonstrations, it was not unsuccessful.

The political crisis, however, was not over. Pipinelis won a vote of confidence and announced a general election for November; but in deference to the opposition's refusal to regard him as neutral, because he had held office under Karamanlis, he resigned in September and gave way to another caretaker government under a senior judge. There could then be no question of the fairness of the elections, but their result was inconclusive. Papandreou's Centre Union (EK) won a small majority over Karamanlis' National Radical Union (ERE), but the balance of power rested with the Communist-sponsored Union of the Democratic Left (EDA), which won thirty seats. Karamanlis resigned the leadership of ERE to his deputy, Panagiotis Kanellopoulos, and left the country. Papandreou formed a minority government, which won a vote of confidence with the support of EDA: but he refused to be dependent on Communist votes, and resigned. Kanellopoulos tried and failed to form a government. King Paul therefore dissolved parliament again, after appointing yet another caretaker government. At the immediately following general election, in February 1964, Papandreou won an unexpectedly decisive victory, with an overall majority of nearly fifty seats.

It was the first time for many years in Greece that a general election had placed a single party in power in succession to another single party. Both parties were, of course, in effect coalitions; but such is usually the case in politics. Papandreou was later to have trouble with both his left and his right wings. But at the beginning of 1964 a watershed seemed to have been passed in Greece's progress towards political stability. It was also marked by a number of changes in the *dramatis personae*. Karamanlis had settled abroad; Sophoklis Venizelos died during the general election; King Paul, striken with cancer, lived only long enough to swear in the new government. The new king was the handsome twenty-three-year-old Constantine II, who had won a gold medal as a yachtsman at the 1960 Olympic Games and was about to marry the beautiful young Danish Princess Anne-Marie. The new reign could hardly have begun under happier auspices. With the traditional republicans in office instead of the traditional monarchists, the young king was assured of an equally loyal government and opposition, which he would not have had in the reverse case.

Old enough to be the new king's grandfather, the new Prime Minister at first displayed a protective benevolence towards him. There seemed no need to revive the traditional quarrel which had divided Constantine I from the Venizelists, and had nearly broken out again between King Paul and Papandreou. The new government was ostensibly more concerned with social justice than with constitutional wrangles. The defence budget was cut by 10 per cent to finance increased expenditure on social services and education. The tempo of releases of Communist prisoners was increased. But on the whole the new government's policy differed only in emphasis from that of its predecessor. Papandreou was hampered by unsolved economic problems, particularly the unwillingness of the western members of EEC to absorb Greece's agricultural surpluses, and of NATO to provide adequate military aid. His policies were also undeniably inflationary. These problems might have been mitigated, however, if the stability of the Greek, political scene had not again been shaken by severe crises. A renewed outbreak of violence in Cyprus overshadowed 1964; and a domestic crisis in defence policy brought down the government and shook the monarchy in 1965.

The new crisis in Cyprus arose from the unworkable character of the constitution imposed by the Zürich-London agreements of 1959. The elaborate system of checks and balances in practice enabled the Turkish minority to frustrate all administration, which they did. After months of friction, Makarios announced at the end of 1963 his intention to revise the constitution unilaterally. The virtual abrogation of the Turkish Cypriots' rights seemed to them only a first step towards *énosis*, as it probably would have been. Communal violence immediately broke out. It was halted for the time being by the intervention of British troops from the bases established on the island, at the request of the Cypriot government; and then by the arrival of a UN emergency force, in which the British troops were incorporated. But the tension continued, aggravated by rumours of a Turkish invasion, followed by Greek counter-manoeuvres in nearby waters. General Grivas returned to Cyprus to take command of all Greek forces in June 1964. Two months later Turkish aircraft bombed Greek positions in the north of the island. The real possibility of war was emphasized by the withdrawal of Greek forces from NATO command, to be held in readiness for action.

The violent phase of the crisis had passed over by the end of the year, and a strange quiet descended on the island, lightly policed by UN forces. But the crisis left an uneasy state of relations between the Greek government and Makarios, whom Papandreou accused of sabotaging the cause of *énosis*. Eventually the two leaders arrived at a new statement of policy, based on unrestricted independence for Cyprus with a right to self-determination. A resolution consistent with this policy was successfully steered through the UN General Assembly at the end of 1965, but it was without effect owing to the large number of abstentions. It became clear once more that the only hope of a satisfactory settlement lay in some kind of bilateral agreement between Greece and Turkey. This was difficult to achieve after the renewed tension of 1964, which had led to the expulsion of many Greek residents from Turkey and some ominous threats directed at the Patriarchate. Negotiations were nevertheless spasmodically renewed between the two governments, though with little to show for them. Since the Greeks persisted in believing that the basis of negotiations was *énosis* for Cyprus, coupled with compensations for Turkey, it was not surprising that they proved abortive.

Embarrassing though the renewed commotion over Cyprus was for Papandreou, it was not this that brought about his quarrel with the young king and the downfall of his government. A still more embarrassing problem was the control of the armed forces, of which the king was the constitutional Commander-in-Chief. After eleven years of right-wing government, it was inevitable that most of the senior officers were in sympathy with the outgoing government which had appointed them. Papandreou sought to replace them with nominees of his own. At the same time, he sought evidence of a conspiracy within the army which he believed had helped to defeat his electoral ambitions in 1961. The quest for conspirators rebounded against him, for evidence emerged of a left-wing conspiracy within the army under the name of *Aspida* ('Shield'), for which eighteen officers were eventually convicted in 1967. Moreover, there were strong rumours that the left-wing officers had been associated with the Prime Minister's son, Andreas Papandreou, a former professor at the University of California, who had renounced his American citizenship to join his father's government and was generally looked on as his political heir. His emergence was linked by public opinion with a distinct incline of his father's policies towards the Left. Apart from the affair of the armed forces, other symptoms were the Prime Minister's acceptance of an invitation to Moscow (though this proved abortive) and the entry into the government of Elias Tsirimokos (once a leader in EAM and now in EDA).

The crisis over the military appointments came to a head in May 1965, when Papandreou dismissed his Minister of Defence for failing to carry out the policy of replacement with sufficient vigour. He then sought to assume the post himself. The king, upon whom the appointment constitutionally depended, accepted the dismissal of the Minister but declined to appoint Papandreou in his place. In so acting, he was within his constitutional rights, though the exchange of letters in which the king and his Prime Minister argued their positions showed that Constantine (who could hardly have framed his letters himself) had been unwisely advised. Constantine believed that he was protecting the armed forces from a demoralizing political purge. Papandreou considered that the young king was meddling in affairs which were not his business. 'The King reigns, but the People rule' was Papandreou's slogan. He offered his resignation in July, expecting that the king would either give way or dissolve parliament. Instead, the king dismissed him and set about forming a new government from the existing parliament. It was a bold move with damaging consequences.

A succession of would-be Prime Ministers tried and failed to form a government. At last Stephanos Stephanopoulos, who had been Papandreou's Deputy Prime Minister, deserted his leader and formed a coalition with the help of Elias Tsirimokos from EDA, Kanellopoulos from ERE, and a considerable bloc of Papandreou's former supporters from the Centre Union. Papandreou reacted angrily. His supporters, abetted by the Communists, organized demonstrations in the streets, strikes and mass rallies. In his speeches Papandreou denounced the new government and the king himself, virtually threatening revolution and the overthrow of the monarchy. For a few weeks the threat seemed real. But the king stood firm, and Stephanopoulos won a vote of confidence in September by a narrow margin. The crisis was temporarily over, but it had had two grave results, for which the king's official advisers were principally to blame. By provoking the disruption of Papandreou's Centre Union, it had destroyed the healthy growth of a two-party system. It had also re-opened the old constitutional wound by establishing a government of 'king's men' opposed by a party of republicans. There were already fears of a reversion to military dictatorship.

No one expected the Stephanopoulos government, with its heterogeneous support and tiny majority, to last long. In fact it survived for nearly a year and a half, at the price of remaining entirely ineffectual. No progress was made in secret talks with the Turks on Cyprus. A succession of strikes by railwaymen, agricultural workers, government employees, teachers and even doctors, emphasized the general discontent. Foreign investors began to lose confidence again, though the economy remained surprisingly buoyant. The government was kept in power chiefly by the reluctance of its supporters to face another general election. The Greeks appeared to be losing the control over their own destiny which had been gained at the price of grim experience. It was almost as if they had grown tired of stability. The situation was too bad to last, but the impulse needed to end it was slow in coming. The resignation of Tsirimokos as Foreign Minister in April 1966 nearly brought down the government, but it was reinforced by the transfer of two votes from the opposition, which led to accusations of bribery. Kanellopoulos eventually withdrew his support at the end of the year. Having lost support on both his left and his right wing, Stephanopoulos had no choice but to resign. He was succeeded by a 'service' government charged to hold elections in May 1967.

The almost featureless interregnum of the Stephanopoulos coalition was notable chiefly for two spectacular trials, each full of political implications. The alleged assassins of Grigorios Lambrakis in Salonika in 1963 were finally convicted, though not of murder or political conspiracy, at the end of 1966. This was a qualified success for the left wing of Greek politics, to whom Lambrakis had become an ideological hero. The trial of the officers alleged to be involved in the left-wing conspiracy (*Aspida*) within the armed forces, ended early in 1967 with numerous convictions and some acquittals. This was regarded as a political success by right-wing politicians, but it was not the end of the story. Their attempts to implicate Andreas Papandreou in the plot had not succeeded; and there were strong pressures in favour of a general amnesty. Andreas Papandreou could not be indicted for complicity with *Aspida* so long as he enjoyed immunity as a Deputy, but this immunity would lapse on the dissolution of parliament. His father then proposed that the new electoral law should extend parliamentary immunity for long enough to cover the electoral period. Kanellopoulos would not agree; and Papandreou refused to support a bill which did not include such a provision. Faced with a deadlock between the two principal party-leaders, the 'service' government resigned.

The Inheritance of Constantine (1952–1967)

The king again passed over Papandreou and invited Kanellopoulos to form a government. He did so, but knew he could not win a vote of confidence in parliament. He therefore asked for a dissolution without facing parliament. In agreeing to his request, the king took an unusual but not an unconstitutional decision, probably influenced by fear that Papandreou would win the election. Polling day was fixed for 28th May, but the poll never took place. Early in the morning of 21st April a group of army officers seized power by a well-organized *coup d'état* to which the king was probably not (as they originally claimed) a willing party. Their justification was an alleged plot by the Communists, which was to be sparked off by a mass rally addressed by Papandreou in Salonika two days later. A number of articles of the constitution were suspended by decree, and a government was formed consisting partly of colonels and generals, and partly of non-political civilians, under the premiership of the senior Public Prosecutor to the Supreme Court, Constantine Kollias. The civilian element in the government was introduced in deference to the king, who would not otherwise have agreed to swear it in. On his first public appearance with his new ministers, he emphasized his desire that parliamentary government should be restored as soon as possible. But he was already a prisoner of his own mistakes.

The new government ran true to form. Like other military dictatorships, its early measures were alternately popular, savage, and ridiculous. Among the initially popular measures were decrees fixing prices, increasing pensions, re-distributing land, and compelling government departments to deal with all complaints within two days. Less popular were decrees forbidding trade unions to meet, or any other gatherings of more than five persons. Worse was soon to follow. Newspapers were submitted to strict censorship and required to publish exactly what was supplied by the government. Many of them, including some of the right wing and centre as well as the left, suspended publication rather than comply.[1] Many thousands of alleged Communists were arrested. Proofs were said to have been found of a Communist plot. Military courts were established in Athens

[1] Among the newspaper proprietors who refused to publish under these conditions was Mrs. Eleni Vlakhou, daughter of the author of the celebrated 'open letter' to Hitler in 1941.

and Salonika. Many parliamentary leaders, including Kanellopoulos, George Papandreou, and his son Andreas were taken into custody. Although some were later released, Andreas Papandreou was indicted for treason. All politicans were denounced as corrupt and unworthy of trust.

The new leaders regarded themselves as the trustees of morality and Christianity. They therefore dismissed the Archbishop of Athens and the Holy Synod which governed the Church in Greece, replacing them with nominees of their own. They also condemned long hair on boys and mini-skirts on girls, and ordered both to go to church. Even foreign tourists were held to be subject to some of these regulations, though the government was anxious not to frighten them away altogether. What they wanted was a moral reformation, for which they set an austere example themselves. It must be counted to their credit that an American corporation, which had broken off negotiations on a plan for the economic development of Crete and the western Peloponnese in 1966, renewed and completed them in 1967; and the success was due to the fact that under the new regime no bribes were found necessary. But like other well-intentioned moralists, the new leaders did not always escape making themselves ridiculous. For example, they deprived the celebrated film-star, Melina Mercouri, of her citizenship for criticizing them; they banned the songs of Mikis Theodorakis, a leading composer who was also a left-wing deputy; and they censored the tragedies and comedies of the classical theatre. Many other crudities and inanities of the eras of Pangalos (1925) and Metaxas (1936) were also repeated.

There were differences, however. In 1967, unlike 1925 and 1936, there was no pre-eminent leader of the *coup* to be identified. It was organized by officers below the highest rank, who differed in that respect from Pangalos and Metaxas. One of their first actions was to retire five of the most senior generals. The revolt of 1967 was in fact a revolt of the colonels, who did not command undivided support among their senior colleagues. This made the consequences and even the intentions of the *coup* harder to assess. The new government was composed of men largely without experience of administrative responsibility at the highest level. In that respect again they differed from Pangalos and Metaxas, each of whom had actually been Prime

Minister already when he seized power. The new leaders of 1967 were virtually unknown men, and they showed some uncertainty what to do with power when they had it. Although they declared their intention to restore democracy of a kind, it was not of the kind that Greece was used to. The road back to a true parliamentary democracy looked as hard and long as in 1936.

This was not because the new rulers of Greece wished to rule unconstitutionally, however contemptuous they might be of the system which they had overthrown. They were careful to obtain the king's endorsement of their acts, and they quickly restored the one article of the constitution (the equivalent of *Habeas Corpus*) which the king had no power to suspend. The fact that their contempt for the professional politicians was widely shared accounts for the comparative docility with which the *coup d'état* was received. But such docility could not be counted on for long. The new government therefore established a commission of jurists and other experts to draft a new constitution, the chief characteristic of which was to be the separation of the executive and the legislature on Gaullist lines. Two long-term consequences were immediately apparent: parliamentary democracy as it had been known for a century, with occasional interruptions, was in abeyance; and the position of the king was gravely, perhaps fatally weakened.

By the end of 1967, things had gone from bad to worse. The dictatorial character of the new government became steadily more apparent, and one of the Colonels, George Papadopoulos, emerged as its strong man. Apart from thousands of detentions without trial, severe pressure was put on those who wished to restore democracy. Two former ministers of the National Radical Union were indicted (though they escaped punishment) for trivial offences; Eleni Vlakhou, the newspaper proprietor, was put under house arrest; civil servants were obliged to sign declarations of loyalty to the government; hundreds of senior officers were prematurely retired; the governor of the Bank of Greece felt compelled to resign; and so, eventually, did four civilian members of the government, including the Foreign Minister. None of these could be accused of holding subversive views. Of those who could, a few dozen were brought to trial later in the year, though Andreas Papandreou was not among them and his father, an aged and broken man, was released. Ugly rumours about the conditions of detention seemed to have some support when the composer, Mikis Theodorakis, arrested in August, was reported unfit to stand trial three months later.

These developments found public opinion apathetic, if not positively contented with the new regime. But they disturbed the king and other prominent figures. Kanellopoulos denounced the government at two press conferences in Athens, and Karamanlis did the same in Paris. The disapproval of Greece's allies was also emphatic. The United States stopped all but a trickle of arms supplies; the European Investment Bank of the EEC witheld a loan already negotiated; the Council of Europe seriously debated the expulsion of Greece. It was not these reactions, however, which brought the crisis to a head, but the perennial problem of Cyprus. The military government sought to re-open negotiations with Turkey at a top-level conference, held near the common frontier in September, but without success. In November General Grivas, as commander-in-chief of both Greek and Cypriot forces, launched a vicious attack on the Turkish minority in the north of the island, as a result of which the Turkish government mobilized an invasion force. War was narrowly averted by allied intervention. The price Greece had to pay was the dismissal of Grivas and the removal of the Greek troops illegally infiltrated since 1963.

Such a fiasco, which appeared to postpone the prospect of *énosis* indefinitely, could be expected to discredit the military government. The king, supported by his civilian Prime Minister, Constantine Kollias, saw the opportunity to dismiss his military bosses and re-establish his own power. But his attempt to do so, on 13th December 1967, was an even more ignominious fiasco than the government had suffered in Cyprus. Leaving Athens in the control of the Colonels, the king flew to the north to rally royalist support. There was little or none to be rallied: the army remained loyal to the dictatorship; and the king fled to Rome within twenty-four hours, accompanied by his family and Kollias. Papadopoulos then appointed a Regent, and had himself sworn in as Prime Minister. But he was careful not to declare the monarchy abolished. The king, he said, had 'voluntarily abstained' from his duties, but he was welcome to return.

The reconstructed military government was in a strong position as a result of these events. They knew it, and acted accordingly. Papadopoulos and his colleagues confidently divested themselves of military rank, as if to emphasize that they had come to stay. They granted a partial amnesty at the turn of the year. It included Andreas Papandreou, who immediately left the country; Mrs. Vlakhou, who had already escaped from house arrest to take refuge in England; and eventually even Mikis Theodorakis, who seemed to be little the worse for his incarceration; but it did not include those designated as suspected Communists. The government also promised to hold a plebiscite on the new constitution, the draft of which was delivered to them by the end of the year; but it was not immediately published, and their displeasure with the work of the drafting commission was unconcealed. Finally, they sent a number of emissaries—or at least allowed them to go—to see the king in Rome and discuss terms on which he might return.

One reason for which they might have wanted him back was to secure their own recognition by foreign powers—a problem which had not arisen after the original *coup d'état*, since the king had endorsed it. But the difficulty was removed early in 1968, when the powers began to accord recognition without more ado. The king, who had at first insisted on the restoration of his constitutional powers as a condition of his return, soon found that if he returned in the immediate future, it would be in a greatly weakened position. After prolonged hesitation, it became clear in the new year that he would not return for the time being. The new government suggested in an indefinite manner that he might do so after the proposed plebiscite had ratified the new constitution during the course of 1968. But in any case the end of an era had come. The 'crowned democracy', as it had been known and with the powers it had enjoyed since 1864, had unmistakably had its day.

CHAPTER XI

The Return of the Republic (1968–1976)

The military dictatorship lasted more than seven years, much longer than any other unconstitutional interruption in Greece's history. Although it finally collapsed in ignominy, during the early years it appeared to be stable, benefiting from popular apathy if not popularity. A critical point was passed with the establishment of a new constitution on 15th November 1968. The document was unworthy of the name of constitution since it was fraudulent in every respect: it was imposed by the Colonels, repudiating the work of their own constitutional commission; it was approved by a blatantly contrived referendum; it was never fully operative; and it was declared null and void on the restoration of democracy in 1974. Nevertheless it provoked surprisingly little internal upheaval or external remonstrance.

The so-called constitution sought to change the regime in a markedly republican direction, and this aspect of it alone was to prove enduring. It sought to regularize a number of arrangements which had already been put into effect on the departure of the king. Although the monarchy was still not abolished, its powers were severely circumscribed. They were to be exercised for the time being by the Regent, an office already held by General Zoïtakis, who had been a tacit accomplice in the military *coup*. But the real power was concentrated in the hands of the Prime Minister. Papadopoulos further increased his ascendancy by assuming other offices from time to time as well. He was also fortunate to secure the support of Pipinelis, formerly constitutional adviser to King George II and briefly Prime Minister in 1963, as Foreign Minister to deal with the crisis in relations with Turkey over Cyprus.

The Return of the Republic (1968–1976)

A certain degree of superficial respectability, or at least of acquiescence, was thus gained by the dictatorship in the eyes of the outside world, and even of some influential Greeks. The United States government began to resume the supply of heavy arms, which had been suspended in 1967, since it was by means of American tanks that the Colonels had seized power. Aristotle Onassis, and later his former brother-in-law and rival in the shipping industry, Stavros Niarkhos, were persuaded to discuss plans for large-scale capital investment with the government. The support of the armed forces for the dictatorship was secured by a far-reaching purge of suspect officers and the conferment of exceptional privileges on those who remained loyal. They were in fact placed above political control, as guardians of the nation, while the rest of the population was subjected to martial law. All publications were liable to censorship, though it was capriciously applied. Most of the articles of the constitution guaranteeing personal rights were suspended: these included freedom of assembly, the formation of political parties, rights of asylum, and freedom from arrest without warrant. The restrictions were accompanied by promises from Papadopoulos, which were repeated in various forms every December, that they were only temporary and that full democracy would be restored as soon as conditions were normal and the Greek people was sufficiently re-educated to justify it.

The Greek people, confronted with overwhelming force and a powerful secret police under military control (known as the ESA), had no alternative but to acquiesce. But there were notable exceptions. At home, the moral opposition was led by George Papandreou and Panagiotis Kanellopoulos, who became national heroes in the eyes of democratic Greeks. Both were put under house arrest for publicly criticizing the dictatorship. When Papandreou died on 1st November 1968, his funeral was the occasion for a vast demonstration in Athens at which Kanellopoulos delivered a memorable address. In 1969 Kanellopoulos made a pact with Papandreou's successor, George Mavros, to work together for the restoration of democracy. The external opposition to the dictatorship had several major spokesmen—Karamanlis in Paris, Papandreou's son Andreas, and the Communist leader Brillakis—but they were less inclined to co-operate with each other.

The Return of the Republic (1968-1976)

There were two notable characteristics of the national and international reaction to the Colonels' regime. Among the Greeks, the Communist Party was not conspicuous in its opposition. It was divided within itself between those in Greece and those abroad, as well as ideologically. At one time no less than five rival groups claimed to represent the true leadership of the KKE. Moreover, several ex-Communists enthusiastically supported the dictatorship, and put their services at its disposal for the preparation of propaganda material. On the whole, opposition to the Colonels was strongest not at the extremes— Communist and Royalist—but among those naturally grouped on the left and right of the Centre. The only serious attempt to assassinate Papadopoulos was made by a loyal and patriotic young officer, Lieutenant Alexander Panagoulis, who belonged at the time to no political party. He was caught and sentenced to death, but reprieved, though kept in barbarous conditions.

Abroad, there was a somewhat similar division in the spectrum of reactions. Neither the United States nor the Soviet governments displayed any particular desire to be rid of the dictatorship. Many European states—not to mention the African dictatorships, which took such things for granted—were inclined to treat the Colonels as a perfectly natural phenomenon. There was even a perverse reaction on the part of Europeans who were tired of hearing Greece called the 'cradle of democracy', to regard the fate of the Greeks as no more than they deserved. Honourable exceptions were the Scandinavians, the Dutch, and more surprisingly the Yugoslavs, at the official level, as well as many individual sympathizers.

The reputation of the dictatorship began to be seriously damaged with the widespread allegation of systematic torture practised on political opponents. The accusations were strongly pressed by the Scandinavian governments in the European Commission of Human Rights, and were investigated under Italian chairmanship during 1968. In spite of obstruction by the Greek government, enough evidence was obtained to leave little doubt that the accusations were true: in fact, they were understated. The responsibility lay mainly on the Military Security Police (ESA) under Brigadier Ioannidis, who was directly responsible to Papadopoulos. In 1969 a further investigation was carried out under Dutch chairmanship on behalf of the Council of Europe, which reported that the Greek regime was 'undemocratic, illiberal, authoritarian, and oppressive'.

The immediate consequence of the two investigations was that the Greek government was forced to resign from the Council of Europe under threat of expulsion—a threat which was supported even by the inordinately tolerant British government. But the western alliance as a whole continued to tolerate the dictatorship, on the grounds that Greece formed an essential part of NATO. Leading Ministers, including successive British Foreign Secretaries, declared that they wished things were otherwise, but they could not interfere in the internal affairs of an allied country. By allowing senior officers and members of their governments to make both private and official visits to Greece, they provided the Colonels with opportunities for propaganda which were skilfully exploited.

The United States government went still further. Allegations that the Central Intelligence Agency (CIA) had helped Papadopoulos to seize power were probably false, although he had benefited from CIA training. But the US authorities were not slow in reconciling themselves to the new regime. From the beginning of 1970, at the latest, when a new Ambassador was appointed in Athens, American policy became one of active support. American and Soviet strategists were engaged in a duel in the eastern Mediterranean. It became more intense after the 'Six-day War' of June 1967 between Israel and the Arab states, which closed the Suez Canal. American strategy required not only Greece's continued membership of NATO, but also bases to protect Israel. The need became greater with the growth of the Soviet fleet in the Mediterranean, the apparent subservience of Egypt to Soviet policy, and the overthrow of the pro-western Libyan monarchy in 1971.

Signs of American support for the Colonels became increasingly clear during this anxious period, but it was far from being unchallenged in the USA. The large and influential Greek population of the USA was divided, so that Congress and the White House were subjected to conflicting pressures. In August 1971 the House of Representatives voted again to suspend military supplies to Greece, but President Nixon overrode the vote on grounds of national interest. Later in the same year Vice-President Agnew, who was partly Greek by descent, paid an official visit to Athens, which was warmly welcomed by the Colonels but bitterly resented by democratic Greeks. The climax of the reconciliation between the two governments came in September 1972, when an agreement was signed by which the US Sixth Fleet would enjoy home-port facilities at Piraeus. Some opposition was expressed in Congress at this new commitment, in the wake of Vietnam, to establish a permanent base on foreign soil.

At the same time the dictatorship was achieving unexpected successes in other directions. There was a marked improvement in relations with the Communist states. Trade agreements were signed in 1970 with the Soviet Union, East Germany, Bulgaria, Rumania and Albania. Full diplomatic relations were established with Albania in 1971, and with Communist China in 1972. An opening into Africa was established by exchanges of official visits with Ethiopia, Libya, Congo-Kinshasa and the Central African Republic. Although the military dictatorship was regarded with strong disapproval by most of the international institutions of Europe—the EEC, the Commission of Human Rights and the Council of Europe—diplomatic relations survived intact with all European countries. Better still, the French Foreign Minister accepted an invitation to Athens and the Greek Foreign Minister was invited to London. These were not inconsiderable successes for Papadopoulos.

His diplomatic successes were marred by some further failures. He had a sharp quarrel with Archbishop Makarios early in 1972, when the latter imported Czech arms into Cyprus. General Grivas was allowed, presumably with the connivance of the Greek government, to return to Cyprus as a thorn in Makarios' flesh. The Czech arms were in the end turned over to the United Nations peace-keeping force, which had been in Cyprus since 1964. Although Papadopoulos won that round, he had made a mortal enemy of Makarios. In other cases his inept diplomacy did further damage to his reputation, especially in dealing with opponents of the regime who enjoyed foreign sympathy. In September 1971 Lady Fleming, a Greek by birth and the widow of the discoverer of penicillin, was arrested while trying to help Lieutenant Panagoulis escape from gaol, and forcibly deported to Britain after being sentenced to sixteen months' imprisonment. In April 1972 a leading figure of the academic resistance, Professor George Mangakis, was released from gaol at the request of the West German authorities because he held a Chair at a German University; but simultaneously the West German Ambassador was declared *persona non grata*. Papadopoulos even contrived to insult the American Ambassador, who was presumably his best friend in Athens.

From first to last, the Colonels showed a total incomprehension of foreign reactions. It was almost impossible to name any Greek of international reputation—at least after the death of Pipinelis in July 1970—who did not regard them with contempt. This meant that every step they took against their opponents was bound to cause them unfavourable publicity abroad. Yet seemingly oblivious of the consequences, they played a cat-and-mouse game with the opposition which oscillated between brutality and farce. The whole intellectual, artistic and political élite of the country were potentially their victims; and these were precisely the people whose fate was bound to attract foreign attention and criticism.

The measures taken to suppress merely vocal opposition varied with the strength of its voices. During 1969 some individual freedoms were restored and press censorship was suspended; but martial law remained in force. A decree limiting the number of trade unions and defining their right to strike was promulgated, and a new press law was drafted, but withdrawn after much criticism and replaced by a new draft in 1970. The enforcement of these restrictive measures was haphazard. Books and articles containing clearly hostile propaganda were sometimes published without retaliation, but at other times editors and journalists were arrested and imprisoned, or their publication frustrated by administrative means. All such proceedings were wholly unconstitutional, since the Parliament nominally established under the 1968 constitution never came into existence. Instead, a purely advisory 'mini-parliament' of fifty-six members, partly elected by corporate bodies and partly nominated by Papadopoulos, but all under his absolute control, was set up in November 1970. Its members were promised increased powers, and the Greek people increased privileges, if they behaved themselves.

Such treatment was humiliating enough. Much more oppressive and capricious were the government's dealings with the active opposition. In 1969 Papadopoulos removed from office twenty-one senior judges and public prosecutors for failing to deliver the convictions and sentences which he required. When the highest court, the Council of State, reinstated them on appeal, he dismissed its President and packed the court with his own nominees. During 1970 he introduced stiffer penalties for so-called terrorism, but also released some 500 detainees. In March of the same year a momentous trial took place of thirty-four members of an organization called Democratic Defence. They included men of the highest repute, for whom Kanellopoulos spoke in their defence; but many long sentences were imposed.

The cat-and-mouse game continued during the next two years. Some concessions were made. The scope of the military courts was reduced; martial law was lifted except in Athens, Piraeus and Salonika; all detainees were released except for fifty 'dangerous Communists'. But still other arrests continued, for activities which would not normally be criminal anywhere outside authoritarian countries. In a number of prominent cases where it would scarcely have been possible to obtain convictions, administrative exile to remote parts of the country was used as a substitute for imprisonment. Still the opposition not only persisted but grew.

At the same time Papadopoulos' personal power also appeared to grow. In August 1971 a reshuffle of his government reduced the number of ministries from eighteen to thirteen and displaced many of the fellow-officers who had helped to bring him to power. His two principal colleagues, Brigadier Pattakos and Colonel Makarezos, who had been Ministers of Domestic and Economic Affairs respectively, were promoted into non-executive posts as first and second Deputy Prime Ministers. All the other Ministers and Secretaries-General were required to resign, and some were appointed to control the seven new administrative regions into which the country was divided. Ostensibly this was a method of decentralizing the government, but it also had the effect of removing rival conspirators from the centre of power.

In March 1972 Papadopoulos dismissed the Regent, General Zoïtakis, who had dared to question some of his decisions, and assumed the office himself. He remained Prime Minister, and held at different times the portfolios of Defence, Foreign Affairs and Education as well. His portrait, and his alone, appeared everywhere in public places. His symbol, the phoenix, replaced the king's head on new coins. His rule became increasingly personal, capricious and even inconsistent. Thus, he reversed the reshuffle of August 1971 in July 1972, bringing back many of his ex-officer colleagues from the provinces to Athens.

His whims were liberal and repressive by turns. During 1972 he released more detainees and suspended martial law in Salonika. But he treated unrest among students and their teachers with extreme severity. Professor John Pesmazoglou, who had negotiated the original Treaty of Association with the EEC in 1961, was dismissed from Athens University for supposedly encouraging student dissidence and other fabricated offences, and was more than once arrested, imprisoned without trial, and exiled. Many other leading academics shared his fate, as did writers, broadcasters, lawyers, parliamentarians, senior officers, trade unionists and everyone who dared to express an independent opinion. In March 1973 the government took power to revoke the deferment of military service for students who neglected their studies, and in the same month the police broke up a 'sit-in' at the Athens Law School. The promise of an eventual restoration of democracy became more and more remote.

It was increasingly evident that Papadopoulos' structure of a 'Greece of the Christian Greeks', as his propagandists called it, was built upon sand. Even what was hailed as Greece's 'economic miracle' was largely fraudulent. The marked improvement of the general standard of living in the early years of the dictatorship was the fruit of measures taken under previous governments, particularly that of Karamanlis from 1955 to 1963. A high growth rate was maintained from 1970 to 1973, reinforced by a boom in tourism from 1971. But the accompanying rate of inflation was a severe penalty: in 1972 it was the highest in Europe, and in 1973 it exceeded 30 per cent. There were also setbacks in the investment programme. The contract with the American Litton Corporation for development in Crete and the western Peloponnese was cancelled, and the agreements with Onassis and Niarkhos for new investment broke down in 1971. The early reputation of the Colonels for financial honesty was marred by suspicions, which were to prove justified, of widespread corruption. A belated prospect of economic recovery, which was opened up by the discovery of oil under the north Aegean seabed, led only to a disastrous deterioration of relations with Turkey.

By 1973 there could be little doubt that the days of the dictatorship were numbered. Papadopoulos was desperately seeking a new device to strengthen his weakening position. An opportunity seemed to present itself in May 1973, when a mutiny took place in the Navy. It was suppressed, though one destroyer escaped to Italy. Papadopoulos convinced himself that the king and his supporters were responsible. He arrested many naval officers and right-wing politicians, including Evangelos Averoff, a former Foreign Minister, who had in fact been in touch with the plotters. He also took the opportunity to abolish the monarchy, introducing a new republican regime under his own Presidency. The republic was ratified by an unashamedly contrived plebiscite on 29th July. Spyros Markezinis accepted the post of Prime Minister which Papadopoulos vacated, but all power remained in the latter's hands. In a show of confidence and magnanimity, he proclaimed a general amnesty, suspended martial law throughout the country, and promised elections in 1974. It was the last shot in his locker.

The first blow in the downfall of Papadopoulos was struck by the Athens students. In November 1973 a 'sit-in' was organized at the Athens Polytechnic. During the night of 16th–17th November armed police, supported by army tanks, were sent to break into the Polytechnic. In doing so they caused heavy casualties, including more than twenty dead. Papadopoulos and Markezinis found it in their hearts to congratulate the perpetrators of this atrocity, but it turned the stomachs of most senior officers. A group among them determined that Papadopoulos must go, but unfortunately the only instrument available for the purpose was Brigadier Ioannidis, head of the Military Security Police. He willingly obliged by arresting Papadopoulos on 25th November, and put in his place the respectable General Gizikis, who in turn became his own instrument. A nonentity was installed in Markezinis' place. The outcome was little improvement in Greece's prospects, for Ioannidis, the real master of power, was a man who would have been perfectly at home in the Gestapo, whereas Papadopoulos had been no more formidable than a Latin-American *caudillo*.

Martial law was at once restored, and repression of the opposition resumed. A respite was gained through the renewed war between Israel and the Arab states in October 1973, which strengthened the American government's anxiety to maintain a stable regime in Greece. On the other hand, the newly elected British Labour government in March 1974 showed signs of firmer antagonism to the Greek dictatorship. The new Foreign Secretary, James Callaghan, cancelled a courtesy visit of the Royal Navy to Piraeus, and the Liberal leader in Athens, George Mavros, expressed approval of his gesture. Ioannidis then arrested Mavros and deported him to a remote island. It was only the most conspicuous of many outrages which filled the first months of the year.

The final crisis of the regime began in April 1974 with a confrontation between Greece and Turkey over rival claims to the Aegean seabed. It seemed to the Greek dictatorship that the only way to restore its crumbling position would be by a spectacular *coup*; and the lot fell upon Cyprus. The intention of Ioannidis' last conspiracy was to assassinate Archbishop Makarios and replace him with a suitable mouthpiece who would proclaim the union of Cyprus with Greece (*énosis*). He chose for the purpose Nicos Sampson, a Cypriot journalist and former member of EOKA who had been condemned to death for murder but reprieved under British rule. Diehards of EOKA had formed a new force called EOKA-B, which together with Greek officers of the Cypriot National Guard provided the executants of the plot. But Makarios had wind of it, as he publicly revealed on 6th July, and it disastrously misfired.

On 15th July Makarios miraculously survived an attack on his palace. He escaped first to the west coast, then to one of the British bases on Cyprus, and finally to Britain. Sampson was proclaimed President, but lasted only a few days, though the US government came near to recognizing him. Turkish forces, which had been mobilized for many months in anticipation of such a contingency, began to land on the north coast of Cyprus on 20th July. The Greek government also ordered mobilization, but the result was a shambles. On 24th July the dictatorship threw in its hand, and President Gizikis invited Karamanlis to return from Paris and assume office.

Karamanlis arrived in Athens the next day in an aircraft put at his disposal by the French government. He speedily formed a coalition government which was without doubt the most popular and probably the ablest that Greece has ever had. The new government immediately declared the constitution of 1968 null and void, and restored the constitution of 1952, with 'the King' replaced by 'the President'. It also suspended martial law, released all political prisoners, and legalized the Communist Party for the first time since 1947. The wave of relief which swept over Greece was unexampled since the end of the Nazi occupation, to which the dictatorship was expressly compared. But the nightmare was not yet over, only shifted to Cyprus.

Under the Treaty of Guarantee of 1960, the three contracting powers—Britain, Greece and Turkey—had an obligation to consult together if the settlement of Cyprus established in that year were overthrown, and a right to act individually to restore the *status quo ante* if joint action proved impossible. Accordingly a conference of the three Foreign Ministers concerned—Greece being represented now by George Mavros—was convened in Geneva. But it proved impossible to reach agreement. The Turkish forces, acting ostensibly under the Treaty, then advanced further still into Cyprus on 14th August, finally occupying some 40 per cent of the island and displacing thousands of Greek Cypriot families. At the same time many Turkish families in the south of the island, displaced in retaliation, took refuge in the British base areas. British action was limited to protecting the bases and rescuing British residents and holiday-makers from the areas of combat.

Although Greek Cypriot forces put up some resistance to the invasion, it was openly admitted in Athens that the Greek forces of the mainland were in no condition to go to war with Turkey. For this aftermath of Ioannidis' criminal blunders much blame naturally fell on Greece's allies. The British government did nothing to fulfil its obligations under the 1960 Treaty; and the US government was legitimately suspected of having backed Ioannidis. The only governments in western

Europe which emerged with credit from this lamentable episode were the Dutch and Scandinavians, but the French were quick to restore their reputation. Having spent eleven years of exile in Paris, Karamanlis was widely believed to have in mind a French style of presidential democracy for the future. He started, indeed, by following French precedent in withdrawing the Greek forces from NATO command (though likewise not denouncing the alliance) in protest at the failure to prevent the Turkish invasion of Cyprus. He also made it clear that the US bases would have to be removed from Greece, except in so far as they served Greek interests.

Cyprus apart, the work of rehabilitation in Greece was initiated with zest and skill. Within a few weeks Karamanlis was able to announce that elections would take place in November, followed by a plebiscite on the monarchy before the end of the year, and thereafter the adoption of a new constitution. An able team of Ministers, some of whom (Mavros, Averoff and Pesmazoglou) had been prisoners of the Colonels, set about eradicating the evils of the dictatorship with almost universal approval. In the Army, however, there were still officers who sympathized with the Colonels and were difficult to remove without demoralizing their units. There were also forces on the left, led by Andreas Papandreou, who criticized Karamanlis for not showing greater severity, for not immediately abolishing the monarchy and for holding elections prematurely. The Communists, by comparison, were restrained and quiescent.

On 17th November 1974 the first general election for ten years resulted in an overwhelming victory for Karamanlis' party called New Democracy. He won 54 per cent of the votes and 220 seats out of 300; the Centre opposition, led by Mavros and Pesmazoglou, won 20 per cent and 60 seats; Papandreou's Socialist party won 13 per cent and 12 seats; and the extreme left collectively won 10 per cent and 8 seats. As the figures show, the electoral system was heavily weighted in favour of the winning party. The Centre parties could hardly complain of that, since their own leaders had been in the coalition government which adopted it. Papandreou could more reasonably complain, however. He could also point to the fact that only a few days earlier the students (few of whom were qualified to vote in the general election) had conducted a poll in which his supporters won a decisive victory.

A few weeks later the Greek people voted firmly but not overwhelmingly against the restoration of the monarchy, by 69 per cent against 31 per cent of the votes cast. A new republican constitution was drafted and published before the end of the year. As expected, it aimed to establish a strong, centralized executive, embodied in the President. Mavros called it 'reactionary' and Papandreou called it 'totalitarian'. Both men and their supporters, after trying to amend the draft in Parliament, boycotted the closing stages of the debate. Some amendments were indeed accepted: for example, the majority needed in Parliament to override a presidential veto on legislation was reduced from a three-fifths majority to a mere majority. But Karamanlis refused to accept what was regarded by the opposition as the most crucial of all the amendments. This was to delete the article which declared that 'the election of the President shall in every case be for a full term' of five years.

The article was crucial because it was widely believed that although Karamanlis did not immediately offer himself as candidate for the Presidency, he intended to do so before the end of the first President's term of office. He nominated for the Presidency, as soon as the constitution was passed by Parliament, his old and faithful friend Professor Constantine Tsatsos, who was already over seventy. It was assumed that Tsatsos would not serve a full term of five years, and that Karamanlis intended to succeed him; but he would not wish simply to complete Tsatsos' term before having to submit himself for re-election. There were therefore seeds of conflict within the constitution from the first. It was also exposed to the same potential embarrassment as the French constitution, that the President and the majority in Parliament might be of opposite political parties.

The election of the new President on 19th June 1975, by a majority of 210 parliamentary votes to 65 for Kanellopoulos, marked the end of Karamanlis' honeymoon period. He already had other major problems to confront. A conspiracy of Army officers sympathetic to Ioannidis and the fallen Colonels had been detected only just in time in February. The students were restive again, and soon civil servants and trade unionists were also, probably not without some Communist stimulus. The left gained some seats in Parliament at by-elections in April, as well as winning handsomely at the municipal elections in March; but in the latter case Karamanlis had refused as a matter of policy to endorse any candidates. There was some talk of reviving the very popular coalition of 1974, since several of the ablest men in Parliament were in the opposition. But the very magnitude of Karamanlis' majority made such a move difficult to justify.

Some progress was made in external relations. The new regime was welcomed with much good will in the West, though relations with the USA unavoidably remained frigid. Karamanlis once remarked that he was himself the Americans' only friend in Greece, and he dared not admit it. The Council of Europe welcomed Greece back, and the EEC unfroze the Treaty of Association. But difficulties lay ahead in negotiating Greece's full integration into the EEC; the Commission recommended against it for the time being, but the Council of Ministers overruled the recommendation and decided to proceed to negotiations immediately. The welcome change in Greece's status was marked by successful interchanges of high-level visits with France, West Germany, Britain and other countries of western Europe. In eastern Europe plans for technical co-operation were resumed: ministerial representatives from Greece's northern neighbours were invited to a conference in Athens at the end of 1975.

But no progress at all was achieved in resolving the Cyprus problem. Makarios, after visiting Washington and the United Nations, passed through Athens in December 1974 on his way back to Cyprus, but his return only hardened inter-communal relations on the island. It was clear that the Turks had no intention of withdrawing their forces altogether. Their presence was bringing about a shift of populations which could only end in a *de facto* partition of the island. It might be concealed in various ways, which were a matter for negotiation between representatives of the Greek and Turkish Cypriots, the former dominated by Makarios and the latter by the Turkish government in Ankara. But whatever the outcome of the negotiations, the large-scale shift of populations would be very difficult to reverse. The Turks were helped in bringing it about by a decision of the British government early in 1975, which allowed the Turkish Cypriot refugees within the British bases to be transferred to the Turkish mainland. There was no doubt that they would subsequently be moved into the Turkish-occupied north of the island, where they would settle in the homes from which thousands of Greek Cypriots had been driven out. The Greek government could do nothing to avert this outcome.

Since the British government had virtually abdicated its responsibilities under the Treaty of Guarantee, only the US government could exercise effective pressure on the Turks. In an effort to do so, arms supplies to Turkey were suspended after the invasion of Cyprus, but instead of yielding the Turks retaliated by denying the use of the American bases and facilities in Turkey. During the long and bitter arguments which followed, the Turkish government changed; but the new government was a precarious coalition which neither dared nor wished to defy the militant policy of the General Staff. A compromise was reached in 1976, from which the Cypriots gained nothing. The Americans resumed supplies to Turkey on the understanding that the arms would not be used for aggressive purposes, and they recovered control of their installations on payment of rent. After Greek protests at this agreement, a compensatory agreement was made with Greece. It provided for the supply of arms to maintain the balance of forces in the eastern Mediterranean, the continued use of some American facilities in Greece, and an undertaking that the USA would oppose any attempt at a military solution of the Aegean problem and would seek to obtain 'just territorial arrangements' in Cyprus. But it was clear that the Turkish forces would not withdraw from Cyprus until some form of *de facto* partition was accepted; and time was on their side.

The dispute grew even worse during 1976, when it was extended from Cyprus to the Aegean. There three issues divided Greece and Turkey: control of the air-space, demarcation of territorial waters, and the exploitation of oil-deposits under the sea-bed. A normal interpretation of international law would have operated in favour of Greece on all three points, because almost all the islands belonged to Greece, which made the Aegean virtually a Greek lake. But the Turks insisted that the Aegean was an exceptional case, and the Greek government accepted in principle that they had a case in equity. The Greeks referred the dispute to the International Court, whose jurisdiction Turkey would not accept. During the summer a Turkish exploration-ship was twice sent out into the disputed waters to take soundings on the sea-bed. The Greek government's strong reaction brought the two countries near to war, which Andreas Papandreou in fact urged as the only possible solution.

Intervention by the United Nations brought about a truce, without solving the problem. Both countries agreed to settle the dispute over the sea-bed by negotiation, not by force. Once more the Greeks had to accept that some concessions would be inevitable in order to achieve a compromise, and they did so readily. Among other reasons, this was necessary in order not to prejudice the negotiations with the EEC, some of whose members were alarmed by the prospect that the admission of Greece would involve them in the Greco-Turkish disputes. Later in the year the Greeks were encouraged by the outcome of the American election to believe that they would have new friends in Washington, and would no longer be continually coerced into concessions. President Carter had spoken favourably of Greece's rights, and his Secretary of State, Cyrus Vance, had had earlier first-hand experience of the Cyprus problem.

Alongside these intractable problems, Karamanlis had also to liquidate the criminal legacy of the dictatorship. It was made particularly difficult by the residual sympathy in the Army for Ioannidis, Papadopoulos and the rest. At first they were not even placed under arrest. Then a vote was sought in Parliament on the legality of the action initiated by them in April 1967, which was a sensitive matter because it was known that a number of senior generals (one of whom was now a member of Karamanlis' government) had been prepared to take similar action, subject to the King's approval, at the same date. In January 1975 Parliament finally determined that the action had been a *coup d'état* and not a revolution: it was therefore illegal. The way was then clear for the prosecution of Papadopoulos and his colleagues—twenty-four in all—but the trial did not begin until May. It resulted in the conviction of eighteen of the accused, three of whom (Papadopoulos, Pattakos and Makarezos) were condemned to death. They were immediately reprieved by the President on the government's recommendation. The opposition protested at this leniency, but it was thought necessary for the morale of the Army. It was also fair to remember that the *coup* of 1967 had at least been bloodless.

There followed a series of other trials: in July, for the abortive plot of the previous February; in August, for the torture of political prisoners; in October, for the atrocities at the Polytechnic. In every case there were many convictions but some acquittals, as well as a number of surprisingly light sentences. Ioannidis had the grim distinction of being involved in every one of these trials, and received more than one life sentence. He would also have been the principal defendant in yet another trial—for the attempt to assassinate Makarios—if it had not been postponed on grounds of national interest. One of the grounds was generally believed to be that Ioannidis was in a position to reveal evidence that his conspiracy in Cyprus had been backed by the CIA. The American Ambassador in Cyprus and a CIA official in Athens paid with their lives for the bitterness of anti-American feeling in these years.

At least there could be no doubt that the conduct of the trials reflected great credit on Greek justice, as well as on the maturity of the political world. Constitutional government was restored as if the tragic interlude had never occurred. Karamanlis showed more flexibility and tolerance than during his first tenure of power. His measures of social reform, coupled with his conciliatory policy towards Greece's Communist neighbours, even led some right-wing critics to accuse him of succumbing to Soviet influence. Pessimists were inclined to say that Greece had reverted to its normal condition of instability. One of the weaknesses of Greek democracy in the past had been that parties consisted simply of adherents to a leading personality, without continuity of policy or discipline. Hence they were very fissile coalitions. Already in 1975 there were such signs in the opposition parties; and it might be doubted whether Karamanlis' own party would survive his personal ascendancy.

It did not necessarily follow that the old instability had returned. There were significant differences from the last previous crisis. Greece was now taking a further major step towards complete assimilation with Europe. A leftward shift of the whole political spectrum meant that the parties reflected more faithfully both the real instincts of the Greek people and the prevalent atmosphere of Europe. The left-wing parties had a more mature leadership, and with the end of the monarchy the right-wing parties were a mere shadow. This did not mean that the constitution was invulnerable: if the opposition parties of 1975 were to win a future election, it might well be amended. But the prospect was one of evolution. Greece was evolving a political structure which included elements of the French, West German and British systems, in a characteristically national framework.

There had been moments in Greece's earlier history when a similarly optimistic prognosis could have been made: under George I and Venizelos in 1911, under Paul and Karamanlis half a century later, and even under Constantine II and George Papandreou in 1964. All had been upset by de-stabilizing factors of the same kind: royal interference, great-power rivalries, and a national habit of growing tired of stability. The first of these factors was eliminated by the plebiscite of December 1974. The second remained active, so long as the balance of power between the USA and the Soviet Union in the eastern Mediterranean was unsettled. Much depended on the third, which alone was under Greek control. At least they could never forget the bitter lesson they had suffered in the decade between 1965 and 1975.

CHAPTER XII

The Trial of Democracy
(1977–1985)

B y the beginning of 1977 the trials and purges in the aftermath of the military dictatorship were more or less finished. Karamanlis could claim to have liquidated the
discreditable past and to be ready to move Greece forward to the
widening horizons of the future. His aim was to establish for his
people a distinctive and accepted place in the modern world. To
achieve it there were two requirements: to rehabilitate and
expand Greece's international relations and commitments, and
to bring Greek society and infrastructure up to date.

The fact that Greece, in the person of Karamanlis, had been
welcomed back into civilized society eased some of his problems,
but by no means all. Relations with Turkey over Cyprus and the
Aegean remained in a deadlock which seemed irresoluble. Negotiations for a new relationship with NATO moved very slowly, in
part because of difficulties raised by the Turks. Negotiations with
the Americans over their installations in Greece were even more
difficult, thanks to the hostility of public opinion towards the
USA. Karamanlis' wish to join the EEC was also handicapped by
the fear of existing member states that favourable terms granted
to Greece would become a precedent for negotiations later with
Spain.

In every case further problems were created by the obduracy of
Papandreou, whose Socialist party (PASOK) was growing in
public favour at the expense of the Centre Union (renamed
EDIK) since the 1974 election. Papandreou, a much more formidable figure in opposition than Mavros, was more anti-Turkish,
anti-American and even anti-European than any other political
figure, not excepting the Communists.

Karamanlis trusted in patience and firmness to overcome these problems, provided that Greece maintained her democratic course. He also launched a parallel policy of establishing Greece's position in less familiar parts of the international scene—with the neutrals and the people's democracies. He and his ministers carried out a wide-ranging programme of visits and initiatives during his last six years in government.

He proclaimed a policy of making the Balkans into a 'zone of peace' in contrast with its traditional role as the 'powder-keg of Europe'. He visited almost all of the East European capitals and received their senior ministers in return. He held two inter-Balkan conferences on technical co-operation which attracted all Greece's neighbours except the Albanians; and even with Albania he was able to establish bilateral contacts. Agreements were negotiated on a wide variety of interests: trade, communications, tourism, culture, consular facilities and clearing arrangements between banks.

Relations with the major Communist powers also improved. Soviet warships were welcomed at Piraeus; Chinese officers were invited to military manoeuvres. The Russians were allowed to anchor ships off Crete and to put into Syros for repairs; Aeroflot opened a weekly air service to Athens. An ascending level of personal exchanges culminated in visits to Moscow as well as to Prague and Budapest by Karamanlis in October 1979. A month later he also visited Peking. In both cases he was the first Greek Prime Minister ever to do so.

His policy of *rapprochement* extended even further afield. Greece's relations with the Arab states had long been friendly, in part because Israel had never been recognized *de jure*. Now a great expansion of trade, investment and political activity took place. Karamanlis and his ministers visited most of the Arab states, and he himself travelled still further into Asia, including Pakistan, Thailand and India, as well as China. At the same time Papandreou was establishing contact with the more revolutionary Arabs in Libya, Syria and the PLO. So the Greeks had two strings to their bow in the Middle East.

In relation to Greece's major aspirations, which lay within the western alliance, these developments were marginal but not negligible. It would be advantageous for NATO that the northern frontier of Greece should cease to be a potential battle front. It might be useful for the EEC to have, through Greece, an economic bridgehead in the Middle East. But these advantages would be seriously offset if at the same time NATO continued to be weakened by the Greco–Turkish quarrel and if the admission of Greece to the EEC compelled the Community to become involved in that same quarrel or, perhaps even worse, to have to contemplate admitting Turkey as well.

For all these reasons negotiations on Greece's place in the western alliance and the European Community both took several years. In the case of NATO Karamanlis did not have the satisfaction of completing a settlement before he left the premiership in 1980, chiefly because the matter was complicated by uneasy relations with the USA and Turkey. But he did succeed in his ambition to bring Greece into full membership of the EEC.

Negotiations with the Commission began in Brussels in July 1976, after the hesitations of the Commissioners had been overruled by the Council of Ministers, under strong pressure from Karamanlis. But formidable difficulties, both internal and external to Greece, had to be overcome before Greek membership became a fact four and a half years later.

Besides the persistent opposition of PASOK, the main internal handicap was the economic and social backwardness of Greece. Karamanlis declared that he was determined to industrialize Greece and to Europeanize the Greeks, 'if necessary by force'. He did not, of course, use force, but he told his people of their shortcomings in blunt language which no other Prime Minister would have dared to use. It was a hard and painful struggle to modernize Greece, and it had not been completed by the date of accession. On the way Karamanlis antagonized many vested interests: businessmen, bankers, trade unions, the academic establishment and the ecclesiastical hierarchy. Only his unique prestige made it possible.

Before he finished he had introduced substantial and irreversible reforms. He took into public ownership the country's national airline and its major oil refinery; he imposed strong discipline on the banks; he set up the first infant industries for armaments production; he laid the foundations of a welfare state; he enforced modernization on the educational system, giving priority to technical and commercial training; he made demotic Greek the official language in place of *katharevousa;* he appealed to the young by reducing the voting age and the length of national service; he brought the status of women more nearly up to date by

315

abolishing the dowry system, by introducing divorce by consent, by recruiting girls to the police and armed services and by making provision for their conscription in times of emergency; he challenged the Church over diplomatic recognition of the Vatican and nationalized much ecclesiastical land.

Perhaps the most far-reaching, though least conspicuous, of his innovations was to try to establish his party, New Democracy, on a permanent basis, independent of his personal leadership. No Greek party other than the KKE had previously been anything more than a group of adherents surrounding a patron. In May 1979 Karamanlis addressed the first national party conference ever to be held by delegates elected from constituency associations; and he made the party also hold regional conferences on the same model, from which he deliberately absented himself. This was a notable step away from the past, but one whose later prospects were precarious.

While Karamanlis was trying to prepare the conditions for Greece's participation in the EEC, he was also negotiating with most of the same allied governments on terms for Greece's re-entry into NATO. In this case almost all the problems arose from Greece's relations with two allies who were not part of the EEC: the USA and Turkey. From the Greek point of view, these two countries seemed to be linked in a tacit inner alliance. Senior American officers did not hide their belief that Turkey was strategically more important, as well as militarily stronger, than Greece; and they were supported by Dr Luns, the Dutch Secretary-General of NATO. A shift of American sympathies towards Greece when Carter was elected President in 1976 was short-lived, as *Realpolitik* soon reasserted itself.

Separate but concurrent negotiations were also in progress over the status of American installations in Greece. Karamanlis could not afford to insist that they should be entirely removed, because in that case the major beneficiary would be Turkey, but he insisted that they must be under Greek control. What that meant precisely required minute discussion. In the meantime, the Turks received $1,000 million in military aid in return for the renewed use of American bases in Turkey. When the Greeks protested, they were offered $700 million for the use of the installations in Greece, subject to negotiation on the precise terms. It was understood that the same proportion between aid to Greece and Turkey would be maintained in future. But the discussion of control dragged on. An agreement between Greece and the USA was initialled in July 1977 but never ratified.

Circumstances had given the Turks a virtual veto over the negotiations between Greece and NATO, which the American Supreme Commander was reluctant to override. Another paradoxical constraint on Karamanlis was the very weakness of Turkish democracy. Turkish governments, which alternated in kaleidoscopic fashion, could hint that if they did not get their own way, the country might collapse into Communism, military dictatorship or sheer anarchy. Karamanlis' uncontested mastery of Greece precluded any such argument on his side.

Similar difficulties frustrated negotiation of the Greco–Turkish disputes over Cyprus and the Aegean, however much the western allies, and indeed the whole international community, wished to expedite them. The two cases were distinct because Cyprus itself, being an independent state whose policy could not be dictated in Athens, was a separate party to the one dispute but not to the other. It was one of the sadnesses of Karamanlis' later career that despite many references to the United Nations and countless diplomatic exchanges and conferences in different capitals during his last six years as Prime Minister, no progress whatever was achieved towards a satisfactory settlement in Cyprus, either between Greece and Turkey or in inter-communal relations.

Equally disappointing was the persistent coolness in personal relations between Karamanlis and Makarios, the Archbishop and President of Cyprus. The death of Makarios in August 1977 did nothing to ease matters. Indeed it even made them worse, since the Turks refused to recognize his elected successor to the presidency as any more than the national leader of the Greek Cypriots.

The problems of the Aegean were only marginally less intractable. Whether Ecevit (who had launched the invasion of Cyprus in July 1974) or Demirel (who sent out the oil-exploration ship in July 1976) were in office, Turkish policy was equally unyielding. Karamanlis had personal meetings with each of them and more than once offered Turkey a non-aggression pact. Talks at official level were apparently amicable but extremely slow in producing results.

In ascending order of difficulty, there were three Aegean problems: control of the air space, the extent of territorial waters and rights on the continental shelf under the sea. The last of the three gave rise to the most serious incidents because of the prospect of oil deposits (which were in fact found in commercial quantities close to the indisputably Greek island of Thasos). Air-traffic control was eventually settled in Greece's favour, as it had been before 1974; and the issue of territorial waters was tacitly left dormant after the Greek government indicated that it had no intention of extending its limits unilaterally. But there remained the Turkish grievance that the Aegean was virtually a 'Greek lake' under the existing law of the sea. Karamanlis sympathized with the Turkish attitude in equity, but his offer to submit the matter to the International Court was unsuccessful, since the Turks rejected its jurisdiction.

By the autumn of 1977 Karamanlis felt that all these issues were reaching a critical point, which would have to be confronted by a government with a fresh mandate. He accordingly asked the President for an early dissolution of Parliament. A General Election was held on 20 November, at which Karamanlis was returned to power but with a reduced majority. New Democracy won 173 seats, but PASOK increased its strength to 92, and Papandreou became leader of the official Opposition. Mavros resigned the leadership of EDIK, which was reduced to 15 seats. The Communists won 11 and the right-wing Nationalists 5, the latter taking votes mostly from New Democracy.

Although the result was disappointing to Karamanlis, he could still claim a mandate to continue the various negotiations. But Papandreou could claim a mandate to oppose them vigorously. He threatened that if PASOK won the next election, he would withdraw Greece from both the EEC and NATO; he also promised a much tougher line with the USA and Turkey. His language became more moderate, however, as he came closer to the realities of power.

After much hard bargaining, and many personal interventions by Karamanlis in the western capitals, the Treaty of Accession to the European Communities was signed on 28 May 1979 and presented to Parliament for ratification four weeks later. Papandreou refused to take part in the debate, and PASOK boycotted the vote on 28 June, when the Treaty was approved by 191 votes to 2.

The negotiations with NATO proceeded at a slower pace, due to difficulties with the Turks. At least one draft agreement, settled between the Greek General Staff and the Supreme Commander and approved by the rest of the NATO governments, was vetoed by Turkey. In the event it was not until late in 1980 that an acceptable conclusion was reached. By then two major changes had occurred.

The first was Karamanlis' decision to stand for the presidency when Tsatsos' term of office expired in June 1980. His election was opposed by PASOK but was finally carried by Parliament on the third ballot. He resigned immediately as Prime Minister and leader of New Democracy and assumed his new office on 15 May. George Rallis, the Foreign Minister, succeeded him after a closely contested election against Evangelos Averoff.

The second major change took place in Turkey. On 12 September 1980 the Chiefs of Staff brushed aside the charade of parliamentary democracy and assumed power themselves. This *coup* by the generals (and other service chiefs) in Ankara was as welcome, both in Turkey and abroad, as the Colonels' *coup* in Athens thirteen years earlier had been unwelcome. The terms of Greece's re-entry to NATO were then quickly settled and ratified by the Greek Parliament on 24 October. No problem of ratification arose in Ankara.

There still remained the problem of the US installations in Greece. Negotiations were begun and suspended several times between 1977 and 1983. More than once new obstacles to agreement arose: in April 1978, when the US government announced its intention to lift the last remaining restrictions on arms supply to Turkey; and in February 1983, when US aid to Turkey was doubled without (at first) any corresponding increase to Greece. On the former occasion Karamanlis issued a reproachful public statement; on the latter, a large demonstration assembled in Athens to demand the total removal of what were called the 'imperialist bases'. But by that date another major change had occurred.

The Greeks have a habit of following the example of the French. So it was in 1981, when the French Socialists were voted into power under President Mitterrand. It seemed then that a victory of PASOK in the elections which were due by the end of the same year was predestined (though in Greece this would not affect the presidency). Parliament was dissolved in September; polling day was 18 October. Papandreou based his campaign on the simple slogan *Allagì* ('Change'). It was successful: PASOK won 172 seats, New Democracy 115 and the Communists 13. All other parties were eliminated. Rallis then resigned the leadership of New Democracy and was succeeded by Averoff.

Papandreou thus became the head of Greece's first truly Socialist government. But the changes were less sweeping than seemed to have been promised. His attitude to the EEC was perhaps modified by the fact that in elections to the European Assembly on the same day PASOK fared less well, winning only 10 seats out of 24. He addressed a memorandum to the Commission emphasizing the difficulties incurred by Greece as a result of membership. The Commission in due course sent a conciliatory reply proposing certain alleviations; and there the matter rested for the present, with no further threat of withdrawal. In July 1983 Greece duly took her turn at the presidency of the EEC's Council of Ministers.

Papandreou's attitudes towards NATO and the US presence in Greece were also modified by the impact of responsibility. In the summer of 1982 he had high-level meetings—with President Reagan, the Supreme Commander and the American Ambassador—at which undoubtedly the issue of the bases was discussed, but without threats or antagonism. Early in 1983, when Papandreou briefed the other party leaders on his discussions with the Americans, it quickly became known to the Athens press that the signs pointed to a *rapprochement.*

It was not only in his dealings with the western allies that Papandreou's stance became more moderate, but also with Greece's eastern flank. He was conciliatory towards Israel and even towards Turkey. In July 1982 the Greek and Turkish governments jointly declared a moratorium on provocative acts. Six months later, in a public speech, Papandreou made a friendly reference to the Turks in the context of the Aegean. On the other hand, his relations with the Greek-Cypriot government were somewhat distant. But although there was no deterioration in Greco–Turkish relations as a result of the change of government, there was no visible progress either. The deadlock was as irresoluble as it had been under Karamanlis and Rallis.

In domestic policy also changes were not fundamental. Papandreou was a declared Marxist but also a democrat. He no longer talked of the 'nationalization' but of the 'socialization' of industry. In practice this was to be achieved by a tighter control over the banks. Almost the only act of true nationalization was the compulsory purchase of large forestry estates. He also believed in enforcing party control of the government apparatus, as in the Soviet system. In consequence his ministers found themselves flanked by PASOK officials, sometimes known colloquially as the 'Green Guard' *(Prasinophrourà)*, since green was the party colour. Opponents suspected that he was preparing the way for a one-party state.

Real changes in economic policy, however, were few. There was a sharp increase in public expenditure, which naturally led to an increase in the annual rate of inflation. The government responded with deflationary measures of a conventional kind: tighter credit, devaluation of the drachma and exchange controls. When workers went on strike for higher wages, Papandreou told them that they were undermining his policy of *Allagì*. But the workers had not noticed any change. They were also shocked to discover that 'worker participation' entailed severe restrictions on the right to strike.

Since fundamental change seemed impossible, Papandreou resorted to distractions, many of which only continued the policies of his predecessors under a new guise. He often annoyed his allies by the sympathy he displayed towards the East European governments; but Karamanlis himself had initiated the policy of *rapprochement* with them. He entertained the Soviet Prime Minister in Athens; but that was merely a return of the visit which Karamanlis had made to Moscow. He promised further decentralization of local government; but almost every recent Prime Minister had done the same.

Other distractions also were not altogether new. The introduction of civil marriage carried Karamanlis's process of secularization a step further. A campaign for the return of the Elgin Marbles from the British Museum was no innovation, though now graced by the leadership of Melina Mercouri, the film star who had become Papandreou's Minister of Culture. A more hazardous distraction was Papandreou's promise to 'open the Cyprus file' on the *coup* of July 1974 against Makarios. But on reflection he evidently concluded that it would do no good (since the major criminals were already in gaol) and might make relations with the USA dangerously worse than they already were.

Conservative Greeks relied, not altogether in vain, on President Karamanlis to exercise restraint on his former opponent. There were signs, however, that Karamanlis was disappointed at the end of his career that the stability which he had hoped to introduce into Greek politics was not completely achieved. The danger of a breach with the western alliance had been averted; the economic and social modernization of Greece had made substantial progress; but at the heart of Greek politics there were still causes for anxiety. Much of the euphoria of 1974 had been dissipated.

Not all Greeks shared Karamanlis' view that the plebiscite of December 1974 had settled the constitutional issue for good. When Queen Frederika died in February 1981, the government permitted her burial alongside King Paul at Tatoi, near Athens, but ex-King Constantine and other mourners were allowed to attend the funeral only on condition that they left Greece the same day. A large royalist demonstration nevertheless gathered at Tatoi. Later in the year Karamanlis refused to attend the wedding of the Prince of Wales in London when he learned that Constantine was invited as 'King of the Hellenes'. The fact that the ex-King had settled permanently in England cast a slight but noticeable shadow over Anglo–Greek relations.

Echoes of the ancient conflict between royalists and republicans were perhaps of no great moment. But despite the success with which Karamanlis had guided Greece back from military dictatorship to democracy, there were still disquieting features in the period of transition. One was the revival of political violence. Another was the reaction to the change of government in 1981. To some extent these two features were linked.

Political violence took many forms: anti-American demonstrations, ugly scenes in Parliament, bombs, arson and even murder. Some incidents were due to private vengeance, some to anarchist elements of the right and left, some to international terrorism, some to unidentifiable causes. The worsening trend reached a peak early in 1983. Rumours spread in February of an imminent *coup* within the Army, which led PASOK to incite a massive *synagermòs* (state of alert) by all the left-wing parties. In March the proprietor of the newspaper *Vradyní*, George Athanasiadis, a close friend and supporter of Karamanlis, was murdered by an unknown hand. In the same month a local meeting of New Democracy in the north-east was disrupted by a bomb, fortunately without casualties.

Some Greeks thought that Papandreou enjoyed provoking antagonism. But he made at least one serious effort to lay to rest an older antagonism which had survived from the wartime Resistance and the Civil War. He abolished the annual celebration of the final victories which crushed the Communist-led rebellion in 1949; and he introduced legislation to confer official recognition on all the Resistance organizations, including the extreme left.

He chose as the focus of reconciliation a nationwide celebration of the fortieth anniversary of the attack on the Gorgopotamos railway viaduct, 25 November 1982. But the right-wing opposition in Parliament, led by the implacable Averoff, refused to support the legislation, and the survivors of the nationalist Resistances, EDES and EKKA, boycotted the ceremony at the scene of the action. Consequently the occasion became virtually a left-wing celebration, increasing rather than reducing tension. The Greeks, it seemed, would not forget the past.

There were things which Papandreou too would not forget. The bitter past, for him, included Greece's experiences at the hands of the United States and Turkey, and also the domestic political feuds of the 1960s. He resented the semi-colonial status to which Greece had been reduced since the Second World War, and he still had reservations about Greece's membership of the western alliance, including the EEC as well as NATO. In contrast with his earlier days in office, from 1983 onwards these memories seemed to exercise a dominating influence on his policies, which were increasingly marked by a trend towards neutralism abroad and autocracy at home.

The last stage of his conciliatory period in dealing with the United States came in September 1983, when he signed an agreement to extend the lease (but to restrict the scope) of the American defence facilities, which he had once denounced as 'imperialist bases'. Even this agreement was hedged with ambiguity. Whereas the English text said that it was to be 'terminable' after five years, the Greek text said that 'it terminates' at that date. From the day of signature, Papandreou repeatedly emphasized his own interpretation. He seemed also to lose all concern for improving relations with the United States, or even with Greece's other allies, except for those which had left-inclined governments.

In both NATO and the EEC, the Greeks often frustrated unanimity. In 1982, after a NATO foreign ministers' meeting, the Greek representative blocked the publication of a *communiqué* for the first time, because the other ministers refused to give a guarantee of Greece's frontier with Turkey. In the same year, Papandreou refused to support EEC sanctions against Poland over the imposition of military law, and dismissed a minister who failed to veto the decision. In 1983 he refused to condemn the Libyan intervention in Chad, or the destruction of a Korean civilian aircraft by the Soviet Air Force. In 1984 he held up an agreement on British, French and Italian participation in a Middle East peace-keeping force, and criticized the United States' intervention in the Lebanese conflict. In general, he showed a marked hostility to any defence initiative by the United States, and a corresponding tolerance towards the Soviet bloc.

Characteristically, he criticized the installation of cruise and Pershing missiles in Europe (although Greece was not one of the countries where they were to be installed), and he refused to allow a new NATO headquarters to be established at Larisa. He protested against US naval flights over the Aegean; he cancelled a 'war games' exercise with the US forces as an irrelevance; and he sought to restrict the relay of broadcasts to Greece by the Voice of America. Most serious of all, he withdrew Greek forces from a NATO exercise in 1983 because the Turks insisted, with the support of the Supreme Commander (an American general), that the island of Lemnos should be excluded on the grounds that it had been fortified illegally by the Greeks.

On the other hand, Papandreou's friendliness towards the Soviet bloc was almost ostentatious. This naturally raised suspicions among opposition Greeks, who regarded him as virtually a tool of the Communists. A striking example of the domestic reconciliation with Communism was the return from exile of Markos Vaphiadis, who had led the rebellion in 1946–9, and his appearance on the platform at a PASOK party rally. He was received with enthusiastic applause, but opposition opinion was shocked and alarmed. Among other such gestures were the visits made by Papandreou to Warsaw and Moscow at times when allied relations with both capitals were very cold; and his support for a Romanian initiative to establish a nuclear-free zone in the Balkans, in opposition to NATO policy. The Soviet Union responded significantly by appointing the son of the late Party Chairman, Andropov, as Ambassador in Athens.

It was possible to offer a reasoned justification for such shifts in Greece's foreign policy. It could be argued that in many respects Papandreou was continuing a movement which Karamanlis himself had initiated; but he was certainly going further and faster than Karamanlis would have done. A more convincing argument used by Papandreou's supporters was that in the past Greece had been too subservient to the West, and therefore too hostile to the Soviet bloc. Papandreou was only redressing the balance and asserting Greece's independence. But in western eyes the process of redressing the balance was seen as exaggeratedly pro-Soviet and anti-American, and even anti-European. It is not surprising that Greece's six-month tenure of the presidency of the EEC in 1983 was considered decidedly – even deliberately – unsuccessful. It was punctuated by unprecedented criticism of the government in the chair; but this did Papandreou no harm with his own electorate.

A more positive aspect of Papandreou's foreign policy was his cultivation of governments with kindred sympathies both in Europe and in other continents. In October 1983 he entertained the Socialist Prime Ministers of Portugal, Spain, France and Italy in Athens. In 1984 he visited Finland, Libya, Sweden, Syria, Jordan and India. Partly as a result of these visits, and partly from other diplomatic contacts, a neutralist group of six countries was formed to oppose nuclear armaments, comprising Greece, Sweden, India, Argentina, Mexico and Tanzania. The most curious of Papandreou's independent initiatives was a meeting in Crete, which he contrived in November 1984, between the French and Libyan heads of state, Mitterrand and Gaddafi, supposedly to settle their conflict in the civil war in Chad.

Papandreou could again claim that he was following the example of Karamanlis in assuming a wider role for Greece on the international stage. But Karamanlis had done so without offending the United States and other allies; Papandreou appeared not to care whether he offended them or not. By 1984 the US administration had begun to become impatient with him. It was hinted that the sale of military aircraft to Greece might be halted. The proportion of seven to ten between military aid for Greece and Turkey, which had been established under Karamanlis, was also judged to be at risk. A statement in December 1984 that Greece's armed forces were to be re-deployed, on the assumption that the threat to national security came from Turkey rather than the Warsaw Pact, aggravated the suspicion in Washington that Greece was seceding by degrees from the western alliance.

This was not Papandreou's real intention, however. He intended to remain in the alliance because the disadvantages of secession would far outweigh the advantages of neutrality. But he wanted to have the best of both worlds, western and eastern. It was a risky policy, because he could not be sure at what point Greece would be written off by her allies. But he would not willingly sacrifice the material benefits. of membership in either NATO or the EEC by withdrawing from them. If he withdrew from NATO, the chief beneficiary would be Turkey; if he withdrew from the EEC, the only loser would be Greece.

In Papandreou's eyes, Turkey was simply a regional surrogate of the United States. He assumed that he would receive no support from the Americans in any dispute affecting Turkish interests. This was apparent when, in November 1983, the Turkish Cypriot leader, Raouf Denktash, proclaimed the establishment of an independent state in northern Cyprus. Only a strong reaction from Washington could have forced a reversal of this step, but none was forthcoming. Although no government except that of Turkey recognized the new state, the international reaction was limited to an adverse resolution at the United Nations.

The UN Secretary-General then tried to reconcile the two parts of Cyprus in a federal state. He brought together Denktash and the Greek Cypriot President, Kyprianou, to sign an agreement early in 1985. But Kyprianou refused to sign, saying that he had been misled about the nature of the agreement. For this he was widely criticized, and censured even in his own parliament. Later in the year, the Turkish Cypriots confirmed their separate status by a constitutional plebiscite, and by electing Denktash their president and establishing a representative assembly. The Cypriot problem thus became even more intractable.

This intractability was to the advantage of the Turks, who still occupied more than one third of the island. To Papandreou, who in this respect spoke for all Greeks, it seemed impossible to believe that the US administration would ever take effective measures to end the Turkish military occupation of Cyprus. The Greeks felt alienated and misunderstood. They took it for granted that, because Greece was smaller and weaker than Turkey, American sympathies would always tend to be against them in principle, and against Papandreou personally, in any conflict with the Turks. This was again apparent in March 1984, when an incident between Greek and Turkish warships nearly led to an armed clash in the Aegean. After initially over-reacting, Papandreou was left without support and with no alternative but to retreat, and to accept Turkish assurances that they had no aggressive intentions.

The Trial of Democracy (1977–1985)

Greece's isolation from the alliance was not confined to relations with Turkey and the United States. The British government also protested at Greek support for the anti-nuclear campaign of the Soviet satellites. The West German government warned Greece that the new policy of treating Turkey as the main potential enemy would inhibit the supply of German military aid. Both NATO and the EEC gave collective indications of disapproval. In 1984 NATO's Annual Defence Review had to omit all reference to Greece and Turkey because of the unresolved dispute over the status of Lemnos. At the same time indignation was expressed within the EEC over Greece's veto on the admission of Spain and Portugal to membership, until a favourable settlement was reached on the Greek claim to increased finance for what were called the 'Integrated Mediterranean Programmes'.

The essential programme in this context was concerned with agriculture, which was much the most important industry in Greece. The national economy in general had not been strong enough to bear the strain of entry into the EEC, as Papandreou had predicted. But Greece was a beneficiary of EEC funds on a large scale, and most of the benefit was channelled to the farmers. So Papandreou was able to exploit membership of the EEC to attract the agricultural vote at home, while treating his European colleagues in Brussels with condescension. He was well qualified to do both, being the only head of government who had an international reputation as a professional economist; though like other political economists before him, he had only modest success in controlling his own economic problems.

His often arrogant attitude towards his allies suited the Greek national temperament better than Karamanlis' Europeanism had done. In this respect, even the Communists found it hard to criticize him; and his individual conception of socialism aroused little hostility. Threats of a general strike against the limitations imposed on strikes in the public sector petered out without effect. Although Papandreou prudently refused a proposal from the KKE of formal co-operation with PASOK, he accepted Communist support at every critical juncture, including votes in parliament when necessary. The official Opposition had great difficulty in making headway against the creeping tide of 'socialization'.

The first opportunity to pass a national verdict on Papandreou's government came at the elections to the European Assembly in June 1984. The result was indecisive. Both PASOK and New Democracy increased their votes, the latter by a wider margin. PASOK retained the same number of seats, while the conservative party, New Democracy, gained one but still remained behind PASOK. More seriously for ND, a new right-wing party, EPEN (formed under the patronage of Papadopoulos from his prison cell), won one seat. The Communist vote declined, but the divided KKE retained its seats. It was clear that the PASOK vote, unusually for a Socialist party, was firmly based in the rural areas.

Greek politics were now polarized around the two major parties. Apart from the small minority of Communists, these were the only parties represented in the Greek parliament. Such a bi-polar concentration of political strength was unusual in post-war Greece. Also unusual was the fact that New Democracy seemed less sure of itself. In September 1984 the party underwent its third change of leadership in less than five years, when Averoff resigned on grounds of ill-health. His successor was Costa Mitsotakis, who had played a distinguished role in the Cretan Resistance during the German occupation. He had in fact been captured and con-demned to death by the Germans, until he was saved by a timely British intervention.

The election of Mitsotakis as party leader revived another bitter memory for Papandreou. Mitsotakis had been a leading member of the so-called 'apostates' from the Centre Union, who in 1965 abandoned Papandreou's father, the prime minister of the day, to support a government under Stephanopoulos. In Papandreou's eyes this act of treachery had opened the way to the military *coup d'état* of April 1967. He made it clear that this was not forgotten or forgiven in 1984. Characteristically, he refused to invite Mitso-takis, as leader of the Opposition, to a banquet in honour of the visiting President of the Austrian Republic. This gesture was also embarrassing to Karamanlis, both as President and as founder of the party of which Mitsotakis was now leader.

Karamanlis found it daily harder to manage his relationship with his headstrong Prime Minister; but it was a relation which public opinion regarded as indispensable to the maintenance of political stability. The presidential powers included in the 1975 Constitution – for example, to dissolve parliament, to order a referendum on controversial policies, to declare a state of emer-gency – were welcomed as a safeguard in the background, though

Karamanlis was seen to be reluctant to use them. Papandreou, on the other hand, while treating Karamanlis with outward respect, treated parliament with none, and was seldom seen there. The fear that he was preparing the way for a one-party autocracy was once more gaining ground among both conservatives and traditional liberals.

It was clear long in advance that 1985 would be a critical year, because a presidential election would fall due in May and parliamentary elections must be held at latest by October. The seemingly amicable relationship between Karamanlis and Papandreou was assumed to imply that the former would be re-elected for a second term as President with the support of PASOK as well as New Democracy. Papandreou more than once virtually promised this outcome, if Karamanlis were willing. There was therefore less anxiety than there might have been about the continuation of political stability, whichever party might win a majority in parliament.

In this mood of national confidence, a new electoral law was passed in January 1985, with the support of both major parties. It provided for election by 'reinforced proportional representation', a system which tended to favour larger parties. For this reason, it was opposed by the Communists, the third party in parliament. But in other respects Papandreou was becoming more and more dependent on the Communists, not only to increase his vote in parliament but also to support PASOK in public demonstrations and propaganda campaigns.

Within two months of passing the electoral law, Papandreou made a dramatic *volte-face*, probably under pressure from the left wing of PASOK, which in turn was anxious not to be outflanked by the KKE. On 9 March, less than twenty-four hours after privately reassuring Karamanlis of PASOK's support for his re-election, Papandreou announced his intention to nominate a rival candidate for the presidency. The man he chose – who also knew nothing of it until the day before – was Christos Sartzetakis, a distinguished lawyer with no prior record in politics. Karamanlis immediately presented his resignation to the President of the Chamber, who automatically became acting President of the Republic in his place.

Papandreou's choice was a shrewd one. Sartzetakis had made his name as the examining magistrate in the investigation of the death of Lambrakis in 1963. His emergence as a candidate there-

fore revived yet more bitter memories of the past, just as Mitsotakis' election to the leadership of New Democracy had done. In
the case of Sartzetakis, the memories were of the campaign which
the Left and the Centre Union (led then by George Papandreou)
had launched against Karamanlis over the death of Lambrakis. It
seemed as if there was a deliberate intention to stage a replay of
the feuds fought out twenty years earlier.

In order to secure Sartzetakis' election, Papandreou would
need the support of Communist as well as Socialist deputies.
There was no prospect of success in the first two ballots, which
required 200 out of 300 parliamentary votes; but in the third
ballot only 180 votes were required. To make sure of left-wing
support, Papandreou announced his intention to make constitutional changes which would virtually eliminate the executive
powers of the President and transfer them to parliament. These
would have to be enacted in two successive parliaments. Even
with left-wing support, however, Papandreou could not be sure of
Sartzetakis' election unless the vote of the President of the
Chamber (a PASOK deputy) were included. Some constitutional
lawyers argued that this would be irregular, since as acting President he was debarred from holding any other public position; but
other lawyers disagreed. Papandreou therefore declared that the
matter would be resolved by a vote of parliament itself, which naturally accorded with his wishes.

Sartzetakis was accordingly elected President on the third
ballot by the absolute minimum of 180 votes. Mitsotakis
announced that New Democracy would not recognize his election
as valid. He also demanded an immediate dissolution of parliament. Papandreou was ready enough, provided that he could first
enact his constitutional changes for the first time. This was
achieved on 7 May by a slightly enhanced majority of 182. Parliament was then dissolved for a General Election on 2 June.

The election was bitterly fought, with malice on both sides. On
the left, an attempt was made to suggest that Mitsotakis had been
a collaborator with the German occupation. On the right, it was
argued that a victory for PASOK would probably be followed
either by another civil war or by another military dictatorship. In
each case the blame lay only with unrepresentative extremists,
but it was the official parties which would gain or lose votes as a
result. Karamanlis' only intervention was to issue a statement
(which the government-controlled media suppressed) urging the

Greeks to use their vote with great care.

PASOK had twice doubled its vote in the three elections since its foundation (1974, 1977 and 1981). Obviously these achievements could not be matched in 1985, but Papandreou won a new term of office, although with a reduced majority. He lost eleven seats, and New Democracy (which now included several former Liberals and Social Democrats) gained the same number. Their relative strength in the new Parliament was thus 161 to 126. The Communists retained thirteen seats as in 1981, but this time one of the seats was won by the dissident KKE (Interior), which had broken from the official KKE over the latter's policy of strict obedience to Moscow. Fortunately for New Democracy, the right-wing EPEN made no further progress at its expense, and won no seats.

After the election, Papandreou confirmed that his government would complete the process of revising the Constitution. In other respects, too, policy would continue on course, but the Council of Ministers would be re-organized, to reduce the number of departments from over fifty to ten. So at last *Allagì* (Change) was to become a reality. Mitsotakis announced that in the new circumstances the Opposition would recognize the election of Sartzetakis as President, since it could hardly do otherwise; but he forecast that the duration of parliament would be short. Karamanlis issued a statement that he would take no further part in public life.

Although Papandreou forecast 'calmer waters' in Greece's relations with the West after his re-election, a new crisis occurred almost immediately. An American civil airliner in transit from Cairo was hijacked by two Shi'ite Muslim gunmen who boarded it unhindered at Athens airport. A third gunman, who failed to obtain a seat in the aircraft, was arrested but released by the Greek authorities, as the price of freedom for a group of Greek passengers. The Greeks were bitterly criticized in Washington, and less severely in other western capitals, for lax security and for yielding to the hijackers. An immediate, though temporary, consequence was a significant reduction in tourist traffic to Athens.

On the other hand, Papandreou was equally under criticism from Moscow at the same date for allowing a Soviet diplomatist, who defected in Athens, to be secretly conveyed out of the country to the United States. These episodes were characteristic of the way in which opposing pressures from the super-powers helped to maintain Papandreou's balance on his tightrope course between them.

Perhaps as a consequence, his speech in presenting his new government to parliament was comparatively mild and non-aggressive. Both New Democracy and the KKE nevertheless voted against the motion of confidence, but for opposite reasons: the conservatives because the policies were still seen as anti-western, anti-capitalist and authoritarian; the Communists because they were not more so. The government was confirmed in office with a comfortable majority of 23. But a number of deputies elected on the main parties' lists subsequently declared themselves independent, which reduced PASOK's overall majority for the future to 14.

The democracy restored by Karamanlis had now passed its first major test by making possible, without adverse reaction, the election and consolidation of Greece's first government committed to socialism. It remained to be seen whether it would also make possible, at a later election, the return of a government committed to the opposite course; or whether socialism, once fully established, would prove itself irreversible.

CHAPTER XIII

The Eclipse of Socialism (1985–1990)

Socialism never meant the same to Papandreou as it meant to the Communist Parties of Eastern Europe. He may have been a Marxist as a young man, but he was no Leninist as Prime Minister. He never intended to establish a one-party state, whatever his opponents believed. He had no inclination to a dictatorship of the proletariat. He did not intend that the state should control all the means of production, distribution and exchange. His only approach to totalitarianism lay in the discipline which he imposed on his party and the use of telephone-tapping against his supporters as well as his opponents.

In his economic policies there was little trace of doctrinaire socialism. He preferred to control industrial activity, like other Prime Ministers before him, through the constraints imposed on the banking system by the central Bank of Greece. The very high proportion of the national economy controlled by state corporations was part of his inheritance, but it continued to grow under his administration. When his government took control of private companies, which it did in many cases, the motive was not ideological but simply to save jobs threatened by bankruptcy, or on grounds of national security. The outcome was nevertheless that public expenditure grew as a proportion of the gross domestic product from just over 30 per cent in 1980 to nearly 45 per cent in 1989.

But even in 1985 Papandreou did not call this 'socialism' any longer. His policy statements spoke rather of 'socialization' and the 'welfare state'. They also spoke of 'healthy competition', 'self-management', and 'strengthening small and medium-sized businesses'. His first intervention in economic affairs after the election was much as any government, left-wing or right-wing, would have made in the circumstances. It was the introduction of an austerity programme, intended to last two years at least, to confront a crisis of inflation running at an annual rate of 25 per cent, and overseas indebtedness equivalent to £11 billion.

The austerity measures of October 1985 were, generally, orthodox and extremely painful. The drachma was devalued by 15 per cent; importers were obliged to deposit between 40 per cent and 80 per cent of the value of their imports for six months at the Bank of Greece, without interest; the system of indexed wage increases was sharply restricted; a reduction was imposed on public sector borrowing; and the introduction of Value Added Tax, as required by membership of the European Community, was postponed. The only measures that could be considered specifically socialist were price controls and a tax on profits.

Naturally, the parliamentary opposition and the business community were indignant at these symptoms of a crisis which had not been revealed during the general election; and so were the trade unionists in PASOK. A one-day strike by nearly a million workers followed on 21 October, and more strikes before the end of the year. In elections to the Council of the General Confederation of Greek Workers (GSEE), PASOK lost control to the KKE.

The budget published in November gave effect to the measures outlined, but exempted education, health and welfare from the cuts in public expenditure. It still forecast a deficit amounting to £4.4 billion, together with higher unemployment, higher inflation, and zero economic growth. But there was at least a prospect of reducing the deficit in the balance of payments, largely thanks to a six-year loan from the European Community. The budget frankly admitted what had always been the case, that receipts from the Community considerably exceeded Greece's contributions.

During a major debate in Parliament on 6 December, Papandreou conceded that the Community had been helpful. He still considered that Greece's entry had been premature, but there was no longer any question of withdrawal. This decision was reinforced by an opinion poll at the same date, which showed that two thirds of all Greeks were in favour of membership. But Papandreou did not intend to be wholly dependent on Western aid.

He was negotiating already a project with the Soviet government to establish an aluminium plant near Delphi, the whole production of which would be bought by the USSR; and in the following year he also began negotiating a twenty-five-year contract with the Soviet government to supply natural gas by way of a pipe-line through Bulgaria, in return for which the USSR would use Greek shipyards for repairs and buy Greek agricultural produce. These were characteristic examples of Papandreou's policy of balancing commitments between East and West, though they were inevitably to fall foul of the 1989 revolutions in the Communist bloc.

In the budget debate the government forecast that inflation would be reduced in 1986 to an annual rate of 16 per cent. Remarkably, the actual outcome was less than one point above that figure, which showed that the austerity measures were working. But the resentment of industrial workers and public employees made itself felt in frequent strikes; and even the farmers, who had been the chief beneficiaries of entry into the EEC, demonstrated against the inadequate prices payable for their produce. By November 1986 it was found necessary to impose a general price freeze until the end of January. In December the Minister of National Economy announced a 'salvage programme' for six of the largest public corporations, comprising power, telecommunications, railways, air and road transport, and water supply. But at the World Economic Forum at Davos in January 1987, Papandreou put a different gloss on the salvage programme by speaking of ambitious investments to create jobs, including a giant bridge across the narrowest gap in the Gulf of Corinth, a new international airport for Athens, a diversion of the River Acheloos to expand hydro-electric power, and an improvement of the motorway system. Most of these projects proved abortive.

In September 1987, after an improvement in the rate of inflation and the balance of payments, Papandreou declared that the austerity programme, painful as it was, had also been successful. He promised to reduce restrictions and the level of taxation to attract foreign investment. Free wage bargaining would be allowed in the private sector, and the indexation of wages would be restored. On the last provision, however, the Minister of National Economy dissented; Papandreou overruled him, and he thereupon resigned. His successor introduced an optimistic budget for 1988, providing for a generously increased investment programme with help from the European Community.

Nonetheless, there were recurrent strikes in 1988, involving not only industrial workers but teachers, doctors, bank employees and civil servants. The level of inflation never fell below an annual rate of 12 per cent during Papandreou's second term. What was remarkable was that foreign investment still flowed abundantly into Greece, and Greek industrialists were also able to make major investments abroad, especially in the field of agricultural produce. The resilience of the battered Greek economy was astonishing. But it owed little to socialism. Papandreou's measures were much the same as any democratic economy in the capitalist world would have taken. After his loss of office in mid-1989, the task of dismantling such of his socialist structure as still survived fell to his successors.

Like all political parties, both PASOK and ND were coalitions of interests with unanimity on very little. Perhaps the one item of national policy on which all agreed was the recovery of the Elgin Marbles, but a formal request to this effect was rejected by the British government less than six months after Papandreou's re-election. Culture, indeed, was common ground for all Greeks as a matter of ancestral pride, and the Minister of Culture, Melina Mercouri, was the most durable of all Papandreou's colleagues. She campaigned tirelessly for her causes: debating the Elgin Marbles at the Oxford Union; opening an exhibition of Byzantine art in London (and taking time off to inspect the Marbles); successfully opposing the location of the proposed aluminium plant too close to Delphi. As the only woman holding a senior post in the government, she was naturally also involved in the promotion of legislation to permit abortion, which became law in June 1986. Her one rival in the field of social and cultural politics was another woman, Margaret Papandreou, whose efforts on behalf of women's rights were ill-rewarded by her husband.

The abortion law was not the only enlargement of personal freedom of choice which came about under Papandreou's government. Another was the concession made to conscientious objectors, allowing them alternatives to military service. This was particularly valuable to Jehovah's Witnesses, of whom there were many in Greece. A more surprising concession was made to the so-called Slavo-Macedonians, who had been deeply involved on the Communist side in the civil war of 1945–49. According to the Slovene member of the Yugoslav presidency, after a visit to Greece in 1986, the government had agreed to allow the official use of the Macedonian language in bilateral relations. These were small but significant accretions to Papandreou's otherwise dwindling reputation for libertarianism.

In general, he was autocratic in both political and personal relations; it was only his ruthlessness that held PASOK together. One of his first measures after re-election was to re-organize the structure of government, reducing the numbers of the Council of Ministers. He transferred the displaced Ministers to the party organization, thus separating government and party and placing himself in sole control of both. In the process he earned much ill will; it was not long before secessions and even expulsions from PASOK followed.

Such upheavals were not uncommon in Greek politics. The opposition was suffering similarly: many members left ND, among them Constantine Stephanopoulos, who formed a new party called Democratic Renewal. Mitsotakis felt the need to secure his position as leader of ND by resigning in August 1985 and offering himself, successfully, for re-election. In 1987, however, he suffered a more serious blow when the former Prime Minister, George Rallis, also resigned from ND, and sat in Parliament as an independent.

Of the two leaders of the major parties, Papandreou was the more ruthless and resourceful in imposing his will. After re-organizing the machinery of his party and government, he returned to the Constitution. He now had his own nominee as President, though he was not wholly satisfied with Sartzetakis, who had been chosen in extreme haste for want of a candidate more acceptable to PASOK. The powers of the presidency were debated in Parliament during January 1986, and the promised legislation to reduce them was ratified in March. A curious paradox of Papandreou's manoeuvres was that after reducing the President to a figurehead, he later sought to displace Sartzetakis in the presidency himself.

He also challenged another of the pillars of Greek society by publishing a bill to expropriate Church property. The Synod of Bishops proved a tougher antagonist than Sartzetakis, retaliating by excommunicating seven Ministers; and in addition the Bishop of Syros forbade the removal from one of his churches of a newly discovered early El Greco, intended for the Byzantine exhibition in London. In the end, however, a more or less satisfactory compromise was reached; but the Bishops remained indignant at the abortion law.

During these years there began to appear signs that Papandreou was losing his grip on power, though his conduct was as arrogant as ever. In March 1986, after less than a year from the election, he carried out a re-shuffle of his government; and it was only the first of many, which came on average two or three times every year. By

337

October dissatisfaction with the government was widespread, more particularly on the left of PASOK. This was clearly illustrated by the local elections in that month. PASOK lost control of the three principal cities (Athens, Piraeus and Salonika), where representatives of ND were elected as Mayors. But they won only by default, because the KKE refused to support PASOK candidates at the second ballot, as they had normally done in the past. PASOK nevertheless retained control in thirty-one out of the fifty-one counties.

A major consequence of the shift of power in the cities was the introduction of independent radio stations. Television was under state control by law, but the new Mayor of Athens, Miltiadis Evert, found that radio was not. His new venture in Athens came on the air on 31 May 1987, with such success that it was followed by other such stations all over the country. As the government could not prevent their inception, it responded by introducing legislation to create a unified radio and television service under state control, and to impose certain limitations on the private radio stations. Their range of audibility was restricted, to ensure that they would be merely local; but in a sense this was an advantage, because it kept them closer to public opinion than the national service. Independent television stations were also permitted from 1989.

In this case, Papandreou appeared to be reacting to events rather than controlling them. A further symptom of diminishing confidence was the gruesome wave of terrorism, both indigenous and foreign, which flooded Greece during his last years in office. The security authorities seemed helpless to arrest or even identify the criminals. As often happens when things are going wrong for a government, the very elements seemed to turn against it. A major earthquake in September 1986 destroyed much of Kalamata in the Peloponnese, causing over 300 casualties and at least 120 deaths; and in the following summer an exceptional heat-wave destroyed trees and crops, cut down industrial activity, and caused many deaths in Athens.

A sense that Papandreou had lost the initiative in controlling events, whether logical or not, affected businessmen, trade unionists, public employees, and members of PASOK itself. But there was also a general feeling that, under Mitsotakis, the opposition did not offer a vigorous or effective alternative. The former liberal parties had virtually vanished, their supporters split between PASOK, ND, and independents. A striking phenomenon of the time was the growing respect for the KKE, judiciously led by Kharilaos Florakis, who had once been a junior commander in the Democratic Army under Markos Vaphiadis. The unexpected result was that when Papandreou lost office in 1989, the Communists were accepted, for the first time since 1944, as partners in a coalition with ND. To that result, short-lived as it was, Papandreou had himself contributed, both by the corruption within his government and by disappointment with his economic expertise. In only one area of policy between 1985 and 1989—foreign affairs—did Papandreou enjoy reasonably general approval.

Papandreou's foreign policy continued to be expansive and opportunistic. Formal exchanges of visits with other states throughout the world, though not necessarily productive in themselves, showed by the levels at which they took place (heads of state, prime ministers, foreign ministers and others) the calculated gradations of importance which he attached to international relations. The first important visitors to Athens after his re-election were Presidents Zhivkov of Bulgaria and Honecker of East Germany. Early in 1986 Papandreou himself visited Belgrade, Delhi and Cairo. He took care to nurture the Group of Six countries formed in 1984 (comprising Greece, Sweden, India, Argentina, Mexico and Tanzania), which held conferences in Mexico in 1986 and Sweden in 1988. Its activities were various: it won an award in California in 1985, offered its services to mediate in the Gulf War between Iran and Iraq in 1986, and sent a joint message to Presidents Reagan and Gorbachov in 1987 on their agreement to reduce nuclear weapons. But the Group could hardly claim to have achieved any particular successes on its own initiative.

In March 1986 Papandreou had the melancholy duty of attending the funeral of the murdered Swedish Prime Minister, Olof Palme, whom he had known when he lived in exile in Sweden during the military dictatorship. In the first half of the same year he received in Athens the Australian and Chinese Prime Ministers, the President of Syria, and the Polish and Nicaraguan Foreign Ministers. Gorbachov himself accepted an invitation to Athens in principle, but no date was ever fixed.

It was clearly Papandreou's policy to pursue friendly relations outside Greece's traditional area of alliances, preferably with foreign leaders who could be loosely described as socialists. In September 1986 he visited Rumania and Bulgaria, and Sartzetakis returned the visit of the East German President. In October the Czech President visited Athens. In November three Soviet warships visited Piraeus, and in the same month an agreement was reached between the Greek and Soviet governments by which the latter would buy the total output of the planned aluminium plant, to be built north of the Gulf of Corinth with Soviet aid.

Gradually the pace of reciprocal visits relaxed, and their complexion slightly changed. In December 1986 the Prime Ministers of Spain and Egypt were in Athens; in March 1987 the Iranian Foreign Minister, whose visit was returned in June; in July the West German President came to Athens, but Papandreou counter-balanced the visit by going himself to East Germany early in 1988. Meanwhile the Polish President, General Jaruzelski, who was in bad odour with the Western Allies after the suppression of the Solidarity movement, was welcomed in Athens by Papandreou, who also refused to support allied sanctions against Poland. On the other hand, with few exceptions Papandreou limited his contacts with the Western Allies and their associates to diplomatic exchanges through embassies, to bilateral meetings on specific agenda, or to the formal gatherings of NATO and the European Community.

This did not imply that he treated Greece's Western connections as merely formal and unimportant. On the contrary, he took both NATO and the European Community seriously, while often disagreeing with their decisions. In both organizations Greece faced difficulties: the essential difference between the two from the Greek point of view being that NATO included Papandreou's two main antagonists—the USA and Turkey—whereas the European Community did not. Hence allied relations in NATO were often disrupted by wrangles about issues affecting its south-eastern front, in which Greece and Turkey could mutually frustrate each other. In the European Community, on the other hand, Greece could frustrate Turkey's ambition to become a full member, but also had difficulties of other kinds in which Turkey played no role.

Papandreou could claim to have fulfilled Greece's obligations to the Community as dutifully as the national economy allowed. In February 1986 he signed the Single European Act, committing Greece to the far-reaching extension of the Community's progress to complete unification. A year later he somewhat belatedly introduced Value Added Tax. He also had the satisfaction of presiding over the Council of Ministers for the second time in 1988, from July to December, an opportunity for favourable publicity which he exploited to the full. But although subsidies from the Community—in particular, the Integrated Mediterranean Programme—greatly exceeded Greece's contributions, Papandreou often complained about the handicaps imposed on the country's underdeveloped industry.

Although he accepted, contrary to his previous beliefs, that Greece's future lay in European integration and the Western Alliance, he continued to push his diplomatic relations further afield. In doing so he overrode a number of fixed points in post-war policy. One remarkable example was an initiative to end the formal state of war since 1940 with Albania, which had still been regarded as an enemy even after peace was made with Italy. The process began at an unofficial level with an agreement in November 1985 on co-operation between the Academies of Athens and Tirana. Diplomatic discussions began eight months later, and culminated in a formal termination of the state of war in August 1987.

The first visit of a Greek Foreign Minister to Albania took place in March 1988, reciprocated a few months later. A useful outcome of this initiative was that when a Balkan Conference was convened at Belgrade in 1988, Albania was represented for the first time since the Second World War, together with Yugoslavia, Greece, Bulgaria, Rumania and Turkey. But this progress was accompanied by signs of dissent from the opposition, anxious over the rights of the Greek population in southern Albania (known to the Greeks as Northern Epirus).

Other delicate problems arose from Papandreou's plan to upgrade the qualified state of relations with Israel, which Greece had never recognized *de jure*. The process began with a visit to Athens in January 1986 by the Director General of the Israeli Foreign Ministry. Negotiations continued slowly but favourably for more than a year, the Greeks being anxious not to compromise their friendship with the Arab world. In November 1987 the first visit of a Greek Foreign Minister to Tel Aviv took place, and full diplomatic relations were discussed. But with the outbreak of the Palestinian *intifada* (uprising) and the Israeli reaction to it, the negotiations were broken off in 1988 by the Greeks. They were successfully concluded in 1990.

Relations with the Arab world, although carefully nurtured for economic reasons, were also not always easy. They were complicated during Papandreou's second term by a wave of terrorism which had many disturbing features. Undoubtedly its roots lay in the Middle East, but no one could be sure exactly where: Palestinians, Libyans, Syrians, Lebanese, Jordanians, Iranians were variously suspected.

Their attacks were aimed more at Greece's allies than the Greeks themselves, but they often took place on Greek territory. The problems were aggravated by the existence of several Greek terrorist organizations as well. To crown the dangers, the Greek police found it virtually impossible ever to identify or capture a single one of the criminals involved. Only in 1990 was there some success.

Papandreou discounted the Allies' speculative identifications of the sources of terrorism. He took few overt steps against the Arab countries, but Western governments suspected that clandestine bargains were struck to divert them from operations on Greek soil or against Greek targets. In July 1986 the Libyan government was persuaded to reduce its pseudo-diplomatic representation in Athens from fifty to twenty. But Papandreou refused to support American claims that Gaddafi was responsible for attacks on US servicemen, and sharply criticized the American bombing of Libya in retaliation. He also rebutted US complaints of Greek contacts with the Palestinian group of Abu Nidal.

To the annoyance of the US and British governments, Papandreou allowed his Foreign Minister to visit Syria, and himself received a spokesman of the Palestine Liberation Organization. In April 1988 he sent a message of condolence to the PLO on the murder of one of its leading members. Such gestures were formally quite normal, but they were not balanced by any reprehension of the suspect Arab governments. Nor did they guarantee Greece immunity from embroilment in the quarrels of the Middle East. In December 1987 the Iraqi *chargé d'affaires* in Athens was shot and wounded in the office of the Arab League. In July 1988, a Greek cruise-ship was attacked by Arab terrorists, whose apparent (though unsuccessful) purpose was to seize hostages in order to secure the release of another Palestinian, Muhammad Rashid. His case was important, because his extradition from Greece was requested by the US government on a charge of sabotaging a civil airliner.

The case of Muhammad Rashid caused Papandreou special anxiety, because the Greek courts advised that he should be extradited; but an appeal to the Supreme Court still remained open. In the second half of 1988 the wave of bombing by unknown hands became greatly aggravated. These alarming developments led to Papandreou's decision in November to deport another Palestinian to Libya, the country of his choice, rather than to accede to the Italian government's request for his extradition. This timid recourse gave little respite: a senior magistrate and two public pro-secutors were shot early in 1989, nobody knew by whom.

When the Supreme Court upheld the advice on Muhammad Rash-id's extradition to the USA in May 1989, the imminence of a parlia-mentary election gave the government a last excuse for postponing action. In effect the postponement was indefinite, because the next ten months were a practically unbroken period of electoral manoeuvres. Terrorism did not abate, however, but the responsi-bility for it shifted (so far as the lack of evidence allows speculation) from foreign to indigenous terrorists. It was Americans who pro-vided the main targets, and they attracted the enmity of Greek as well as Arab conspirators.

The number of Greek terrorist organizations is not certain, but at least half a dozen were known by name. Some took their names from the calendar, the best known being called after 1 May and 17 November. Their motives were inscrutable, and their occasional outbursts of propaganda almost meaningless. They all hated the Americans, but not the Americans alone. Their victims included a leading official of the Trade Union Confederation (GSEE), a wealthy Greek businessman, an official of the British Council, the US Defence *attaché*, and a much-respected Deputy of ND who was the son-in-law of Mitsotakis. They also blew the statue of President Truman off its pedestal; it took Papandreou more than a year to insist that it must be restored.

The affair of Truman's statue encapsulates Papandreou's dilemma, the two horns of which were his hostility towards the US government and his dependence on it. His foreign policy oscillated between the two throughout his second term of office. The main issues between Greece and the United States were all related to defence, but they were complicated by a basic divergence: the potential enemy for the Americans was the USSR, whereas for Greece it was Turkey. Many particular issues arose between the two sides: nuclear weapons, air bases, technical installations, equipment supplies, security guarantees, terrorism; but the basic divergence of defence policy overshadowed them all.

Defence discussions began early after Papandreou's re-election, with visits in October 1985 by the Greek Foreign Minister to Washington and by the US Under-Secretary for Political Affairs to Athens. In the same month it was announced that all nuclear weapons stored in Greece were finally to be removed, although their presence had never been formally admitted. The first exchanges of visits were not yet concerned with US bases but chiefly, apart from disagreements on the sources of terrorism, with the purchase by Greece of American military aircraft. A ban on their purchase was lifted early in 1986, in return for a guarantee by the Greek government to block the leakage of technology to the Soviet Union.

The future of the US bases in Greece was first raised in February 1986. Papandreou insisted that they must be closed at the end of 1988, in accordance with the 1983 agreement. He added that if the Americans wished to retain them, negotiations must start afresh from 'zero', as if no prior agreement existed. He added that any new agreement would be submitted to a popular referendum. He also raised the need for security guarantees against Turkish aggression, and for the removal of Turkish armed forces from Cyprus. These were all recurrent and interminable issues.

For some months, after the attack on the Truman statue in March 1986 and the US air raid on Libya in April, relations were very cold between Athens and Washington; negotiations were at a standstill. A thaw in November made it possible for the two governments to sign a defence agreement on co-operation in the production and maintenance of weapons, and in technological research. The agreement for Greece's purchase of forty American fighter aircraft was signed in January 1987. But it was not until the middle of that year that the question of a renewed agreement on the bases was raised again by the US Secretary of State, during a meeting of the NATO Council in Brussels.

Meanwhile strong feelings had re-emerged between the two governments over their differing attitudes towards Turkey and Cyprus. Greco–Turkish disputes over their rights in, under and above Aegean waters, and over the Turkish occupation of northern Cyprus, were as bitter as ever. In the Greek view, the Americans were prejudiced in favour of the Turks. The Greeks retaliated by blocking co-operation in NATO exercises, and by delaying the re-activation of Turkey's treaty of association with the European Community, which had been suspended when the Turkish Generals seized power in 1980. On several occasions in 1986–7 there were clashes on the land frontier between Greece and Turkey, narrow escapes from serious accidents in Aegean air-space, and sharp disagreements over rights to prospect for oil under the continental shelf.

Matters came to a head in February 1987, when the US Secretary for Defence admitted that the Turks had been allowed to deploy

American weapons in Cyprus, a decision which he justified on the grounds that the Turkish presence there was not aggressive. The Greek government strongly protested, and again demanded that the Turkish forces should be removed from Cyprus altogether. When an agreement was concluded (but not yet signed) in the same month for the continued operation in Greece of two relay stations of the 'Voice of America', Papandreou threatened to cancel it if the US government failed to enforce 'corrective measures' on the Turks in Cyprus.

For internal consumption, Papandreou regularly used hostile language about the United States, but it was seldom followed by decisive action. He claimed that the US government was arming Turkey to replace post-revolutionary Iran as the 'gendarme of the Middle East', and had secretly breached the conventional proportion of 7 to 10 in the supply of arms to Greece and Turkey, in favour of the latter. Nevertheless, Greece's relations with the United States survived Papandreou's rhetoric. At the end of July 1987 the US Under-Secretary for Political Affairs arrived again in Athens to prepare for negotiations on the bases. The first formal meeting between the negotiating teams was held in November.

The negotiations pursued a slow and intricate course for more than a year. There was a tacit assumption on both sides that they would not end in a complete rupture, so it was no surprise that the terminal date of the original agreement, 31 December 1988, arrived and passed without any final conclusion. But important steps had already been taken. Construction work at the bases was halted in January 1988. In early August the Greek government announced that the US air base at Hellenikon, outside Athens, was to close in December. Although taken by surprise, the Americans accepted the decision, and went even further when they announced early in 1990 the closure of a nearby installation at Nea Makri, as a consequence of plans to reduce defence expenditure worldwide. By then Papandreou was out of office, and the initiative had passed out of the Greeks' hands.

There were several reasons for the indecision of the Greeks and the fluidity of the situation which had developed. One was that the official date of termination fell only six months before the statutory date of a parliamentary election (June 1989). Papandreou was seriously ill in the latter part of 1988, and the survival of his government was in doubt. No successor government could be bound by his declared intentions if they had not yet been embodied in contractual form. In any case, even if the agreement on the bases were not renewed, the Americans were entitled to a period of seventeen months to remove all their installations. There was therefore no reason for hurry.

In the event, nearly a year was spent—from May 1989 to April 1990—in a succession of electoral campaigns. So it caused no surprise when Papandreou announced in April 1989 that the negotiations were suspended, nor when it was further announced in January 1990 that the deadline for the removal of the bases was extended for six months from May of that year. But the agreement to suspend the decision was not unconditional, at least on Papandreou's part.

Apart from his persistent assertion that any new agreement would be subject to a referendum, he also insisted that it should include binding safeguards of Greece's security and territorial integrity. This stipulation was of course aimed at the Turks. Throughout the whole period of negotiation, Turkey had been regarded as the Mediterranean surrogate of the United States, and Greco–Turkish relations had fluctuated in parallel with Greco–American relations. For the sake of public relations, whether or not in reality, the threat of Turkish aggression had still to be regularly emphasized. It led in early 1986, for the first time, to the appointment of a senior Minister for the Aegean.

A few weeks after that appointment, Papandreou and Özal, the Turkish Prime Minister since 1983 (and later President), met for the first time at the annual World Economic Forum in Davos. Their mutual reaction was described at the time as 'negative', though Davos was later to be the scene of a more positive encounter. Initially the main subjects of complaint were, on the Greek side, that the Turks were illegally in occupation of northern Cyprus and were persistently trespassing into Greek air-space and territorial waters; on the Turkish side, that the Greeks were frustrating the normalization of Turkey's relations with the European Community and were illegally fortifying the island of Lemnos.

On the latter issue, Özal made threatening remarks at a NATO Council meeting in May 1986, to which Papandreou delivered a public retort at a dinner in Athens in honour of the Syrian President. A month later Özal announced his intention to visit northern Cyprus, which he carried out in July. Papandreou next raised the subject of Cyprus at the summit meeting of the European Community, where it was not technically relevant. Soon afterwards the

Turkish armed forces carried out exercises in the Aegean, which led to numerous violations of Greek air-space, and even to the firing of warning shots. The Greeks considered that Turkey was being deliberately provocative.

A new source of friction emerged in November 1986, on the land frontier between eastern and western Thrace, when the Turks forcibly deported across the frontier a number of Iranian refugees, and the Greeks drove them back again. Özal tried to make amends by offering to sign a treaty of friendship with Greece, including a guarantee of Greek frontiers; but Papandreou was only interested in a collective guarantee by NATO, which was not to be had. The matter became more serious in December 1986, when an armed clash on the Thracian frontier led to the deaths of two Turks and one Greek. A joint enquiry into the incident was inconclusive, but fortunately restraint was shown on both sides.

The Aegean sea-bed was the next subject of dispute, in March 1987. Papandreou proposed to bring under government control the North Aegean Petroleum Company (NAPC), which was under American management, as a matter of national security. This proposal was denounced by the Turkish government as an infringement of a protocol signed at Berne in 1976, by which both governments had agreed not to take any unilateral initiative over the continental shelf. The Turkish response was to send out a scientific research vessel among the Greek islands, and to authorize the Turkish Petroleum Company to explore for oil outside territorial waters.

The Greeks protested in their turn, promising resistance 'not merely by words'. The Turkish government declared a state of alert; Papandreou declared that if hostilities began, the US bases would be closed; but Özal retreated from the brink of war, and the two Prime Ministers agreed that neither party would prospect for oil in the disputed waters. Papandreou also proposed that the dispute over the continental shelf should be referred to the International Court of Justice, but this was a proposal which the Turks had rejected more than once before. They responded by publishing a map of the Aegean which appeared to divide the sea into equal halves. The dispute, in fact, was far from being over.

A period of cautious quiescence followed. At the end of November 1987 Papandreou congratulated Özal on his re-election. A continuing exchange of messages between them was putting Greco–Turkish relations on a more even keel, though not one of the specific problems was actually solved. In January 1988 public attention was drawn to the fact that the two Prime Ministers were to meet again shortly at Davos during the World Economic Forum. The publicity was especially significant because in the same month there was a number of contentious episodes which could almost be described as normal: a violent clash between the police and the Muslim minority at Komotini in western Thrace; and a challenge by the Greek government of the European Community's right to release a package of economic aid to Turkey, under an agreement made before Greece became a member.

Much attention was therefore given in anticipation to the meeting of Papandreou and Özal at Davos on the last two days of January. It was described in the press as the 'Davos Summit', and Papandreou spoke of its outcome as a 'no-war programme'. No substantial changes took place, but there were procedural innovations. A 'hot line' by telephone was to be established between the two capitals; two joint committees were created to handle political and economic relations; and the two Prime Ministers agreed to meet at least once a year in each other's capital.

A few concessions were also made on each side. Özal rescinded a decree of 1964 freezing Greek property rights in Turkey, though without retrospective effect. Papandreou withdrew objections to the re-activation of the treaty of association between Turkey and the European Community. But he disappointed the Turks' expectation that Greece would support their application for full membership of the Community. Özal, on his side, refused to withdraw troops from Cyprus or to accept the jurisdiction of the International Court on the continental shelf. At least, however, the two Prime Ministers were able to attend the Balkan Conference in Belgrade at the end of February in an amicable mood.

The 'Davos Summit' caused some uneasiness both in Athens and in Cyprus. In the course of a parliamentary debate on 11 March 1988, Mitsotakis was critical of Papandreou's 'secret diplomacy' and sceptical (rightly, as things turned out) about its lasting effect. In Cyprus a new President, George Vasiliou, took office at the end of February, and visited Athens two weeks later. He argued that the Greek government ought to be pressing for the withdrawal from Cyprus not only of Turkish troops but also of Turkish settlers from the mainland. At the end of March he also visited London, to remind the Prime Minister that Britain was still a guarantor power of the island. He also made it clear that he intended to meet Özal in Ankara before he met Denktash, the nominal President of the self-proclaimed state of Northern Cyprus, thus emphasizing his view of the realities of power.

The two new committees created at Davos duly met on several occasions between March and September 1988, but achieved little. High-level visits were exchanged between the Mayors of Athens and Istanbul; Melina Mercouri was also invited to Istanbul; Özal visited Athens in June, but met with a hostile reception from the Greek public. Papandreou shrewdly stated that he would return the visit at a date to be determined, but on assuming the presidency of the European Community's Council of Ministers (for the second time) on 1 July, he made it clear that his visit to Ankara would not be possible during his six-month term of office. In the event he was spare this particular embarrassment by his own serious illness later in the year and by the approach of the election in 1989.

Since the Turks refused to discuss the question of Cyprus either in the political committee set up under the Davos agreement or in the Association Council of the European Community, the subject was temporarily adjourned between Athens and Ankara and left in the hands of the Cypriot leaders themselves. At the invitation of the UN Secretary-General, Vasiliou and Denktash met at Geneva in August 1988, and several times in the following months. The Secretary-General proposed that June 1989 should be the deadline for their formal negotiations. It was a forlorn hope, especially as June was to be the month of the Greek parliamentary election. No progress was in fact achieved.

Meanwhile the so-called 'spirit of Davos' was soon dissipated, with inevitably adverse effects on relations between the Greek and Turkish Cypriots. In July the fruitless talks between Vasiliou and Denktash were broken off by the latter, pending the adoption of a declaration which he demanded, containing a reference to the Turkish Cypriot community's right of self-determination. The UN Secretary-General continued to hold separate discussions with each of them, and invited both to New York in February 1990. But their talks broke down almost at once over Denktash's demand for recognition of the independence of Northern Cyprus.

The dissipation of the 'spirit of Davos' had already begun. In March 1988 the Greeks were protesting once more at Turkish violations of Greek air-space, and in May they protested at such violations by both US and Turkish aircraft during a NATO exercise. Later in May two Turkish diplomatic cars in Athens were damaged by bombs. At the end of the month a meeting of the Association Council of

Turkey and the European Community was cancelled because the Turks opposed the inclusion of a reference to Cyprus in the opening statement. Meetings of the two joint committees under the Davos agreement took place from time to time, but their proceedings were perfunctory.

In September 1988 the political joint committee met in Ankara and the economic joint committee in Athens, both of them for the last time. Renewed recriminations followed. In October the Turkish government blocked a proposal that NATO should finance a defence project on Rhodes, which was particularly annoying for the Greeks since Papandreou was shortly due to preside at a meeting of the European Community Council of Ministers on the island. At the end of October a spokesman for the Turkish Foreign Ministry publicly accused the Greeks of frustrating the 'spirit of Davos'. Early in November the Turks and the Greeks successively blocked each other's initiatives at the NATO Defence Review Committee. Soon afterwards their official spokesmen made mutually contradictory statements on the unresolved issues between their two governments. In addition to the usual complaints, the Turkish spokesman significantly stressed the status of the Turkish minority in western Thrace.

That last point was significant because the Greeks did not recognize the minority as Turkish but only as Muslim. The dispute over a single word was to lead to more severe conflict a year later. Leaders of the minority insisted on their right to call themselves Turks, contrary to a ruling of the Supreme Court in Athens. At the end of January 1990 a violent fight broke out at Komotini between about 1,500 protesters and Greek citizens and police. Fortunately no one was killed, but the Turkish Consul was expelled and in retaliation the Greek Consul-General was expelled from Istanbul.

At the same time the two governments were embroiled—Turkey directly and Greece indirectly—in another international conflict close to their common frontier. The Communist government of Bulgaria had adopted in 1984–85 a policy of compulsorily assimilating their own Muslim minority, ordering them to adopt Bulgarian names, to speak the Bulgarian language, and forcibly closing many of their mosques. The enforcement of this policy led in 1989 to a mass flight of Bulgarian Muslims across the frontier to Turkey. At first the Turks welcomed them, but when the number of refugees had reached some 300,000 they halted the influx and forced large numbers back into Bulgaria. The Greeks, who were simultaneously facing an influx of Greek refugees from southern

Russia, took measures to ensure that none of the Bulgarian refugees should cross their own frontier. Fortunately the downfall of President Zhivkov in November 1989 led to the abandonment of Bulgaria's previous policy.

This episode was only one symptom of the indirect impact on Greece of the astonishing series of revolutions in eastern Europe during 1989. The Greeks had escaped from the threat of Communist domination forty years earlier, but they could not ignore the upheavals among their northern neighbours. Yugoslavia had escaped from Stalinist domination in 1948, while remaining ideologically Communist; but by 1989 its federal system was breaking down and the artificial country was itself in danger of disintegration, if not civil war, on ethnic lines. Since both Yugoslavia and Bulgaria had once made claims on Greek Macedonia, which still remained latent but not extinct, the turmoil in northern Macedonia could not fail to cause anxiety in Greece. Nor could the turmoil in Serbia, which included a large and rebellious Albanian minority. Albania itself was still a closed and inscrutable society during the revolutions of 1989. There were conflicting rumours about a state of emergency, and then about some degree of relaxation. But the Greek minority was still reported to be suffering repression.

Just as the disorder among foreign neighbours affected Greece, so also Greek disputes could affect international relations elsewhere. This was naturally the case above all with the Greco–Turkish conflict. In the autumn of 1989, for example, the presentation of allied proposals for the mutual reduction of conventional forces by NATO and the Soviet government was hindered by a disagreement between Greece and Turkey over the exclusion from verification procedures of the area round the southern Turkish port of Mersin. The Turks wanted the area excluded, and the Greeks wanted it included: neither of them had forgotten that it was from Mersin that the Turkish invasion of Cyprus in 1974 was launched. The apparent impossibility of negotiating a satisfactory settlement was equally exasperating to the Soviet and the Western sides.

Further north, the revolutionary changes in eastern Europe, and within the Soviet Union itself, did not impinge so directly on Greece, where the press and public opinion were preoccupied with the country's seemingly endless series of scandals and elections. But although Greece was the odd man out in the year of eastern Europe's revolutions, the country could not remain permanently unaffected by the consequences. The future of NATO and the

Warsaw Pact were obviously at stake; so was the American military commitment to Greece and Turkey. The question would also have to be faced whether the newly liberated ex-Communist countries were to be accepted into the European Community, at least initially as Associates. If so, what would be the effect on Greece's fragile economy, and on Turkey's prospect of full membership? Greece's government would have to develop both cautious and farsighted policies in response to such questions; but Greece hardly had a government at all when the neighbouring revolutions were passing through their climactic phase, from the middle of 1989 to the spring of 1990.

It was in the middle of 1988 that Papandreou began to lose the initiative and control of events, though the rot had set in at least a year earlier. His second term of office was marked initially by his personal domination to an even higher degree than the first. He treated his Ministers with contempt, overruling their decisions, transferring or dismissing them or forcing their resignation at will. His Council of Ministers underwent almost innumerable reconstructions, the outcome of which was that at the end of eight years of power only one senior colleague (Melina Mercouri) had been in office with him throughout. More than one Minister, after losing office, was expelled from PASOK; others resigned from the party after serious disagreements. Even with Sartzetakis, his nominee as President, Papandreou's relations were uneasy; but he could find no alternative nominee when Sartzetakis' term of office ended in 1990.

The most remarkable manifestation of Papandreou's dominant personality was the confidence and relative ease with which he overrode the public and private scandals which plagued his final years. The public scandals began to emerge openly as early as mid-1987, when allegations of the misappropriation of public funds by PASOK officials led the Opposition in Parliament to table a motion (unsuccessful, of course) for the appointment of a select committee to investigate them. Soon afterwards a close associate of Papandreou, George Louvaris, was forced to resign as president of the International Trading Company, a state agency, because of allegations of bribery in connection with the purchase of French missiles. Allegations were also made against a senior PASOK Minister of forging documents to allow Yugoslav grain to be represented as Greek in origin for sale to the European Community, in order to attract subsidy. This case led to the imposition of a fine on Greece by the Community.

The Eclipse of Socialism (1985–1990)

Far more serious accusations were to be brought later against Papandreou personally. One was that he had illegally arranged the tapping of telephones not only of his political opponents but also of his own party colleagues. More serious still was the scandal which became public in June 1988 involving the Bank of Crete, then the second largest private bank in the country. Here the central figure was George Koskotas, a young entrepreneur who had acquired a dubious fortune and bought control of the bank among many other enterprises (including the newspaper *Kathimerini* and the football team *Olympiakós*). In October, when Koskotas was under suspicion of embezzlement, the central Bank of Greece put in a Commissioner to control the Bank of Crete. Koskotas was forbidden to leave the country and placed under surveillance, but not arrested.

He nevertheless contrived to escape from Greece, first to Brazil and then to the USA. In Boston he was arrested on unrelated charges arising from his earlier career. The Minister of Public Order in Athens resigned for having failed in his responsibilities; the Minister of Justice also resigned, but remained in office as Minister to the Prime Minister, until he too was forced to resign under suspicion of personal involvement in Koskotas' activities. Other resignations and expulsions from the party followed. Papandreou disclaimed all personal knowledge of the affair, and blamed hostile intrigues. An application for Koskotas' extradition was made to the US government, but in the meantime Koskotas began to speak freely to the media and friends, repudiating Papandreou's claims of personal innocence. He claimed to have made huge payments to the party funds of PASOK out of the proceeds of his embezzlement, either directly to the Prime Minister or to his deputy, Agamemnon Koutsoyiorgas, or through agents such as Louvaris.

In February 1989 the Public Prosecutor in Athens ordered an enquiry into Koskotas' allegations, and Papandreou, in self-defence, appointed a parliamentary committee to explore the facts. But no substantial progress had been made before the dissolution of Parliament in May. Although both New Democracy and the Communists (now re-united in a Left Coalition) treated the scandal as major issue in the subsequent election, it did not seem to have a serious impact on the result. Nor did a scandal in Papandreou's private life which was running concurrently with it.

While Papandreou was in Britain for serious heart surgery in September 1988, it was announced that he intended to divorce his American wife and to marry a Greek, Dimitra Lianis, who had accompanied him to London. Their liaison had been known for some time, and provoked public reactions ranging from outrage to ribaldry. There was much sympathy for Margaret Papandreou, who had loyally supported her husband's career. She accepted her displacement with dignity, and returned to the United States. Dimitra Lianis accompanied the Prime Minister everywhere, including the Summit meeting of the European Community on Rhodes in December. His divorce and re-marriage, however, were only just accomplished before the parliamentary election on 18 June 1989.

Papandreou clearly did not expect to win an overall majority again. So he had introduced a new electoral law based on a variant of proportional representation, even more complex than usual, which virtually guaranteed that New Democracy could not win an overall majority either. He also created 100,000 new jobs in the public sector during May 1989, to improve PASOK's chances. There was little new in the parties' programmes for the election, except that ND asserted its intention to conduct a more thorough investigation into the financial scandals. This intention was supported by the Left Coalition, led jointly by Kharilaos Florakis of the KKE and Leonidas Kyrkos of the former KKE (Interior), and joined by a number of former members of PASOK, including two ex-Ministers.

The outcome of the election was the expected deadlock. New Democracy won 145 seats, PASOK 125, the Left Coalition 28, the rest two. A coalition government was inevitable; it was ironically only with the Conservative ND that the Communists could join forces against their *bêtes noires*, the Socialists. After prolonged negotiations, the principal leaders renounced office personally to allow a coalition to be formed under a retired naval officer, Tzannas Tzannetakis, who had been elected for New Democracy. He undertook to hold office only for three months, with the express purpose of carrying through a parliamentary investigation into the charges against Papandreou and his Ministers. A parliamentary commission voted decisively for the indictment of Papandreou on the charge of telephone-tapping, and of both himself and five of his Ministers on charges of corruption. Parliament voted to lift their immunity from prosecution, and was then dissolved for a fresh election on 5 November.

Most notably, the short-lived government had not attempted to introduce a new electoral law. It would have been impossible for the Left Coalition to agree to such a change, since Papandreou's law favoured small parties. The Communists were likely to lose votes in any case, simply for having combined with the Conservatives. The result of the second election of 1989 was therefore another deadlock. New Democracy and PASOK each gained three seats, and the Left Coalition lost seven. The most interesting novelty was the election of a single Green candidate, who was a woman. But the generally unsatisfactory character of the electoral system could be judged from the fact that ND failed to gain an overall majority of seats even with more than 46 per cent of the poll, whereas in 1985, under a different system, PASOK had gained a substantial overall majority of seats with an almost identical percentage of the poll.

The deadlock made another election inevitable in the New Year. Protracted negotiations on the formation of an interim government led to a different result in November 1989 from that in June, because the Left Coalition was unwilling to risk another partnership with ND. The outcome was an unusual experiment which seemed unworkable from the start. All parties agreed to support a Prime Minister outside Parliament, and the choice fell on Xenophon Zolotas, an eighty-five-year-old economist and banker of great distinction.

His Council of Ministers was to consist of Deputies proportional to the parties' representation in Parliament. It was agreed, though not without dissent on the Left, that the duration of Parliament should again be limited in advance. The date of 8 April 1990 was fixed for the third election within ten months. In fact the coalition broke down in February; all the Ministers withdrew, led by ND, and Zolotas completed his term of office with a Ministerial Council consisting entirely of non-parliamentary technical experts.

Although no stable government could be formed in the Parliament of November 1989, it was still responsible for the election of a new President of the Republic, since Sartzetakis' term of office was due to end on 30 March 1990. Mitsotakis hoped that Karamanlis would emerge from retirement to become a candidate, but he at first refused. When the first ballot was held on 18 February, Sartzetakis himself was the only candidate, but he failed to reach the required minimum of 200 votes out of 300 Deputies. Greece was therefore in danger of being left, in the following month, with neither a stable government nor an elected President.

The election of 8 April was held in conditions of great tension, still under the system devised by Papandreou a year earlier to create a deadlock. The campaign was overshadowed in its closing stages by the publication of a letter from the President of the European Commission to Zolotas, containing a devastating criticism of the chaotic state of Greece's economy and threatening the suspension of subsidies from Community funds until drastic remedies were imposed. A few days later a report was published by a group of eminent economists defining what those unwelcome remedies would have to include.

It was still doubtful until the last moment whether the election would produce a government capable of decisive action. In the event, the ND under Mitsotakis won exactly half the seats in Parliament (150 out of 300) with over 47 per cent of the votes—the highest percentage won by any governing party in Europe. Mitsotakis' position was at once reinforced by a promise of support from the single Deputy of the right-wing breakaway party, Democratic Renewal. The mood of the country was swiftly reflected in a sharp rise of prices on the Athens stock exchange.

Mitsotakis made it clear that he would give a high priority to the revision of Papandreou's electoral law, which he described as 'criminal'; and equally to the economic reforms, painful as they would be, which were demanded by the European Commission. His Council of Ministers included an impressive galaxy of technical as well as political talent: economists, engineers, doctors, lawyers, university teachers, and senior service officers. Women were particularly well represented, and if Greece's most famous film star (Melina Mercouri) was inevitably displaced, her loss was balanced by the inclusion of Greece's most popular musician (Mikis Theodorakis).

A sense of renewal, even if achieved by the narrowest margin, was reinforced by the agreement of Karamanlis, on a second approach by Mitsotakis, that he would after all be a candidate for the Presidency. He was duly re-elected, in his eighty-fourth year, to the post from which he had been unceremoniously ousted by Papandreou five years earlier.

Papandreou's defeat in June 1989 can be regarded as the death-knell of socialism in Greece. It was not a revolution, like the demise of socialism in eastern Europe, which began almost immediately afterwards. Indeed, the very word 'socialism' has quite different meanings in the two contexts, since Papandreou's never ceased to be democratic, which Stalin's never began to be. But there was a common feature in the socialism of both kinds: neither of them ever worked. Every eastern European country except Greece had to learn this fact the hard way. The Greeks may have thought that theirs was a hard way too. They had a hard time escaping from Stalinism in

1943–49; again under military dictatorship in 1967–74; and again in shaking off the legacy of Papandreou in 1989–90. But they only had to look northwards to see how much harder their fate might have been in other circumstances. The contrast between Greece and the rest of eastern Europe exemplified a plain lesson—that democracy alone contains an inbuilt mechanism for correcting potentially disastrous mistakes.

Bibliography

The following bibliography is confined to books available in English, in order to keep it within reasonable compass. It can be extended into other West European languages by reference to the bibliographies contained in many of the books listed. But it would need to be supplemented also by reference to a growing number of scholarly works in Greek, upon which I have freely drawn, though they are not listed in detail because they would not be generally accessible to readers other than professional historians with a knowledge of Greek.

Certain works span several chapters of this survey, as follows:

Chapters I–III

N. H. Baynes and H. St. L. B. Moss, *Byzantium: An Introduction to East Roman Civilization* (Oxford, 1948).

J. B. Bury, *A History of the Later Roman Empire, A.D. 395–800*, 2 vols. (London and New York, 1889).

Cambridge Medieval History, vol. IV, parts 1 and 2 (Cambridge, 1966–67).

Edward Gibbon, *The Decline and Fall of the Roman Empire*, 7 vols. (edited by J. B. Bury, London, 1926).

J. M. Hussey, *The Byzantine World* (London, 1957; New York, 1961).

G. Ostrogorsky, *History of the Byzantine State* (Oxford, 1956; New Brunswick, N. J., 1957).

Tamara Talbot Rice, *Everyday Life in Byzantium* (London and New York, 1967).

A. A. Vasiliev, *History of the Byzantine Empire, 324–1453* (Oxford, 1952).

Bibliography

Chapters I–VI

George Finlay, *History of Greece*, 7 vols. (edited by H. F. Tozer, Oxford, 1877).

Chapters I–X

W. A. Heurtley, H. C. Darby, C. W. Crawley and C. M. Wood-house, *A Short History of Greece from Early Times to 1964* (Cambridge and New York, 1966).

Sir George Hill, *History of Cyprus*, 3 vols. (Cambridge, 1948).

Chapters IV–IX

L. S. Stavrianos, *The Balkans Since 1453* (New York, 1958).

Chapters V–VIII

Douglas Dakin, *The Unification of Greece, 1770–1923* (London, 1972).

Bernard Lewis, *The Emergence of Modern Turkey* (London, 1961).

John Campbell and Philip Sherrard, *Modern Greece* (London, 1968).

W. Miller, *The Ottoman Empire and Its Successors, 1801–1927*, with appendix for 1927–36 (Cambridge, 1936).

The following works are also valuable for special subjects which run through the whole or the greater part of the story:

M. S. Anderson, *The Eastern Question, 1774–1923* (London and New York, 1966).

H. A. R. Gibb and Harold Bowen, *Islamic Society and the West*, vol. 1 in two parts (Oxford, 1950–57).

G. L. Lewis, *Turkey* (3rd Ed.; London and New York, 1965).

Philip Sherrard, *The Greek East and the Latin West* (Oxford, 1959).

Timothy Ware, *The Orthodox Church* (Baltimore, Ma., 1963; London, 1964).

The following contain source-material in addition to the above for particular chapters:

Chapter I

Jacob Burckhardt, *The Age of Constantine the Great* (London and New York, 1949).

Bibliography

A. H. M. Jones, *The Decline of the Ancient World* (London and New York, 1966).

Chapter II

Paul J. Alexander, *The Patriarch Nicephorus of Constantinople* (Oxford, 1958).

J. B. Bury, *A History of the East Roman Empire, A. D. 802–867* (London, 1912).

F. Dvornik, *The Photian Schism* (Cambridge, 1948).

Romilly Jenkins, *Byzantium: The Imperial Centuries, A. D. 610 to 1071* (London, 1966; New York, 1967).

Chapter III

W. Miller, *The Latins in the Levant* (London, 1908; New York, 1964).

W. Miller, *Trebizond: The Last Greek Empire* (London, 1926).

D. M. Nicol, *The Despotate of Epirus* (Oxford, 1957).

D. M. Nicol, *The Last Centuries of Byzantium, 1261–1453* (London, 1972).

Steven Runciman, *The Sicilian Vespers* (Cambridge and New York 1958).

Steven Runciman, *A History of the Crusades*, 3 vols. (Cambridge and New York, 1951–54).

Steven Runciman, *The Fall of Constantinople 1453* (Cambridge and New York, 1965).

P. Wittek, *The Rise of the Ottoman Empire* (London, 1938).

Chapter IV

George Finlay, *History of Greece*, vol. V (Oxford, 1877).

W. Miller, *Essays on the Latin Orient* (Cambridge, 1921).

W. Miller, *The Turkish Restoration in Greece, 1718–97* (London, 1921).

Chapter V

C. W. Crawley, *The Question of Greek Independence 1821–33* (Cambridge, 1930).

Douglas Dakin, *British and American Philhellenes During the War of Greek Independence, 1821–33* (Salonika, 1955).

Douglas Dakin, *British Intelligence of Events in Greece, 1824–1827* (Athens, 1959).

Bibliography

Domna Dontas, *The Last Phase of the War of Independence in Western Greece, 1827–1829* (Salonika, 1966).

Thomas Gordon, *History of the Greek Revolution* (Edinburgh, 1832).

Stephen A. Larrabee, *Hellas Observed—The American Experience of Greece 1775–1865* (New York, 1957).

W. Miller, *A History of the Greek People, 1821–31* (London, 1922).

C. M. Woodhouse, *The Greek War of Independence* (London, 1952; New York, 1975).

C. M. Woodhouse, *The Battle of Navarino* (London, 1965; Chester Springs, Pa., 1967).

Chapter VI

Domna Dontas, *Greece and the Great Powers, 1863–1875* (Salonika, 1966).

Romilly Jenkins, *The Dilessi Murders, 1870* (London, 1961).

E. Prevelakis, *British Policy Towards the Change of Dynasty in Greece* (Athens, 1953).

Chapter VII

G. F. Abbott, *Greece and the Allies, 1914–1922* (London, 1922).

Chapter VIII

Charles B. Eddy, *Greece and the Greek Refugees* (London, 1931).

A. A. Pallis, *Greece's Anatolian Venture and After* (London, 1937).

Dimitri Pentzopoulos, *The Balkan Exchange of Minorities and its Impact upon Greece* (Paris, 1962).

David Walder, *The Chanak Affair* (London, 1969).

Chapter IX

G. M. Alexander, *The Prelude to the Truman Doctrine,* (Oxford, 1982).

R. V. Burks, *The Dynamics of Communism in Eastern Europe* (Princeton, 1961).

J. O. Iatrides, *Revolt in Athens* (Princeton, 1972)

J. O. Iatrides, *Greece in the 1940s* (Hanover and London, 1981)

D. George Kousoulas, *Revolution and Defeat: The Story of the Greek Communist Party* (Oxford, 1965).

Edgar O'Ballance, *The Greek Civil War, 1944–1949* (London and New York, 1966).

Bibliography

General Alexander Papagos, *The Battle of Greece, 1940–41* (Athens, 1949).

Floyd A. Spencer, *War and Post-War Greece* (Washington, 1952).

Bickham Sweet-Escott, *Greece: A Political and Economic Survey, 1939–53* (London and New York, 1954).

C. M. Woodhouse, *The Struggle for Greece, 1941–1949* (London, 1976).

Stephen G. Xydis, *Greece and the Great Powers, 1944–1947* (Salonika, 1963).

Chapter X

Theodore A. Couloumbis, *Greek Political Reaction to American and N.A.T.O. Influences* (New Haven, 1966).

Chris Jecchinis, *Trade Unionism in Greece: A Study in Political Paternalism* (Chicago, 1967).

Stanley Mayes, *Cyprus and Makarios* (London, 1960).

Robert Stephens, *Cyprus: A Place of Arms* (London and New York, 1966).

Stephen G. Xydis, *Cyprus: Conflict and Reconciliation, 1954–1958* (Columbus, Ohio, 1967).

Chapter XI

Richard Clogg and George Yannopoulos, *Greece Under Military Rule* (London, 1972).

Christopher Hitchens, *Cyprus* (London, 1984)

Keith R. Legg, *Politics in Modern Greece* (Stanford, California, 1969).

Andreas Papandreou, *Democracy at Gunpoint* (New York, 1970; London, 1971).

Laurence Stern, *The Wrong Horse* (New York, 1977)

C. M. Woodhouse, *The Rise and Fall of the Greek Colonels* (London, 1985)

Kenneth Young, *The Greek Passion* (London, 1968).

Chapter XII

Richard Clogg, *Greece in the 1980s* (London, 1983)

George Th. Mavrogordatos, *Rise of the Green Sun: The Greek Election of 1981* (King's College, London, 1983).

Stanley Mayes, *Makarios: A Biography* (London, 1981).

C. M. Woodhouse, *Karamanlis: The Restorer of Greek Democracy* (Oxford, 1982).

Bibliography

Chapter XIII

Richard Clogg, *Parties and Elections in Greece* (London, 1987)

G. N. Yannopoulos (ed.), *Greece and the EEC: Integration and Convergence* (London, 1986).

Index

365

Index

Index

Index

Index

Index

Index

Index